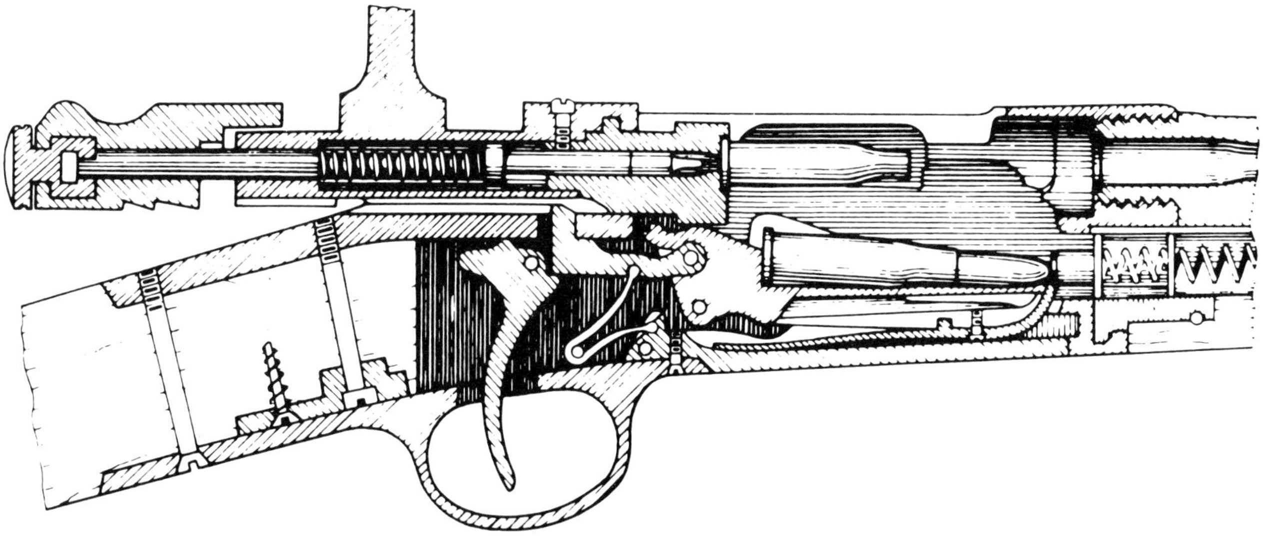

PICTURE CREDITS
Australian War Memorial: 135B
Barnaby's Picture Library: 171
Christchurch, Oxford: 6/7
Geoffrey Boothroyd: 168/9
BSA Guns Ltd: 170/1
Camera Press: 42
Cooper-Bridgeman Library: 94/5, 120/1, 154/5
DOE/Crown Copyright: 14/5, 16
Galleria di Capodimonte: 8/9
Gunshots: 10, 22, 32T&B, 38/9T&B, 40/1, 43B, 50, 54, 98, 112/3, 126/7, 126B, 138/9, 139, 142/3, 158/9, 173, 174/5
Hart Associates: 157, 170
Ian Hogg: Title page, 49T&C, 61, 62, 65, 70/1, 75, 75/6, 85, 87, 93T&B, 96, 100, 101, 105, 118, 120TL&BR, 125, 128/9, 129, 130B, 131T&B, 134/5T, 147C, 160, 158/9, 163T, 163B 185
Angelo Hornak: 64/5, 106/7, 132/3
Mansell Collection: 11, 66
MOD/Crown Copyright: 162, 181
Kevin McDonnell: 84
Masami Tokoi: 150/1
Milbro Ltd: 172B
National Army Museum: 25TR
Novosti: 145B
Picturepoint: 78/9, 90/1, 102
MM Rathore: 182
Remington Arms Co Ltd: 130
H Roger-Viollet: 82/3
Royal Artillery Institute: 67
Royal Military College of Science: 176
Imperial War Museum: 112, 113, 114T, 122, 147T
Sarah Errington/Camera Press: 154
Sonia Halliday 9
Sotheby's: 25L
US Marine Corps/JG Moore Collection: 108/9
USAF: 167
Courtesy Wadsworth Atheneum: 44/5
JS Weeks: 147B
Western Americana: 35, 45, 55, 116/7
Whitney/Western Americana: 26/7

ARTWORK CREDITS
Jim Bamber: 23, 30, 31, 36, 49B, 53, 57, 75T, 97, 99, 104T, 111, 115, 121, 128B, 160/1, 161B, 172
Jim Marks: 52/3, 88, 89, 144/5, 156/7
Tom McArthur: 17, 18/9, 28/9, 30/1, 34/5, 62/3, 72/3, 80/1, 81L&R, 110/2, 124/5
Malcolm McGregor: 15B, 20/1, 21, 24, 33, 76, 77, 114B, 130/1, 136, 153, 158
Nigel Osborne: 118/9
Osborne/Marks: 178/9
Sarson/Bryan: 122/3, 180

S.&W. 357 MAGNUM
IN U.S.A.
REGISTRADAS
WESSON
FLD. MASS.

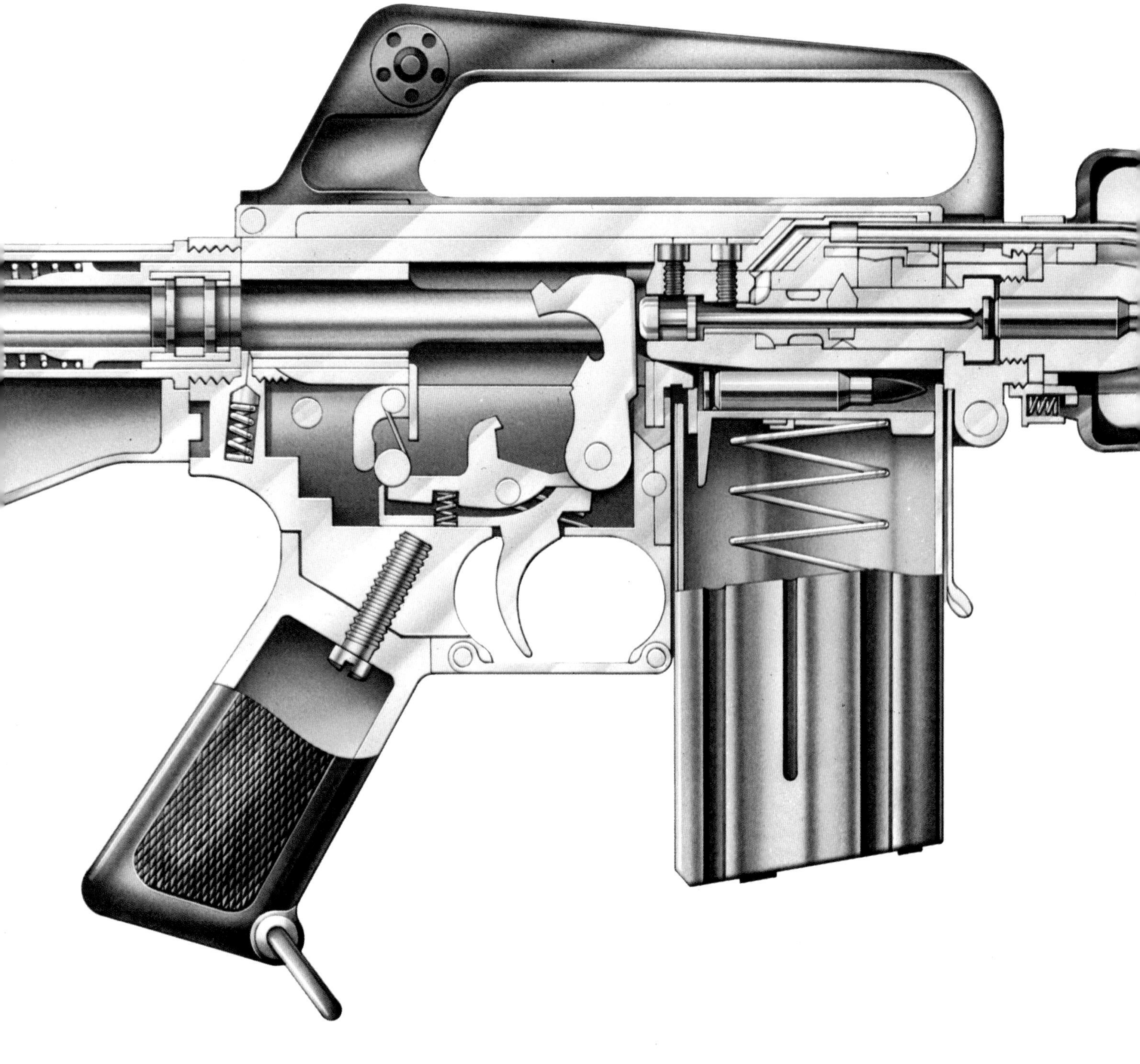

GUNS
and how they work

Ian V. Hogg

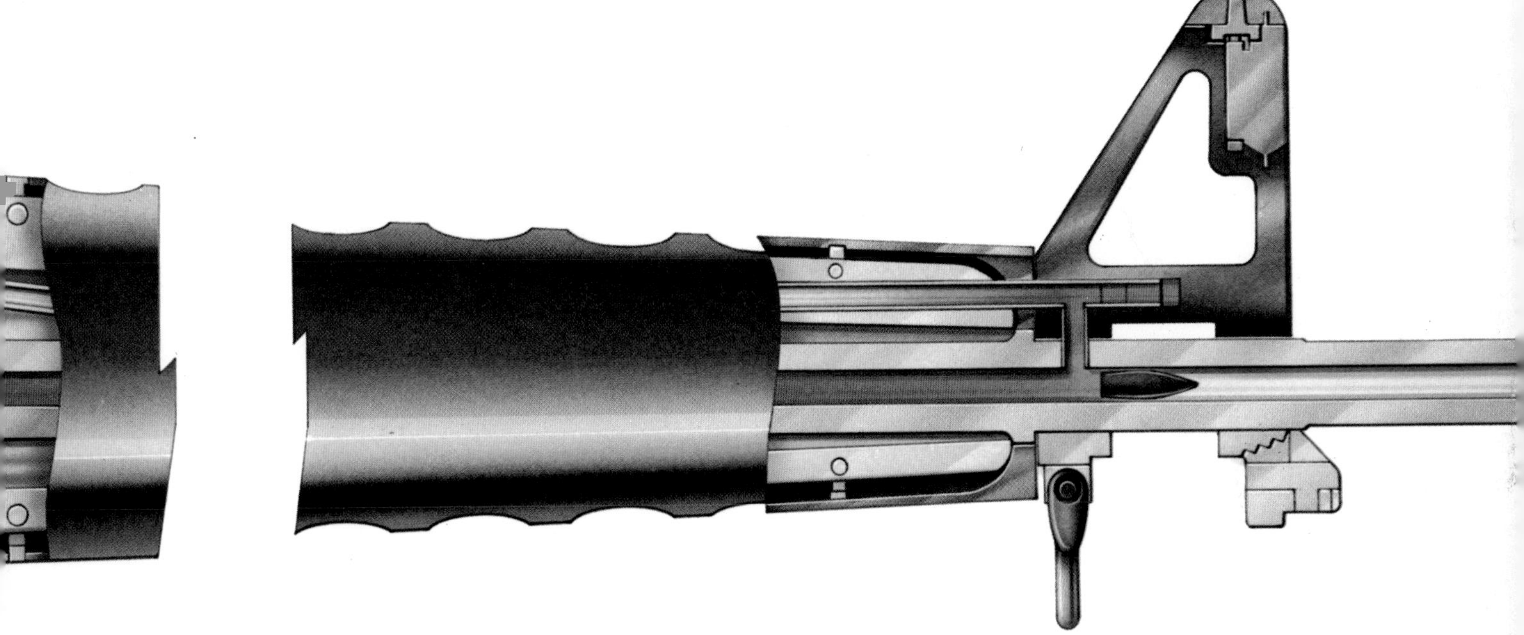

CAVENDISH HOUSE

Editor: **Robin L. K. Wood**

Assistant Editor: **Randal Gray**
Designer: **Jim Bamber**
Picture Researcher: **Mark Dartford**

The Browning .30in Model 1919A4 air-cooled MG on the standard M2 tripod.

Endpapers *Smith and Wesson .357 Magnum revolver.*

Published by Marshall Cavendish Books Limited
58 Old Compton Street
London W1V 5PA

First printing 1979
Second printing 1981
Third printing 1984

Printed and bound in Hong Kong by Dai Nippon Printing Company

ISBN 0 85685 492 1

This volume is not to be sold in North America

INTRODUCTION

This book is about how guns work. Leaving aside, for the moment, the moral and psychological aspects, whatever else you may think of firearms you have to admit that they are remarkable mechanical achievements. Just consider, for example, what goes on inside a machine gun twenty times a second – the cycle of firing, unlocking, extracting, ejecting, reloading, relocking and firing again, for thousands of rounds on end. An automobile half as reliable as the Vickers machine gun would be hailed as the ninth wonder of the world.

That being the case, we have, in this book, tried to bring out some of the mechanics of firearms and show how the various technical problems were overcome, whilst not losing sight of the broad spectrum of historical development. Inevitably, with a subject so vast, we have had to compress and omit, but without, we hope, losing any of the essentials.

Highlighted in the book are twenty-four of those guns worthy of the title 'famous' – because of their performance, their historical significance, or sheer charisma. For those unfamiliar with some of the terms and verbal shorthand associated with firearms, we have appended a section at the end of the book which will explain the mysteries of calibre notation and conversion.

Ian V. Hogg

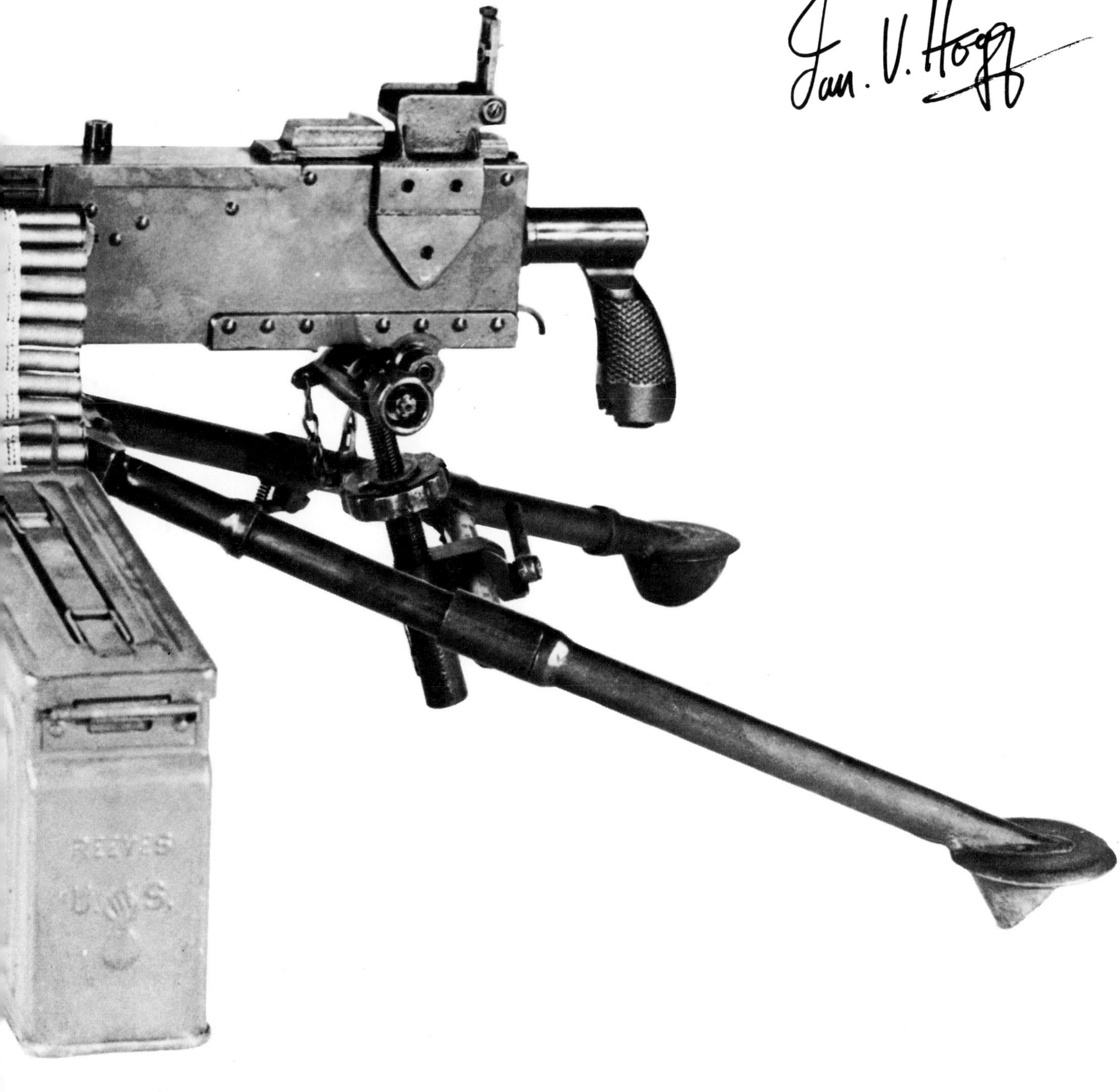

CONTENTS

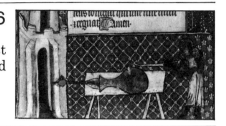

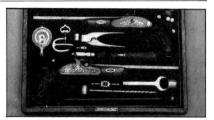

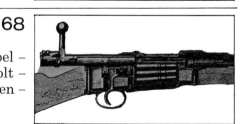

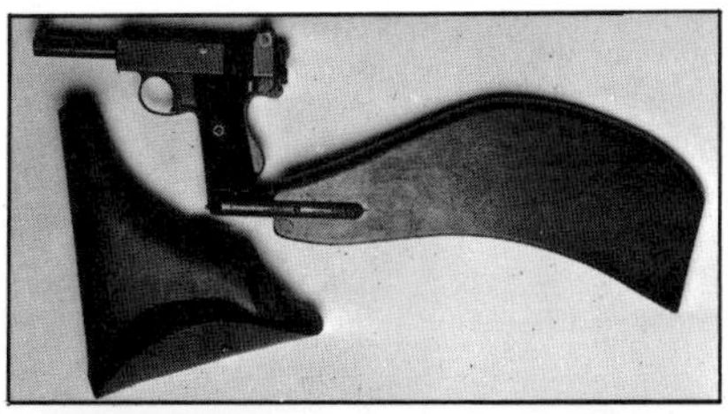

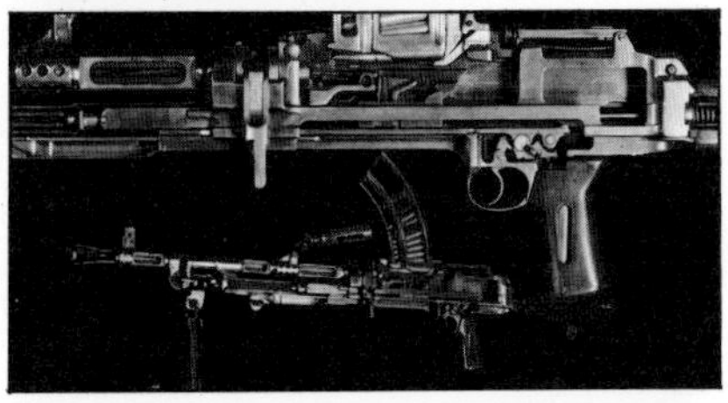

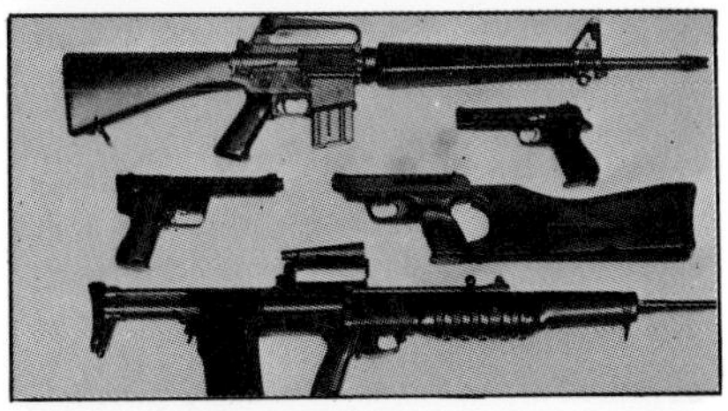

THE DEVIL'S INVENTION

THE DEVIL'S INVENTION/Gunpowder

JUST WHO INVENTED gunpowder and the gun is one question which is likely never to be resolved satisfactorily. Images of hell conjured up by the fearful flash and explosion of the crude first guns led churchmen to denounce them as the invention of the devil himself. The invention of gunpowder has been credited to the Chinese, the Arabs, the Indians, even the lost people of Atlantis, but nothing in the way of solid proof has ever been forthcoming. In the latter part of the nineteenth century, the contemporary improvements in guns led to a certain amount of interest in the history of firearms, particularly in England. A Royal Artillery officer, Lieutenant-Colonel Henry W. L. Hime, spent many years researching in the museums and libraries of Europe in an attempt to solve the question of gunpowder's origins once and for all.

One of the sources he checked was a manuscript by an English scholar, Roger Bacon (c.1214-94), entitled *De Mirabili Potestate Artis et Naturae* (On the Marvellous Power of Art and Nature) written in 1242. Bacon's name had often been put forward as the possible inventor of gunpowder, or, if not the inventor, at least someone who had a hand in its acceptance. Nothing in his writings, however, appeared to support this claim.

Among the various philosophical observations in Bacon's manuscript, Hime was struck by a string of apparently meaningless words which he came across just as Bacon appeared to be warming to the subject of explosives. After much study, Hime realized that the nonsensical phrase was actually an anagram which, when reassembled and punctuated properly, read: '*But of saltpetre take 7 parts, 5 of young hazel twig and 5 of sulphur, and so thou wilt call up thunder and destruction if thou know the art.*'

Bacon had concealed the formula for gunpowder in this manner because of the danger he would have run in openly revealing such knowledge. He was a Franciscan friar, and in 1139 the church authorities had expressly forbidden the discussion or manufacture of 'fiery compositions' for military purposes. Had Bacon published his formula in defiance of this decree, his life would have been in danger. As it was, his outspokenness on other subjects led to a suspicion that he was a practitioner of the Black Arts, and in 1257 he was ordered into cloisters in Paris where he remained shut off from the world.

In 1266, however, Pope Clement IV requested Bacon to write a series of treatises on the current state of scientific knowledge, and among these was a text entitled *Opus Tertius*. A portion of the manuscript was discovered in 1909 in the Bibliothèque National in Paris by Professor Pierre Auhem of Bordeaux University. When translated, it read as follows:

'*From the flaming and flashing of certain igneous mixtures and the terror inspired by their noise, wonderful consequences ensue which no one can guard against or endure. As a simple example may be mentioned the noise and flame generated by the powder, known in divers places, composed of saltpetre, charcoal and sulphur. When a quantity of this powder, no bigger than a man's finger, be wrapped up in a piece of parchment and ignited, it explodes with a blinding flash and a stunning noise . . .*'

Bacon makes no claim for having discovered 'the powder' in this, the first known reference in plain language to gunpowder. What is most significant, he refers to it as being 'known in divers places' – in other words, a matter of common knowledge. So in a matter of 24 years gunpowder had moved from being something of which learned men spoke in riddles to something which was relatively commonplace. It seems reasonable to assume that, if gunpowder had been discovered several hundred years before, as some theories insist, it would have come out into the open much sooner, and would not have been hidden until the middle of the thirteenth century. Irrespective of the inventor, it would seem improbable that gunpowder was known much before the year 1200.

This is not to deny that various pyrotechnic compositions were known and employed well before that date. For example, Greek Fire, an inflammable mixture first used by the Byzantine Greeks to set fire to Saracen ships at the Siege of Constantinople in 673, and various firework compositions attributable to the Chinese undoubtedly existed; but there is a great deal of difference between these and the explosive effect of gunpowder.

Gunpowder (or 'black powder' as it is also known) has changed since Bacon's day. His formula calls for 41.2% saltpetre (potassium nitrate), 29.4% sulphur and 29.4% charcoal, and these three constituents were ground fine, independently of each other, and then mixed. The resulting fine powder was called 'Serpentine' and suffered from various defects: when transported in barrels, for example, the heavier saltpetre and sulphur tended to settle at the bottom of the barrel, leaving the lighter charcoal at the top, a process which ruined the effectiveness of the powder. Moreover, when loaded into the barrel of a gun, the fine powder tended to pack tightly and resist ignition, while it was also susceptible to damp.

In efforts to improve the performance, the formulation gradually changed, increasing the saltpetre at the expense of the other two ingredients. Although not understood at the time, such a move was sound sense, since saltpetre provides the oxygen necessary for combustion while charcoal provides the fuel in the form of carbon. In Bacon's formula there was an excess of charcoal, which was inefficient, but gradually reducing the charcoal and increasing the saltpetre brought the mixture to the point where there was a balance, with just enough charcoal to be burned efficiently by the action of the available oxygen in the saltpetre. The sulphur reduces the temperature of ignition (making the powder easier to light) and also increases the temperature of the explosion, which, by generating more gas, enhances the effect of the powder.

Today the formula stands at 75% saltpetre, 15% charcoal and 10% sulphur. Moreover, the powder is no longer the fine dust of Bacon's day but is made in 'grains' by mixing the ingredients in wet form, drying them into a solid cake, breaking up the cake

Previous page *The Millimete manuscript has the earliest accepted illustration of a gun. It shows the mailed gunner applying a metal rod holding a glowing match to the vent of the vase-shaped cannon firing a crossbow-type bolt.*

Above *Tall-hatted Janissaries, special escort of the Turkish Sultan, Suleiman the Magnificent. By 1500 the Janissaries were using the arquebus, making them the first body of troops in the world to use firearms on a large scale.*

and screening it through a sieve to obtain grains of the required size. This system, followed by coating the grains with graphite and polishing them, renders the powder less susceptible to damp, easier to ignite because of the interstices between the grains when the powder is in the gun, and less likely to form troublesome dust.

The invention of gunpowder lies shrouded in distant history. We are no wiser on the question of who first thought of using gunpowder to propel a missile out of a closed tube – that is, who invented the first gun. A longstanding legend attributed the discovery of gunpowder's propulsive force to Berthold Schwartz, a German monk of Freiburg-in-Breisgau popularly known as Black Berthold. According to the story, he pounded together a mixture of saltpetre, charcoal and sulphur in a mortar one day, causing it to explode and blow the pestle out of the vessel. This, it is said, gave him the inspiration to invent the gun. Unfortunately for the legend, the dates which writers of old ascribe to this event are neither in agreement nor are they within several years of the first authentic records of firearms. Moreover, modern research tends to show that Black Berthold was as much a legend as his famous discovery.

A claim long considered to be authentic was an entry in the *Memorialbuch der Stadt Ghent* – a sort of day-diary of events in the city of Ghent during the Middle Ages – which, in 1313, claimed that 'in this year the use of "bussen" was discovered in Germany by a monk'. The word 'bussen', which approximates to the later 'buchsen', was taken to mean cannon. A further entry in 1314 said 'bussen and krayk (powder) were despatched to England'. But later research showed that these entries had been added many years after the claimed dates, and they can no longer be considered as valid.

The first unquestioned reference to a gun comes in 1325, when Walter de Millimete wrote a treatise for the young Prince Edward, later King Edward III of England (1327-77), entitled *De Officiis Regnum* (On the Duties of Kings). Millimete included in his manuscript a pictorial representation of an early cannon. Unfortunately, he did not expound on this in the text, but the drawing is sufficiently clear to leave no doubt of what is being depicted. In the following year there is an entry in the records of Florence which authorizes the manufacture of brass cannon and iron balls for the defence of the commune camps and territory of Florence, so we can be quite certain that by the first quarter of the fourteenth century the cannon had appeared on the scene.

The first guns were cannon, to be fired at arm's length by a bold gunner, in the hope of hitting something . . . anything. Shaped rather like a vase, with a rounded breech end and a flared muzzle like a bell-mouth, the projectiles launched were the traditional arrow (bound round with leather to make it a snug fit in the bore) or stone or iron balls. These cannons were not, at first, very large: a bore of perhaps 7.5cm (3in) seems to have been the average. The science of gun-making was in its infancy, and the makers were feeling their way.

Very early guns were cast using the techniques already known in bell-founding, but when (as was natural) bigger guns were wanted, the founding technique was not sufficiently advanced to allow the casting of a sound piece of metal of the requisite size. A new technique was then applied, the gun being constructed in accordance with the system used for making barrels. A number of wrought-iron staves were laid together and kept in place by hoops (also made of wrought iron). The whole barrel was then bound with hides and ropes to form a resistant tube, and a solid breech piece riveted into the end. By this method it proved possible to build quite large guns. At the Siege of Odruik in 1377, a cannon firing stone balls weighing 90kg (200lb) was used by the Duke of Burgundy, and later in that year he employed a cannon firing a 200kg (450lb) ball, which is roughly equivalent to a calibre of 560mm (22in).

While this sort of weapon was suited to battering at the walls of a castle, it was a cumbersome device to cart about the countryside and its applications were limited. Something lighter and more handy, capable of being used against armoured knights and men on foot was desirable, and in 1382 we have a record of the men of Ghent setting forth to do battle with the citizens of Bruges, taking with them a number of 'ribauldequins', light carts mounting a number of small-calibre gun barrels. These were placed in the front rank of the army to protect the men from sudden attack. Their field of fire was circumscribed by their fixture to the cart, and reloading them was a slow performance. It would seem likely that at about this time someone had the idea of taking these small cannon from the cart, fitting them with wooden stocks, and placing them in the hands of individual soldiers so that they could point them in whatever direction a threat appeared. The handgun was born.

Before proceeding further it might be well to pause here to consider the basic features of a gun and to define some of the terms used when speaking of firearms. Like any other technical subject, the study of firearms is replete with technical terms. Many of these are in everyday use; many of them are not. What is worse is that many of them are not used correctly and can thus give the wrong impression when they are placed in their proper context.

A gun consists basically of a tube closed at one end, inside which an explosion takes place in order to eject a missile. The tube is called the *barrel*; the hole down the middle of the barrel is the *bore*, the closed end the *breech* end, and the open end the *muzzle*. The missile discharged by the gun is broadly called a *projectile*, though in *smallarms* – which are weapons whose bore is less than 15mm (0.6in) in diameter – the projectile is usually called the *bullet*. The bullet is ejected from the gun by the explosion of a *propelling charge*, which may be of *gunpowder* or *smokeless powder*, and the complete combination of all the requisites to fire one shot from the gun – bullet, propelling charge and means of ignition – are collectively referred to as a *cartridge* or *round*. If the cartridge is inserted into the gun from the muzzle end, then the gun is a *muzzle-loader*, while if it is possible to open the breech in some way and insert the cartridge from that end, then the gun is a *breech-loader*.

The most essential and descriptive measurement used in referring to a gun is its *calibre*, which is the diameter of the internal surfaces of the barrel: that is, the width of the bore. If the gun is a *smooth-bore*, the measurement is simple. If the gun has grooves cut on the internal surface, for the purpose of spinning the bullet, then it is said to be *rifled*, and in this case the calibre is measured from the bottom of one *groove* to the surface of the opposite *land* (the metal left between grooves). Somewhat confusingly, the calibre is sometimes used as a measure of the length of a gun barrel. Thus, a gun with a calibre of 0.5 of an inch and having a barrel 10 inches long could be said to be *20 calibres long*, but this method of description is not commonly applied to smallarms.

The performance of the gun relies on the efficiency with which the propelling charge is converted to gas. The powders used in charges are technically known as *low explosives* because they do not detonate (undergo molecular disruption) but burn extremely rapidly and progressively so as to generate gas at high speed. This gas, expanding behind the bullet, forces it out of the barrel, and the speed at which the bullet leaves the barrel is called the *muzzle velocity*, usually quoted in metres (or feet) per second. The kinetic energy contained in the bullet is the *muzzle energy*, defined in kilogram-metres (or foot-pounds). Both velocity and energy are reduced as the bullet flies through the air.

The efficiency of the charge would, of course, be reduced if any of the generated gas were to leak away and not be used in propelling the bullet. This could occur in a muzzle-loader because the bullet obviously must be slightly less than the gun's calibre in order to allow it to be forced down the bore. This difference in diameter between the bullet and the bore is known as *windage*, through which some gas can escape. In the case of a breech-loader, however, the bullet can be a tight fit, and the problem becomes one of efficiently sealing the breech against the unwanted escape of gas, such sealing being called *obturation*.

Finally, it is not sufficient merely to have a metal tube – it has to be mounted in some way so that it can be handled and used. So the basic gun is mounted into a *stock*, usually of wood, shaped so that the *butt* can be placed against the shoulder to support the rear end, and the other end supported by holding the *fore-end*. A *trigger* is provided with which to fire the weapon and *sights* with which to aim it. Other such refinements as traps to hold cleaning materials, swivels to attach some sort of carrying strap or *sling*, and so forth are referred to as *furniture*.

Top left *Old Swedish handgun with reinforced barrel. The socket at the rear is for the supporting stave, and the firing vent is visible.*

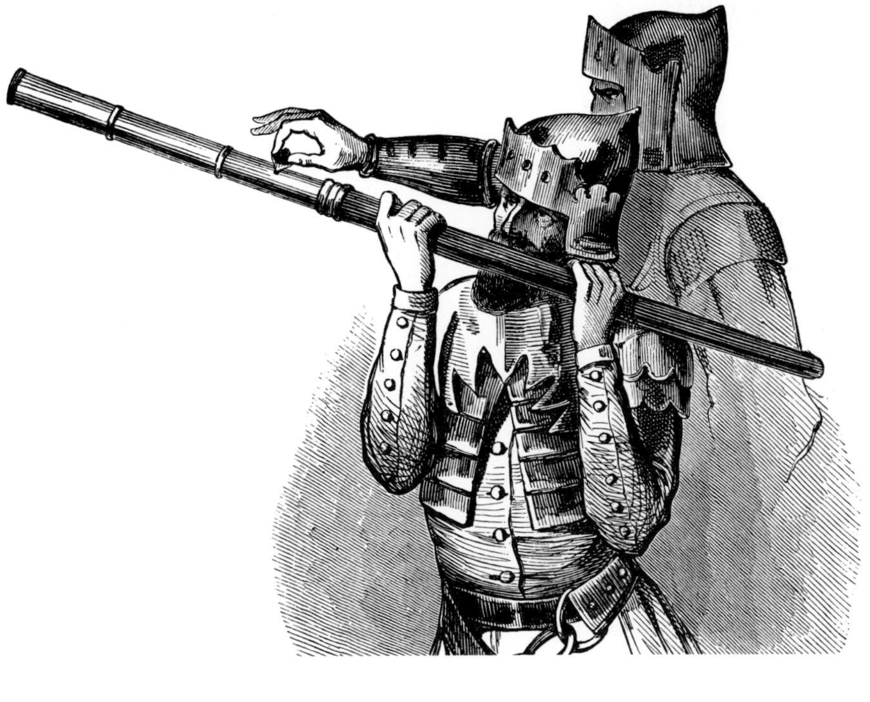

Right *A Victorian impression of a two-man team firing a handgun. One man holds the tube while the other applies a red-hot ember to the vent. English troops are first recorded as using handguns in 1369. By* c.*1475 stocks were being fitted to guns. Effective range was only about 50 metres.*

8873

MUZZLE LOADERS

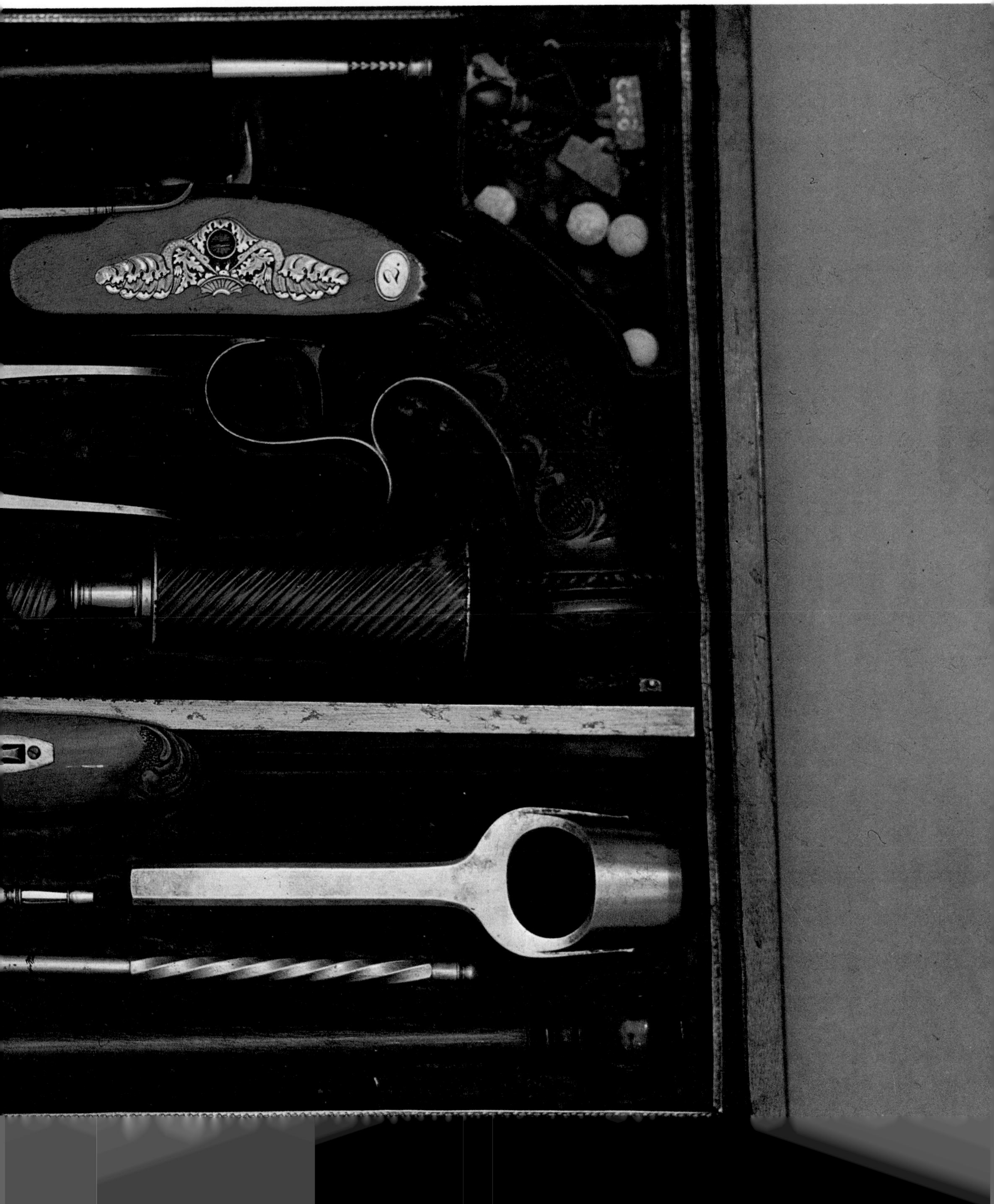

Previous page *A cased pair of fine Bavarian-made duelling pistols. These percussion muzzle-loaders' accessories include a powder flask, mallet, ramrods and bullet mould. The owner would make his own ammunition to meet the guns' exact requirements.*

Below *A German-made matchlock of 1537, an unusually early attempt at breechloading. It bears the cypher and arms of King Henry VIII.*

Bottom right *A late 16th century Spanish arquebusier with match-lock and slow match.*

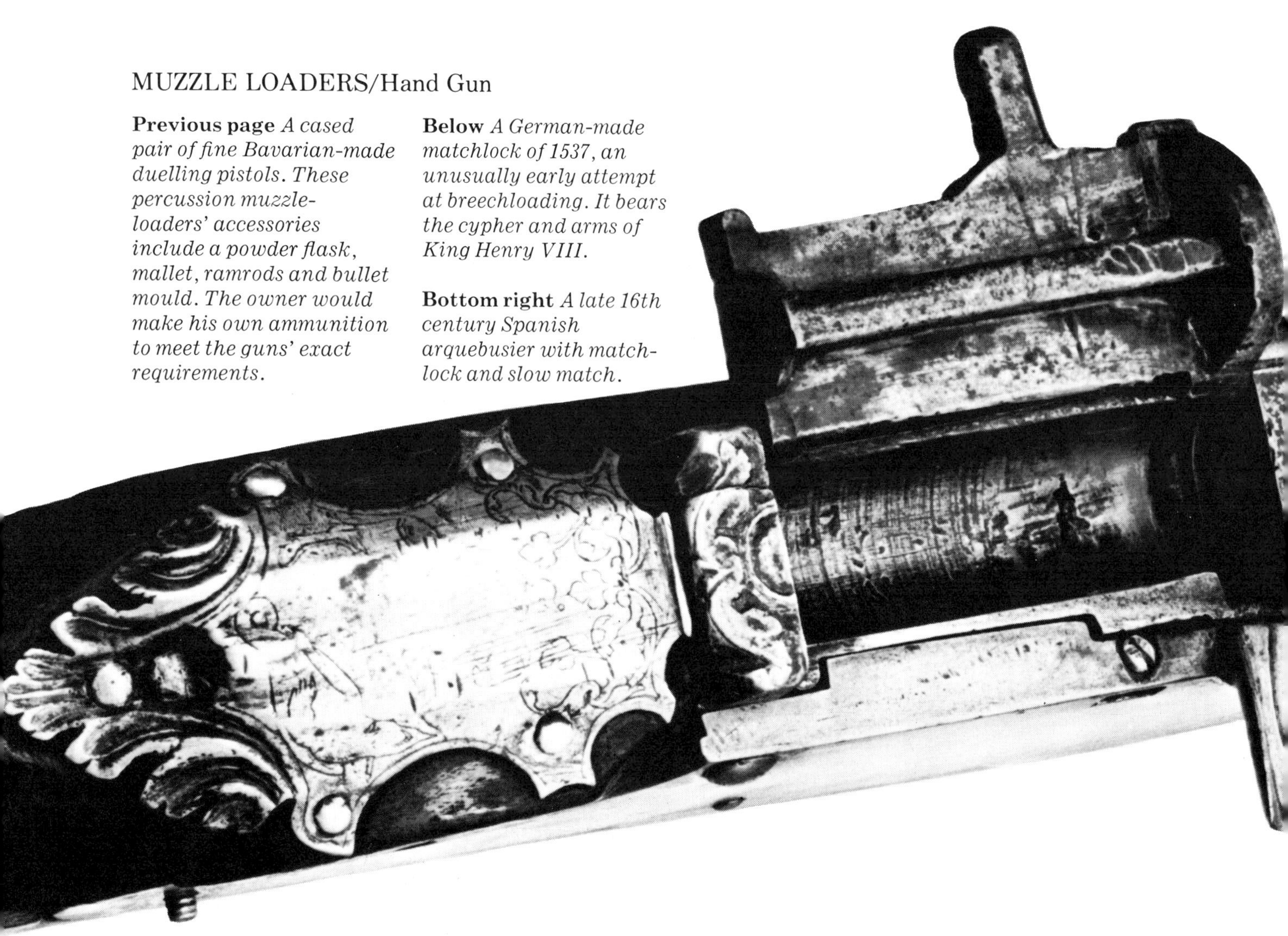

THE FIRST HANDGUNS were cumbersome and rather ineffective. They were simply tubes about 30cm to 90cm (1-3ft) in length, 2.5cm (1in) or so in calibre, strapped to a wooden pole from 1m to 1.5m (3-5ft) long. They were loaded through the muzzle in exactly the same way as the contemporary full-sized cannon. A charge of gunpowder was tipped into the barrel and followed by a 'wad', a small ball of rags or straw. This was forced down to the breech end of the barrel by a ramrod, the wad acting as a retainer to keep the gunpowder in place beneath the vent or touch-hole. The ramrod was withdrawn and a ball dropped into the barrel and again rammed down. If the ball was a good fit, that was enough, but if it was a poor fit – as was likely in those days – then another wad would be rammed on top to hold everything in place.

The vent was a fine hole bored through from the outside of the barrel to the end of the bore, the outer end of the vent being widened into a saucer-like depression. Into this went a sprinkling of gunpowder, some of which would find its way into the vent. Finally the handgun was touched off by applying a burning brand of hot iron to the exposed powder at the end of the vent. The explosion of this powder would flash down the vent, into the bore of the gun, and ignite the powder which in its turn would explode and discharge the ball.

In order to accomplish all this the firer had to load and then grasp the gun just behind the breech with his left hand, tucking the stock under his left elbow and clasping it to his side. Then with the right hand he applied the burning brand to the vent. As can be imagined, the firer would be concerned more with watching where he put the brand, so as to avoid applying it to his left hand by accident, than he would be with pointing the gun, so the accuracy of these early weapons is open to some doubt.

Gradually the stocks were shortened, and since these weapons were frequently designed for use in defending towns and castles, a hook was forged underneath the muzzle so that the gun could be hooked on to the wall and thus relieve the firer of the recoil (the sudden rearward thrust caused by the reaction of the gun to the explosion and expulsion of the ball). Such hooked guns became known in Old German as 'hackenbuchse', from which, by corruption, came the English name 'arquebus' or 'hackbut'. For firing when no wall was available, a forked stick was adopted, on to which the muzzle could be laid to support the weapon. The stock was now shaped so that the firer could rest it against his shoulder or, in many cases, against his chest.

Improvements in these early days followed in the wake of the cannon. The first development to appear was when some unknown experimenter found that, by soaking a piece of twine in a solution of saltpetre, he could make a 'slow match' which, once ignited,

would burn very slowly and thus provide the cannon gunner with a ready source of ignition without having to resort to plucking burning brands from a fire or to heating up irons. The hand gunner also adopted the slow match, commonly carrying it, burning, in his hand so that it was always ready to apply to the vent of his arquebus. This, though, was inconvenient, and soon a mechanical contrivance – the matchlock – was devised. An S-shaped metal arm, known as the serpentine, was hinged to the stock of the arquebus and the top end formed into a clamp which would hold a piece of burning match. The vent of the gun was enlarged to form a 'pan', into which the burning end of the match would fall when the lower end of the holder was pulled. Now the firer could devote his attention to the direction in which his gun was pointed, knowing that on pulling on the lever, the match would light the powder in the vent and fire the gun.

This simple mechanical arrangement was soon improved by cutting off the lower half of the 'S' of the serpentine, putting a spring behind it to force the match-holder toward the vent, and then fitting a stop, controlled by a trigger, to hold the match away until ready to fire. This was the snapping matchlock, the subsequent history of which is rather peculiar. It did not last long in Europe, but specimens were taken to the Far East by Portuguese merchant venturers and introduced into Japan. Shortly after this, Japan closed her borders to foreigners and the subsequent developments in firearms bypassed that country. As a result, the snapping matchlock remained in use there for another two centuries.

In Europe the gradual introduction of various mechanical devices into everyday life was echoed in the development of firearms, and by about 1517, doubtless due to the influence of the skilled clockmakers of southern Germany, the wheel-lock was invented. In this lock a thin, serrated wheel was connected, by a fine chain, to a spring. The axle of the wheel was finished in a square boss on to which a key could be fitted, and the wheel wound back so as to place the spring under tension. Once fully wound, the wheel was then held against the pull of the spring by a trigger-operated catch and the key removed. An angular arm, known as the 'cock' from its shape and from the appearance of the head, held a piece of iron pyrites and this was swung forwards to press against the edge of the wheel. When the trigger was released, the spring spun the wheel and struck sparks from the pyrites; the sparks fell into the powder-filled pan and thus fired the gun. The same principle survives today in the cigarette lighter.

The wheel-lock was an elegant solution to the ignition problem. Compared with the matchlock, it was safer against accidental discharge (provided the cock was clear of the pan), surer in all weathers, and easier to handle. But it was expensive and proved too delicate for the rough and tumble of ordinary warfare and it was never adopted as standard issue to the foot soldier. The wheel-lock did see some use in cavalry pistols, as it was assumed that these would be better cared for by their owners. But many more were turned out by gunsmiths as private orders for wealthy individuals, especially sportsmen, and as a general rule the wheel-lock was a stylish and richly-decorated weapon.

During the period of the wheel-lock, with guns being made to rather better standards of accuracy, the problem of fouling (a deposit left on the inside of the barrel by the burning of gunpowder) became acute. In early guns, where the fit between barrel and ball was generous, fouling made little difference, but when gunsmiths began to make weapons with little clearance between the bore and the bullet, then a layer of fouling could make reloading a difficult matter. An ingenious Swiss devised a system of cutting longitudinal grooves into the inner surface of the barrel, so that the fouling went into the grooves and the ball travelled on the 'lands' or the raised portions between the grooves. This necessitated making a patch of cloth to go beneath the ball to seal the grooves against the escape of gas, and it meant that loading the gun was a little more strenuous, but it appeared to improve the accuracy.

Below *A wheel-lock gun, probably late 16th century, showing the degree of embellishment commonly found on these hunting weapons. This one has two triggers – one 'sets' the mechanism and the second fires it with minimum risk of the gun drifting off target.*

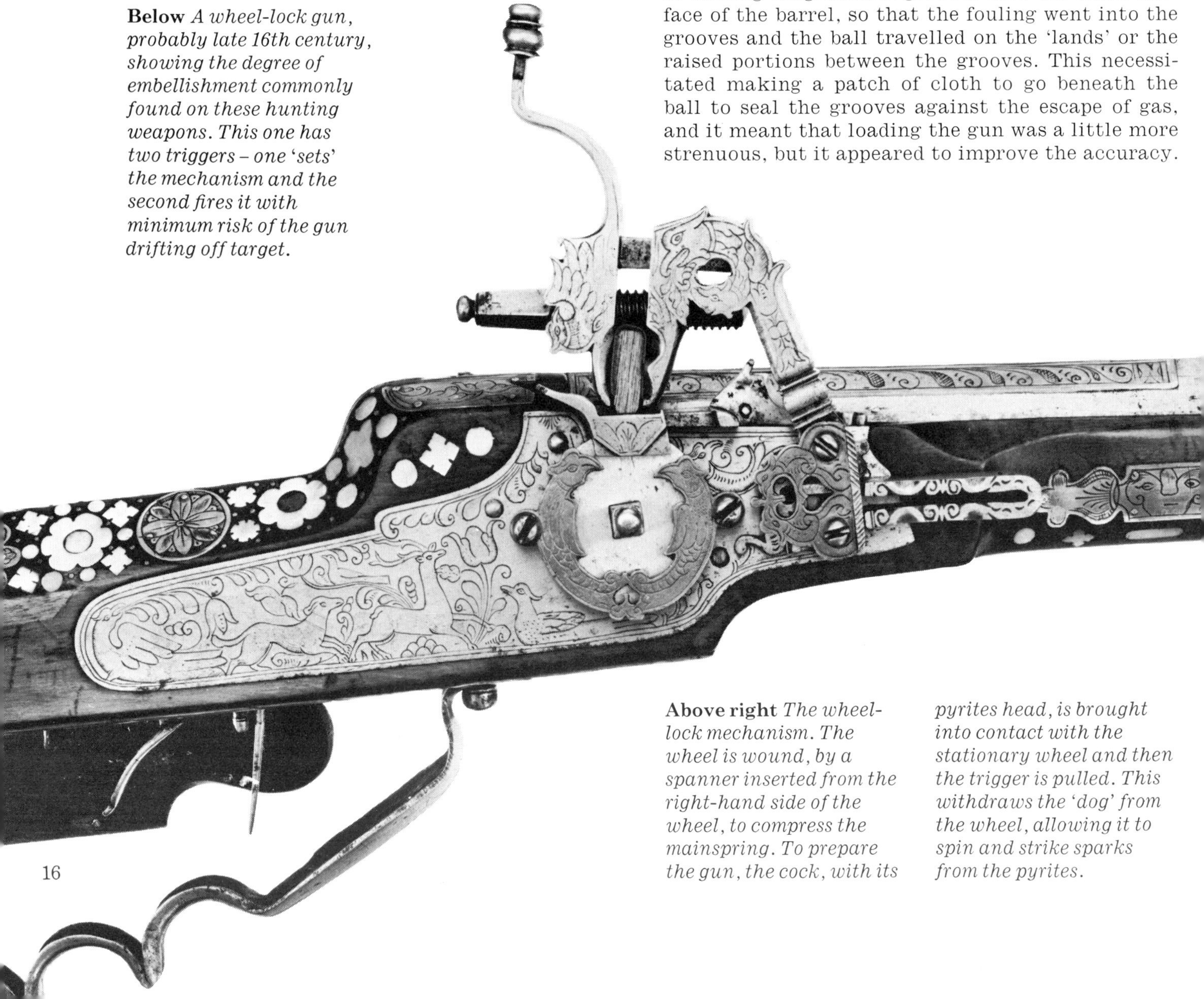

Above right *The wheel-lock mechanism. The wheel is wound, by a spanner inserted from the right-hand side of the wheel, to compress the mainspring. To prepare the gun, the cock, with its pyrites head, is brought into contact with the stationary wheel and then the trigger is pulled. This withdraws the 'dog' from the wheel, allowing it to spin and strike sparks from the pyrites.*

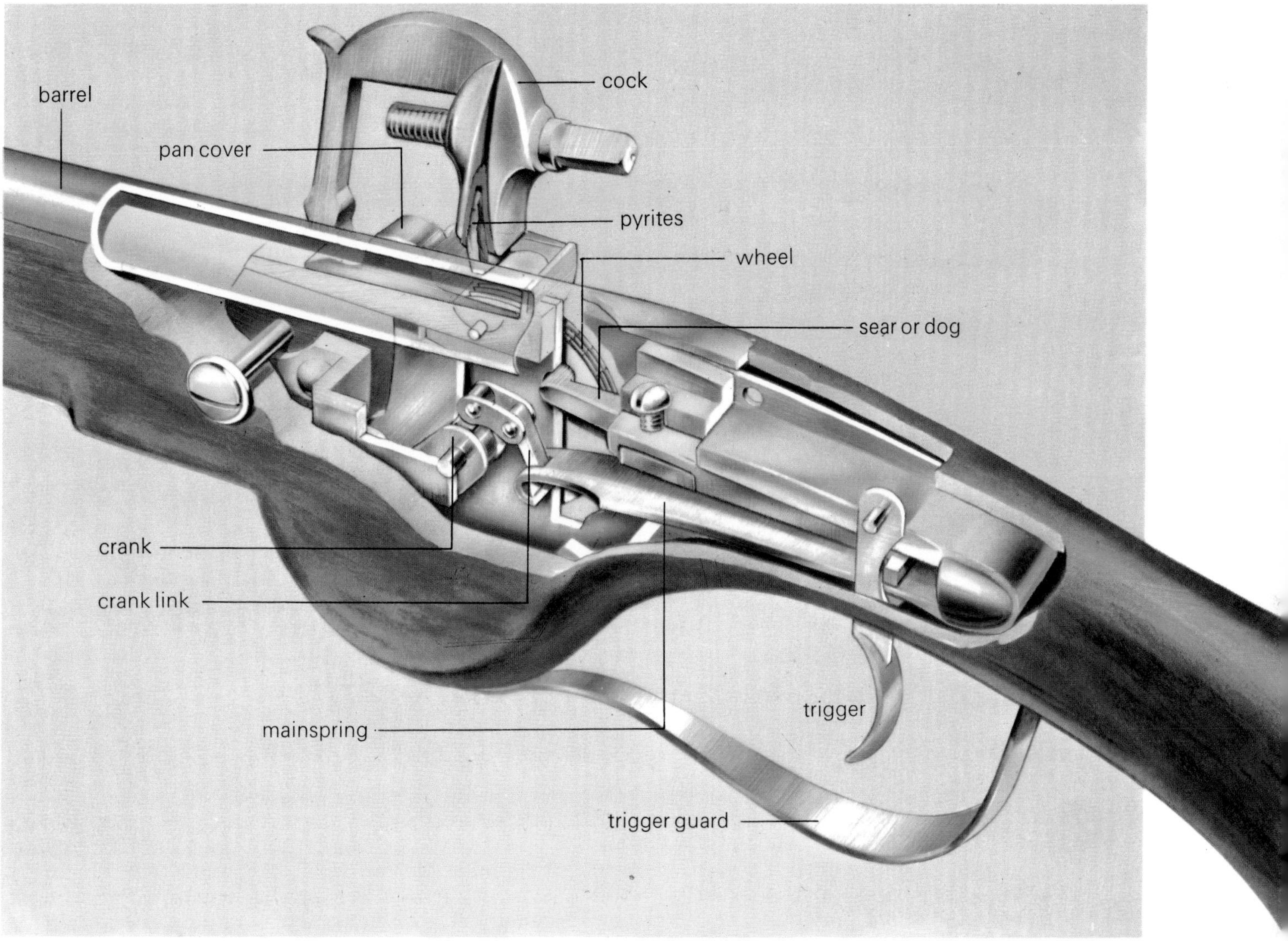

A more significant advance came when an unknown genius decided to give the grooves a slight twist and invented the rifled barrel. The spiral grooving inside the barrel gave a spinning motion to the ball, endowing it with gyroscopic stability during flight. This tends to equalize any abnormality of flight caused by irregularities of shape or density and also gives the flying bullet a better ability to resist changes in direction due to wind or air density. Knowledge of the advantages of rotational flight for projectiles was ancient – long before the first guns were made, archers and javelin-throwers used to cause their missiles to spin in flight – but an accurate explanation of the phenomenon came later.

The spinning principle was to increase in importance when spherical balls were replaced by elongated bullets, since only gyroscopic stabilization keeps such bullets flying point-first. Today, in general usage, the word 'rifle' implies a weapon fired from the shoulder and using a relatively small-sized, high-velocity bullet. But in the days before the invention of machine tools, cutting the rifling grooves was a difficult business, one of the 'mysteries' of the gunsmith's profession, and rifled guns were, in the first instance, strictly for the wealthy few.

At the beginning of the sixteenth century a new system of ignition appeared in Spain – the Spanish 'miquelet' lock or 'snaphance'. It combined the simplicity of the snapping matchlock with the spark ignition of the wheel-lock. One drawback of the wheel-lock was that the iron pyrites material was soft, did not last long in use, and was difficult to come by. The Spanish lock used a cock with a double jaw into which a shaped piece of flint could be clamped. A leaf spring, bearing against the heel of the cock, provided the power to drive it forwards, and a cross-bolt, coupled to the trigger, slid over and held the cock against the spring when it was pulled back by the firer. The pan, at the right side of the breech, was closed by a cover which turned up into a vertical face at the rear edge of the pan and was held tightly over the pan by another small leaf spring. The cover could be flipped open, against the spring, and powder poured into the pan, after which the cover snapped back. The spring had sufficient tension to hold the pan securely closed so that carrying or handling the weapon would not shake the powder out of the pan. To fire, the trigger was pulled, and this removed the cross-bolt from the path of the cock. The cock fell, and at the end of its

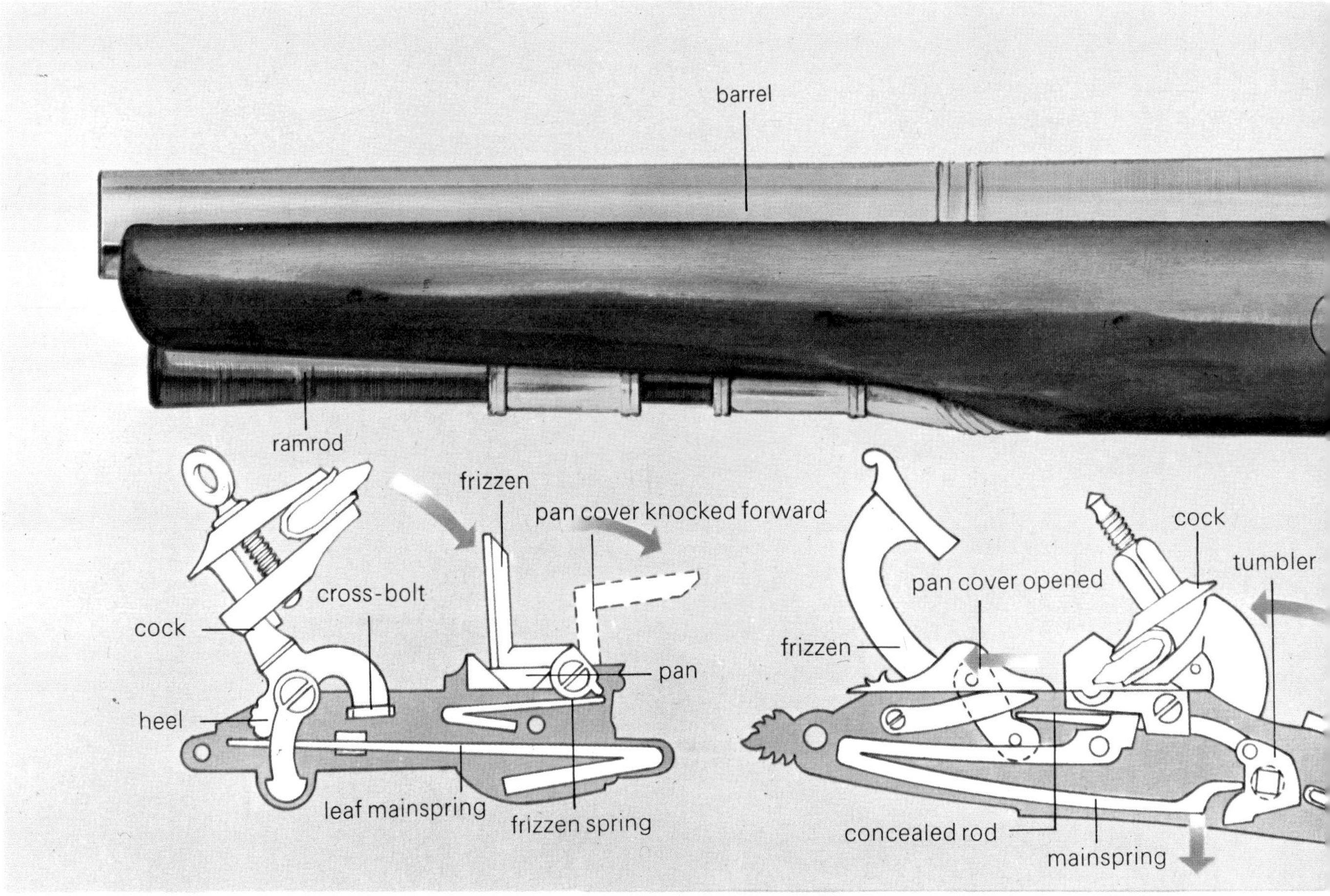

travel brought the flint into grazing contact with the vertical face of the pan cover. This contact both struck sparks between the flint and the steel of the cover, and also knocked the cover forwards so as to allow the pan to be exposed and the sparks to fall into the powder and fire the gun.

The Spanish lock was strong, simple and as reliable as could be hoped for at the time. It soon travelled throughout Europe, gathering improvements as it went. The Netherlands were then under Spanish occupation and influence, and the next step came with the Dutch Snaphance lock. In this design the pan cover was separated from the 'frizzen', that piece which struck the spark from the flint. The pan cover was a sliding cover which had to be slid open and closed when loading the pan but which was linked to the cock by a concealed rod. The mainspring was now concealed inside the lock and bore on the 'tumbler', a shaped metal piece on the axle of the cock. The action was more or less the same: as the cock fell, released by a catch operated by the trigger, so the connecting rod pushed the pan cover open. The flint struck sparks from the frizzen, the sparks fell into the open pan, and the gun fired.

The perfected design was known as the 'French' or 'Flint Lock', the earliest known examples dating from about 1610. This lock combined the internal spring and tumbler of the Dutch lock with the combined pan cover and frizzen of the Spanish design to produce the most reliable mechanism of its kind, one which was to remain the standard until the end of the spark ignition era. The flint would last for about 50 or 60 ignitions, after which it was generally discarded. Even removing it and resharpening it gave little more life. As a result, 'knapping' or the manufacture of flints became a major industry in those parts of Europe where suitable flints were found, and a skilled knapper could produce two or three thousand flints a day.

Once the flintlock became popular, firearms began to become more common, since the cheaper and simpler flintlock lowered the price and reduced the degree of skilled workmanship demanded. The flintlock smooth-bore musket became the standard weapon of the armies of the day, the flintlock pistol armed the cavalry, and also became a civilian arm. Flintlock sporting guns appeared.

Loading weapons such as the British service 'Brown Bess' or the Charleville musket of the French Army was a complex performance, drilled into the soldiers of the day until they could do it in the heat of battle without having to stop to think about it. The following drill for recruits – taken from the official British *Exercise of the Firelock* of the late eighteenth century – gives a fascinating glimpse of what was involved in handling a flintlock musket:

'Upon the command "Prime and Load"; make a quarter turn to the right . . . at the same time bringing down the firelock to the priming position, with the left hand at the swell, the side-brass touching the left hip, the thumb of the right hand placed in front of the hammer with the fingers clenched, the firelock nearly horizontal. Open the pan by closing the elbow to the side . . . Upon the command "Handle Cartridge"; 1st, draw the

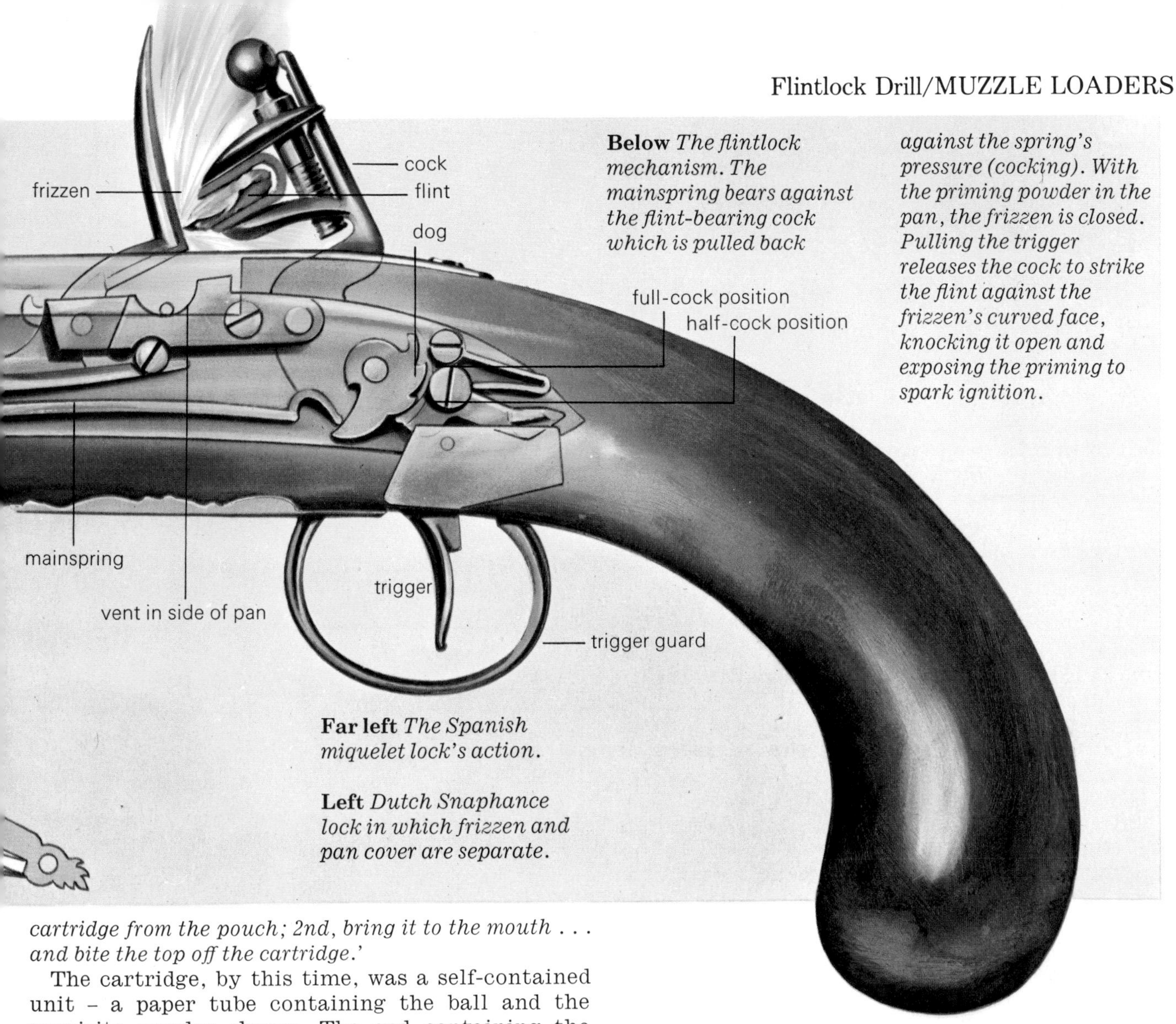

Below *The flintlock mechanism. The mainspring bears against the flint-bearing cock which is pulled back against the spring's pressure (cocking). With the priming powder in the pan, the frizzen is closed. Pulling the trigger releases the cock to strike the flint against the frizzen's curved face, knocking it open and exposing the priming to spark ignition.*

Far left *The Spanish miquelet lock's action.*

Left *Dutch Snaphance lock in which frizzen and pan cover are separate.*

cartridge from the pouch; 2nd, bring it to the mouth . . . and bite the top off the cartridge.'

The cartridge, by this time, was a self-contained unit – a paper tube containing the ball and the requisite powder charge. The end containing the powder was closed by twisting the paper and dipping it in wax or grease. It was possible to undo it by hand, but biting it off was the accepted and fastest method. It was also the reason why the British Army insisted on recruits having sound teeth.

'Upon the command "Prime"; 1st, shake out some powder into the pan and place the last three fingers on the hammer (frizzen). *2nd, shut the pan . . .*

'Upon the command "About"; turn the piece nimbly round to the loading position . . .

'2nd, place the butt on the ground without noise, raise the elbow square with the shoulder, shake the powder into the barrel, putting in after it the paper and ball.'

The paper was inserted first as a tight bundle, to act as a wad over the powder. Some of it would wedge between the ball and the interior of the barrel and thus act to retain the ball after loading.

'3rd, drop the right elbow close to the body and seize the head of the ramrod . . . Upon the command "Draw Ramrods"; 1st, force the ramrod half out and seize it back-handed exactly in the middle . . . 2nd, draw it entirely out . . . turning it at the same time to the front, put one inch into the barrel.

'Upon the command "Ram Down Cartridge"; 1st, push the ramrod down until the second finger touches the muzzle. 2nd, press the ramrod lightly towards you and slip the two fingers and thumb to the point, then grasp as before. 3rd, push the cartridge well down to the bottom of the barrel. 4th, strike it two very quick strokes with the ramrod.'

It will be appreciated that ramming could have been done more simply. Much of the detail insisted on here was to produce a uniform technique and drill movement which could be more readily checked by the non-commissioned officers and also to drill into the recruit a system of loading which would ensure that he would perform it automatically in response to orders during a battle.

'Upon the command "Return Ramrods"; 1st, draw the ramrod half out, catching it back-handed . . . 2nd, draw it entirely out . . . turning it to the front, put into the loops and force it as quickly as possible to the bottom . . . after a pause . . . bring the firelock in one motion to the same position as the word "Prime and Load".

'Upon the command "As Front Rank, Ready"; place the thumb of the right hand on the cock and finger behind the guard, and cock the piece. Then take a grasp of the butt, fixing the eye steadily upon some object in front.

'Upon the command "Present"; bring the firelock up to the present slowly and independently until in line with the object the eye had fixed upon; then pull the trigger without a jerk, and when fired remain looking on the

aim until the word "Load" is given . . .
'Too much pain cannot be taken to prevent the recruit from raising his firelock with a jerk; it must be deliberately raised until aligned with the object that the eye is fixed upon and so that he may lay his right cheek on the butt without too much stooping of the head; particular care must be taken that the recruit in this position shuts the left eye in taking aim, looking along the barrel with his right eye . . .'

It will be noticed that there is no question of using any sight – the firer looks along the barrel.

One of the most important features of the flintlock was the distinct sequence of events once the trigger had been pulled. The first time a flintlock is seen in action, the flash and smoke are so spectacular that the individual events go unnoticed, but after becoming used to it, it is possible to distinguish three separate actions. First comes the strike of sparks from the flint; then the ignition of the powder in the pan; and finally, after a distinct pause, the ignition of the main charge, the actual firing of the gun. The natural reaction for an unaccustomed firer is to flinch when the powder fires in the pan, thus disturbing his aim by the time the main charge fires, and this was a matter which received particular attention in the training of soldiers:
'The recruit having acquired the habit of readily aligning the firelock with any object selected by the eye, he is next taught to burn priming without winking, or the slightest degree altering the composure of his countenance . . . The instructor must watch the recruit minutely in this practice, which must be continued until the eye is perfectly indifferent to the flash caused by the ignition of the powder.'

But even if the firer became 'indifferent' to the flash of the priming powder, the same could not always be said of the target. Game birds and beasts were often alarmed by the initial fizzing and flash and frequently managed to make their escape during the short delay – known as 'hang-fire' – before the cartridge fired and sent a charge of shot in their direction, much to the chagrin of shooters 'for the pot'. One of these frustrated sportsmen was the Reverend Alexander Forsyth of Belhelvie, near Aberdeen in Scotland, who began, in about 1800, to apply his scientific bent in a search for a more certain and speedy method of ignition.

Towards the end of the eighteenth century, probably spurred on by the Napoleonic Wars, a number of people had begun to investigate various chemical substances which could be made to explode without the use of flame or spark to initiate them. Among them was the English chemist Edward Howard who, in 1799, discovered fulminate of mercury, a compound so sensitive that it could be exploded by the impact of a light blow. Forsyth began experimenting with fulminate and eventually discovered that a mixture of fulminate and potassium chlorate reduced the sensitivity of fulminate alone and also provided a stronger flash from the detonation. His next problem was to design a lock which would take advantage of the 'detonating powder' and in 1807 he patented his first percussion lock.

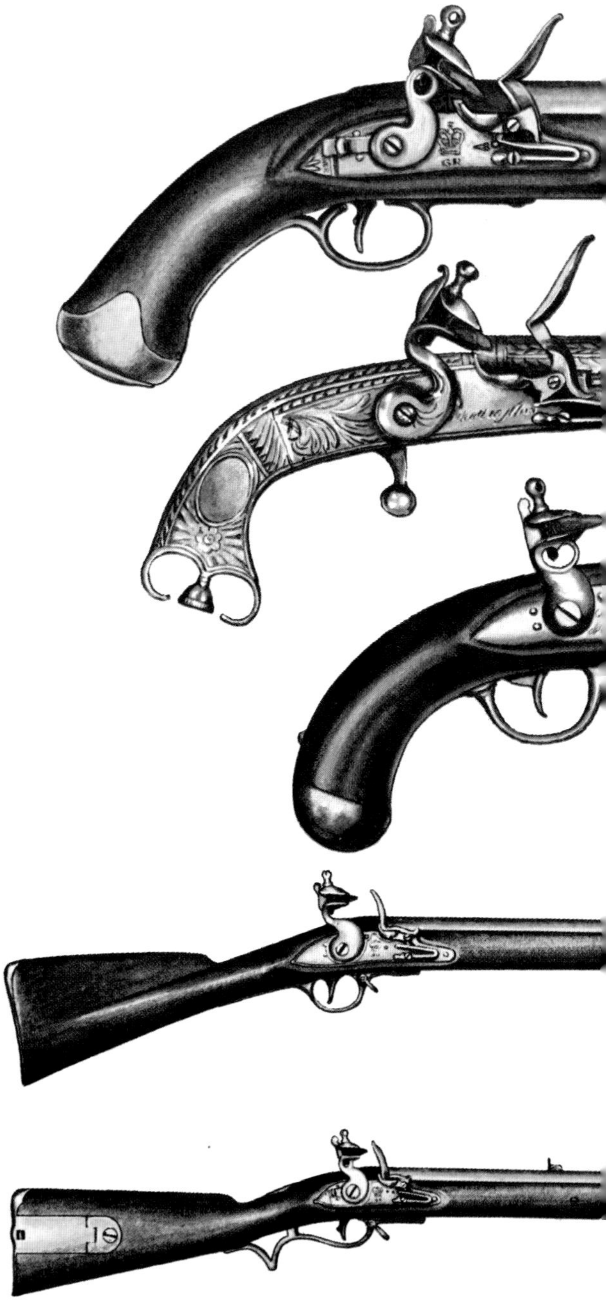

Forsyth's lock consisted of a tubular 'magazine' containing detonating powder in one half and a vertical pin in the other. It was mounted vertically just in front of the vent which ran from the breech of the gun – in other words in the position occupied by the pan and frizzen in a flintlock. The cock of the flintlock was replaced by a similar device but one which was tipped with a plain end, rather than with the double jaw to hold the flint. With its new function came a new name: it ceased to be known as the cock and became the 'hammer'. To operate the Forsyth lock, the magazine was charged with a quantity of detonating powder and the gun loaded in the usual way. Then the lock was rotated on its vertical axis

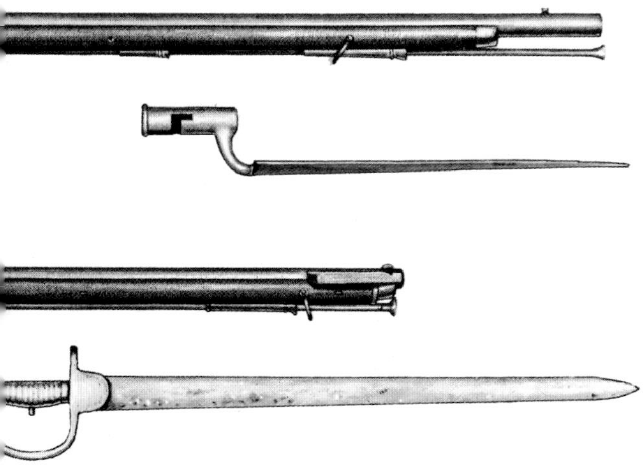

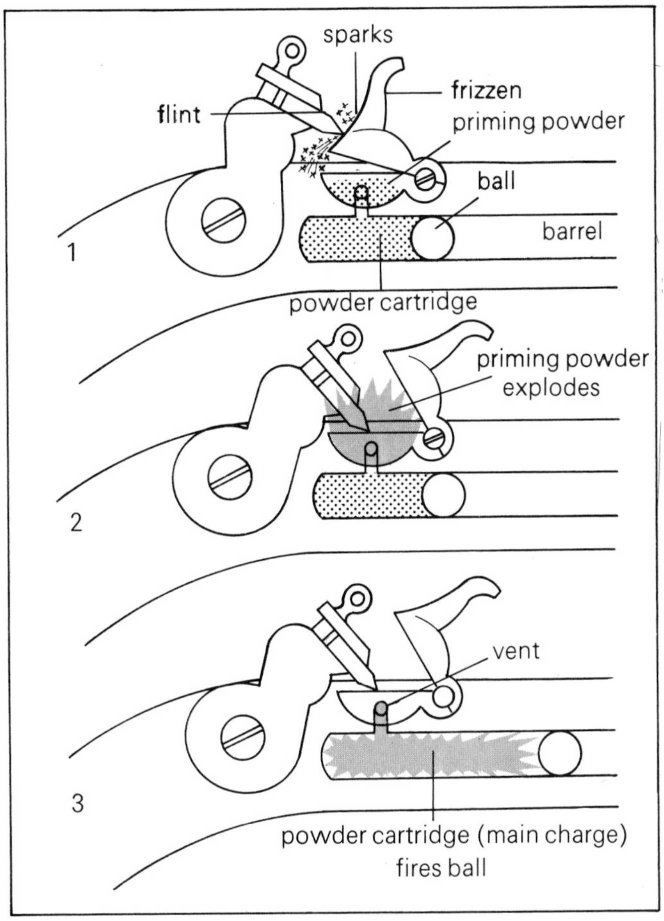

Far left *From top to bottom: a British light cavalry pistol of 1800-pattern with 'stirrup' ramrod attachment; an all-metal Scottish pistol of .7in calibre with 'rams horn' butt; an 1804 French .67in cavalry pistol; a British 1797 'India' pattern Brown Bess musket of .75in calibre, weighing 3.8kg (8.5lb) and measuring 137cm (54in) without the 45cm (18in) bayonet; a British 1800-pattern Baker Rifle with 61cm (2ft) sword bayonet. The Baker, of .615in calibre, was the British Army's first general issue rifle.*

Left *The three stages of flintlock ignition. (1) The flint strikes the frizzen, igniting the priming powder (2), which, via the vent, sets off the main charge (3). 'Hang-fire' is the delay from (1) to (3).*

so as to bring the magazine section over the vent. This deposited a small amount of powder in the vent. The lock was then revolved back, which brought the vertical pin above the powder in the vent. When the trigger was pressed, the hammer fell, struck the vertical pin, and drove it down on to the powder in the vent. This detonated, and the flash passed down the vent to fire the charge in the gun's chamber.

What this meant in practice was a far more efficient system of priming and ignition than that allowed by the flintlock. The magazine could be loaded with enough powder to fire 30 or 40 shots; the vent could be primed with a quick twist of the fingers; and when the trigger was pulled, the reaction was almost instantaneous. The birds of Belhelvie were extremely surprised when the good Reverend appeared among them with his new shotgun.

Forsyth's second design of lock has gone down in history as the 'scent bottle lock' because of its shape: the side view resembled a waisted bottle of the sort used in the eighteenth century for perfume. This lock was widely copied on the continent, notably by the French gunsmith Prelat. Continental designers then set about making the locks 'automatic' by linking the magazine with the hammer so that as the hammer was drawn back to cock, so the magazine was pulled to prime the vent with powder. Then, as the hammer came forwards on the firing stroke, it pushed the magazine out of the way and directly struck the powder in the vent.

Loose powder, however, was an inconvenient method of working and several minds were now applied to producing something easier and safer to handle. The first and most obvious solution was to compress the powder into pills which could simply be placed into a suitable vent, doing away with the expense of the magazine-type lock. This was not entirely satisfactory, since the pills were prone to crumble into powder when carried around for any length of time. Moreover, they were easily dropped or could be shaken out of the vent after loading. Forsyth himself overcame this handicap by pasting the pills between two strips of paper to make a string which could be carried rolled in some suitable receptacle on the lock and pulled out to present one

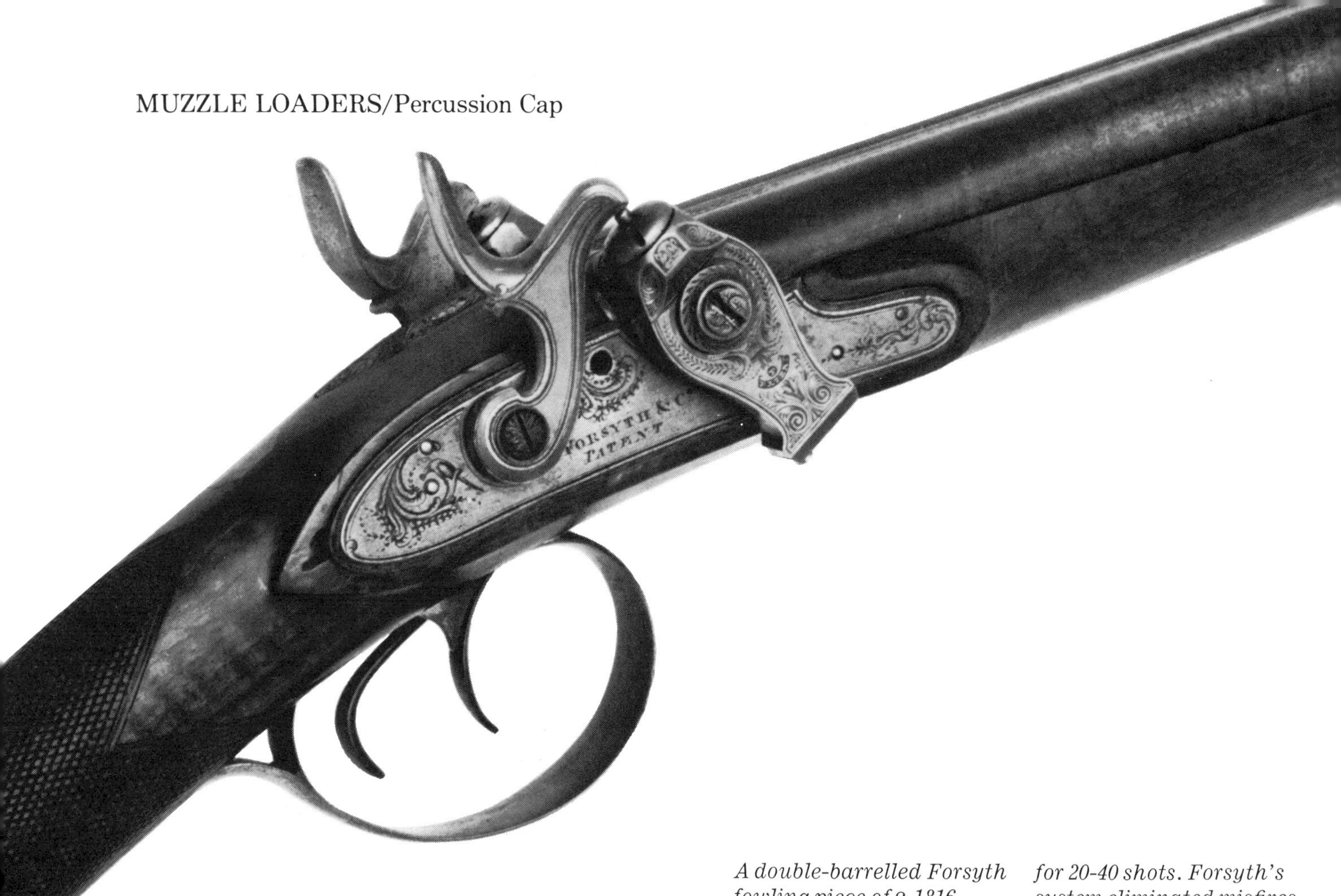

A double-barrelled Forsyth fowling piece of c.*1816 with the 'scent bottle' percussion lock. The lower half, or magazine, took enough priming powder for 20-40 shots. Forsyth's system eliminated misfires, multiplied rate of fire and allowed all-weather use, unlike the flintlock's open ignition.*

pill at a time to the vent. In fact the idea was the forerunner of the roll of paper caps or 'amorces' used by children in toy guns to this day. The idea of tape priming failed to catch on at first, though it was to reach a degree of success several years later in the United States when Dr Edward Maynard, a Washington dentist, used it in his carbines.

A better solution came in 1818 from Joseph Manton, a noted English gunsmith, when he placed a measure of detonating powder in a thin copper tube. He then bored the vent into the side of the gun chamber and placed a protruding peg in the position of the pan. The copper tube was then pushed into the vent so that a portion of it was exposed and supported by the peg. On pulling the trigger the hammer fell, to crush the tube against the peg and fire the detonating powder, flashing down the vent and firing the charge.

At much the same time, Manton, together with Joseph Egg, another London gunmaker, produced another idea. Presumably he backed both horses in the hope that one of them would win. This second idea was the percussion cap, which resembled a small top-hat made of copper. Inside the crown was a layer of detonating powder, retained there by a thin tissue and a coat of varnish. The gun now had the vent bored diagonally into the top centre of the breech, and into this was screwed a thin tube which stood proud of the breech and in line with the hammer. The open end of the percussion cap was slipped over the open end of this tube – or 'nipple' – and fitted sufficiently tightly for it not to be easily dislodged. When the hammer fell it simply crushed the powder between itself and the edges of the nipple, and the subsequent flash went through the nipple and vent directly into the chamber to fire the charge. Since there was a danger of the detonating cap flying to pieces and showering the firer with fragments of copper, the face of the hammer was recessed so as to shroud the cap at the instant of detonating.

In all fairness it should be said that the idea of the percussion cap appears to have struck several people at much the same time – a common enough occurrence with good ideas. Captain Joshua Shaw of Philadelphia patented a similar idea in 1814 and various European inventors have claimed priority. But whoever started the idea, it spread very rapidly and the days of spark ignition were largely over.

In general, the weapons of the early percussion period were simply those of the flintlock era, but with a hammer and nipple replacing the cock and frizzen. Indeed, the similarity was so great that many hundreds of flintlock guns were simply converted to percussion by removing the pan and frizzen and screwing in a nipple and holder, and replacing the cock with a hammer. In some cases the work was so well done that it is almost impossible to detect, but in many it was cheaply performed and the conversion is obvious. Many of these conversions appear in sale-rooms and collections today, and, it is regretted, many have been re-converted by dealers and owners to make them into 'genuine flintlocks' once more and thus command higher prices.

The perfection of the percussion lock was a considerable step forwards, sufficient to allow inventors to turn their attention to something else as an outlet for their talents. One of the next things to claim their attention was the question of the bullet. By the 1830s rifling had become universally accepted and the smooth-bore gun, except for the shotgun, was a thing of the past. Yet the problem still lay in producing a bullet which would pass down the bore easily when rammed but which would expand – 'set up' is the technical expression – into the rifling on its way out again to emerge with spinning flight. An early solution was the Delvigne system, in which the chamber at the breech-end of the weapon was of smaller internal diameter than the rest of the barrel. When the round lead ball was dropped in, it came to rest on this constriction, and a few hard blows with the rammer caused the lead to deform into a 'skirt' which bit into the rifling. The constriction prevented the ball from being driven down into the powder and possibly firing it by friction. Unfortunately, while this worked, it also deformed the ball. As a result, flight was even more inaccurate than usual, so that the system tended to defeat itself.

Gustave Delvigne appears to have appreciated the point, and he went on to produce a conical bullet with a cavity in the base. The exploding powder set up pressure behind the bullet and some of the pressure caused the thinned-out sides of the base cavity to expand into the rifling, without deforming the bullet. Then came the Thouvenin system, in which the gun chamber carried a steel pillar in its centre. The conical bullet was dropped down and, again, pounded with the rammer. Since the bullet came to rest on the tip of the pillar, the blows of the rammer forced the pillar onto the base and thus spread the base outwards into the rifling. This pillar became known as the 'tige' and the French Army adopted the 'carabine á tige' which used it. The same system was also used with British Army percussion pistols.

Finally, in 1849, came the famous 'Minié ball' developed by Captain Claude-Étienne Minié of the French Army. Minié fashioned a conical-cylindrical bullet with an iron cup let into a cavity in the centre of the grooved base. On firing, the iron cup was driven into the base of the bullet by gas pressure, and this forced the side of the base outwards to bite into the rifling. Minié had great success with his invention – he was paid the princely sum of £20,000 by the British Government for the use of his idea, and similar sums came from many other European governments. The Minié ball became the primary rifle bullet of the American Civil War, being generally used by both sides in that conflict.

Below *A percussion weapon's principle of operation. The hammer and nipple are shown, with the connection to the gun chamber.*

Bottom *The Maynard type (invented 1845) of tape-primed percussion lock, with the lock cover open to expose the roll of tape and showing how it feeds up to the nipple. The priming pellets of fulminate of mercury are embedded in paper or linen. The Model 1855 US Pistol-Carbine had this system.*

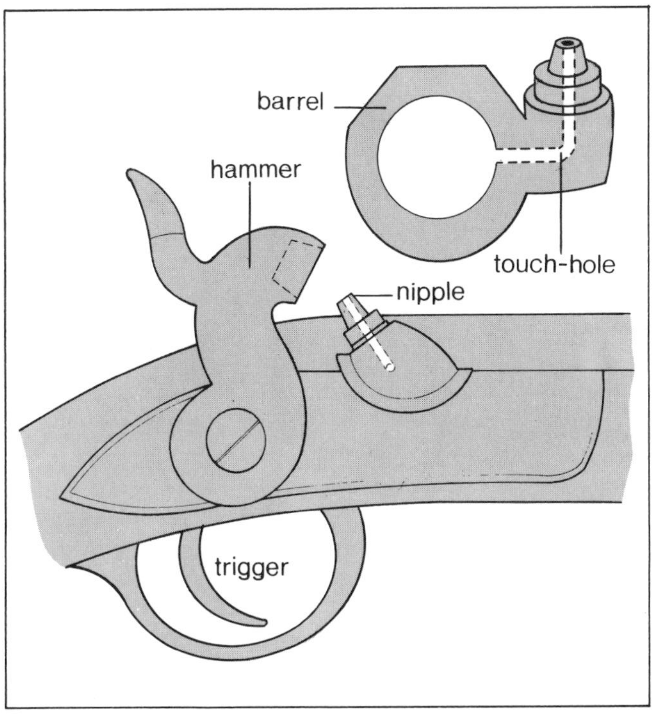

Brown Bess

Nobody knows where the British Army's famous musket, the Brown Bess, got her name; certainly not from 'Good Queen Bess' (Elizabeth I), who had been dead for over a century when the musket was first issued. 'Brown' certainly came from the colour of the barrel, chemically treated to resist corrosion and to prevent glare. 'Bess' probably came from simple alliteration.

The origin of the gun itself is equally indistinct. No definite date of approval has ever been discovered. The earliest date definitely ascribed to a specimen is 1720. It was formally known as the 'Long Land Service Musket' and was of .753in calibre with a 116cm (46in) barrel. It fired a 31.75g (490grain = 1.12oz) lead ball by means of an 8g (124gr = 0.28oz) powder charge. At 5.32kg (11.75lb) weight it was a heavy weapon, a good deal heavier than a 20th century magazine rifle, but it was primarily designed to be utterly soldier-proof. The British Army of those days was liable to find itself fighting in any corner of the globe, far from an armourer's workshop, so that robustness and reliability were of paramount importance.

The effective range was considered to be about 180m (200yd), within which it was as accurate as could be expected of a smoothbore. The markmanship test of the period called for a trained soldier to hit a 203mm (8in) circle at 180m (200yd), firing from the standing position, which is a fair performance.

In the mid-1760s the Long Land Service Musket was supplemented, and then gradually replaced, by the 'Short Land Service Musket', which had a 106cm (42in) barrel. This fired the same bullet but used a 4.53g (70gr = 0.16oz) charge in order to reduce recoil. It had a steel ramrod to replace the Long Land's wooden one. The Short Land Service Musket was a better-balanced and more easily handled weapon.

The shortage of muskets at the outbreak of war with France in 1793 led to the British Army buying them from the Honourable East India Company. This slimmer, slightly shorter and lighter 'India pattern' musket with a 99cm (39in) barrel became the regulation arm in 1797. A 'New Land Service Musket' followed in 1802; it was almost a complete return to the 'Short Land Service' model. They remained the standard British long arms until the arrival of the percussion muskets in 1842. And these, to the confusion of historians and students ever since, were still called 'Brown Bess'.

Left *A War of 1812 British redcoat with the 1797 India pattern Brown Bess. He has his 18in (45cm) bayonet fixed and would carry 60 rounds in his cartridge box.*

Below *An India pattern musket.*

Bottom *The 1802 New Land Service musket.*

LONG LAND SERVICE MUSKET

Calibre .753in
Length 155.2cm (61.125in)
Weight 5.32kg (11.75lb)
Barrel 115.5cm (45.5in)
Rifling Smoothbore
Foresight Blade
Rearsight None
Action Muzzle-loader
Rate of fire 2-3rpm
Muzzle velocity 182m/sec (600ft/sec)
Bullet weight 31.75g (490gr)

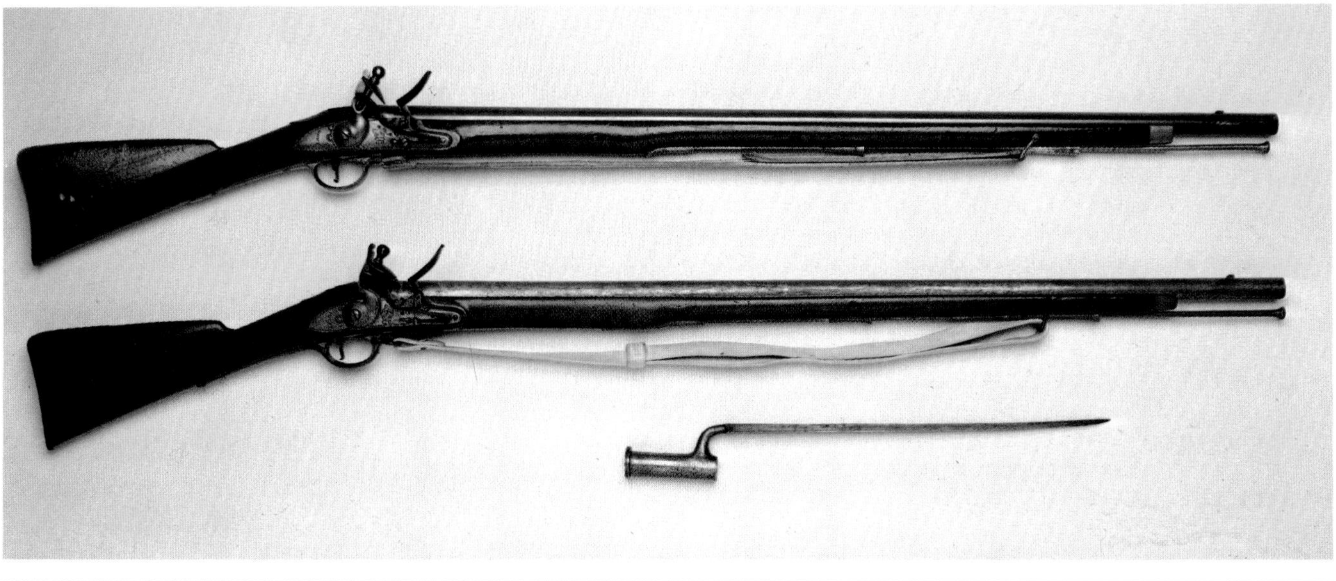

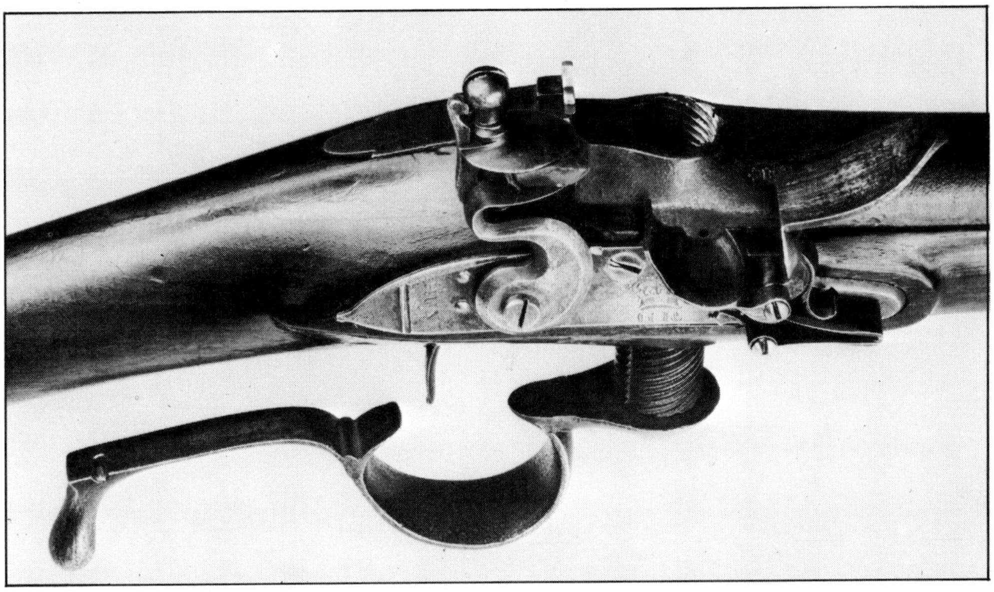

The Ferguson was the first breech-loading rifle to be adopted officially by the British Army, and, but for the death of its inventor, might have replaced Brown Bess. It was invented by Captain Patrick Ferguson of the 70th Foot (later the East Surrey Regiment) who adopted and improved an earlier French breech-loading idea. The breech of the rifle was closed by a screwed plug which ran vertically and was actuated by a lever which formed the trigger guard. The eight-grooved barrel was 86.6cm (34.1in) long, the whole rifle being 125.4cm (49.3in) long overall and weighing 3.1kg (6lb 14oz), almost one-third less than Brown Bess.

The Ferguson operated in very simple fashion. The breech was opened by swinging the lever in three-quarters of a circle clockwise, which, due to the fast pitch of the screw on the breech plug, lowered the plug and exposed the rear end of the chamber. The ball was then dropped in, being prevented from going too far into the barrel by the rifling, and a charge of loose powder was poured in. A turn of the lever then closed the breech once more, the flintlock was cocked and the pan primed, and the rifle was ready to fire. It was possible for the average soldier to load and fire three rounds a minute, while a skilled man could get off five or six shots in that time. In addition to the speed, the accuracy was far better than that of the contemporary muskets.

After demonstrations by Ferguson, the rifle was accepted by the Board of Ordnance in 1776, and 100 were made in London under Ferguson's personal supervision. A special Light Company of 100 men was formed, Ferguson was placed in command, training with the new rifles was completed, and the unit was then dispatched to North America to fight in the War of Independence. There, unfortunately, the first engagement of the Ferguson Rifle turned out to be its last, though not from any defect in the weapon.

Ferguson and his green-uniformed Light Company led a diversionary attack at Brandywine Creek on 11th September 1777. They acquitted themselves well until Ferguson was shot in the arm. With the guiding hand removed from the field, the Light Company (having lost 40 killed and wounded) was split up after the battle and the men dispersed to their former regiments. Their rifles were removed and subsequently vanished; very few have ever been seen since. Although Ferguson recovered from his wound, he was killed at the Battle of Kings Mountain (7th October 1780) before he could begin to reconstitute his rifle company.

A Ferguson is shown open for loading. The trigger guard has swung the twist-threaded plug down about 22mm (.875in).

FERGUSON RIFLE

Calibre .702in
Length 125.4cm (49.375in)
Weight 3.13kg (6.9lb)
Barrel 86.6cm (34.125in)
Rifling 8 grooves, r/hand
Foresight Blade
Rearsight V-notch (some weapons had no rearsight)
Action Screw breech
Feed system None
Muzzle velocity (est.) 228m/sec (750ft/sec)
Bullet weight 29.11g (450gr)

BREECH LOADERS

Previous page *Custer's Last Stand, the Battle of the Little Big Horn (25 June 1876) as most accurately illustrated by E. S. Paxson. The US 7th Cavalry were armed with a single-shot .50in calibre, cam-locked Springfield carbine, an obsolete weapon. Though few Indians had firearms, some had Winchester or Henry repeating rifles. Both sides used the Colt .44 revolver. One trooper is trying to unjam his carbine.*

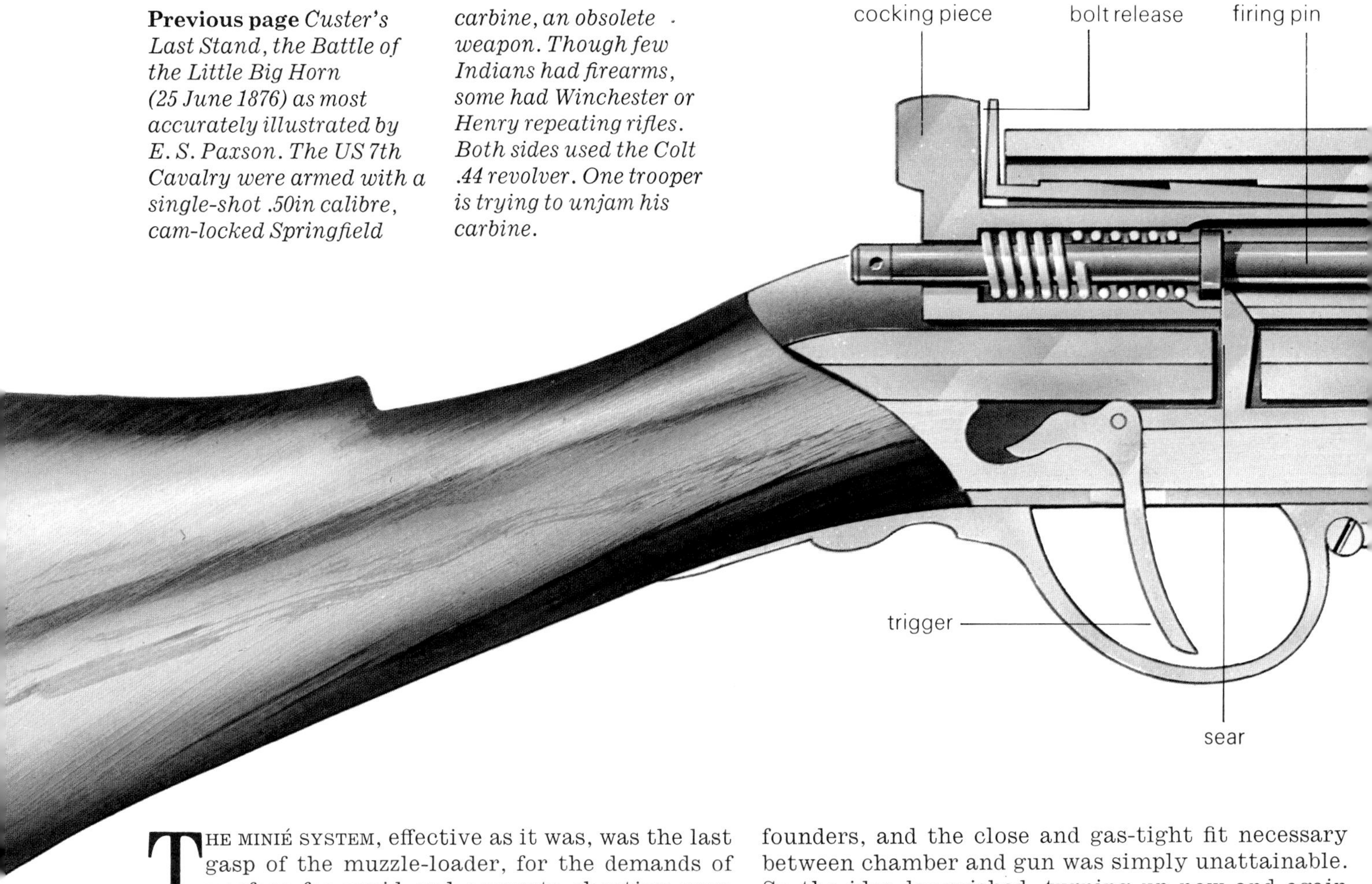

THE MINIÉ SYSTEM, effective as it was, was the last gasp of the muzzle-loader, for the demands of warfare for rapid and accurate shooting were becoming too insistent to ignore. The slow loading and inherent inaccuracy of the muzzle-loader were bad enough, but the full tally of disadvantages which went with it tend to be forgotten today. They were lovingly tabulated by William Greener, writing in the late nineteenth century of the advantages '*possessed by the breech-loader over the best of muzzle-loading guns. There is no danger when loading; no possibility of the ramrod being shot through the hand or of caps flying into the eye; no nipples to foul; no powder-flask and shot-flask to carry, no caps to fumble with and no need to tear paper into wadding. There is stronger shooting because there is no escape of gas through the nipple-hole, and because the powder is unimpaired by the fouling which, with the muzzle-loader, used to be forced down upon the charge by the wad . . .*' Because of these drawbacks, and because of the promise of better things, the records of the second and third quarters of the nineteenth century abound with ideas for breech-loading arms.

The whole idea of loading from the breech was not new. Some of the earliest cannon had been made with separate chambers which could be pre-loaded with powder and ball and then placed behind the open breech of the cannon, locked in place with wedges, and fired. The empty chamber could then be quickly removed and replaced by a loaded one. The idea was sound, but the degree of technology demanded was not within the reach of the early gun-founders, and the close and gas-tight fit necessary between chamber and gun was simply unattainable. So the idea languished, turning up now and again as new inventors tried to make it work. It was not until the nineteenth century, with its advances in mechanical engineering and consequent improvement in fit and finish, that breech-loading became practical. Even then, it took much trial and error before inventors realized the magnitude of the forces of explosion and heat that they were playing with, and appreciated that what was an elegant solution on paper very often failed to work on the firing range.

The prime requirement was still a gas-tight seal, and simply making flush-fitting faces to the barrel and breech-piece was not good enough. Moreover, so long as the cartridge was no more than a lead ball and a pinch of powder, loading was still almost as difficult by the breech as it was by the muzzle. The self-contained cartridge – a paper sleeve with the ball and powder on a single unit – was a step in the right direction, but the eventual answer was to construct the cartridge so that it performed two tasks. Not only was it to carry the propellant powder and the missile, but it was to be interposed between the chamber and the breech to act as a seal, one which was renewed every time the gun was reloaded and thus was never likely to wear out.

As early as 1812, a Swiss gunsmith named Samuel Johannes Pauly, working in Paris, had developed a single-shot pistol using a remarkable self-contained cartridge which included its own means of ignition.

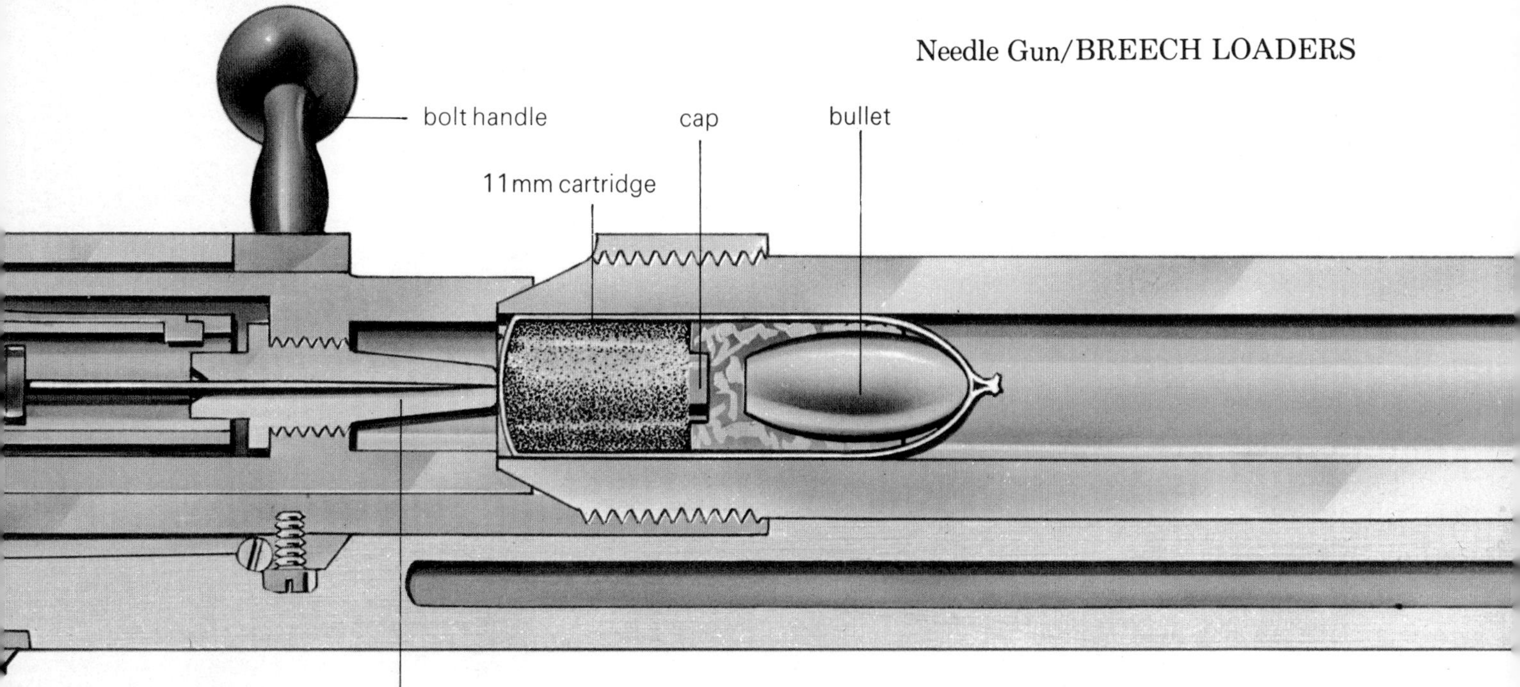

The mechanism of the Dreyse Needle Gun. To load, the bolt release is pressed and the cocking piece pulled out. The bolt is then opened by lifting the handle and pulling it back. The self-contained cartridge is inserted into the chamber. The bolt is closed and the handle turned down, the cocking piece thrust into the bolt to compress the spring. The trigger releases the needle to penetrate the cartridge and strike the bullet base.

A cylindrical brass or iron base formed the support for a tube of paper, into which the powder charge and the bullet were inserted. The brass base was centrally bored and carried a pellet of detonating powder in a recess at the outer end of this boring, secured in place by a covering of varnished paper. Pauly's pistol had a 'break action' (similar to that of the modern shotgun) which lifted the rear end of the barrel and allowed direct access to the breech. The cartridge was inserted, and the barrel closed on it, cocking a firing pin within the breech as it closed. On pulling the trigger the pin was released to go forwards and strike the detonating powder. This flashed through the base of the cartridge to fire the charge. The firer then opened the breech and removed the brass base-piece – the paper, of course, had been largely consumed in the firing. He was now ready to reload with another cartridge, and at the end of the day faced the prospect of sitting down and cutting up the necessary paper to make up a fresh lot of cartridges on the fired bases.

Pauly, however, was ahead of his time. His invention received little attention in France and after the occupation of Paris in 1814 following the defeat of Napoleon Bonaparte, he went to London. He still failed to find acceptance of his ideas and he died in poverty in 1817. Although one or two gunsmiths toyed with his idea, it lapsed into obscurity, but Pauly deserves remembering as the inventor of the self-contained, centre-fire metallic cartridge.

The first practical system of breech-loading to be adopted for military use (which, after all, is the criterion of any system of firearms) was the bolt action 'needle gun' of Johann Nikolaus von Dreyse. Von Dreyse, a Prussian, had been apprenticed to Pauly in Paris and he set up in business as a master gunsmith in Sömmerda, Prussia. In 1827 he developed his needle gun, but it took several years work to perfect and not until 1835 did he manage to produce a reliable weapon. After thorough trials, it was taken into service by the Prussian Army in December 1840, and this acceptance marked the arrival of what we might call 'modern' weapons into military service.

Von Dreyse's breech mechanism was based on the common door-bolt which, when turned sideways against a lug, resists opening. Through von Dreyse's bolt ran a long 'needle' or firing pin, propelled by a spring, and controlled, through the agency of a 'sear' or intermediate lever, by the trigger. The bolt lay in prolongation of the breech of the rifle, and its face carried a chamfered lip which made tight contact with the correspondingly chamfered rear face of the breech to give a fairly efficient gas-tight joint. Behind the barrel, and surrounding much of the bolt, there was a metal framework – the 'receiver' or the body of the gun – and this was cut away to allow the bolt handle to be turned down through 90° when the bolt was slid forwards and closed, so that the handle lay in front of a metal surface and thus locked the bolt in the closed position.

The heart of von Dreyse's system lay in the ammunition. A special cartridge was prepared, consisting of a cylindrical bullet with a rounded nose and a pellet of detonating powder in its flat base. The bullet was contained in a paper cartridge which extended well behind the bullet base to contain the propelling charge of gunpowder. The percussion pellet was thus in front of the charge. This self-contained cartridge was loaded into the breech of the rifle and the bolt closed behind it. Prior to closing the bolt, the needle was pulled back into the bolt. After the bolt was closed and locked, the needle was then placed under pressure by pushing in an inner sleeve of the bolt which cocked the firing spring. Pulling the trigger released the needle which was driven forwards by the spring. It penetrated the base of the paper cartridge and continued until it struck the percussion pellet, crushing this against the base of the bullet and igniting the charge. After firing the soldier pulled out the inner bolt sleeve to withdraw the needle and remove pressure from the spring. He then unlocked and opened the bolt, ready to reload.

The Prussian Army had taken a major technical step by adopting von Dreyse's gun, but the rest of the world's armies were in no hurry to follow suit. They were quite content to wait and see how the new system proved itself over the course of a few years of use before they committed themselves. Moreover, they were now confronted with a problem which has recurred whenever a new idea has appeared: how to justify the scrapping of a vast and valuable stock of weapons and the expense of re-equipping with new ones? The armies of Europe were stocked with hundreds of thousands of weapons, most of which had just been converted from flint ignition to percussion at great expense, and the thought of throwing all this away in order to spend huge sums on a new and untried system was repellent. Nevertheless, it soon became obvious that breech-loading had arrived and intended to stay, so the economy-minded men who controlled the military purse-strings began looking for some way of converting percussion muzzle-loaders into percussion breech-loaders as cheaply as possible.

The list of proposals for converting existing weapons runs into several hundreds, some of which were practical, but most of which bordered on the lunatic. The general tendency was to cut off the breech of the rifle and replace it with a solid block which was hinged so that it could be swung out of the way to allow a paper cartridge to be loaded into the breech and then swung back again and locked. The block was bored with a vent and provided with a nipple for taking a percussion cap, and it was generally arranged so that the nipple fell in the same relative position that it had done on the muzzle-loading original gun, so that the hammer did not need to be altered. Probably the most famous of these conversions were those of Erskine Allins and Jacob Snider. Allins' conversion hinged forwards and was adopted in 1865 by the Americans for the Springfield rifle, familiarly called the 'Trapdoor Springfield'. The Snider conversion of 1867, although designed by an American, was applied to the British Enfield musket. (The Enfield was officially called a musket, though it was, in fact, rifled and not a smooth-bore.)

While the military authorities were thus groping slowly towards the breech-loading era, the civilian shooters – less inhibited by convention and without vast stocks of arms to be converted or disposed of – were moving rather more rapidly. In 1832 a Parisian, Casimir Lefaucheaux, designed a new shotgun for hunters. This had the barrel hinged to drop down, lifting the rear end clear of the standing breech which contained the firing lock. A special cartridge was developed by Lefaucheaux to suit the gun. It consisted of a cardboard tube and base supported by a brass outer cap, the two being firmly held together by a thick card wad pressed into the interior. The tube contained the charge of powder and the shot, while a percussion cap was fixed into a recess in the brass base so that it could flash through a hole and ignite the charge. This cartridge laid the foundations for all subsequent development of shotgun ammunition, and the pattern has changed only in minor details up to the present day.

In 1846 another Frenchman, Bernard Houllier, patented a self-contained cartridge which was essentially a percussion cap with a tiny bullet in the

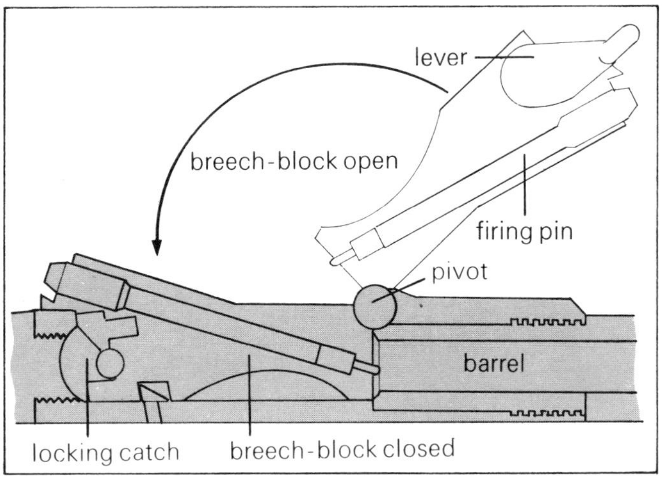

Above *The Springfield Trapdoor conversion. The breech-block is released by a thumb-catch to allow loading. Locking brings the firing pin under the cocked hammer.*

Below *Some early self-contained cartridges. From left to right: the Needle Gun; the Maynard, ignited by an external cap, the spark passing through the base hole; the early*

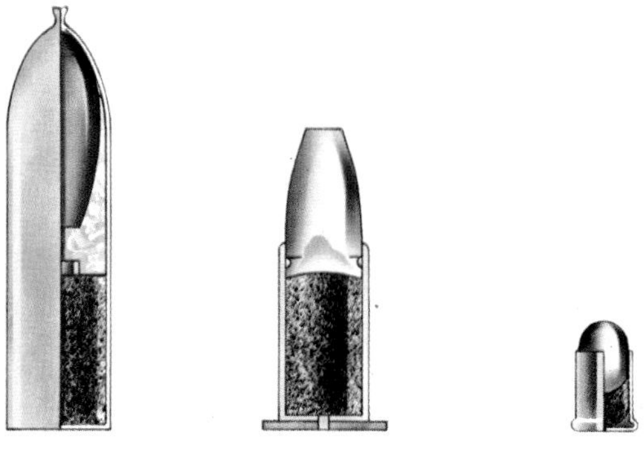

front. Houllier had improved matters by making the cap with a folded hollow rim, into which the detonating powder was packed. The powder was ignited by hammering the rim against the edge of the breech. The small cartridge – the bullet was 5mm calibre – has gone down in history as the Flobert cartridge, because Houllier appears to have been less interested in manufacture than he was in invention, and the exploitation of the idea came from Louis Flobert who produced a range of 'saloon' rifles and pistols for indoor target practice. The design has, in fact, survived to the present day, being known today as the BB Cap (BB for 'Bulleted Breech').

Not content with this, Houllier came up with another idea in the following year when he produced a cartridge in which the percussion cap was ignited by a pin which passed through the side of the cartridge base. The breech of the gun was slotted to allow the pin to protrude when the breech was closed. The gun hammer fell on to the pin which, in turn, crushed the cap and fired the cartridge. This, for obvious reasons, became known as the 'pin-fire', while his earlier idea became the 'rim-fire'.

Both were widely adopted in Europe, but the rimfire tended to be confined to low-power weapons

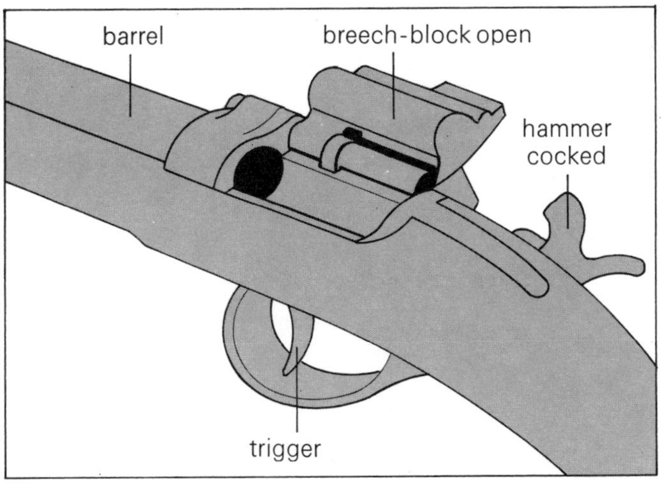

Flobert rimfire; a pinfire shotgun; a Pottet shotgun centre-fire; a Boxer, the anvil is part of the cap; and a Berdan, the anvil is part of the cartridge case which has two flash holes.

Above *British Snider conversion open for loading. The breech-block is hinged to the right in order to open. This is done by pressing a thumb catch. An extractor was fitted.*

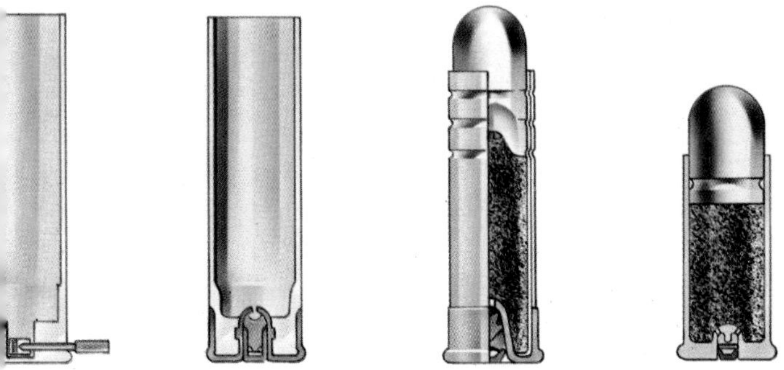

since there was always the danger of the rim blowing out and injuring the firer if any great amount of pressure was developed inside the case. The pinfire was safer in this respect: even if internal pressure tried to blow out the pin – which was unlikely – the pressure of the hammer resisted it.

In the United States an interesting but aberrant form of cartridge had been developed as the 'Volcanic' cartridge. This was a conical bullet with a recessed base containing a charge of powder and a percussion cap, and it was allied with the Volcanic repeating pistol and rifle first made in 1854 by two gentlemen named Horace Smith and Daniel Wesson. The Volcanic used a lever beneath the trigger to operate the breech-block; when the lever was pushed down the breech-block was pulled away from the barrel and, in moving back, it cocked the hammer. At the same time a 'lifter' lifted a cartridge from a long tubular magazine fixed below the gun barrel (rather like a second barrel) and presented it to the breech. Pulling the lever back thrust the breech-block forwards and pushed the cartridge into the breech, lowering the lifter to pick up a fresh cartridge. Ingenious as it was, the Volcanic failed because of two basic defects. Firstly, the cavity in the base of the bullet did not have sufficient room to carry a worthwhile amount of propellant, so the velocity and accuracy were poor. And secondly, the closure of the breech was not gas-tight, so that much of the propulsive force leaked out, reducing the velocity even further. Smith and Wesson were astute enough to see these defects before most other people, and they sold out in 1856 and went off to design a better pistol.

It will be recalled that the armies of Europe were sitting on their percussion muskets and waiting to see what sort of results the Prussians got from their von Dreyse-designed needle gun. Its efficiency was to be well demonstrated in the Austro-Prussian War of 1866. But before then a French mechanic, Antoine Chassepot, foreman at a French arsenal, developed his version of a bolt-action rifle which was adopted by the French Army in 1866. Chassepot's rifle showed some improvements over the needle-gun design. In the first place, the firing pin was automatically cocked as the bolt was closed, doing away with the separate cocking movement required of the firer by the von Dreyse design. In the second place, the obturation (sealing) of the breech was made more effective by using a washer-like plug of india-rubber around the end of the bolt which fitted tightly into the breech when the bolt was closed. And, thirdly, Chassepot had developed a cartridge which carried the percussion cap centrally in the base, so that the firing pin no longer had to pass entirely through the cartridge to strike the cap. This reduced damage to the pin which, in the von Dreyse design, was subjected to strain by the heat of the explosion.

The Franco-Prussian War of 1870 allowed the observers to see what results were achieved when two first-class armies armed with bolt-action breech-loaders met each other. The results proved quite conclusively that the breech-loading rifle was a

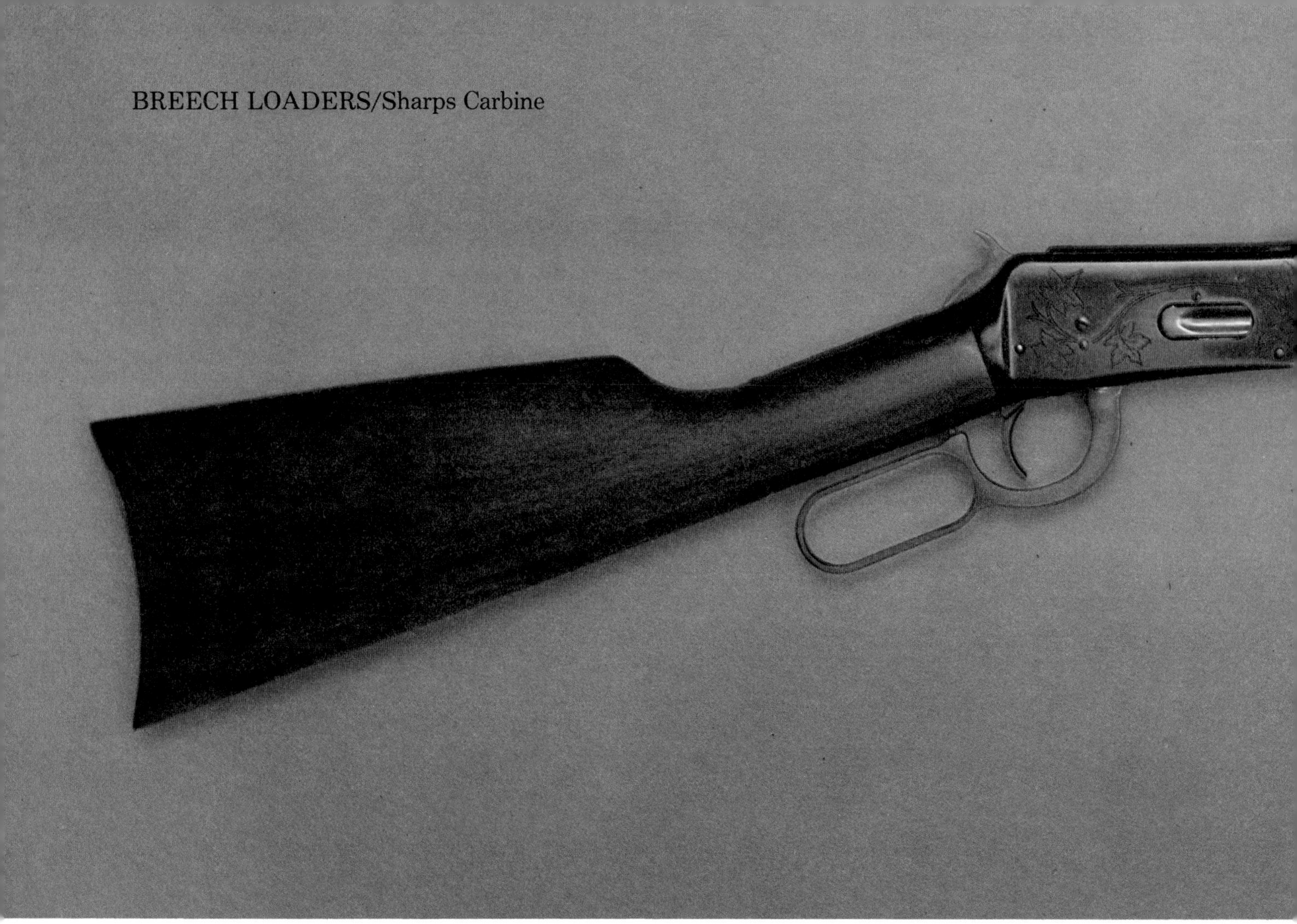

necessity in modern armies, and the rest of the world busied itself with testing competing designs.

There were, of course, ways of closing the rear end of the rifle other than using the bolt action. One of the most successful early designs was that of Christian Sharps, a Philadelphian gunmaker who, in 1848, patented a rifle with a breech-block which dropped in guides in the frame to expose the rear of the chamber. The movement was controlled by a lever beneath the trigger. The block carried a vent and nipple, and an external hammer was fitted. With the block lowered, a paper cartridge containing charge and bullet could be inserted into the chamber. As the block was raised, the front edge cut the end from the paper cartridge and thus exposed the powder inside to the flash from the cap, coming down the vent. One advantage of the design was that when the block became too difficult to operate due to fouling, it was quite possible to treat the weapon as a muzzle-loader and revert to the method of ramming the charge and bullet down the barrel and placing a cap on the nipple. After figuring prominently in the American Civil War, the Sharps' carbine (as it is popularly called) became the buffalo hunters' gun – used by professional hunters in the large-scale slaughter of the buffalo to obtain food for the railroad gangs.

Another system of closing the breech was exemplified by the American Maynard rifle in which the barrel dropped away from the breech in shotgun

Top *The Model 1894 Winchester Rifle, the first to use smokeless powder ammunition. Over three million have been made and production continues.*

Above *The Model 1895 Box Magazine Winchester's trigger lever guard fully open. The hammer is thereby cocked and the breech-pin rod retracted.*

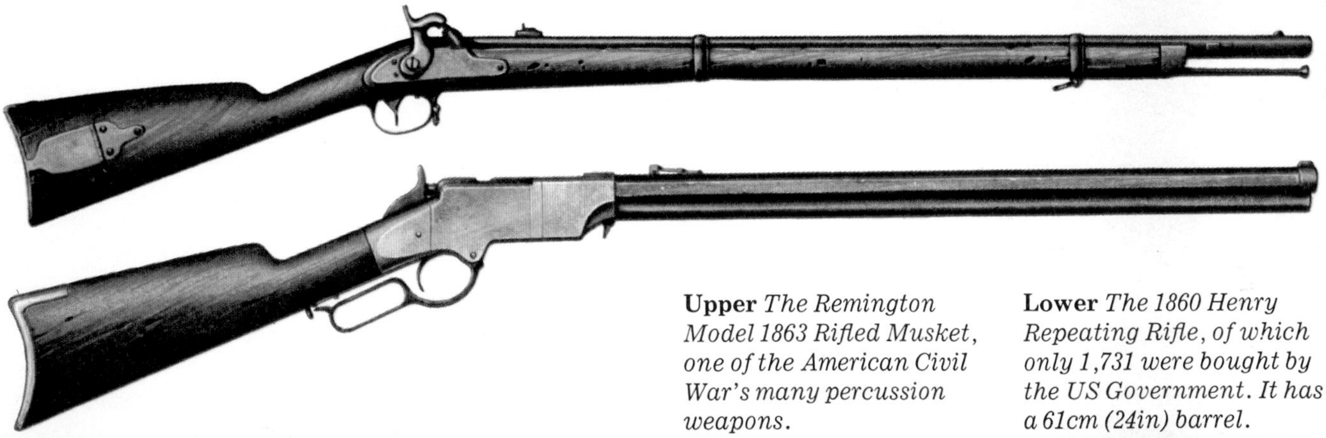

Upper *The Remington Model 1863 Rifled Musket, one of the American Civil War's many percussion weapons.*

Lower *The 1860 Henry Repeating Rifle, of which only 1,731 were bought by the US Government. It has a 61cm (24in) barrel.*

fashion and was loaded with a metallic cartridge which, however, did not contain its own ignition system. It merely had a hole in the base, covered with thin paper. A percussion cap and nipple on the standing breech provided the flash, which passed down the vent, through the hole in the cartridge, and fired the charge. The cartridge had a large rim which allowed the empty case to be extracted, after which it could be reloaded when the firer had time.

One of the most important designs to appear during this fertile period of American firearms manufacture was that of the Winchester lever-action rifle – perhaps the most famous of all repeating rifles. It will be remembered that the Volcanic rifle used a lever action to cock the arm, feed a cartridge and close the breech. The Company went bankrupt in 1857 and was bought by Oliver Winchester, a major shareholder. Winchester was a haberdasher who knew little or nothing about firearms design, but he had the sense to find a man who did know something and hired him to run the factory. Benjamin Tyler Henry was the man, and he took the Volcanic rifle, gave it a thorough overhaul, and produced the immortal Winchester. The basic system was the same: the under-lever opened the breech, cocked the hammer, and brought up a fresh round from the tubular magazine below the barrel. But Henry improved the mechanism to make it more reliable and designed the gun to use the rimfire, and later the centre-fire, cartridges.

A contemporary of the Winchester – and probably more renowned in its day – was the Spencer carbine. This too was a lever-action weapon – indeed, it was patented a few months earlier than Henry's design – but it was loaded by means of a magazine tube inserted into the butt. A supply of 7-shot loaded tubes could be carried by the soldier and rapidly inserted so that he could keep up a high rate of fire. Christopher Spencer, who was only 20 years old, managed to gain the attention of President Lincoln, and the Spencer carbine was adopted for use by the Union Army during the Civil War, over 60,000 being delivered in .52 calibre. The Henry design, on the other hand, never managed to attract official attention, though it was widely purchased by State authorities to arm their militia regiments. But when the Civil War ended, so did orders for the Spencer, and Winchester bought out Spencer.

Another lever action of the time, though not a repeating weapon, was the Peabody rifle, invented by a Bostonian in 1862. Here the breech-block was hinged at its rear end and, when the lever beneath the stock was operated, moved so that the front end of the block fell clear of the chamber, leaving sufficient room for a cartridge to be slid down over the block and into the breech. Peabody's first model used an external hammer to strike a firing pin in the breech-block, and was chambered for a .45 calibre rimfire cartridge – remarkably big for a rimfire at that time. The design was a great success and Pea-

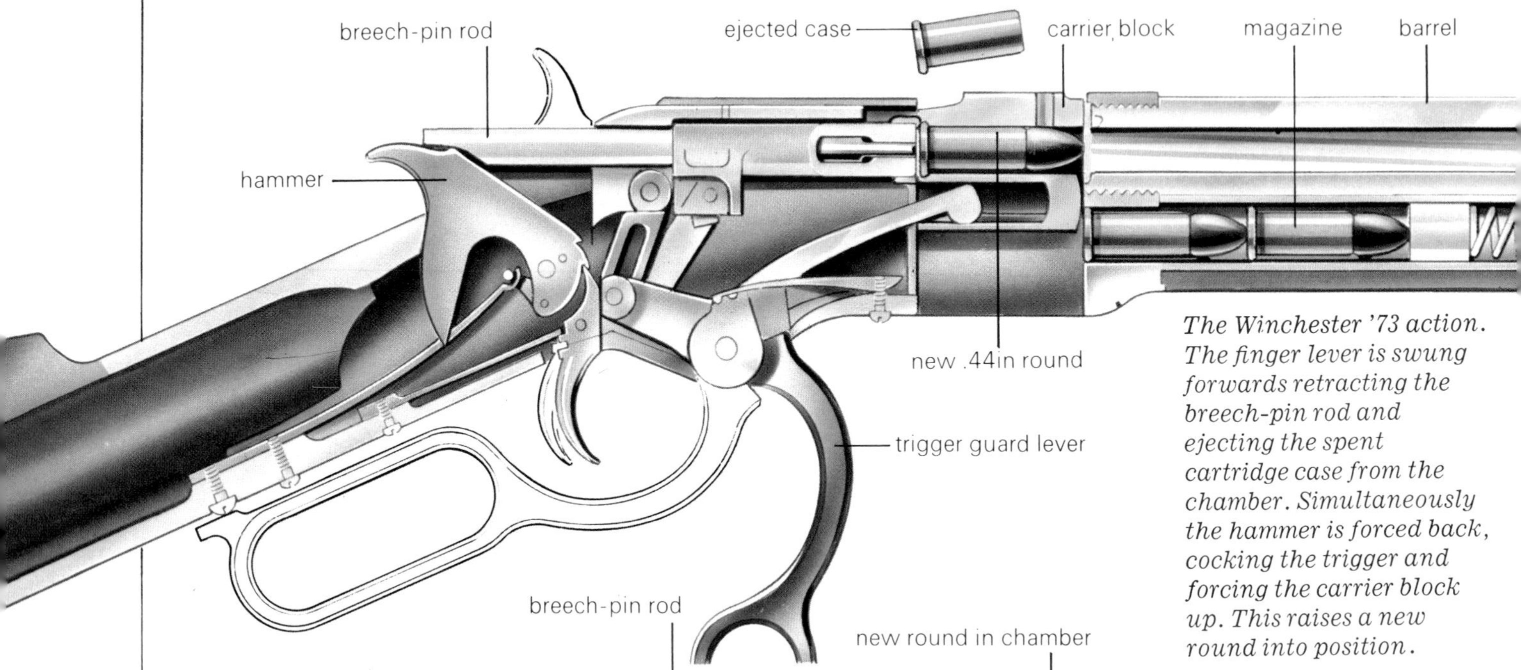

The Winchester '73 action. The finger lever is swung forwards retracting the breech-pin rod and ejecting the spent cartridge case from the chamber. Simultaneously the hammer is forced back, cocking the trigger and forcing the carrier block up. This raises a new round into position.

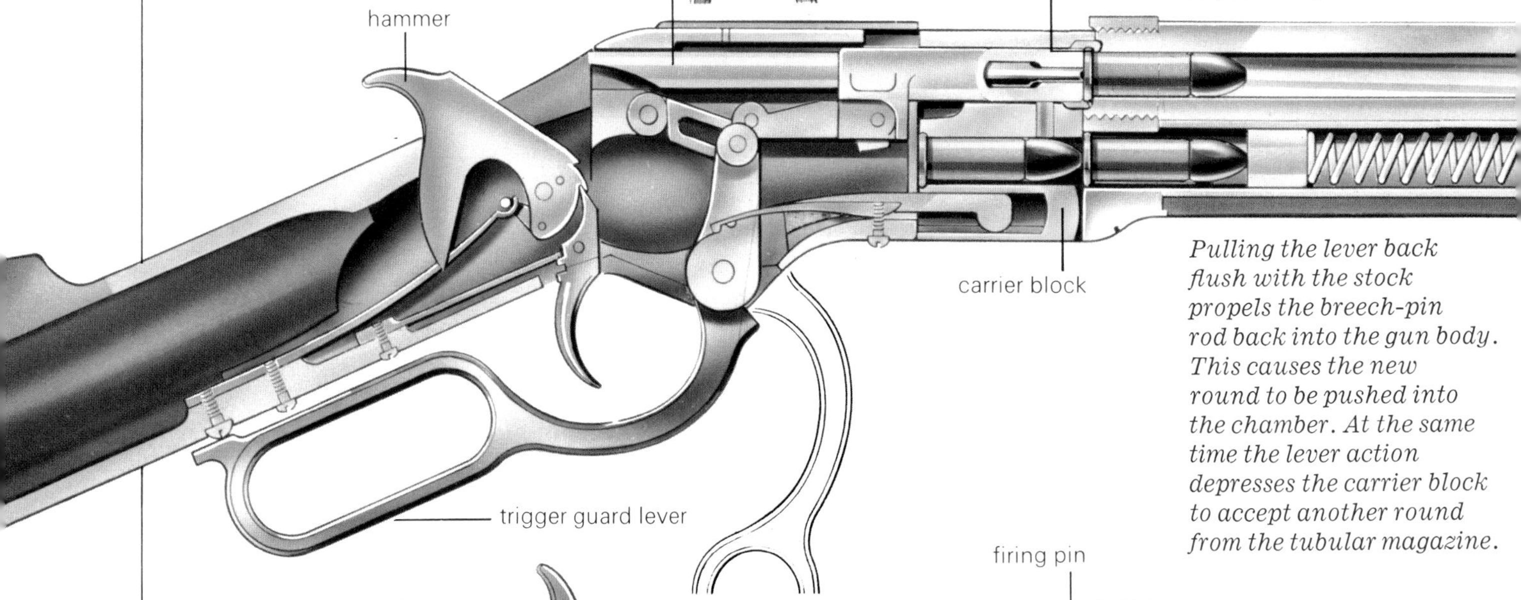

Pulling the lever back flush with the stock propels the breech-pin rod back into the gun body. This causes the new round to be pushed into the chamber. At the same time the lever action depresses the carrier block to accept another round from the tubular magazine.

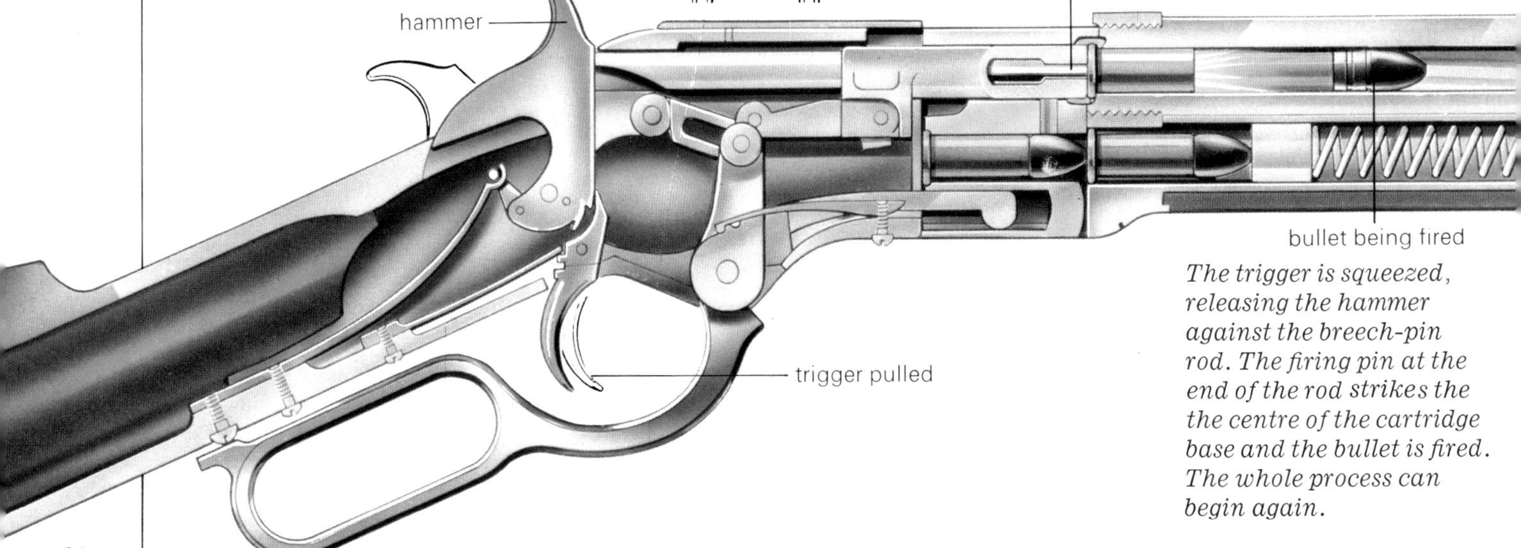

The trigger is squeezed, releasing the hammer against the breech-pin rod. The firing pin at the end of the rod strikes the the centre of the cartridge base and the bullet is fired. The whole process can begin again.

Oliver F. Winchester (1810-80) began life on a farm, was apprenticed to a carpenter and became a master builder. He then went into haberdashery and patented a new method of making men's dress shirts which made him moderately rich. Casting around for somewhere to invest his money, he came across the moribund Volcanic Arms Company and bought stock in it in 1855.

Volcanic had gone into business to make and sell a lever-action rifle which had a tubular magazine beneath the barrel and which locked the breech by a toggle joint. The projectile was a combined bullet and cartridge, the bullet having a hollow base and percussion cap. The weapon worked but was not very efficient, having low velocity, short range and poor accuracy. Sales were few and the company went bankrupt in 1857. Winchester, though, was convinced that there was some good in the weapon and bought out the remaining stock. Hehired Benjamin Tyler Henry, a first-class gunsmith to make something of the Volcanic design.

Henry made considerable changes. He first discarded the Volcanic bullet and developed a .44in rimfire cartridge, in memory of which every Winchester cartridge to this day has the letter 'H' impressed on its base. Henry then overhauled the mechanism to make it more reliable and robust, though he retained the essential feature of the toggle joint. This lies behind and beneath the the bolt and its centre joint is linked to the operating lever beneath the rifle stock. As the lever is pushed down and forwards, the centre joint of the toggle is pulled down, breaking the lock behind the breech and drawing the block back. As it comes back, so the hammer is cocked and another attachment to the lever raises a cartridge. As the lever is pulled back, the bolt is thrust forwards, ramming the cartridge into the chamber and the toggle is lifted up behind the bolt to form a shield strut to resist the force of recoil against the bolt. The cartridge lifter drops into line with the tubular magazine and a spring forces another round into the lifter. Finally the trigger is pulled, releasing the hammer to fall on the firing pin and fire the cartridge.

Issued first in 1860 as the Henry Rifle, this met with little success but sales of about 10,000 during the American Civil War were sufficient to keep the Winchester Company going. An improved version, in which the magazine could be charged from the rear by a trap in the side of the gun body, instead of from the front by removing the end of the magazine tube, was introduced in 1866. In .44in rimfire the Winchester Model 1866 was widely bought by the pioneers of the American West, and it achieved considerable military fame during the Russo-Turkish War of 1877-78 when the Turks at Plevna inflicted over 30,000 casualties on the attacking Russians with their Winchesters.

In 1873 a centre-fire version appeared, the famous Winchester '73 model. In subsequent years it was chambered for just about every sporting centre-fire and rimfire cartridge on the market. It enjoys wide popularity to this day and is essentially unchanged from Henry's original design of 1860.

Left *'Deadwood Dick', Negro cowboy Nat Love, poses with his M1866 Winchester in the 1870s.*

WINCHESTER '73

Calibre .44-40in
Length 106.7cm (42.0in)
Weight 3.85kg (8.51b)
Barrel length 609mm (24.0in)
Rifling 6 grooves, r/hand
Foresight Barleycorn
Rearsight V-notch, adjustable to 600yd (548m)
Action Lever, sliding bolt
Rate of fire 15rpm
Feed system 15-round tubular magazine
Muzzle velocity 396m/sec (1,300ft/sec)
Bullet weight 12.96g (200gr)

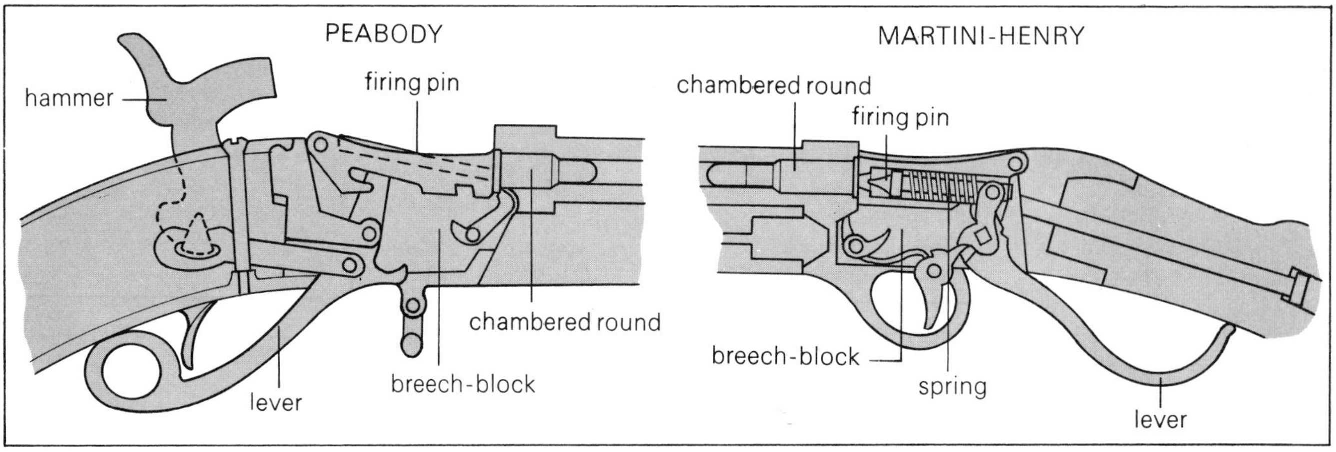

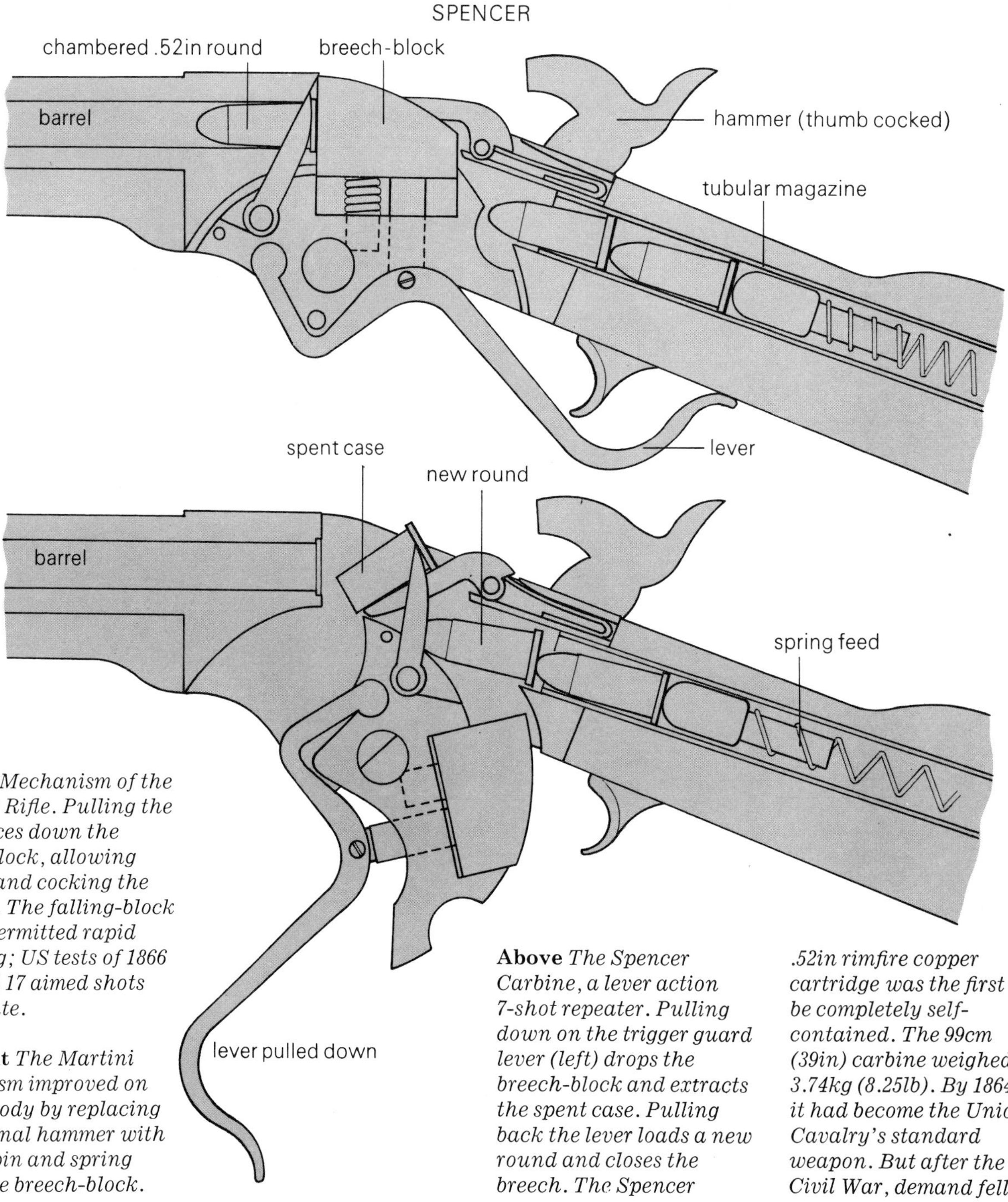

Top left *Mechanism of the Peabody Rifle. Pulling the lever forces down the breech-block, allowing loading and cocking the hammer. The falling-block system permitted rapid reloading; US tests of 1866 achieved 17 aimed shots per minute.*

Top right *The Martini mechanism improved on the Peabody by replacing the external hammer with a firing pin and spring inside the breech-block.*

Above *The Spencer Carbine, a lever action 7-shot repeater. Pulling down on the trigger guard lever (left) drops the breech-block and extracts the spent case. Pulling back the lever loads a new round and closes the breech. The Spencer .52in rimfire copper cartridge was the first to be completely self-contained. The 99cm (39in) carbine weighed 3.74kg (8.25lb). By 1864 it had become the Union Cavalry's standard weapon. But after the Civil War, demand fell off.*

body rifles were sold in their thousands throughout the world. In Switzerland the Peabody design was modified by Frederich von Martini, a skilled designer who did away with the external hammer and fitted an internal firing pin and spring inside the breech-block. This made for a much neater weapon and one which was remarkably fast in its action, for there was the very minimum of delay between pulling the trigger and firing the cartridge. Since this feature is highly desirable in competitive shooting, the Martini action can still be purchased today in small-bore target rifles.

The British Army adopted the Martini action in 1871, and allied it to a barrel rifled according to the design of Alexander Henry of Edinburgh. The .45 calibre Martini-Henry was a notable weapon which served the Army well throughout the British Empire for many years. However, although this rifle, the Peabody and the Winchester were widely adopted as military weapons, they all had one serious drawback. When the firer was lying down, they were well-nigh impossible to operate. At the time of their adoption, no one gave this much thought, since warfare was still something of a gentleman's pastime in which it was the accepted practice to stand up to shoot . . . and be shot at. But as warfare moved into a less formal pattern, the lever action soon fell out of favour. Probably its 'finest hour' occurred during the Russo-Turkish War in 1877-78 when the Turks, armed with Peabody and Winchester rifles, delivered a devastating fire against the Russians, notably at the Siege of Plevna, and cut them to ribbons. The fearful fire-power of the Peabodies and Winchesters showed that a repeating rifle was a necessity, but that lever-action was not the way to go.

Throughout the period of early development of breech-loaders, the metallic cartridge was being gradually refined and improved. The pinfire, good as it was, suffered from the defect of the protruding pin. This was dangerous since any impact could fire the cartridge, and this meant that the user could not simply stuff a handful of pinfires into a pocket or pouch – they had to be carried in specially fitted boxes which protected the pins. Moreover, the hole in the case through which the pin passed was a potential source of failure. The gas could leak from it or the pin could be blown out, both reasons for restricting the pinfire to low-powered rounds.

The rimfire was similarly restricted. The tight folding of the case metal in order to produce the hollow rim set up weak spots which frequently blew out on firing. In addition, it took several years of experimentation to perfect the accurate distribution of the priming compound around the rim, and thus early rounds were prone to misfire.

The first centre-fire cartridges were developed for shotguns, since these weapons developed the lowest breech pressures and the size of the case was such that experimental designs could easily be made. This led to the familiar metal base, with percussion cap in the centre, extended by a cardboard case to carry the powder and shot, a design which has only changed in small details since its introduction in the 1860s. During almost the same period, work on military cartridges followed a similar design but used a light metal section in place of the cardboard, so as to support the rifle bullet. Scores of variations and modifications entertained the minds of gunsmiths until the final result was achieved, but by about 1870 the drawn metallic cartridge, complete with integral percussion cap in the centre of the base, had arrived. Subsequent design of firearms was based entirely on this form of ammunition.

The success of the von Dreyse and Chassepot rifles in the fighting between French and Prussian troops in 1870 led a number of inventors to look at the bolt system to see whether it was capable of improvement, and the advent of the metallic cartridge removed most of the more serious problems. One of these inventors was Peter Paul Mauser of Oberndorf in Germany. He had served his apprenticeship as a gunsmith and in 1859 was conscripted into the army, where he came into close contact with the needle gun. He began contemplating improvements and, after finishing his military service and returning home, continued his work until, in 1865, he had perfected a fresh design. The most important features of this design were that the firing pin was withdrawn and cocked as soon as the bolt began to open, and the bolt was securely locked to the breech by two lugs on its front end which were engaged as the bolt was turned at the end of the closing stroke.

Paul Mauser, and his brother Wilhelm, now set out to interest some European military power in their design. They did not succeed, since most of the armies had but recently adopted new designs of one sort or another. However, through the agency of the Austrian Minister of War, whom they had approached, an American entrepreneur called Samuel Norris got in touch with them.

Norris was the European representative of the Remington company and was pushing hard for sales of their 'Rolling Block' single-shot rifle. The Remington rolling block was a simple and robust weapon which had been adopted by the US Navy in 1866, and thereafter was sold widely and used in several European armies. Nevertheless, Norris was astute enough to see that a bolt action was fundamentally stronger than the rolling block and would be a useful acquisition for future use. He had the idea of convincing the French Government to adopt Mauser's bolt action in place of the Chassepot rifle, which shows how little Norris knew of French military psychology. He therefore got in touch with the Mauser Brothers and entered into a contract with them in which they transferred to him their entire rights in the design, plus their rights in any future invention they might make, in exchange for a payment of 80,000 francs spread over a period of 14 years. Rarely has a more onerous contract been committed to print. Norris, moreover, left himself a safety clause in case things failed to turn out to his satisfaction. Should he ever fail to pay the annual instalments of the 80,000 francs, then the contract became void except that Norris retained the French rights to the invention.

Naturally the French, who like most conservative armies would never willingly accept any foreign invention, turned Norris down. He then tried to sell the Mauser design to Remington but they were not interested. Norris had signed the contract with the Mauser brothers in 1867. By 1870 it was obvious that the French were not about to change their policy and, exercising his escape route, he reneged on the payment due to the Mauser brothers for that year – a matter of $1,000 US – and thus terminated the contract. It is ironic that the one nation in which Norris retained his rights – France – was the one country in which Mausers never sold a single weapon to the government.

Although Norris's contract tied the Mausers for three years, it nevertheless rescued them from poverty at a critical time. They now returned to Oberndorf and submitted their rifle to the Prussian Royal Testing Commission at Spandau. The War of 1870 revealed the defects in the ageing needle gun and Mauser's design appeared to fill the bill. In December 1871 their design was officially accepted as the future service rifle of Germany provided a few modifications were made. These were done, and in 1872 production began.

Mauser's bolt action was so significant that it deserves some detailed study. When it is considered that for the next 100 years the Mauser bolt was the standard to which all other bolt actions were referred, then the magnitude of the invention becomes more clear.

Von Dreyse had shown how the bolt could be made to work. Chassepot had incorporated a self-cocking motion which cocked the firing pin as the bolt was closed. Mauser now improved on these in the following respects. Firstly, leaving the cocking action

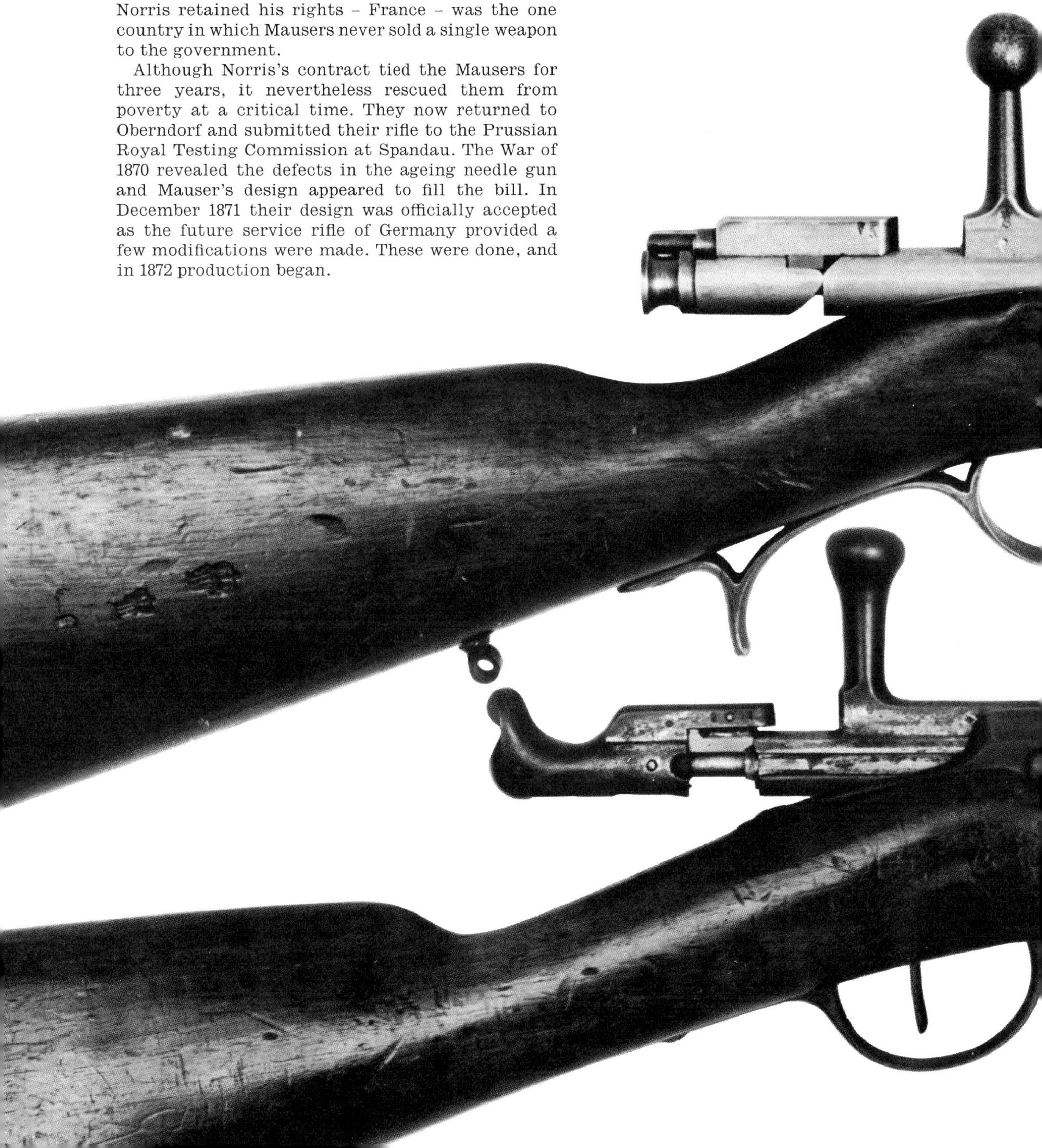

until the bolt closed was dangerous with a central-fire cartridge, since should the firing pin stick then it would strike the cap as the bolt went forward and probably fire the cartridge before the bolt closed. Mauser got around this by withdrawing the firing pin as soon as the bolt began to open. Secondly, the existing method of locking the bolt closed (by turning down the handle in front of a lug on the receiver) was weak, and by forming two opposite lugs on the bolt head which would lock into recesses in the chamber itself, Mauser made the strongest bolt possible.

Mauser's third improvement was to incorporate an elastic extractor made of spring steel which would automatically grip the rim of the cartridge as the breech closed and infallibly extract it as the breech opened. In order to aid this action, he arranged the working surfaces of the bolt so that, as the handle was lifted to open, there was a minute but powerful rearward movement, sufficient to lever the tightest cartridge from the chamber. Fourthly, he fitted a positive ejector which actively threw the empty case out of the way and did not simply rely on the soldier picking it from the boltway. And fifthly, the bolt was fitted with a safety catch which could be applied after the bolt had been closed and the rifle loaded, so that the soldier could carry it safe, but ready for immediate action.

The German Army was so convinced of the superiority of this rifle that it arranged financial assistance for the Mauser brothers and gave them the use of the rifle factory at Oberndorf to produce the Model 1871. Once the Army's supplies were assured, they were given more financial help so that they could step up production for overseas sales. While Paul Mauser superintended the factory, Wilhelm became the salesman and negotiated sales as far afield as China. The Mauser rifle had begun its rise to prominence.

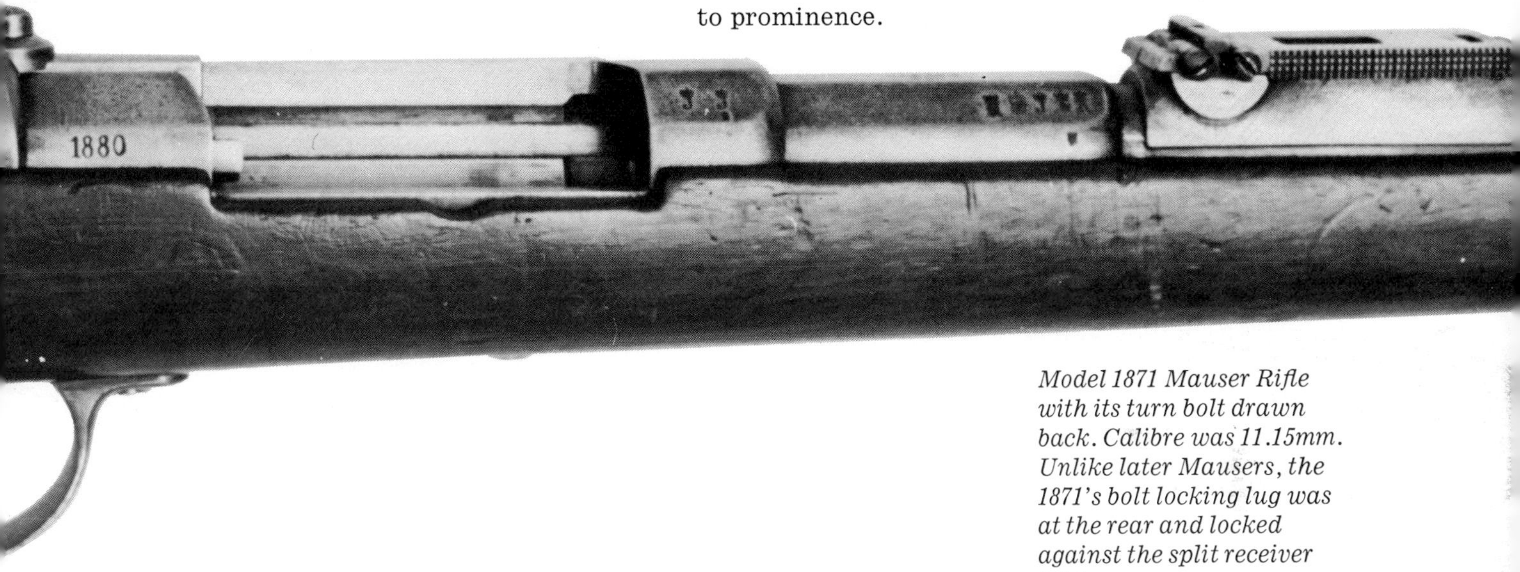

Model 1871 Mauser Rifle with its turn bolt drawn back. Calibre was 11.15mm. Unlike later Mausers, the 1871's bolt locking lug was at the rear and locked against the split receiver bridge.

French Chassepot Rifle of 1866, an 11mm calibre weapon that outranged the Needle Gun in the Franco-Prussian War (1870-71) and thus stimulated the Mauser's introduction.

REVOLVERS

WHILE THE NATIONS of continental Europe were arming themselves with breech-loading, bolt-action rifles to settle their disputes, Americans out in the Wild West were growing accustomed to occasionally resolving their personal disputes in a blaze of fire from a very different weapon – the revolver. Commonly known there as an equalizer – it was said that 'the Colt makes all men equal' – the revolver as introduced to America by Samuel Colt put a 'shootin' iron' in the hands of the outlaw and law-abider alike.

Revolvers are popularly associated with the Wild West of the cowboy era, but they did not originate there. Inventors worldwide had been occupied for many years with the problem of obtaining more than one shot from a weapon without having to go through all the process of reloading. The simple and quick answer, which had been employed for years, was the double barrel (tried out on a variety of pistols, muskets and rifles) and this sufficed for a long time. But as gunsmiths became more skilled, they also became more venturesome and a variety of multiple-shot weapons were put forward. Most of them fell by the wayside, since devising a means of providing multiple firing when the ignition system was the flintlock demanded a very high standard of design and manufacture.

One simple solution was the 'Mob Gun' or 'Duck's Foot' pistol of the late eighteenth century, a pistol in which the breech led into a metal block from which four or five barrels sprang, pointed in splayed fashion over an arc of some 30° or so. One large charge delivered pressure to all the barrels, so pulling the trigger fired a spreading arc of bullets well suited to dealing with a mob. It is said that these pistols were especially favoured by ships' captains, fearful of a rush of mutineers.

The drawback to the Duck's foot pistol was, of course, that once you had pulled the trigger, it was empty. If the mutineers kept coming, all you could do was throw the empty pistol at them and dive over the side.

A better idea was to devise a pistol from which a single shot could be fired several times in succession, allowing the firer to space out his shots and aim each one individually. Several attempts at this were made in very early days, but the first practical weapons were the 'pepperbox' revolvers which appeared in about 1780. These used a cluster of barrels, usually six because this gave a symmetrical arrangement, which revolved ahead of the butt. Each barrel had its own pan and frizzen, while the cock and trigger were carried on the butt. The barrels were revolved by hand, aligning one barrel with the cock and firing it, before revolving the cluster to present the next barrel. Provided the pan covers fitted tightly the system worked, but if the springs lost their tension there was always the danger of the shock of discharge of the first barrel jarring open all the pan covers and dumping their priming on the ground.

With the introduction of percussion ignition, the

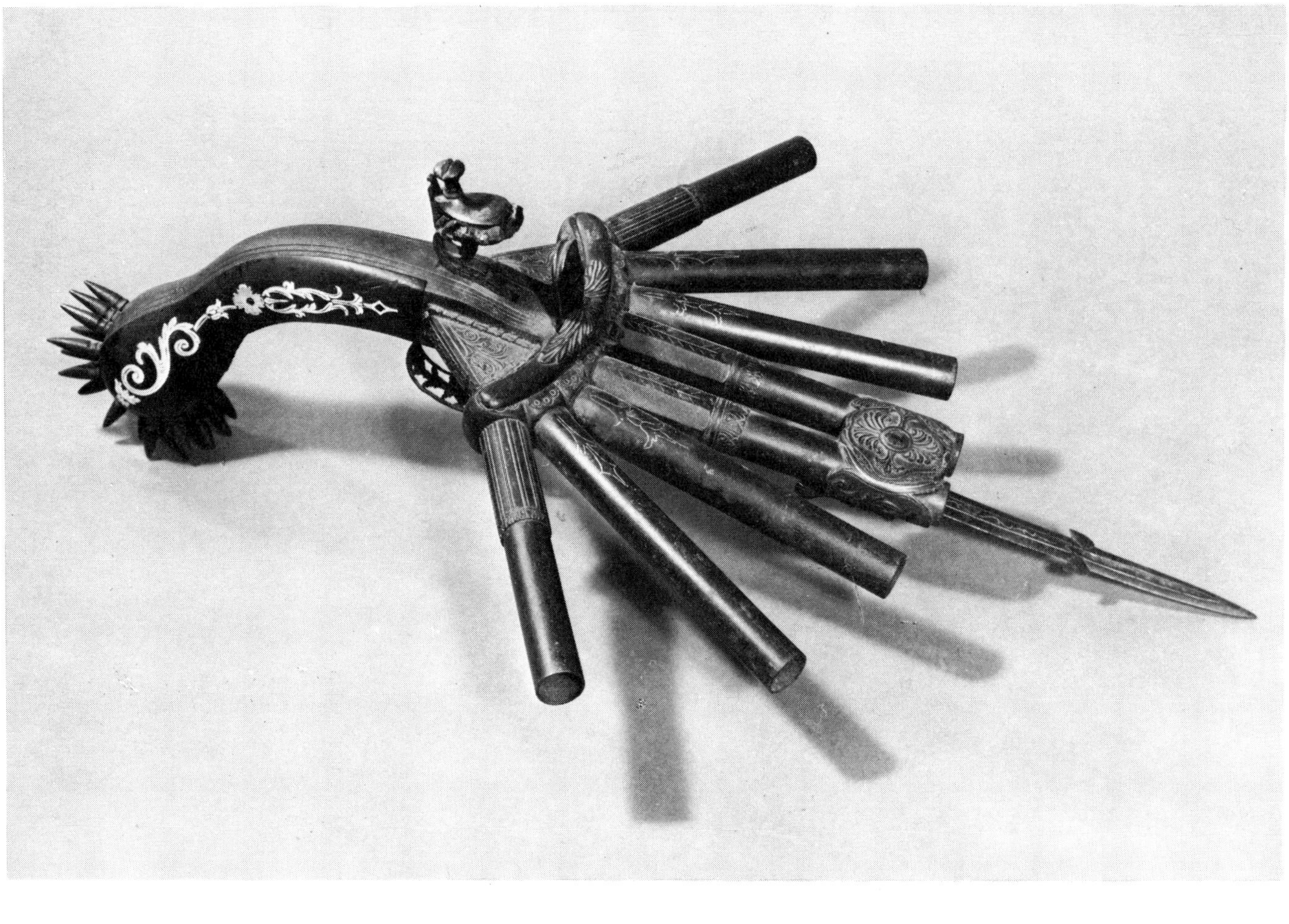

pepperbox, although still bulky and muzzle-heavy, became rather more practical and was widely manufactured and used, especially between the 1830s and 1850s. Just at the dawn of the percussion period, however, came an inventor whose name was destined to become a household word – Samuel Colt.

There can be no doubt that the rapid spread of the revolver as the common hand-weapon was due to Samuel Colt's inspired publicity and salesmanship, but the image of Colt as the inventor of the revolver is far from accurate. The legend is that Colt, as a youth, worked as a cabin boy on the sailing ship *Corvo* and was inspired by the spoked ship's wheel to invent a revolver mechanism. This he whittled from wood; then he perfected it and kept it secret until he was old enough to obtain a patent.

In fact this tale was purely a publicity stunt invented by Colt in later years. He did serve a spell as a cabin boy; he then went on the road in America as 'Doctor Coult', selling patent medicines and titillating the yokels with laughing gas. He probably saw the need for a reliable pistol during his travels, and from the profits of his medicine show he engaged a gunsmith and in 1834 set him up in a small workshop in Baltimore. This gunsmith, John Pearson, developed the first pilot models of the Colt revolver, though it appears that Colt had previously attempted to have a gun made by Anson Chase, a gunsmith of East Hartford, Connecticut. The Anson Chase model came to grief when one day the cap cross-fired all the other caps on the cylinder and blew up the

Previous page *The Beaumont-Adams Model 1855 Revolver that introduced the 'double-action' lock to handguns. Its calibre is .45in and barrel length 146mm (5.75in). The cylinder held five rounds. Loading, with a paper cartridge, was from the front. The nipples for the copper percussion caps can be seen on the cylinder.*

Left *An unusual and fearsome 'Duck's Foot' pistol with eight barrels, the centre pair being parallel.*

Above *Samuel Colt (1814-1862) cocks one of his percussion revolvers.*

Right *A revolving pepperbox pistol. The hammer is concealed within the butt and percussion nipples prolong the chambers.*

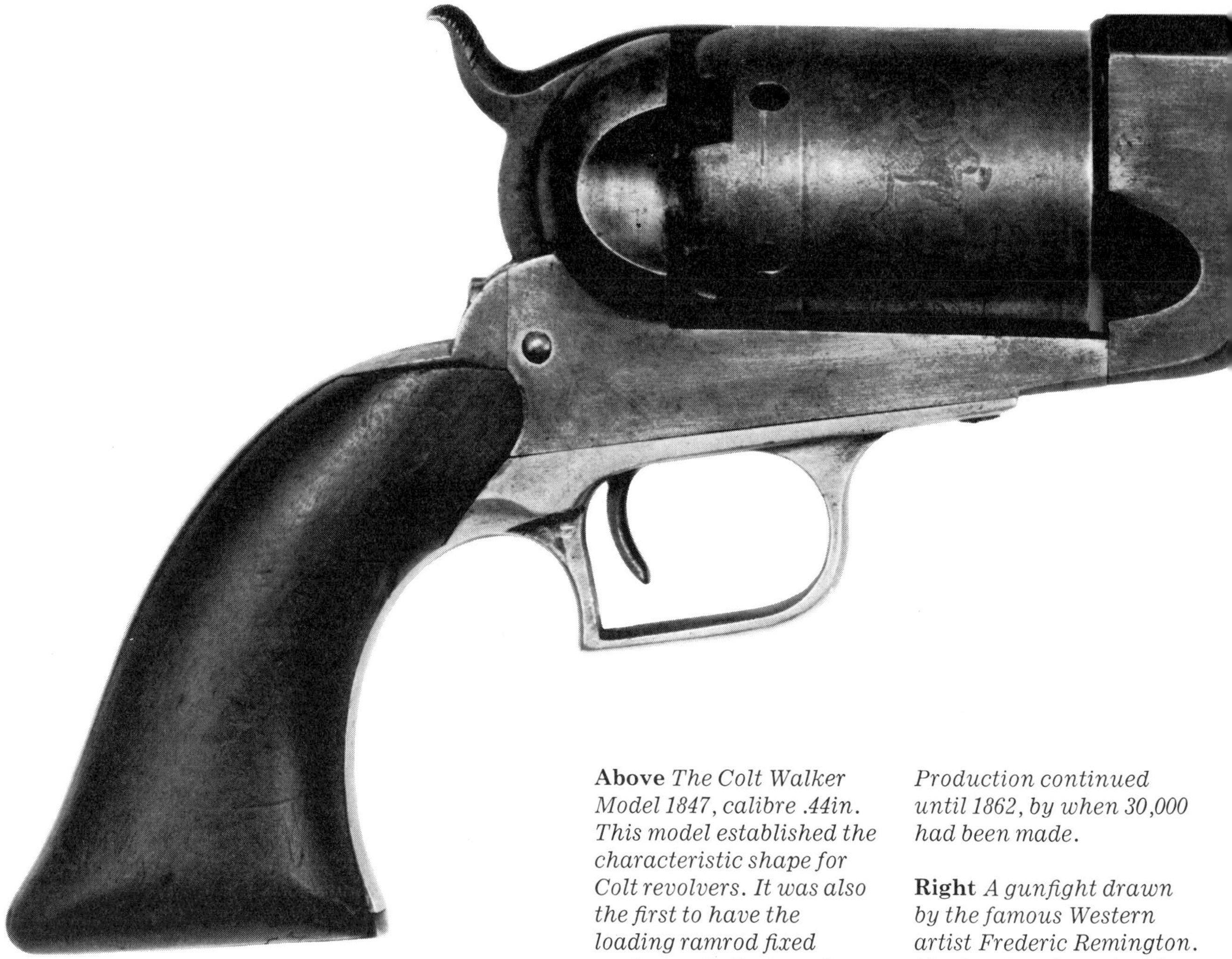

Above *The Colt Walker Model 1847, calibre .44in. This model established the characteristic shape for Colt revolvers. It was also the first to have the loading ramrod fixed underneath the barrel. Production continued until 1862, by when 30,000 had been made.*

Right *A gunfight drawn by the famous Western artist Frederic Remington. No shooting from the hip.*

entire pistol. Learning from this, Pearson designed his model with partitions between the nipples to prevent cross-firing. In 1835, Colt went to England and took out his first patent, then returned to America and patented the design there in 1836.

None of the individual features covered in Colt's patent were really original. His cylinder rotation system, for example, can be seen in a flintlock revolver made in London and dating from the time of Charles I (1625-49). Nevertheless, his patent was accepted and, since it was so worded as to cover any method of mechanical rotation of a cylinder, Colt had effective monopoly of revolver manufacture until the expiry of his patents, which occurred in 1849 in England and 1857 in the United States.

The English patent was allowed to lie on the files and was never worked, merely remaining as a block to possible competitors. But in America Colt obtained financial backing and in 1836 set up the Patent Arms Manufacturing Company at Paterson, New Jersey, to make revolving pistols and rifles. The first production pistol was the five-shot 'Texas' model in .36 calibre, otherwise known as the Paterson. This model exhibited all the features of later Colt revolvers, plus one or two unique points of its own. The basic form was an 'open-frame' revolver, in which the top of the cylinder was exposed. The butt, firing mechanism and hammer were in one unit; the cylinder revolved on a central 'arbor', pushed round by a pawl attached to the hammer; and the octagonal barrel unit was fitted to the front, aligned by contact with the lower part of the frame and by slipping over the front of the cylinder arbor where it was locked by a cross-bolt passing through the barrel support and the arbor. The barrel and cylinder were removed so that the cylinder could be loaded by prepared paper cartridges containing powder and ball, inserted at the front of each chamber. The nipples were capped with small copper caps filled with fulminate and the cylinder slipped back on to the arbor and the barrel then locked in place. It was, of course, possible to load the chambers with the gun assembled, but a normal method of operation was to have a second cylinder (supplied with the pistol) loaded and carried in the pocket.

To fire, the hammer was drawn back with the thumb, which rotated the cylinder and locked it in alignment with the barrel. A light pressure on the trigger then released the hammer to fall on the cap. The trigger was of a folding pattern which lay close under the frame until the hammer was cocked, when it dropped into the ready position.

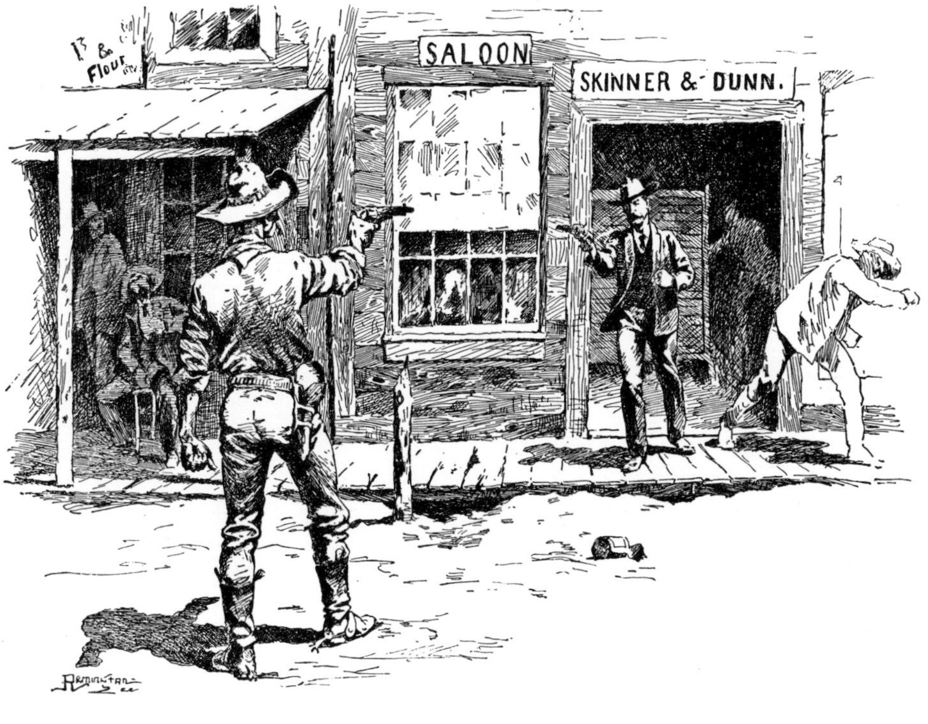

Colt also manufactured a number of rifles and carbines (short rifles for use by mounted men) which were simply the pistol mechanism provided with a long barrel and a wooden butt-stock. These were less successful, since the heavier loadings needed to obtain reasonable performance from a rifle frequently gave rise to excessive flash at the cylinder-barrel joint. This flash passed to the other chambers and was liable to ignite their charges if the bullet was a poor fit.

Even the revolver – good as it was – failed to catch the public's attention, and in 1843 Colt's financial partner went bankrupt. This forced the Patent Arms Company into liquidation and the plant, tools and stock were sold at auction for just over $6,000 – a price which one Paterson revolver would realize quite easily at an auction today.

In 1846, war broke out between Mexico and the United States. This led to a demand for weapons and in 1847 Colt received an order for 1,000 revolvers for use by the U.S. Mounted Rifles. Colt, guided by suggestions from Captain Sam Walker of the Texas Rangers, improved on his 1836 design to produce a robust and heavy .44 calibre pistol known variously as the Model 1847 or the Whitneyville Walker Model. The name arises from the fact that Colt, at this time, had no manufacturing facilities and had to contract the manufacture out to Eli Whitney jr of Whitneyville, a noted American gunmaker. Whitney was particularly famous as the originator of mass-production methods and interchangeability of parts in the gun trade, and his manufacturing techniques produced Colt's design in good time and also opened Colt's eyes to the virtues of modern production methods. Until that time the production of firearms was largely by 'out-workers'. One man produced barrels, another frames, another cylinders and so on, and the maker's factory was simply a small workshop in which all these hand-made components were fitted together. Because they were hand-made, fitting the parts together demanded considerable skill, since it was necessary to file or otherwise modify the components to obtain satisfactory fit and working. Whitney changed this by assembling all his workers under one roof, and by providing them with machine tools which would produce the specific items to a constant pattern. This meant less hand-fitting in the assembly and also gave the factory the ability to provide spare parts.

The Walker Colt was a heavy weapon, weighing 2kg (4lb 9oz), and was 393mm (15.5in) long with a 230mm (9in) barrel. The cylinder had six chambers and a lever rammer was incorporated beneath the barrel. This allowed the cylinder to be reloaded (from the front) without having to be removed. A prepared paper cartridge was dropped into the chamber and was then forced down by the use of the rammer. The single-action lock, in which the hammer had to be cocked by the thumb before the trigger was released, was still used, with a conventional trigger and guard.

The Walker Colt was so successful that a second order for 1,000 was received, and the profit from these orders allowed Colt to set up his own factory in his home town of Hartford, Connecticut, in 1848. From then on his success was assured and production of revolvers in a variety of sizes – though all to the same general pattern – got under way. A considerable fillip to his business came in 1849 when gold was discovered in California: most of the prospectors who headed west provided themselves with a Colt pistol or two.

In 1851 Colt introduced one of the best-known of all Colt revolvers, favoured by 'Wild Bill' Hickock and other heroes of the Wild West – the Navy pistol in .36 calibre. This was a six-chambered pistol of open-frame construction with a 190mm (7.5in) octagonal barrel, which took its name not from any official Naval adoption but from the engraving, around the cylinder, of a naval battle scene representing the action between the Texan and Mexican navies in 1845.

Also in 1851, Colt came to England to show his revolvers at the Great Exhibition at the Crystal Palace in London's Hyde Park. With consummate showmanship, he displayed over 100 weapons and gave away presentation guns to people of influence. His larger aim, beside selling the Colt pistol commercially, was to interest the British Government both in his weapons and also in his system of producing interchangeable parts, and he opened a factory in London, beginning production in 1853.

There was, however, a native producer of a revolver who was to become Colt's principal rival. Robert Adams, a London gunsmith, also exhibited at the Crystal Palace in 1851. Adams' design was, in fact, a better weapon than the Colt, because Adams had patented a form of construction which was inherently much stronger. His revolver used a 'solid frame', in which the whole of the pistol – barrel, frame and butt – were forged from a single piece of metal. The barrel was then bored out and a rectangular hole made in the frame to accept the cylinder. In this way the barrel was secured to the rest of the weapon at two points: at the lower front of the frame; and above the 'standing breech' behind the cylinder (from which a 'top strap' passed across the top of the cylinder to the top of the barrel breech). An arbor pin passed through the front of the frame to support the cylinder and, by releasing a simple spring catch, this pin could be withdrawn and the cylinder removed for cleaning or reloading. This made for a much simpler and quicker system than that of the Colt design. (Like the Colt, Adams' revolver was loaded at the front of its six chambers.)

A particular feature of the Adams revolver was the lock, which was totally different to that of the Colt. In the Adams design the hammer (which had no spur) could not be cocked. The firer simply pulled the trigger, which first raised the hammer and rotated the cylinder, and then released the hammer to fire the pistol. This became known as the 'self-cocking lock' and opinions about it were mixed. In formal military trials of comparison between a Colt and an Adams, the Colt was marginally more accurate, as a result of which the British Army and Navy ordered several thousand Colt revolvers. But this accuracy was largely due to the single-action lock of the Colt which allowed the hammer to be cocked and then the firer to take a deliberate aim. The Adams self-cocking lock, due to the long pull on the trigger, tended to move the pistol off its aim during the operation of the lock.

Experience in actual warfare, however, showed that the Adams was more popular because it could be fired much faster, and, moreover, the 38-bore (.497in calibre) Adams bullet was considerably more effective when it came to stopping an opponent than the 100-bore (.36-in calibre) Colt. One British officer in the Crimean War (1853-56) reported that with his Adams revolver he was able to drop four Russians intent upon bayoneting him, while another in the

Indian Mutiny (1857-59), emptied a Colt into an enraged Sepoy and was 'cloven to the teeth' by the unstopped mutineer.

Nevertheless, such few revolvers as were being bought officially for issue to the Army were still those of Colt's pattern, and the reason seems to be that the single-action lock was felt to be more positive; at any rate, only a revolver with thumb-cocking appeared to be acceptable. In 1855 a Lieutenant Frederick Beaumont of the Royal Engineers patented a modification to the Adams self-cocking lock which gave the firer the option of either thumbing back the hammer to cock it and then firing single-action or firing it self-cocking by applying greater pressure on the trigger. Logically, this came to be known as the 'double-action' lock and it was adopted by Adams in 1855, the resulting revolvers being called the 'Beaumont-Adams'. The Board of Ordnance immediately ordered 100 revolvers for trial, and before the year was out had ordered a further 2,000 revolvers for use in the Crimea. The Crimean War created a demand from the British Army for revolvers, and when the war ended in 1856, demand naturally fell. In the following year, Colt closed his London factory.

While the Colt and Adams revolvers served well, they were, of course, loaded with powder and ball (albeit prepared in a paper cartridge). By this time the metallic cartridge was beginning to make its appearance. Revolvers for the Lefaucheaux pinfire cartridge had been made in Belgium, France and Germany in the early 1850s. Flobert of Paris had added a bullet to a percussion cap and had then extended the idea to take in Houllier's patent for placing the percussion powder inside the hollow rim of the cartridge, and had produced small rifles for the rimfire round in 1845. Now it was the time for the metallic cartridge to be introduced to the revolver in America.

Smith and Wesson, who had abandoned the Volcanic

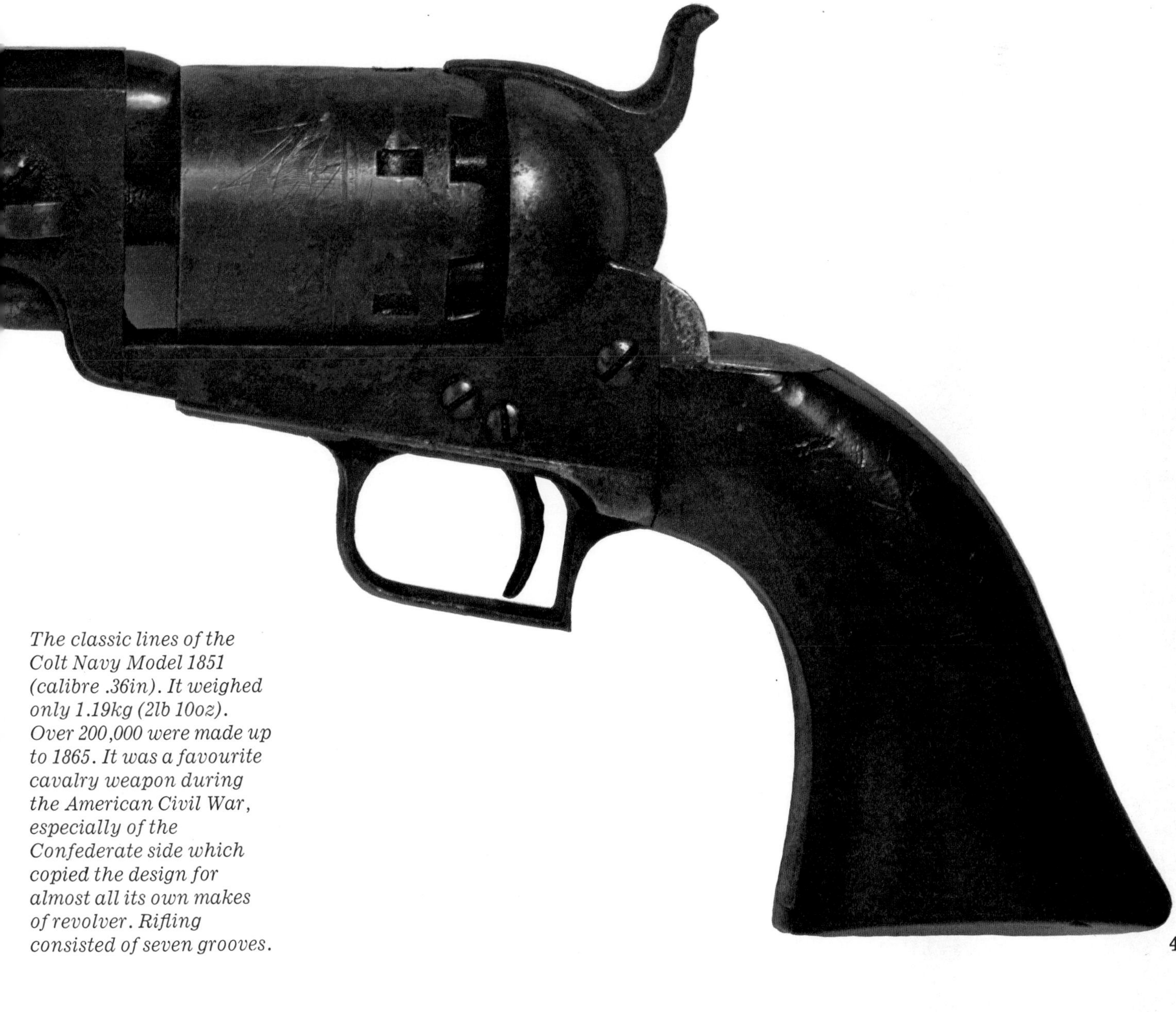

The classic lines of the Colt Navy Model 1851 (calibre .36in). It weighed only 1.19kg (2lb 10oz). Over 200,000 were made up to 1865. It was a favourite cavalry weapon during the American Civil War, especially of the Confederate side which copied the design for almost all its own makes of revolver. Rifling consisted of seven grooves.

repeater in 1856 and turned to making revolvers, saw the possibilities of Houllier's rimfire cartridge. They first extended the case so that a charge of powder could be added, so improving the power, and then they worked on producing a revolver to suit, against the rapidly approaching day (in 1857 in the US) when Colt's master patent would expire. They had seen the legal results of trying to produce pistols which cut across the Colt patent, and one of their first tasks was to sit down and go through the patent files to see if there were any other patents in existence which might cause trouble for them in the future. In this way they discovered the existence of US Patent 12608 of 1855, taken out by a man named Rollin White, an ex-employee of Colt.

White was an indefatigable patentee who always included every conceivable claim in his patents. In this one, which primarily covered an impractical magazine pistol, he had claimed, and had received patent protection for, any cylinder having chambers completely bored through so that the cartridge could be inserted from the rear. This is so fundamental that it is amazing that he ever obtained protection for it. He certainly never managed to patent the idea in England where, it could have been pointed out, several bored-through chambers existed long before 1856. Nevertheless, he did obtain protection in the United States, and Smith and Wesson realized that without control of this patent they were finished before they began. But White was amenable to bargaining, and they eventually bought the patent from him on extremely advantageous terms.

With the Rollin White patent secured, Smith and Wesson gained a monopoly in the United States of breech-loading revolvers until 1869 when their patent expired. Production of their revolver began in 1857, as soon as the Colt patent expired, and the design introduced a new method of construction – the 'tip-up' frame. In general appearance the revolver was like a solid-frame design with a top strap across the top of the cylinder. But at the front of this strap, over the front edge of the cylinder, was a hinge. The lower portion of the frame received the lower edge of the barrel unit, which was locked there by a simple spring catch. The seven-shot .22 calibre cylinder could be removed by pressing in the spring catch and hinging the barrel upwards, after which the cylinder slipped off its arbor. A fixed pin beneath the barrel was then used to punch out the empty cases and the cylinder was reloaded before being slid back and the frame closed down. The lock was single-action, and the trigger was concealed by a spur on the lower part of the frame until the hammer was cocked. Cocking the hammer brought the trigger out of the spur into position for pressing. This design is generally called the 'sheath' or 'stud' trigger and became extremely popular in cheap revolvers in the United States.

While Smith and Wesson concentrated on rimfire revolvers during the period of the Rollin White patent, the centre-fire cartridge had been slowly making its way into the world, notably in rifles and shotguns. Inevitably, several designers got to work on its application to revolvers as soon as they could begin unfettered manufacture. In spite of the rise of the centre-fire cartridge, the rimfire was to remain a popular revolver cartridge for many years, due largely to the pitch of perfection to which it had been brought, as well as its cheapness, and its general satisfactory performance in low-powered revolvers. But where power was needed – as in the heavy-calibre military revolvers – the centre-fire cartridge made its mark.

When the Rollin White patent expired, Smith and Wesson were still in a commanding positon: their pistols were now well-known, they had a large plant and an experienced work-force. Yet by a strange twist of fate they lost their lead in America to Colt within a few years. In 1869, a purchasing agent from the Russian Government visited America with the commission of buying weapons for the Tsar's Army. According to legend, he was taken on a hunting trip by 'Buffalo Bill' Cody and was so impressed by the Smith and Wesson revolver which Cody carried that he went to the factory and placed an order for 215,000 revolvers. Such an order was a manufacturer's dream. For the next five years Smith and Wesson had little time left to do anything but grind out revolvers for Russia without a care in the world. No struggling for markets, no worries about cash flow, just turn them out and get paid. But in those five years the American West was opened up, and the natural demand for revolvers could not be filled by Smith and Wesson. So, by default, it went to the Colt concern (Colt himself died in 1862, aged 48).

The revolver which Smith and Wesson were producing was known as the .44 Russian, and it followed the .44 Model No. 3 or .44 American, the pistol which Cody is said to have demonstrated to the Russian. This model inaugurated a new type of frame to America – the hinged frame. Unlike the 'tip-up' frame (which was hinged at the top of the cylinder), the barrel and top strap were hinged to the frame at the lower front of the cylinder, being locked in place at the top of the standing breech by a spring catch. When the catch was opened, the barrel could be swung down to expose the rear face of the cylinder, and a cam enclosed in the hinge operated an automatic extractor. This was a plate in the centre of the cylinder which formed the inner halves of the chamber mouths and on which the rims of the cartridges rested. When the barrel hinged down, the cam thrust on a central pin and caused this central 'star plate' to lift away from the cylinder face, pushing the empty cases outwards so that they could fall free from the chambers. At the end of the barrel's movement the cam was released and the star plate snapped back, flush with the chamber face, ready for reloading.

The question of the authorship of this design is a very vexed one. Several people had produced 'automatic extracting revolvers' which used star plates, but there seems little doubt that the perfection, as shown by the Smith and Wesson design, was based on the work of an American named W. C. Dodge. He took out patents in the United States and Britain in 1865

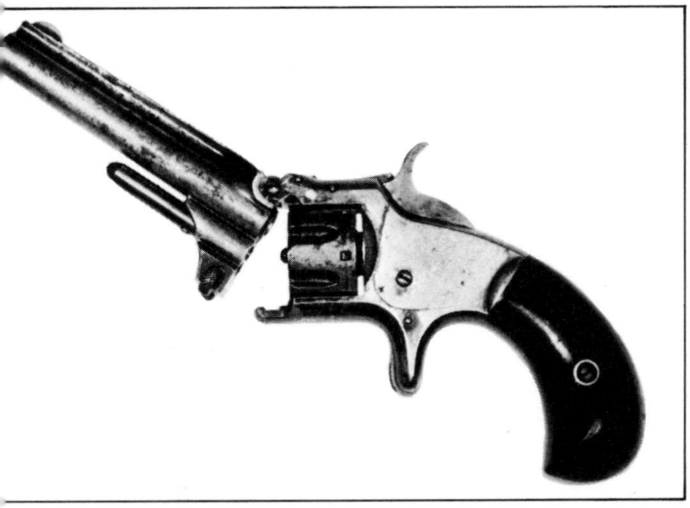

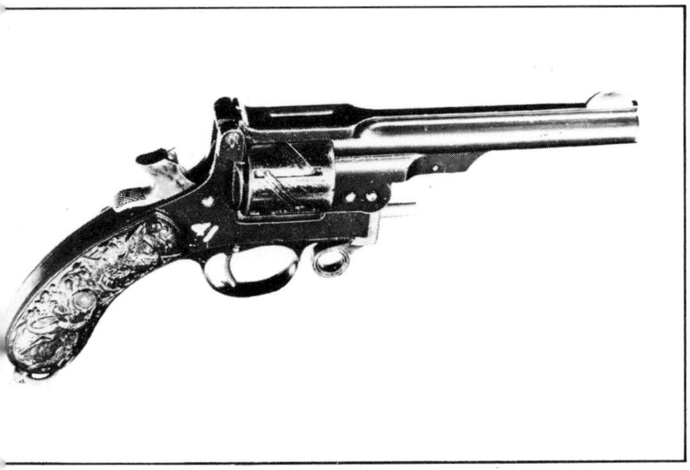

covering his system of 'simultaneous ejection' and the American patent was assigned by Dodge to Smith and Wesson. The British patent was not assigned, but Dodge was late in posting his payment for extending the patent after the first three year period, and his cheque arrived too late. On August 8, 1868 his patent fell void due to failure to pay the renewal fee. (In the US, no further fees were required after the patent had been issued.) It has rankled with American gun historians ever since, who tend to see a touch of 'Perfidious Albion' in the affair.

A wide variety of patent ejection systems appeared in Europe. Paul Mauser ventured into the revolver field, in the hope of a military contract, and in 1878 he introduced an unusual weapon known as the 'Zig Zag' model.

For reasons best known to himself, Mauser decided to eschew the more usual method of revolving the cylinder by using a pawl and ratchet on the rear face. Instead, he adopted a method which relied on a zig-zag groove cut into the outer surface of the cylinder. In the frame, under the cylinder, lay a rod with an upstanding pin which engaged in the zig-zag groove. As the hammer was cocked, either by the thumb or by pulling the trigger, the rod was thrust forwards, and the forward movement of the pin in the groove caused the cylinder to revolve one-sixth of a turn and align the next chamber. As the hammer fell, so the rod was withdrawn and the pin passed down one of the straight sections of groove, ready to act on the next shot.

The other unusual feature was the method of extraction. The barrel unit and cylinder were hinged to the standing breech. A large spring catch held them

Top *The Model 1857 Smith and Wesson .22in calibre, rimfire, 7-shot, 'tip-up', revolver.*

Above *The Mauser Model 1878 'Zig Zag' Revolver.*

Right *The star plate ejection system on a revolver with a plan view of the cylinder.*

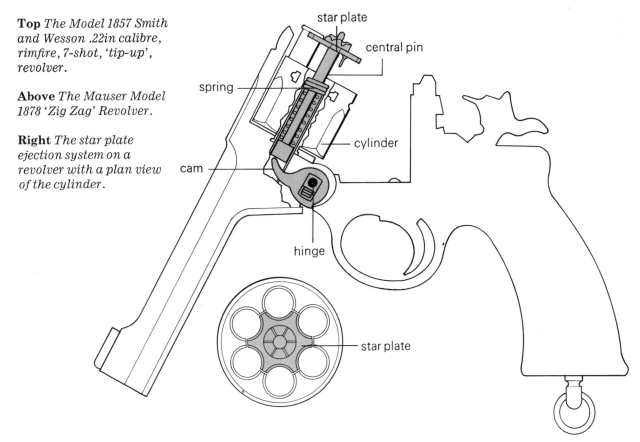

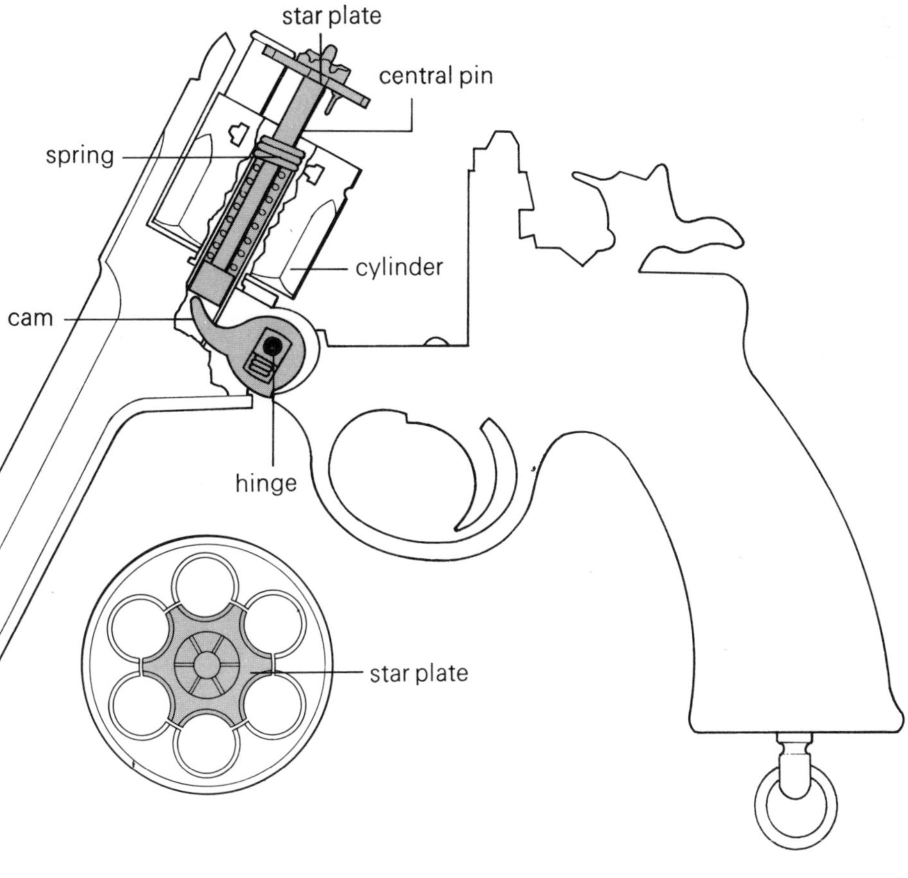

S&W American

In 1870 the Smith and Wesson company, aiming to keep ahead of their rivals, produced the .44 'American' revolver, their first venture into really heavy calibres. The novel feature of this weapon was that it used a hinged frame, with the barrel and cylinder dropping to expose the rear of the cylinder for re-loading, and it incorporated an 'automatic' extractor based on the patents of W.C. Dodge and C.A. King.

Shortly after the introduction of the 'American', the Russian Army decided to equip its cavalry and artillery with a modern revolver, and a purchasing commission was sent to the US in 1869. Though the visitors were impressed with the 'American', modifications were stipulated before an order was placed in 1873. The American .44in cartridge, a 14.12gramme (218grain = 0.49oz) bullet of slightly less diameter than the cartridge case, was not a good fit in the bore, which caused accuracy to fall off after some 45m (50yd). The Russians enlarged the .44in cartridge to make it a tight fit. The new bullet weighed 15.9g (246grain = 0.56oz) and had a muzzle velocity of 228m/sec (750ft/sec), a 30m/sec (100ft/sec) improvement on the American version. Accuracy improved spectacularly. As one commentator later said, the new cartridge was a revelation to an industry in which most ballisticians operated by guesswork and past experience.

With the improved ammunition, some minor changes were made in the pistol. The butt was given a 'pawl' or protuberance at the top rear which prevented the weapon from sliding in the hand during recoil; a finger-rest was added beneath the trigger-guard; and the barrel length was set at 165mm (6.5in). Now satisfied, the Russians contracted with Smith and Wesson for a staggering 215,704 pistols.

Although this contract kept Smith and Wesson so busy that Colt was able to capture much of the Western market, they were able to produce useful variants of the Russian design. The most famous was the .45 'Schofield' Smith and Wesson, named after Lieutenant Colonel George W. Schofield of the US Artillery who made some improvements to the original pattern by strengthening the barrel catch and simplifying the ejector mechanism. About 9,000 Schofields were produced. One became the personal sidearm of Jesse James and another was used by Wyatt Earp in the famous 'Gunfight at the OK Corral'.

Below *The Smith and Wesson Model No.3 .44in calibre single action 'American' Revolver. About 30,000 were made, 1870-73.*

Bottom Left *The Smith and Wesson 'Russian'. It weighed 1.1kg (2.5lb). The pawl and finger-rest distinguish it from its 'American' precursor.*

S&W RUSSIAN
Calibre .44in Russian
Length 305mm (12.0in)
Weight 1.13kg (2.5lb)
Barrel 165mm (6.5in)
Rifling 5 grooves, r/hand twist
Foresight Blade
Rearsight Fixed V-notch
Action Revolver
Rate of fire 12rpm
Feed system 6-shot cylinder
Muzzle velocity 228m/sec (750ft/sec)
Bullet weight 15.95g (246gr)

S&W AMERICAN
-as above except for:
Calibre .44in American
Length 340mm (13.38in)
Weight 1.16kg (2.55lb)
Barrel 203mm (8in)
Muzzle velocity 198m/sec (650ft/sec)
Bullet weight 14.12g (218gr)

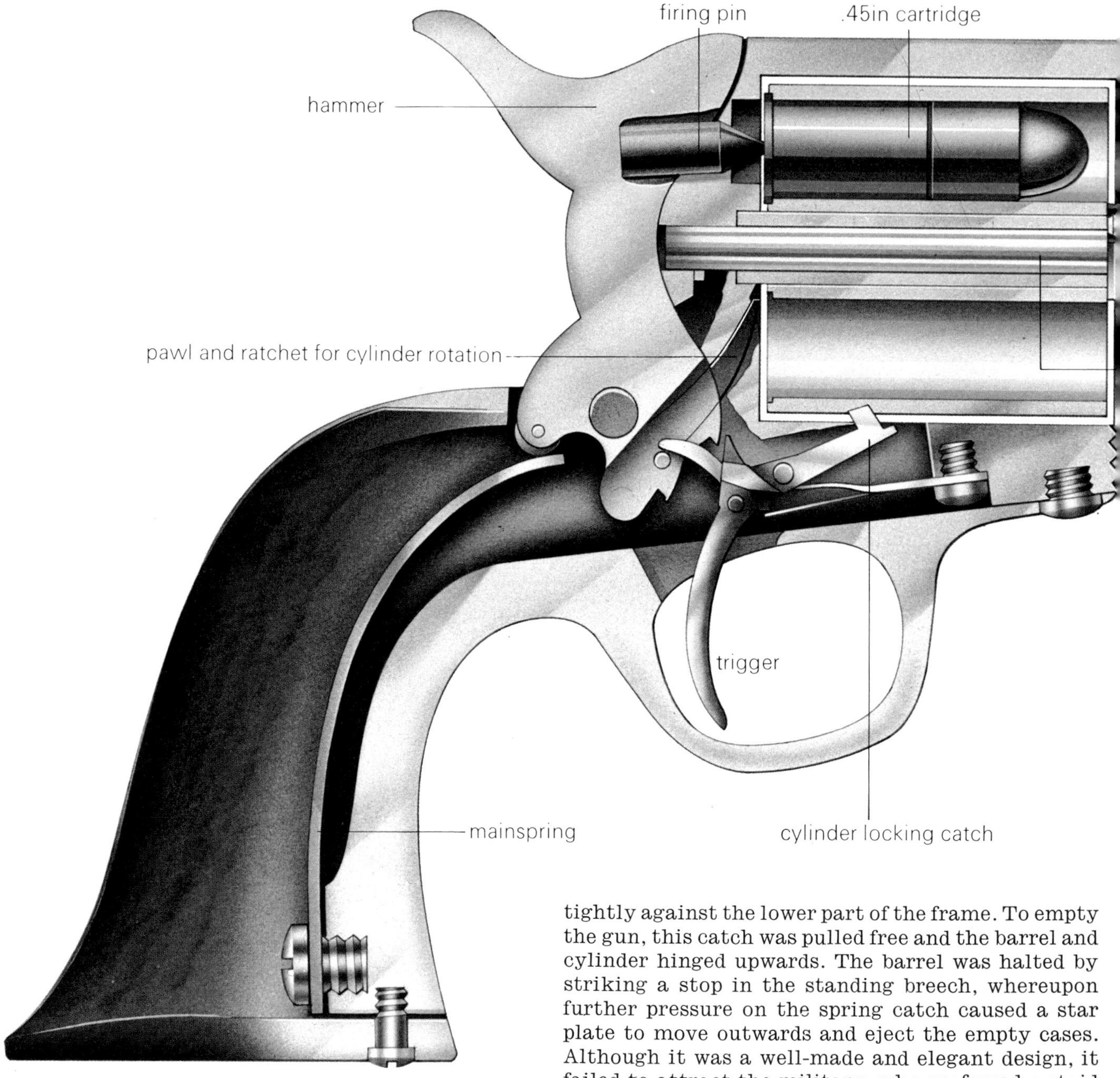

Above *The simple but effective mechanism of the Colt Frontier (M1873 .45in Single Action) revolver. Drawing back the hammer causes the pawl to rise and push the cylinder round, bringing the next chamber into line with the barrel. The cylinder locking-catch then rises to engage in a slot and holds the cylinder in alignment. Pulling the trigger releases the hammer to fire the cartridge. The original ammunition was a .45in blunt-nosed bullet with black-powder cartridge introduced in 1871. At 45m (50yd) the projectile still had an energy of 528 joules (390ft-lb-force), eight times that needed to down a man.*

tightly against the lower part of the frame. To empty the gun, this catch was pulled free and the barrel and cylinder hinged upwards. The barrel was halted by striking a stop in the standing breech, whereupon further pressure on the spring catch caused a star plate to move outwards and eject the empty cases. Although it was a well-made and elegant design, it failed to attract the military, who preferred a staid solid-frame revolver in which the cylinder had to be removed and the cases punched out one by one.

For all the patent ejection systems on offer, Colt strangely enough closed their eyes to all of them when they finally decided to produce a breech-loading, cartridge revolver, and yet they came up with an immortal design which has survived ever since and has been copied all over the world at one time or another. Known properly as the Model of 1873, it also goes under the names of 'Peacemaker', 'Army' or 'Frontier' model, and is among the more instantly recognizable pistols of the world.

The Frontier was a solid-frame revolver (itself a departure for Colt, who took some persuading to drop their open-frame design) with a single-action

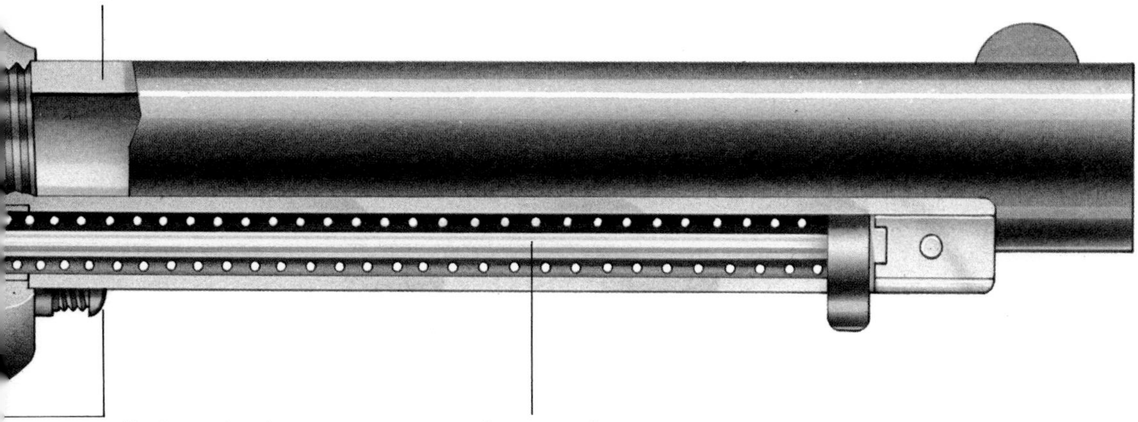

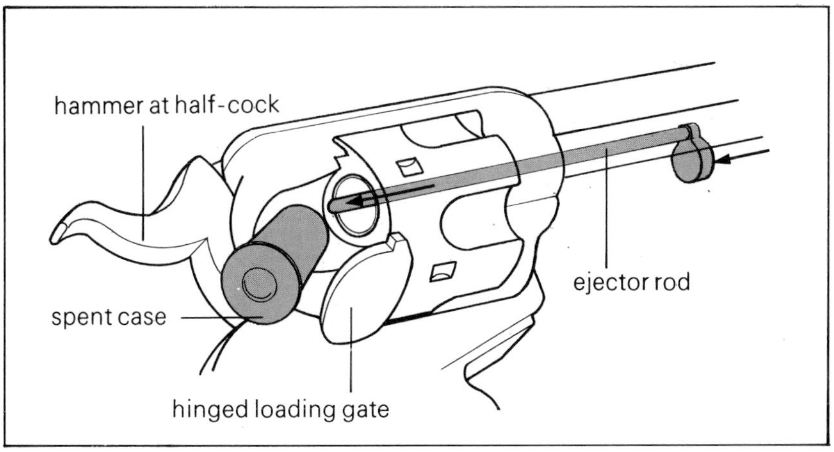

Left *The Colt Frontier's spent case is ejected by pushing it through the hinged loading-gate with the ejector rod positioned below the barrel. The chamber can be reloaded. The hammer has to be at half-cock to allow the cylinder to revolve.*

lock and an ejection system which consisted of a spring-loaded rod carried in a shroud beneath the lower right side of the barrel. This rod was aligned with the upper right-hand chamber of the six-shot cylinder, and behind this chamber the standing breech was cut away and fitted with a hinged 'loading gate'. To load, the revolver hammer was pulled back to a 'half-cock' position which allowed the cylinder to be freely revolved. The gate was then opened and the chambers loaded one by one, turning the cylinder by hand to load each chamber. After firing the gate was opened and the hammer half-cocked. The spring-loaded ejector rod could then be forced back to eject the empty case through the gate; a fresh round was loaded and the cylinder moved round one; the next case ejected and the chamber loaded; and so on.

On coming to the end of their Russian contract, Smith and Wesson found that the market for large-bore revolvers had been fairly effectively tied up by Colt, so they astutely aimed for the pocket revolver market, in which Colt had not, at that time, made much progress. There were innumerable small companies turning out cheap hinged-frame and solid-frame revolvers in this field, but Smith and Wesson soon made their presence felt by their considerably better quality. A notable design was their 1888 New Departure or 'Safety Hammerless' model, a small hinged-frame revolver in which the hammer was completely concealed inside the frame which was built up behind the standing breech. The 'Safety' part of the designation came from the incorporation into the butt of a grip safety device, a moveable backstrap which, when pressed in the firer's hand gripping the butt, removed a blocking lever from the rearward path of the hammer. Thus, unless the butt was properly gripped it was impossible to fire the pistol.

By the late 1880s the Colt solid-frame design with rod ejection was looking distinctly old-fashioned, but the company was loath to give up the undoubted advantage of the solid frame. After much experimentation it produced something quite new in the New Navy revolver of 1889 – a side-swinging cylinder. The arbor of the cylinder was held at its front end by a 'crane', a vertical arm lying in the forward part

The Colt 'Frontier' is one of the immortals and must be one of the most easily-recognized guns in the world. It was originally developed for military use as the 'Single Action Army', adopted by the US Army in July 1873. Two months later it was placed on the civilian market and rapidly acquired the nickname of 'Peacemaker'. These first models were in .45in calibre. During 1878, models in .44in, .38in and .32in calibres were added, chambered for the same cartridges that were being currently used in Winchester carbines. This allowed a man to arm himself with a rifle and pistol taking the same ammunition and, because of this, the Colt was now advertised as the 'Frontier Six-Shooter'

This was one reason why the Colt proved so popular despite its cumbersome action and the tendency of its rod ejector to bend, its lock to break and cylinder pin to loosen. No matter what went wrong you could still fire it. If the trigger spring snapped, you merely thumbed back the hammer and let it slip. The hammer, not the trigger, controlled cylinder rotation, which is why the spectacular and inaccurate pastime of 'fanning' the hammer (slapping it back with the open palm while keeping the trigger pressed) is only feasible on this pistol. If the ejector broke, you pulled out the cylinder pin and used it to poke out the empty cases. And if the mainspring broke, you could always pound the hammer with a rock to make it fire. And, allied to all this, it had that indefinable quality of 'pointability': it seemed to point instinctively at the target, just like fine duelling pistols used to do.

The US Army bought 36,000 Model 1873s and this remained the standard military sidearm until replaced by a double-action Colt in 1892. A total of 357,859 'Frontiers' were sold between 1873 and 1941.

After World War II the demand for the Colt Frontier grew, fostered by Western movies and by the rise of the 'quick-draw' craze. Pre-war Colt revolvers began to command a high price and numerous companies took advantage by turning out copies of the 'Frontier' model. Eventually Colt bowed to public demand and put the Colt Frontier back into production in September 1955 at $125 a copy (compared with the 1873 price of $17). The only sure way to identify a post-war Colt is by the serial number, which has the suffix 'SA'.

Far left *A superb nickel-plated and engraved Colt made in 1886. The ivory butt has a steer's head in high relief. The barrel length is 139.7mm (5.5in).*

Left *Cowboys of the 1880s proudly display their Colts.*

FRONTIER 7.5in Barrel
Calibre .45in
Length 317mm (12.5in)
Weight 1.04kg (2.30lb)
Barrel 190.5mm (7.5in)
Rifling 6 grooves, l/hand
Foresight Blade
Rearsight Fixed V-notch
Action Revolver
Rate of fire 12rpm
Feed system 6-shot cylinder
Muzzle velocity 265m/sec (870ft/sec)
Bullet weight 16.2g (250gr)

of the frame and connected to a rod which entered the frame under the cylinder. The rear end of the arbor slid into a slot in the standing breech and was retained there by a sliding catch on the left side of the gun. When this catch was pulled back, the cylinder could be swung out of the frame, the crane turning about the rod inside the frame as on a hinge, so that the cylinder came to rest alongside the lower section of the frame. Once in this position, pressure on an ejector rod which extended from the front of the cylinder would push out the usual star plate and simultaneously eject all the empty cases.

This design obviously gave the great mechanical strength of the solid frame and yet the simplicity of loading and unloading formerly associated with the hinged frame, and as a result it became almost the standard pattern for American revolvers. The Colt pattern locked into the standing breech, leaving the ejector rod unsupported beneath the barrel. Smith and Wesson adopted the side-swinging cylinder in 1896 but, in order to avoid patent problems, latched their cylinder in place by having the hollow tip of the ejector rod anchored into a lug forged beneath the barrel as well as locking into the standing breech, and it was released by sliding a catch forwards.

Before leaving the revolver, one last important feature deserves to be mentioned. Once the centre-fire cartridge was adopted, it became necessary to withdraw the hammer and its firing pin before attempting to revolve the cylinder, otherwise there was a danger of breaking off the tip of the firing pin. As a result, the 'rebounding hammer' became a standard fitting. In this, the hammer drops to the fullest extent when the trigger is pressed, so striking the cartridge cap, but as soon as the trigger is released, preparatory to firing the next shot, the hammer 'rebounds' a short distance to pull the pin clear of the chamber. It might be noted that the original Colt Frontier models did not have this feature, and it was considered wise to leave the topmost chamber empty and lower hammer on to it, rather than have the firing pin sitting precariously on the cap of the aligned chamber all the time the weapon was carried about.

While the rebounding hammer was a useful safety feature, it still meant that if, by chance, the revolver was dropped so that the hammer struck the ground, it would be driven on to the cap with enough force to fire the aligned cartridge with dangerous effect. In 1896 the Iver Johnson company, who made inexpensive pocket revolvers for the American market, introduced a safety feature which they popularized under the slogan 'Hammer the Hammer', which fairly described the action. The actual hammer did not have the usual firing pin let into its face. Instead, a separate firing pin was carried in the standing breech, spring-loaded to be clear of the cartridge unless actually forced in by the flat face of the hammer. The face of the hammer was shaped, above the 'active' part which touched the firing pin, into a boss which struck against the solid part of the standing breech, in such a manner that the remainder of the hammer face did not make contact with the firing pin. Thus, when the hammer was at rest, no power on earth could force it forwards to touch the firing pin and thus inadvertently fire the pistol. But when the pistol was properly cocked and the trigger pulled back deliberately, a solid strut was thrust upwards by the lock mechanism, into place behind the firing pin, and held there so long as the trigger was pressed. Thus when the hammer fell in deliberate fire it struck this strut which then transmitted the blow to the firing pin and fired the cartridge. A similar device was later adopted by Colt as their 'Positive Safety Lock' and most other manufacturers incorporated similar safety devices into their pistols. They are, in fact, now required by law in all revolvers sold in the United States.

By about 1880, the manufacture of revolvers had become concentrated in the hands of a relatively small number of companies who had the financial strength and mechanical ability to mass-produce at a rate which put the hand-worker out of business. At the same time most of the mechanical features of the revolver were either well-established or so protected by patents as to be unusable by the small manufacturer. (Indeed, except for improvements in manufacturing techniques, there has been little new in the revolver world since the turn of the century. Except for minor refinements, the revolvers sold today by various companies differ very little from the designs sold by those same companies in, say, 1905.)

As a result of the established nature of revolver manufacture, many inventors began to look in other directions to see if, perhaps, there was not some other way to make a handgun. As we have seen, the bolt-action rifle had become established, and it occurred to some designers that the bolt action might possibly be a suitable method of operating a pistol. This led to the rise of the mechanical repeating pistol.

A peculiarity of this pistol is that by far the majority of designs appeared from the Austro-Hungarian Empire, something which has yet to be satisfactorily explained. As a representative specimen of this class of weapon, we might consider the pistol of Erwin Reiger of Vienna, patented in 1889. This used a reciprocating bolt driven by a finger-operated lever which extended below the frame and, being slotted at the rear edge, overlaid the firing trigger when in its rearward position. Ahead of the lock, in the position of the cylinder in a revolver, was a cylindrical casing which contained a rotary magazine, a collection of spring fingers revolving on an arbor into which six cartridges could be clipped. A sliding door on the right side of the pistol allowed this magazine to be slipped out for emptying and loading. When the magazine was in place, the topmost cartridge was aligned with the breech end of the barrel.

To operate the weapon, the firer hooked his forefinger into the ring at the end of the operating lever and thrust it forwards. This rotated and withdrew the bolt to the rear. He then inserted the magazine

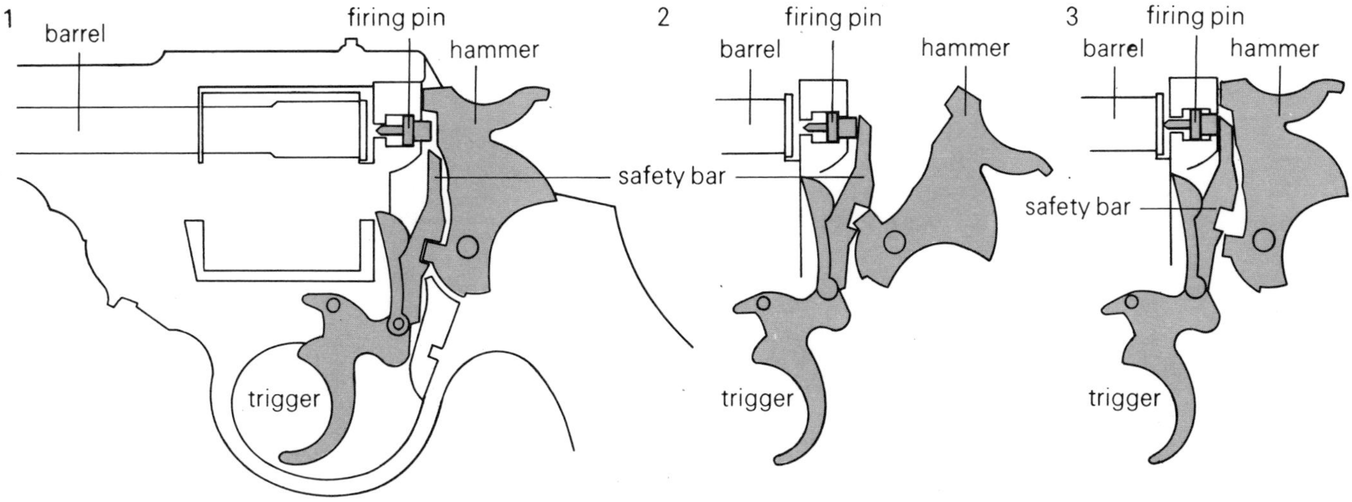

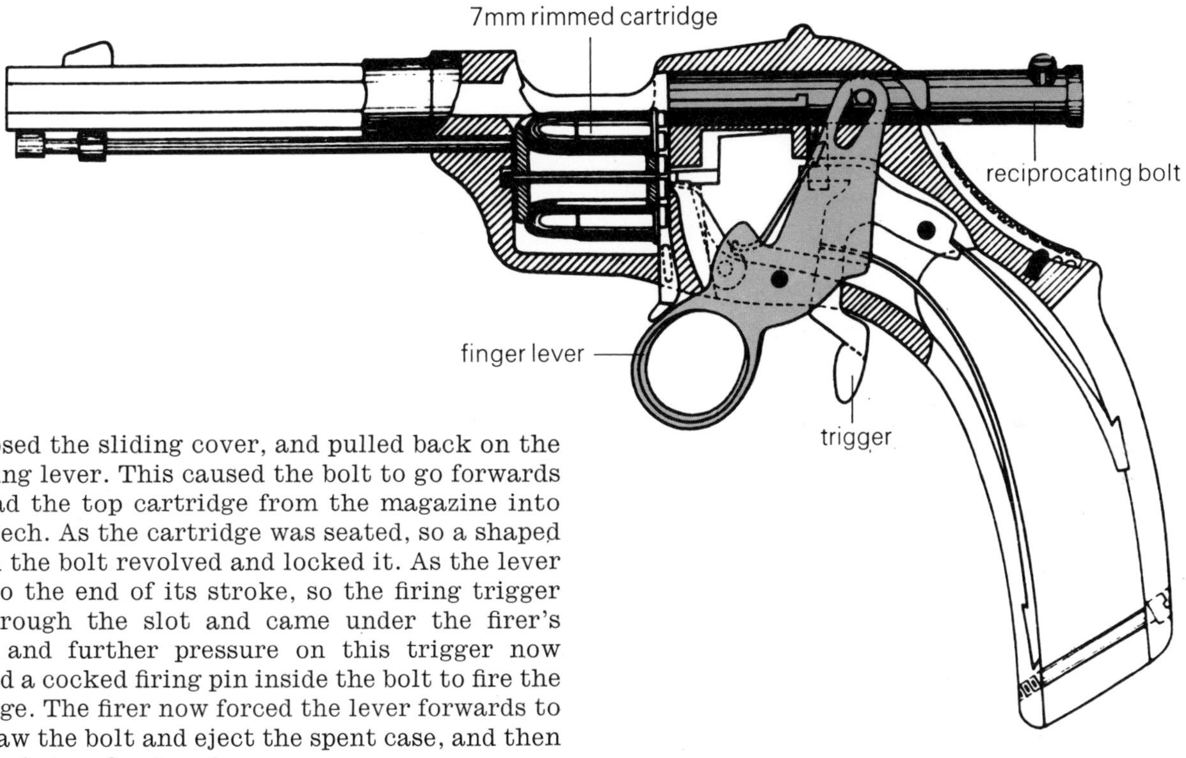

and closed the sliding cover, and pulled back on the operating lever. This caused the bolt to go forwards and load the top cartridge from the magazine into the breech. As the cartridge was seated, so a shaped cam on the bolt revolved and locked it. As the lever came to the end of its stroke, so the firing trigger slid through the slot and came under the firer's finger, and further pressure on this trigger now released a cocked firing pin inside the bolt to fire the cartridge. The firer now forced the lever forwards to withdraw the bolt and eject the spent case, and then back again to reload, and so on.

While this appears to be a sound enough mechanism, there are one or two drawbacks. The most awkward feature is that the ejection of a fired case could be difficult if the case elected to stick in the chamber, and the human finger is not well adapted to delivering pressure in the forward direction. Nevertheless, a number of similar designs were put forward in the late 1880s, by such people as Karl Krnka, Franz Passler, Josef Schulhof and Paul Mauser. None of them appear to have prospered, and they are extremely rare today. But one design, patented by Laumann, formed the basis of the first successful automatic pistol. So, in spite of their short existence and lack of commercial success, the mechanical repeater has a definite place in the history of the firearm.

Top *How The 'Hammer the Hammer' safety feature works. (1) When at rest, the hammer is not in contact with the firing pin. (2) When cocked, the hammer raises a separate steel bar between it and the firing pin. (3) When the hammer is pulled, it strikes the bar which imparts the blow to the firing pin thus firing the cartridge.*

Above *The Passler and Seidl mechanical repeater, patented in 1887. It uses a reciprocating bolt to close the breech, actuated by a finger lever. Pulling the lever forces the bolt home and then revolves it to lock. After firing, a forward movement of the lever unlocks and withdraws the bolt, extracting the spent case ready for reloading.*

MECHANICAL MACHINE GUNS

War has always bred new weapons. But the Crimean War of 1853-56 acted as a very peculiar sort of catalyst in the development of firearms. For the first time, the popular newspapers of the world were able to report the progress of a foreign war – between Great Britain, France, Turkey and, later, Sardinia on one side, and Russia on the other – in an 'up-to-the-minute' fashion, thanks to the electric telegraph. And also for the first time, it was brought home to many people just how dated were the weapons on which the armies relied. The Industrial Revolution was in full swing – mechanical marvels were the order of the day, from steam locomotives to printing presses – and yet here were the military forces of several of the most advanced nations of the world still using weapons which in their essentials were little changed from the days of the first Duke of Marlborough and his battles against the French in the early years of the eighteenth century. The nineteenth century – and the Crimean and American Civil Wars in particular – changed all this. All over Europe and America, inventors began to take a fresh look at weaponry, and we have already seen some of the developments – in rifles, revolvers and cartridges – which stemmed from this.

One area which claimed the attention of a small number of thinkers was that of producing weapons which would fire rapidly and continuously and thus shower the battlefield with bullets – the idea being that by putting up such a screen of flying metal it would prove impossible to wage war at all. The idea was not particularly new. One famous pioneer in this field was James Puckle of London, who in 1718 patented his 'Defence' gun, with the slogan:

'Defending King George, your country and Lawes,
Is Defending yourselves and (the) Protestant Cause.'

Puckle's gun was, in effect, a flintlock revolver of large calibre, mounted on a three-legged stand. By releasing a clamp behind the cylinder, a loaded chamber could be lined up with the barrel and locked in place, thrusting the chamber mouth into the rear end of the barrel to seal the joint against gas leaks. Then a lever was tripped to release the cock of a flintlock mechanism which ignited the charge in the chamber. After firing this shot, the cylinder was unclamped, turned to the next chamber, reclamped, and fired. Cumbersome as it sounds, it was a considerable advance for its time. The *London Journal* of March 31, 1722 reported that the gun was fired in the Artillery Fields 63 times in seven minutes in the rain by one man. But in spite of demonstrating it to the Board of Ordnance, Puckle never achieved any success. The fact that he advertised the gun as being able to fire *round* balls against Christians and *square* ones against Turks – through the same barrel – may have had something to do with this.

The principal drawback to rapid-fire guns in those days was the ammunition: powder, ball and flint did not lend themselves to rapid manipulation. When the percussion cap appeared in the early nineteenth century, interest revived, and this, with the stimulus of the Crimean War, started the ball (or, rather, the cylinder) rolling. One of the earliest designers, and one of the least-known, was Sir James Lillie who put forward his 'Battery Gun' in 1857. This was a framework which carried 12 rifle barrels, each with a revolver-type cylinder behind it, some containing 12 chambers and some 18. A hand crank tripped the hammers of each unit, either simultaneously so as to produce a 12-barrel barrage of fire, or consecutively so as to produce a continuous ripple of fire from each barrel in turn. Spare, loaded cylinders were provided so that fire could be kept up for long periods. Lillie seems to have had little success with his invention. It was never followed up by the military, and the only specimen ever made now resides in the Royal Artillery Museum at Woolwich, London.

The American Civil War (1861-65) brought several inventions to light. Among the first was the Billinghurst-Requa Battery Gun, which was very little more than the fourteenth-century 'ribauldequin' (small cannons mounted on a cart) brought up to date. A simple two-wheeled carriage carried 25 rifle barrels of 15.2mm (0.6in) calibre mounted side by side. They were loaded with a metallic cartridge containing powder and ball and having a hole in the base. The breech plate was then closed to secure all these in their barrels and a single percussion cap was fired into a channel in the breech plate. This flashed through all the holes in the cartridges to produce a ragged volley, after which the battery had to be emptied and reloaded. Although primitive, a number

were built and saw some use in the war. They were frequently called 'Bridge Guns' since their sudden concentrated volley was found useful in defending narrow bridges against a sudden rush.

Another Civil War weapon was the Ager 'Coffee Mill', so-called from the funnel-shaped hopper on top and the crank at the side of the breech. Invented by Wilson Ager, it was a single barrel weapon which had to be fed with a supply of pre-loaded steel tubes which contained powder, bullet and a percussion cap on a nipple at the rear. These were dropped into the hopper and gravity-fed one at a time by rotating the crank, which loaded the tube into the breech, locked the breech-block and then struck the percussion cap. The empty tube fell out as the next was loaded, and the gunner's mate had the task of picking them up and reloading them.

The Ager gun worked quite well, but it was too much of an innovation to be readily accepted. When Ager announced that it would be possible to fire 100 rounds a minute through the gun, the experts derided him. Their view was that such a high rate of fire meant exploding about a pound (0.45kg) of gunpowder a minute inside the barrel, and they were sure that the heating effect would melt the steel in time. They had, in fact, put their collective finger on one of the greatest problems confronting the would-be designer of a machine gun. And because of this view Ager never sold more than about 50 guns.

Today we speak of a 'machine gun' without giving it much thought, but, strictly defined, a machine gun is a gun which once set firing will continue to fire so long as it is provided with ammunition and the firer keeps the trigger pressed. This is an *automatic* machine gun, one in which the energy to load and fire is provided by the gun itself – or, more strictly, by the ammunition. There are two other types of multiple-firing guns. Guns such as the Billinghurst-Requa and the Mitrailleuse (discussed below), which fire the amount of ammunition which has been loaded into their barrels and then have to be reloaded, are *battery guns;* while the Ager and others of the sort which have to be cranked by hand (or, for that matter, by outside machinery) are *mechanical* machine guns.

The heating problem, offered as an objection to the Ager, presented a very real problem – and still does. It has been calculated that a modern machine gun firing at about 1,000 rounds a minute generates some 150 kilowatts (200 horsepower) of work in that time. The ejected bullets represent about 37.5 kw (50 hp) of work, and thus the remaining 112.5 kw (150 hp) is largely dissipated as heat. This heat is absorbed by the mechanism and, in particular, by the barrel. And since the steel of which the barrel is made will begin to melt at temperatures above 550°C, measures have to be taken to keep the temperatures below this figure. Water-cooling, air-cooling, or even making the gun so that alternate barrels are used, giving each barrel time to cool between bursts, are all methods which have been tried.

The other great problem which confronted the machine gun in its youth was the vexed question of how it was to be used. Was it artillery, or was it a small arm? Was it to be employed in batteries, or was it to be used by individuals? Some of the answers to this became apparent when the French Army unveiled their machine gun in the Franco-Prussian War of 1870. This was the Mitrailleuse which had originally been invented by a Belgian, Captain Fafchamps, in 1851. He passed his drawings and ideas to a manufacturer called Montigny who made minor improvements and made several guns for the Belgian fortress defences. He later managed to interest Napoleon III in the gun, and it was purchased for the French Army in 1869. In great secrecy 156 guns were built at the Meudon Arsenal and issued to the Army. Only the officers who would control them in battle were allowed to see them. But the press got hold of the story and, thanks to their boasting of what the secret weapon would do to the Prussians, with whom war was imminent, when the gun finally made its appearance on the battlefield the Prussians were quite ready for it.

The Mitrailleuse consisted of 37 rifle barrels mounted inside a cylindrical casing and carried on a two-wheeled carriage, so that externally it looked very much like a field gun. A separate breech-block carried 37 firing pins and could be slid backwards and forwards inside an extension behind the barrel. A steel plate pierced with 37 holes was loaded with cartridges – the same cartridges as used by the Chassepot rifle – and dropped in behind the barrels.

Previous page *An 1892 depiction of a Gatling with the 26th Middlesex Volunteer Cyclists. The operating handle is misplaced and the bottom barrel, not the top, should be firing.*

Left *Puckle's Defence Gun of 1718 with the chamber unit withdrawn from the barrel for rotation.*

Above *A mitrailleuse machine gun with its crew.*

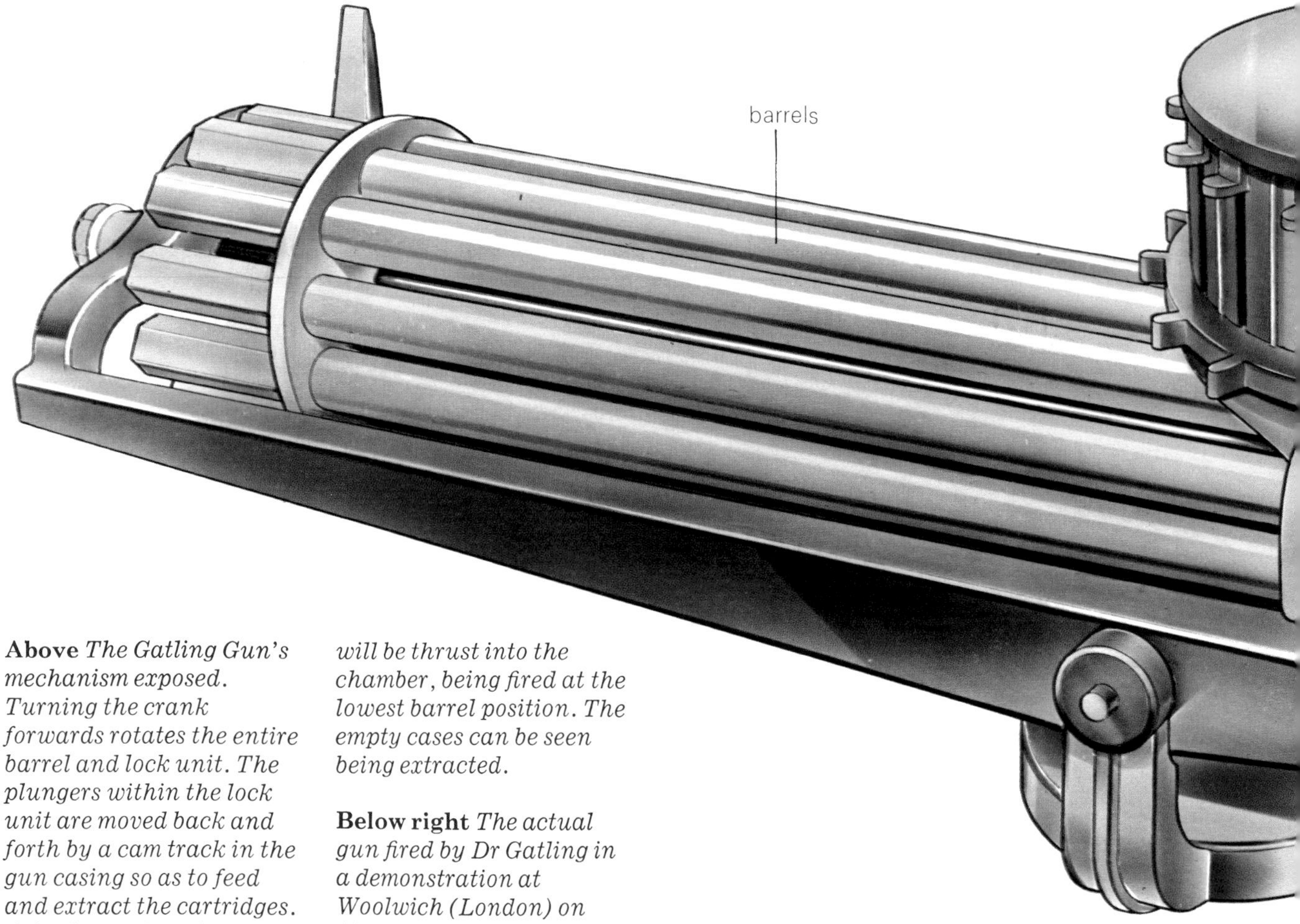

Above *The Gatling Gun's mechanism exposed. Turning the crank forwards rotates the entire barrel and lock unit. The plungers within the lock unit are moved back and forth by a cam track in the gun casing so as to feed and extract the cartridges. A fresh cartridge has just come from the drum and will be thrust into the chamber, being fired at the lowest barrel position. The empty cases can be seen being extracted.*

Below right *The actual gun fired by Dr Gatling in a demonstration at Woolwich (London) on 11 August 1870. The drum held 368 .42in rounds.*

The sliding breech-block was then pushed forwards and locked, forcing the cartridges into the chambers of their respective barrels. Turning a crank at the rear of the gun now caused the 37 firing pins to fall in succession, the rate of fire depending upon how quickly the crank was turned. After the last shot had been fired, the block was pulled back and the cartridge plate removed, a freshly-loaded plate dropped in, the breech closed, and fire could be resumed. A rate of 150 shots a minute could be kept up. The gun's maximum range was 1,800m (1,970yd).

The appearance of the Mitrailleuse in battle was, however, a disaster. The French deployed it like artillery, four or six guns in line to provide covering fire to the infantry. The Prussians dealt with them very easily by countering them with field guns. Since their range was 2,400m (2,624yd) they could stay well away from the French fire while pounding the mitrailleurs into silence.

The first really successful mechanical machine gun was the famous Gatling Gun, and yet even this had a hard time gaining acceptance. Richard Jordan Gatling was an American doctor of medicine (though he never practised as such) whose real vocation was mechanics. He began developing his gun in 1861 and his first version used a hopper-shaped, steel container similar to the Ager gun together with six barrels.

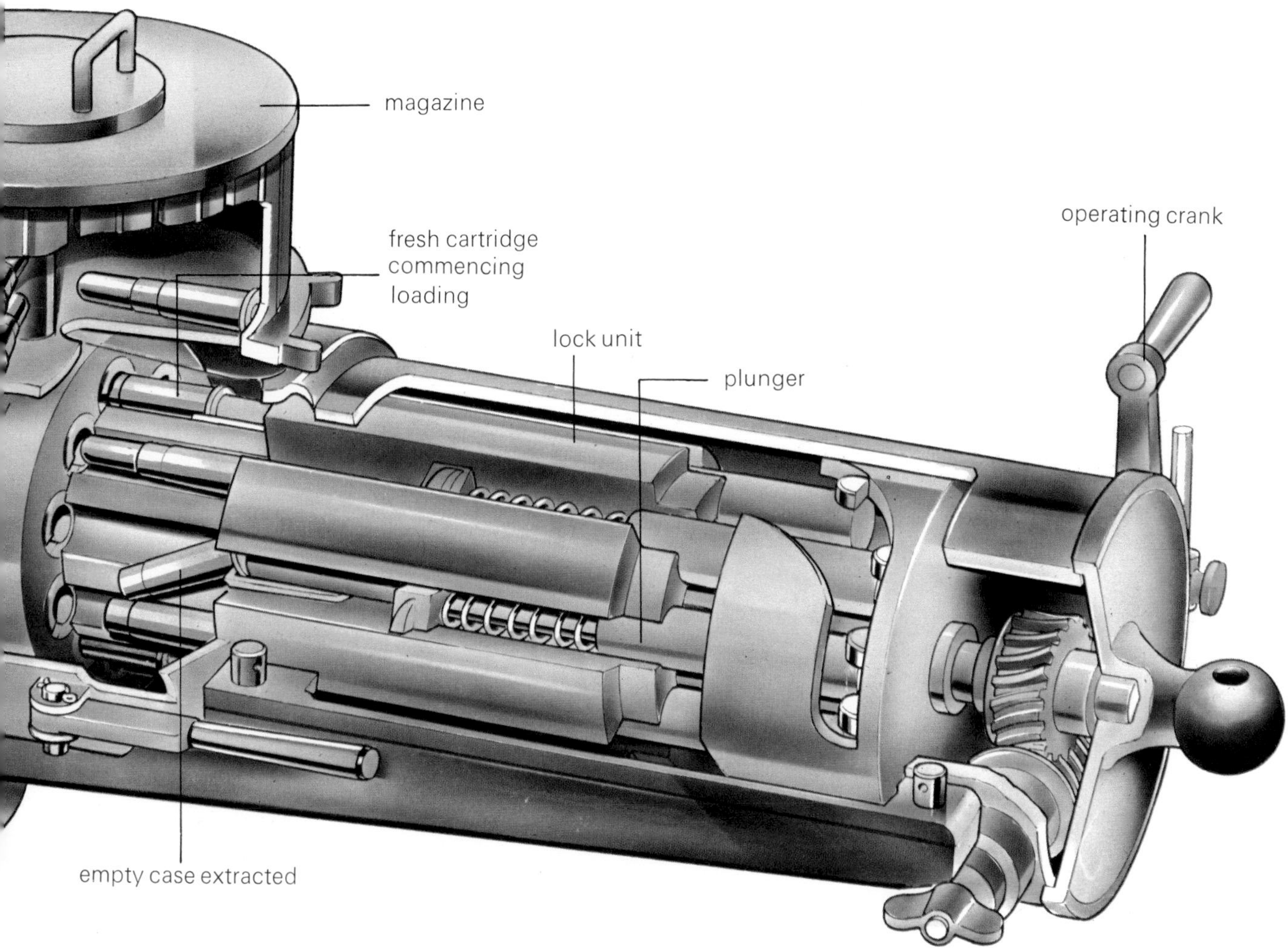

which revolved around a central axis. The charge containers were pressed forwards into contact with the barrels by a cam action and fired at the lowest position of the barrel, the remainder of the rotation being employed to force the cylinders into contact and then withdraw them. In 1862 he demonstrated a gun successfully and made arrangements for six guns to be made for an official test by the Union Army. Unfortunately the factory in which the guns were being made was destroyed by fire, and the guns and all his drawings were lost. Dr Gatling managed to raise sufficient money to have 12 more guns made, and this time he did away with cylinders, using rim-fire cartridges in .58 calibre. But the Union Army failed to adopt the gun. It seems that Gatling had been born in the Confederate state of North Carolina, and his politics were suspect. The Union Army felt that there was something odd about a Southerner offering a gun to the Union, and turned it down. The only military acceptance during the Civil War came when General Ben Butler of Massachusetts personally bought 12 guns for $1,000 each and later put them to good use against the Confederate troops besieged at Petersburg, Virginia.

In 1864 Gatling completely redesigned the gun so that each barrel was formed with its own chamber, thus doing away with the separate cylinder and its gas-leak problems. The gun now fed centre-fire cartridges from a magazine mounted on top. The cartridges were gradually fed into the chamber by cams as the barrels revolved, then fired at the bottom position, and extracted and ejected during the upward movement. As the barrel reached the top it was empty and ready to take the next round. The great advantage of this system was that it divided up the mechanical work between the six barrels so that the machinery was operating at a reasonable speed, and it also allowed each barrel time to cool down between shots.

The new gun was demonstrated to the Union Army in 1865 and finally met with their approval. In 1866 it was officially adopted, 50 guns of one-inch (25.4mm) calibre and 50 of half-inch (12.7mm) calibre being ordered. With this testimonial to his gun, Gatling was soon selling it abroad. One of the more remarkable overseas sales occurred when the Tsar sent General Gorloff to America to superintend the manufacture of 400 Gatling Guns for the Russian Army. Gorloff very astutely had Russian nameplates, bearing his own name, fitted to the guns before they were shipped, and ever since then the Gatling has been known as the 'Gorloff' in Russia.

Gatling's success soon inspired others to try their hand, and one of the first to appear was William

FAMOUS GUNS Gatling and Gardner

The Gatling Gun was the first successful mechanical machine gun, and after a slow start during the American Civil War went on to gain acceptance throughout the world. Dr Richard J. Gatling began work in 1861, but it was not until 1864 that he perfected a centre-fire model which was adopted by the US Army in 1866. The British Army adopted a ten-barrel version in .45in calibre in 1874 and the Royal Navy a .65in version in 1875.

The Gatling's novel feature was its division of firing between a number of barrels, thus allowing each barrel time to cool between shots. Behind the cluster of rotating barrels, and linked to it, was the lock unit which contained plungers driven back and forth, as the unit revolved, by a cam surface inside the outer (stationary) casing. Thus the plunger for a particular barrel would start at the fully-drawn position. A cartridge was dropped into the groove ahead of the plunger and, as the unit revolved, the plunger moved forwards and rammed the cartridge into its barrel, fired it, and then extracted the case and ejected it through the casing.

In spite of Sir Henry Newbolt's famous line about 'The Gatling's jammed and the Colonel's dead', the Gatling jammed relatively infrequently and was considered quite a reliable weapon. In the 1890s Dr Gatling went so far as to mount an electric motor on a Gatling, to achieve the prodigious rate of fire of 3,000rpm. The idea was revived in the Vulcan aircraft Mini-gun of the 1940s.

The Gardner Machine Gun was developed by another American, William Gardner, who had served in the Civil War and who had seen a variety of 'battery' guns and the Gatling.

The Gardner Gun consisted of two barrels mounted side by side and closed by two sliding breech-blocks. These were attached by connecting rods to a crank which was revolved by a handle outside the gun. The crank throws were 180° apart, so that when one breech was closed, the other was open, and the two barrels fired

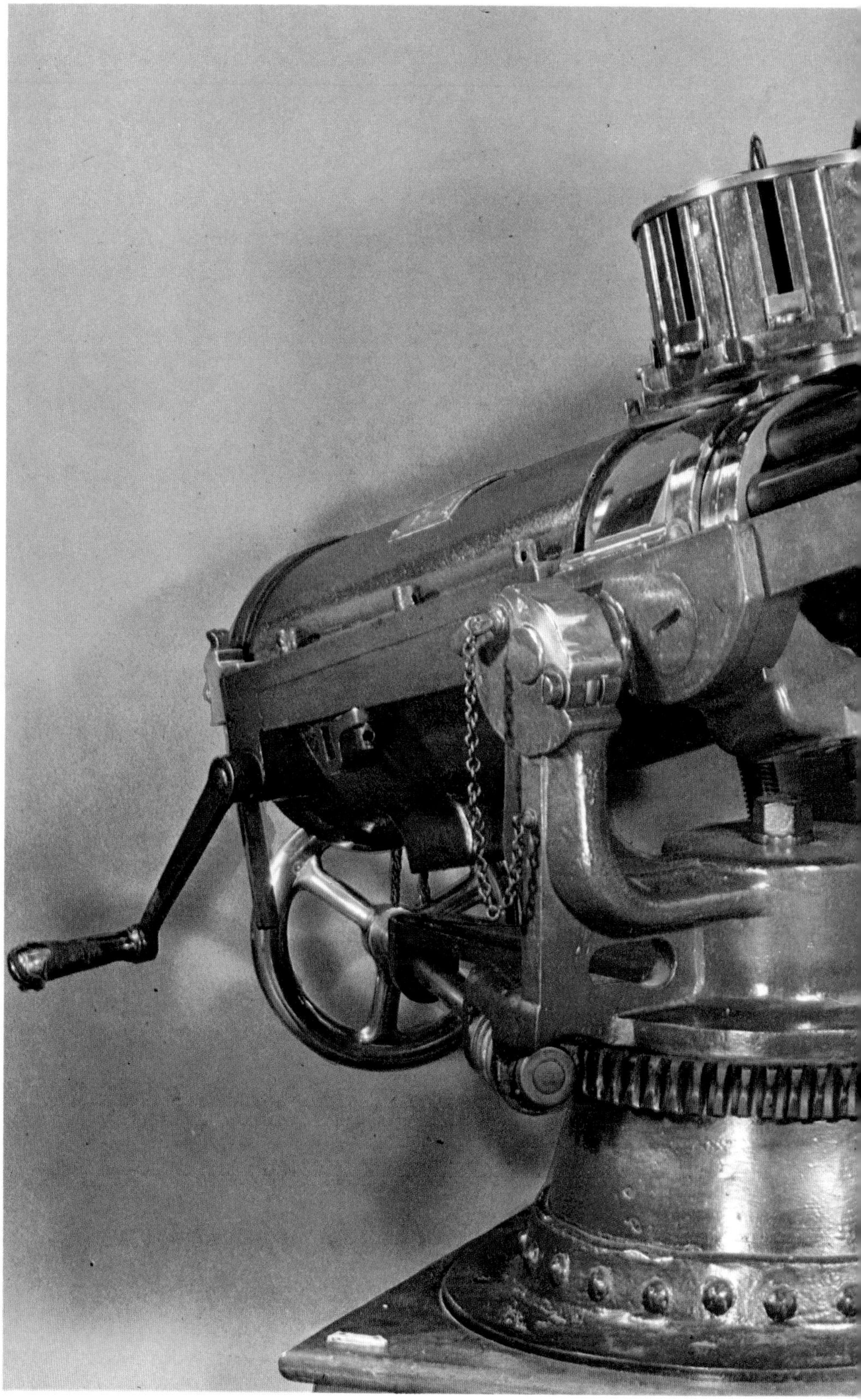

alternately. The cartridges were fed down a slotted feed strip to land on a swinging tray between the breechs. The tray, linked to the crank, fed each breech in turn. A rate of fire of 300rpm was well within the mechanism's capability.

Gardner was unable to sell his gun to the US authorities; they had the Gatling and were satisfied with it. He went to Europe and managed to interest the British Army and Navy in two and five-barrel versions which were adopted in 1882.

Gardner was responsible for introducing the term 'Machine Gun' into official terminology; the Gatling Gun had been introduced simply as the 'Gun, Gatling, 0.45in' but the Gardner became the 'Gun, Machine, Gardner, 0.45in'. These guns were provided with tripods for infantry use, and also with 'Gunwhale Mountings' for firing from small boats by naval landing parties. In spite of being replaced by the Maxim Gun in the 1890s, the Gardner remained on the British Army's inventory until 1926.

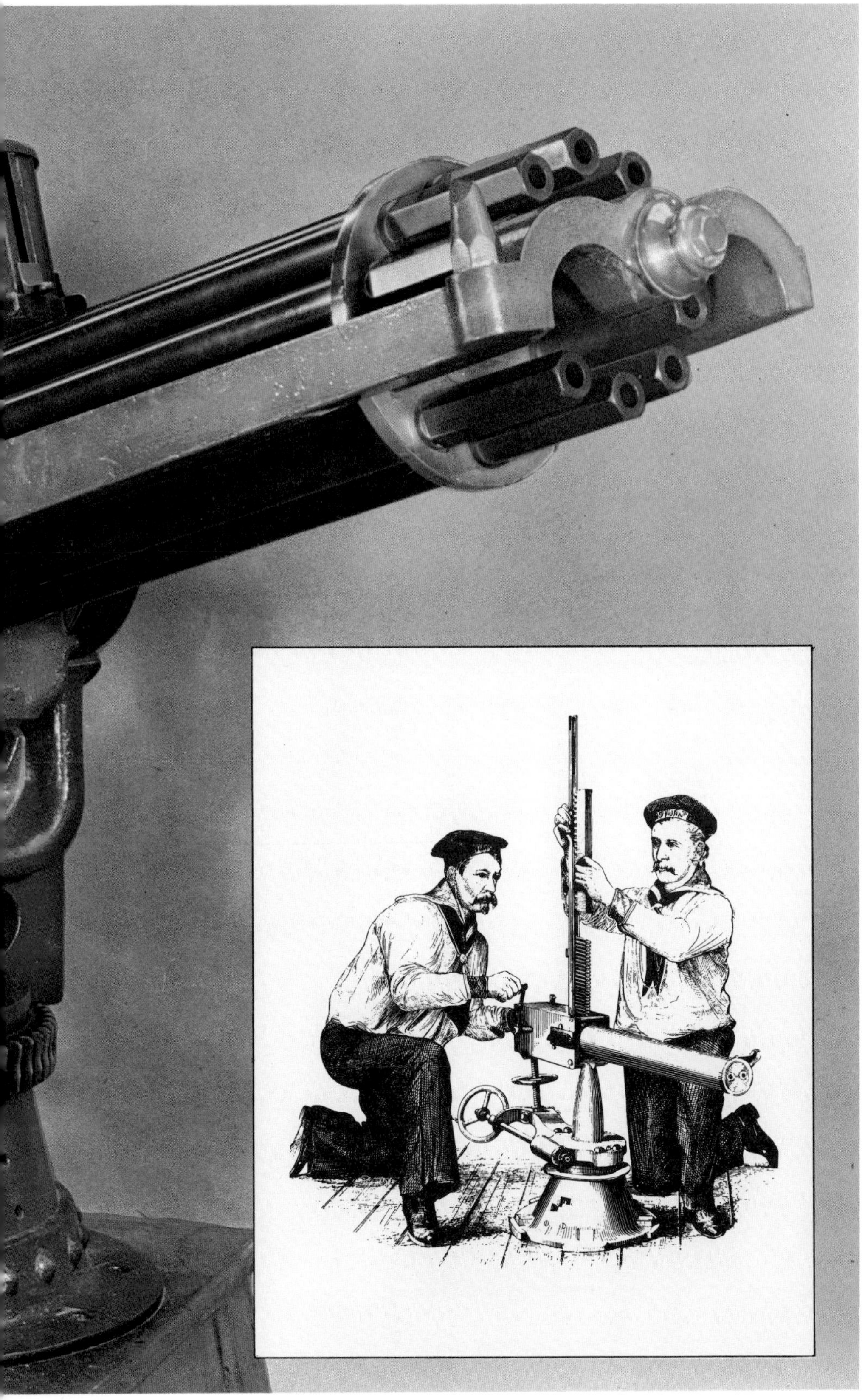

The colour picture is of a .65in 10-barrel Gatling on a naval cone mounting.

Two sailors from HMS Ajax *(a battleship of 1880) are shown operating the twin-barrel M1879 Gardner MG.*

GATLING 10-Barrel
Calibre .45in
Length 150.9cm (59.41in)
Weight 210kg (444lb)
Barrel 81.1cm (31.95in)
Rifling 7 grooves, r/hand
Foresight Blade
Rearsight V-notch, adjustable to 2,000yd (1,829m)
Action Mechanical
Rate of fire 1,000rpm
Feed system 240-round drum
Muzzle velocity 396m/sec (1,300ft/sec)
Bullet weight 31.1g (480gr)

GARDNER 5-Barrel
Calibre .45in
Length 135.9cm (53.5in)
Weight 131.5kg (290lb)
Barrel 838mm (33.0in)
Rifling 7 grooves, r/hand
Foresight Blade
Rearsight V-notch, adjustable to 1,500yd (1,372m)
Action Mechanical
Rate of fire 650rpm
Feed Vertical 50-round magazine
Muzzle velocity 412m/sec (1,350ft/sec)
Bullet weight 31.1g (480gr)

Left *The Gatling gun in naval use as depicted by the* Illustrated London News *in 1878. The weapon is mounted in a ship's protected main top and would have been a lethal anti-boarding weapon.*

Right *A 5-barrel Nordenfelt MG being test fired. A 10-barrel Nordenfelt fired 3,000 rounds in 3 minutes and 3 seconds without a stop on trial in 1882. Like the Gatling, the Nordenfelt was bought by the Royal Navy, and it was produced in many calibres with one to 12 barrels.*

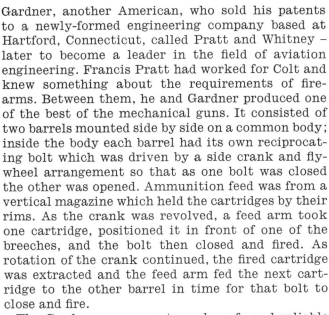

Gardner, another American, who sold his patents to a newly-formed engineering company based at Hartford, Connecticut, called Pratt and Whitney – later to become a leader in the field of aviation engineering. Francis Pratt had worked for Colt and knew something about the requirements of firearms. Between them, he and Gardner produced one of the best of the mechanical guns. It consisted of two barrels mounted side by side on a common body; inside the body each barrel had its own reciprocating bolt which was driven by a side crank and flywheel arrangement so that as one bolt was closed the other was opened. Ammunition feed was from a vertical magazine which held the cartridges by their rims. As the crank was revolved, a feed arm took one cartridge, positioned it in front of one of the breeches, and the bolt then closed and fired. As rotation of the crank continued, the fired cartridge was extracted and the feed arm fed the next cartridge to the other barrel in time for that bolt to close and fire.

The Gardner was an extremely safe and reliable weapon. On trial in 1879 it fired 10,000 rounds non-stop in 27 minutes 36 seconds – a quite remarkable achievement for a hand-cranked gun. But there was no interest in the United States, so Gardner took the gun to Britain where it was quickly adopted. Models with as many as five barrels were constructed though the twin-barrel model was the most usual.

At much the same time the Royal Navy had adopted another mechanical gun, the Nordenfelt. This had been invented by a Swede called Palmkranz who, lacking money to finance his invention, went to Torsten Nordenfelt, a Swedish banker, and named the gun after him in gratitude for his support. This was another multiple-barrelled gun, the number of barrels ranging from two to twelve, arranged side by side in front of the gun body. An overhead hopper magazine carried as many columns of cartridges as there were barrels and delivered them into a 'carrier block' operated by a hand lever. This hand lever was pushed forwards to take the carrier block forwards until the cartridges were lined up with their chambers. A breech-block then moved forwards to force the cartridges home, and an 'action block' containing the firing pins moved in behind the breech-block and lined up with the caps of the cartridges. At the end of the forward stroke of the handle, the firing pins were tripped and fired the rounds. On the return stroke of the lever, the action block moved away, the breech-block pulled clear and ejected the empty cases, and the carrier block went back to pick up a fresh loading of cartridges.

While most of these machine guns were developed for use in land warfare, they found a considerable market among the navies of the world, who saw in them an ideal fast-firing weapon for dealing with the new 'torpedo-boats' which were gaining favour. These light and fast vessels could dash into the middle of a fleet, either in harbour or at sea, and launch two or three torpedoes while the big guns of the fleet were still trying to aim at them. The handy machine gun, firing heavy bullets at a great rate, was an ideal solution to this problem.

One prominent weapon in this application was the Hotchkiss Revolver Cannon, the invention of Benjamin Berkely Hotchkiss, an American living in Paris. Impressed by the Gatling, in 1874 he developed his own revolving gun which used five barrels. But, instead of the continuous operation of the Gatling, he 'stepped' the barrels round and then stopped them for a fraction of a second while the lock mechanism performed the various actions of feed, fire and extract on the different barrels. Firing a 37mm high-explosive shell weighing 0.45kg (1lb), the Hotchkiss Revolver Cannon was, in practice, light artillery rather than small arms. But with this gun as a basis, the company which Hotchkiss founded was to enter the machine-gun business and later become the makers of one of the most widely-distributed designs.

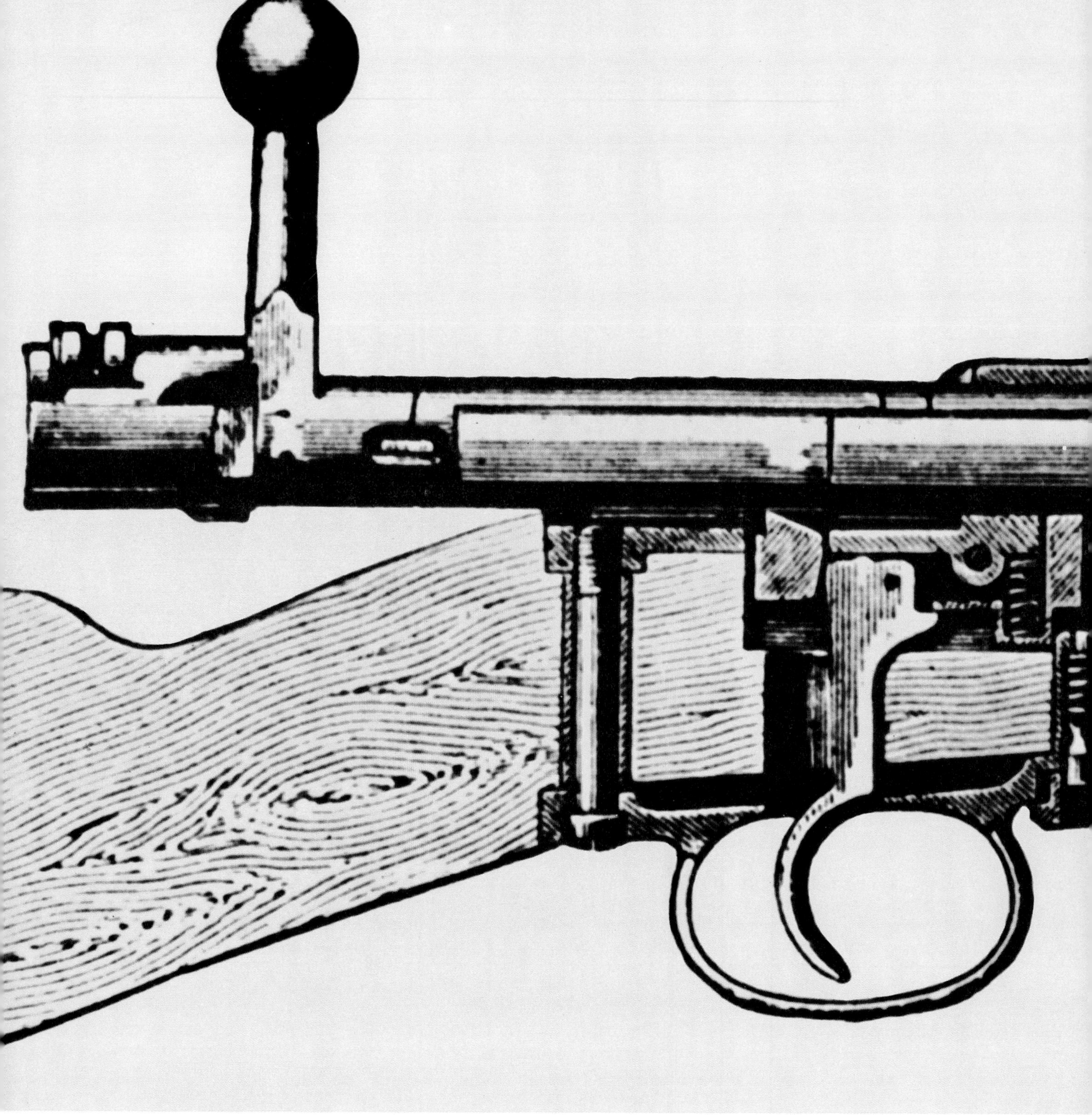

MAGAZINE RIFLES

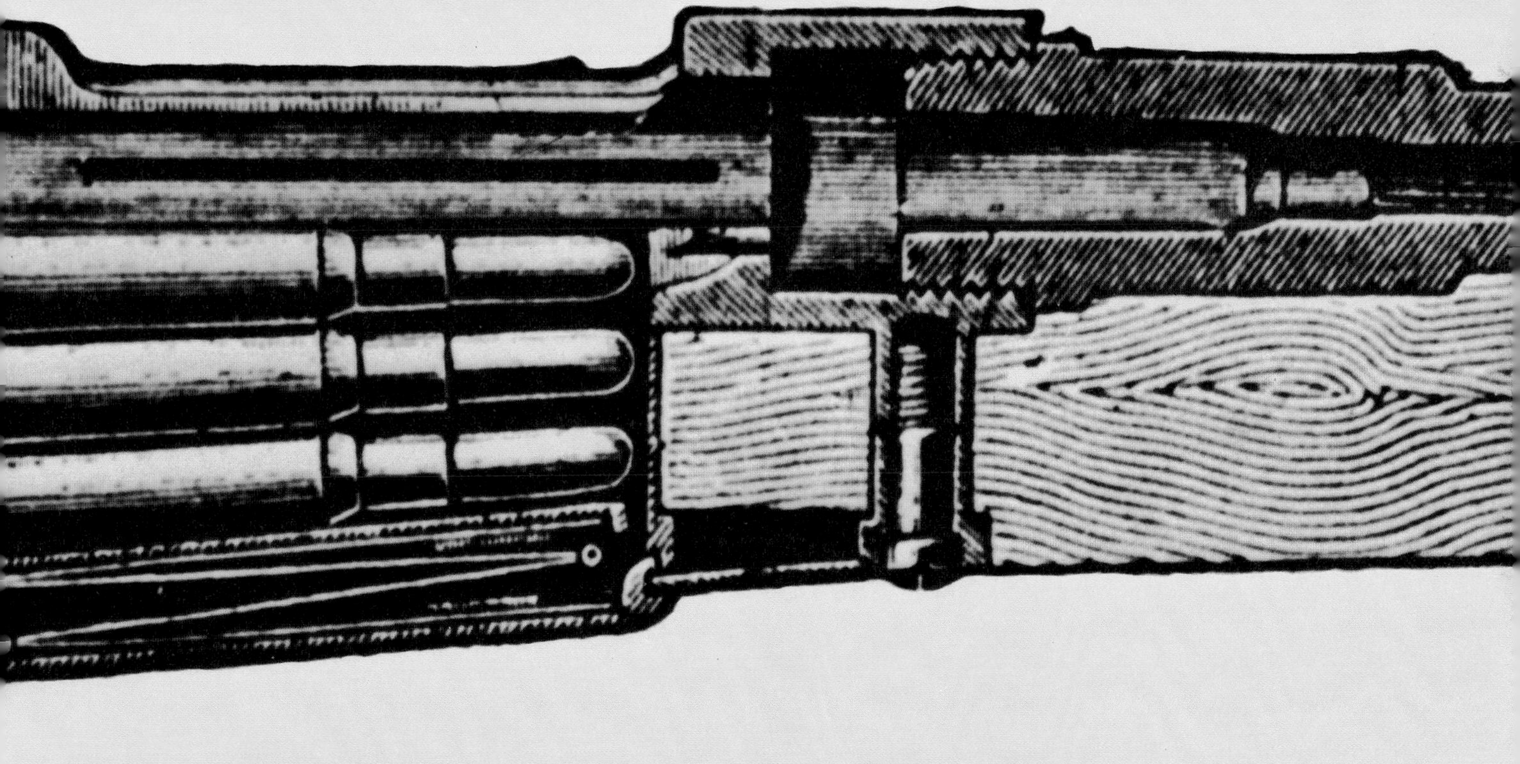

The success of Dr Gatling and his contemporaries in producing guns capable of firing several hundred rounds in a few minutes led to a reappraisal of the basic infantryman's rifle. Infantry units were now being provided with sophisticated machine guns, yet the rifleman was left holding a slow-firing, single-shot weapon.

The Turks with their Winchesters at the Siege of Plevna had shown the value of repeating rifles, but the lever-action, as we have seen, was frowned upon for military work, and the Winchester's tabular magazine had its drawbacks. Still, the first major advance in military rifles came when Paul Mauser took his existing (1871) single-shot model and put a tubular magazine underneath the barrel, linking the bolt action to a cartridge lifter so that opening the bolt ejected the spent case and lifted up a fresh round ready to be rammed in by the return stroke of the bolt. Mauser's magazine rifle appeared in 1884 and was in 11mm calibre, with a magazine capacity of eight rounds. It was enormously successful: in addition to being adopted by the German Army, it was sold abroad in vast quantities, over half a million going to the Balkan state of Serbia alone.

Extensive testing by Mauser indicated that the 11mm calibre was not the optimum for the black powder then in use, and 9.5mm was chosen as giving the best results. In 1886 the Turkish Army took over 500,000 rifles and carbines in this calibre. At the same time as Mauser was producing the acme of black powder rifles, however, other people were at work, paving the way for the next great step forward in firearms technology.

Since the fourteenth century, gunpowder had been the only explosive substance of any worth, used both for firearms and as a blasting explosive. In 1846 an Italian chemist, Sobrero, had discovered nitro-glycerine, and 20 years later Alfred Nobel had produced dynamite followed, in 1875, by Nobel's Blasting Gelatin. As an explosive for use in construction work, gunpowder was finished. With these technical advances to spur them on, chemists now began seeking some substitute for gunpowder in firearms. The defects of gunpowder were well-known – excessive fouling, sensitivity to damp, susceptibility to friction – and anything which promised a relief from these ills would be welcome. In 1886 a French chemist, Paul Vieille, made the breakthrough when he treated nitrocellulose with alcohol and ether to produce a tough impervious material which burned fiercely, but virtually without smoke. Tried as a propellant it was immediately successful, and the smokeless powder era had begun.

At much the same time two Swiss Army officers, Majors Rubin and Bode, had been investigating bullet design. Their prime object was to do away with the problem of lead fouling – the trace of lead left in the grooves of the gun's rifling after the bullet had passed by and which could soon build up and prevent the weapon being fired at all. Various expedients had been tried – paper patches around the bullet, grease pressed into grooves around the bullet, and so forth – but these were only palliatives.

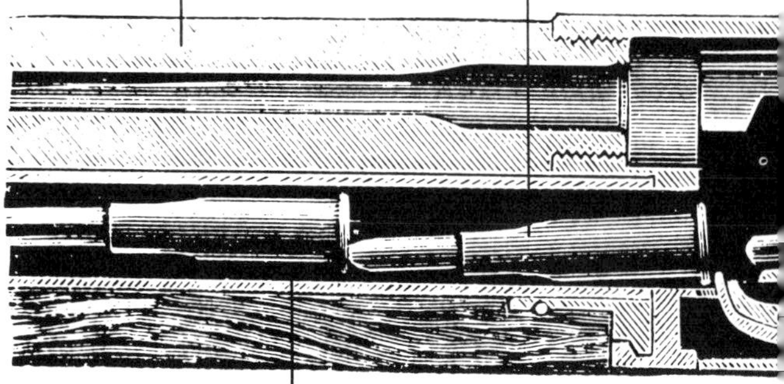

Eventually Rubin and Bode developed the small-calibre jacketed bullet. The bullet had a leaden core, to give the necessary weight, wrapped in a malleable metal envelope which could deform to suit the rifling but would leave little or no trace of its passage. The jacketed bullet could, of course, work equally well in any calibre, but Rubin and Bode pointed out the ballistic advantages of making the bullet thinner and longer: the cross-section was less, so that there was less air resistance, but the mass was still there, giving the bullet a far better trajectory, greater range, and better accuracy. The only trouble was that a small-calibre rifle loaded with black powder fouled up all the quicker, so although the Swiss idea was respected, few military powers were interested in trying it out in practice.

But when Vieille produced his smokeless powder – called 'Poudre B' after General Boulanger, then French Minister of War – here was the opportunity to put Rubin's theories to the test: moreover, the political climate was ripe. France's strained relations with Germany after her humiliating defeat by Prussia in the war of 1870 had been further embittered by Germany's annexation of the French provinces of Alsace and Lorraine. General Boulanger launched a slogan – 'New smokeless powder and revenge for Alsace-Lorraine!' – and demanded a new modern rifle to take advantage of the one and effect the other. Within months the French Army was issued with the 8mm Lebel magazine rifle, the first military rifle to adopt smokeless powder and the small-calibre jacketed bullet. As in so many technical military matters, the French were ahead of the field. And, as with most of the other examples, they sat back self-satisfied and let the opposition overhaul them before they woke up.

The Lebel takes its name from Colonel Nicolas Lebel, a member of the Board which designed the rifle and, it is generally believed, the designer of the

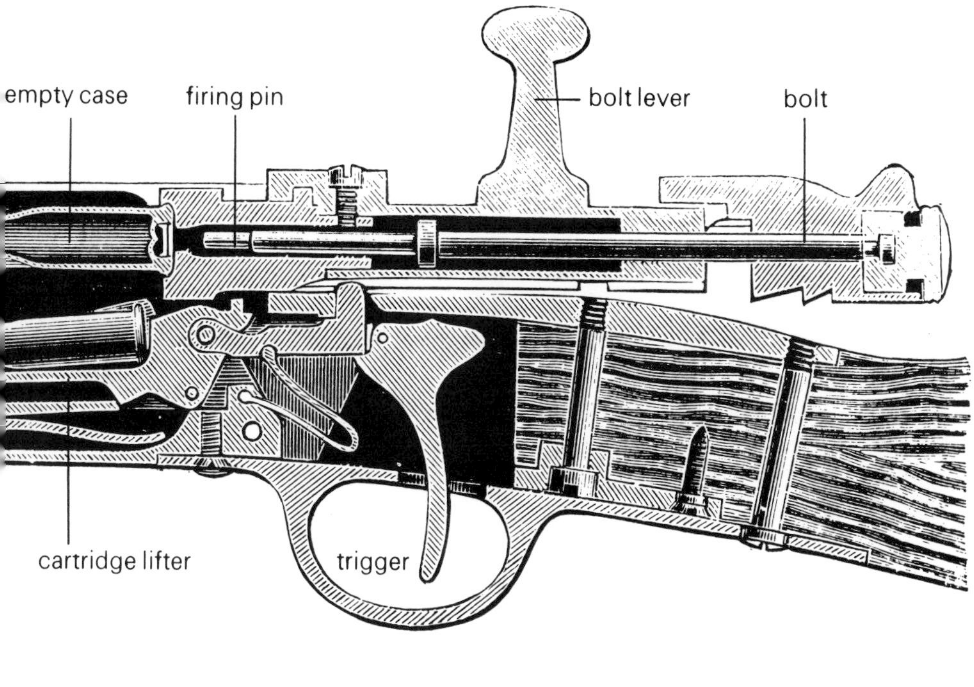

Previous page *The Model 1893 Mauser bolt-action rifle, the first Mauser to have an 'in-line', charger-loaded box magazine instead of a 'protruding' one. It carried five 7mm cartridges.*

Left *The French Lebel Rifle of 1886 allied a bolt action to a tubular magazine. As the bolt is opened, the cartridge lifter brings a fresh round up and aligns it with the chamber, to be rammed in on the closing stroke of the bolt. Smokeless powder and the 8mm Lebel cartridge sparked off a revolution in military arms design.*

cartridge. At the time of its introduction it was far ahead of any other rifle in the world, with a bolt action, a tubular magazine holding eight cartridges beneath the barrel, and the undoubted advantage of smokeless powder and a high velocity bullet. Impressed and alarmed, other European armies looked to their rifles and began to plan improvements.

By this time the drawbacks of the tubular magazine had become fairly apparent. In the first place, the balance of the rifle shifted considerably as the bullets in the magazine were used up, which tended to upset the soldier's aim. And when small-calibre bullets were issued a new hazard appeared. The tip of each bullet was resting snugly on the percussion cap of the cartridge in front, and the shock of firing the rifle often shifted the column of ammunition back with enough force to jam a point against a cap just a fraction too hard, firing the cartridge and setting off a chain reaction inside the magazine. This further tended to put the soldier off his aim. It also put him off tubular magazines.

There is always a reluctance on the part of governments to give money to their armies to buy some new weapon when they have just recently disbursed a sizeable sum for the same purpose. Many European armies had but recently invested large sums in single-shot rifles and now, in the hope of staving off the day when they had to buy magazine rifles, many took to using various 'quick-loader' devices. These began as a sort of clip mounted on the side of the rifle near the boltway; into this clip a number of cartridges could be placed with their bases upward. The soldier, after opening the rifle bolt, could grasp a fresh cartridge by its base, pull it from the clip and insert it into the breech, and then move his hand back to the bolt quite quickly, much quicker than if he had had to reach down to the usual type of pouch on his belt. Such quick-loader devices are still to be found today, used by target shooters who, having got into position, do not wish to disturb themselves by reaching for ammunition. In the 1870s and early 1880s a number of European armies adopted them since they allowed a fair rate of fire to be attained from a single-shot rifle, and without spending too much money.

From the simple side-mounted clip, however, inventors began to get more and more involved, developing boxes with springs inside which clamped alongside the rifle and, by spring pressure, pushed a new cartridge into the top of the box ready to be withdrawn by the soldier. It was not long before it was suggested that cutting a hole into the bottom of the rifle and mounting the box there, so that the spring pushed the cartridge up in front of the bolt, would save the soldier the trouble of pulling each cartridge from the magazine and placing it in the boltway. The idea may sound simple, but some of the attempts to make it work were masterpieces of mechanical complication, none of which attracted military favour. It remained for James Paris Lee, a Scottish-born American, to do the job.

Lee's design was quite simple. The boltway was cut away underneath, and a detachable, sheet-metal box was inserted through the bottom of the rifle. Inside the box a zig-zag spring pushed up a platform, on top of which the cartridges rested. The magazine was loaded and thrust into the rifle, retained there by a spring catch. When the bolt was opened the spring forced the top cartridge up into the path of the bolt, so that as the bolt was closed, this cartridge was swept forwards and placed in the rifle chamber. When the magazine was empty it was removed, and either reloaded or replaced by another full magazine carried by the soldier.

Lee took out a patent on this in 1879 and then made some small improvements. The American Ordnance Commission tested it and approved, and Lee licensed the Remington Company to make use of the patent.

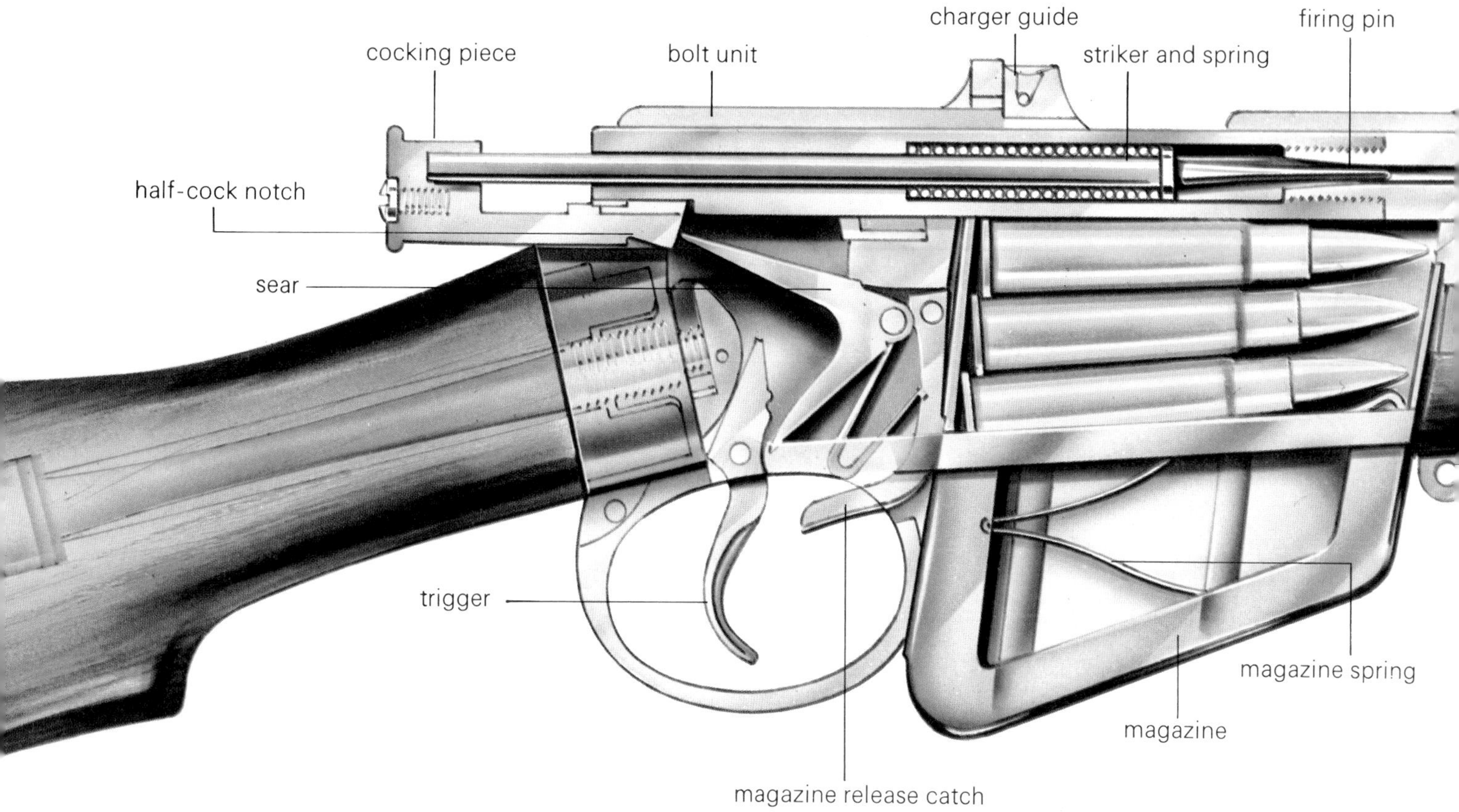

They produced 25,000 Remington-Lee rifles and 15,000 carbines for the Mexican Army in 1884.

Once Lee had shown the way, dozens of other inventors followed his example, though they had to tread warily until his patent expired. One of the most significant developments, though it never was adopted, was a little-known design by an American, Lieutenant A. R. Russel, in 1882. Russel's intention was to produce a system which would allow the weapon to be reloaded quickly once the magazine was empty, and he did this by carrying five or six cartridges in a thin, metal frame. To reload, this pack of cartridges was placed against the top of the magazine, still in position below the rifle, and the cartridges then pushed down, from the pack into the magazine, by thumb pressure. This was a most important step, but it went unrecognized at the time and Russel failed to interest anyone in it. It was some years before the idea was revived and applied almost universally to magazine rifles.

An alternative method of loading a magazine without having to remove it was to use a 'clip' which held five or six cartridges and which was simply dropped into the magazine. A 'follower arm' driven by a spring forced the cartridges up in the clip and, when the clip was empty, it was removed, either by the firer or by having it drop through a hole in the bottom of the magazine. This system was adopted by Ferdinand Ritter von Mannlicher, one of the most prolific arms designers of the nineteenth century, when he introduced the Austrian Model 1885 magazine rifle. Mannlicher's box magazine was fixed in place and a clip was dropped in after the bolt had been opened. Once the last shot was fired, a lever at the side of the magazine ejected the empty clip. In the following year he did away with the ejection lever and simply allowed the clip to drop out of the magazine.

Mannlicher's other notable innovation was the 'straight-pull' bolt. As the name implies, this bolt was operated by simply grasping the handle and pulling it straight back; there was no need to raise the handle in order to rotate and unlock the bolt. Such a mechanism has some advantages, notably that the firer does not have to wave his arm around, and it is theoretically faster than the turn-bolt. The principal drawbacks, however, are that in most designs of the straight-pull bolt there is no slow initial opening movement during the turn, which helps to unseat a sticky cartridge case, and in some designs it is possible to assemble the bolt incorrectly so that the first shot fired blows it out and into the firer's face. The Mannlicher design, though, was extremely reliable and helped to overcome much of the initial resistance to this system.

The Mannlicher bolt carried a hinged block below the rear end. The bolt handle actuated a sliding block in the bolt which carried ribs, and these, when the handle was pulled to the rear, forced the hinged block to rise. At the end of the rising movement the bolt handle drew the bolt back. On thrusting the handle forwards the bolt closed on the cartridge in

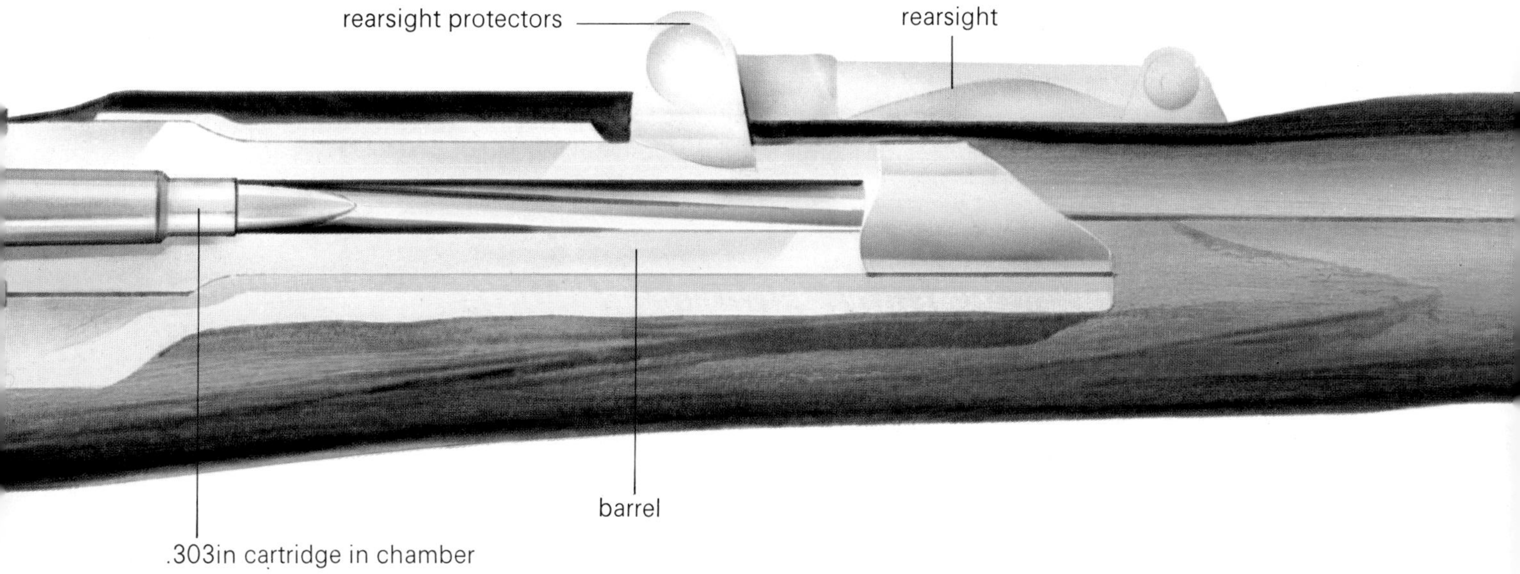

Above *The mechanism of the Lee-Enfield rifle is representative of many contemporary bolt-action magazine rifles. As the bolt goes forwards to load the cartridge, the cocking piece and striker are held back by the sear. This is released by the trigger to fire the cartridge. Pulling the bolt fully back will eject the spent case, raise a new round and re-cock the weapon. Closing the bolt will chamber the new round for firing.*

the breech and the final movement of the handle forced the block forward, so that the ribs drove the locking block down to lock securely in front of a solid portion of the rifle frame.

Motivated by France's adoption of the Lebel in 1886, the German Army had begun looking for a new magazine rifle to replace the tubular-magazine Mauser, and this clip-loading system of Mannlicher's appealed to it. So in 1888 the 'Commission' rifle – so-called as it was designed by a weapons commission – was introduced. This rifle allied Mauser's bolt action with Mannlicher's clip magazine. The only significant alteration was that the clip was so designed that it could be dropped into the magazine either way up. In Mannlicher's original design it could be loaded only one way – a nuisance in the heat of action.

For all its convenience, the clip-loader has one major drawback – it cannot be 'topped up'. If the firer has fired two rounds from his five-round clip, he cannot open the bolt and put in two loose rounds to make it up to five again ready for the next burst of activity. He can only wait until the shooting starts, fire off the three rounds remaining, and then reload with a full clip. Mauser was among the first to see that this was a significant disadvantage and he set to work to develop a magazine which could be topped up. His idea was similar to Lee's box, but instead of being removeable it was securely fixed to the base of the rifle action. The cartridges were held in a thin 'charger' in groups of five. With the bolt open, the charger was positioned in a guide-way and the cartridges then swept from the charger and into the magazine, the empty charger being flicked out of the way by the thumb as it was removed. The bolt was then closed, loading the first round. At any time, the bolt could be opened and loose rounds pressed down into the magazine to fill it.

This system was introduced in 1889 in the 7.65mm Belgian Army Mauser, which Mauser submitted for competitive trial. He won, hands down, and obtained an order for several hundred thousand rifles. Since he did not have the manufacturing capacity to make them, a factory was set up in Belgium which became the renowned Fabrique National d'Armes de Guerre, invariably known as 'F.N.'. His success here was followed by large orders from Turkey, Argentina, Spain, Brazil, Sweden and many other countries.

Also in 1889 came the first of a series of rifles which were to arm the British Army for the next 70 years and which, in slightly modified form, still continue to do so in specialist tasks. This was the Lee-Metford, an amalgam of the Lee bolt and magazine with a barrel rifled according to the principles of William Metford, a foremost firearms theoretician of the day. Although it was a small-calibre weapon – .303in – it still used black powder, since British trials of Vieille's smokeless powder showed that it was unstable when stored in tropical climates and at that time most of the British Army was dispersed abroad in hot countries. The propelling charge was a compressed pellet of extremely fine-grain gunpowder, but, even so, fouling was still a problem and the Metford rifling was intended to combat this. The grooves were wide and shallow, flowing gently up to the lands instead of being sharply incised, so that there were no angles in which fouling could accumulate.

The magazine of the first Lee-Metford held eight cartridges, which were loaded singly. In the Mark 2 model, the magazine held 10 cartridges in a double column, a pattern which was retained after that, though the cartridges were still loaded singly. The original intention for the Lee magazine was that it would be replaced by a full one rather than reloaded through the action, but this idea does not seem to have caught on with the British Army and spare magazines were never issued. Indeed, on many of the early rifles, the magazines, although removeable, were secured to the rifle by chains.

While rejecting the French smokeless powder, the British Army had not closed its eyes to the idea, and experiments went ahead to develop one which would stand up to the rigours of tropical climates. Eventually cordite was perfected, a combination of nitrocellulose, nitroglycerine and mineral jelly which was extruded in the form of thin strands or cords – hence the name. While cordite was exceptionally stable under all climatic conditions, the price which had to be paid for this virtue was a high one. Due to the nitroglycerine content, the flame temperature was high and it was very erosive, fast wearing away the rifling of the barrels. To counter this the Metford rifling was changed to a form having deeper and sharper grooves, less easily eroded. This rifling was developed at the Royal Small Arms Factory at Enfield and thus became known as the 'Enfield' rifling. By extension, the rifles now became the Lee-Enfield rifles.

An interesting feature of both the Lee-Metford and Lee-Enfield rifles was the introduction of a 'magazine cut-off' device. This was a thin, steel plate, hinged at its forward end, which could be swung into the action above the magazine and below the bolt to prevent the cartridges in the magazine from rising and thus be loaded by the action of the bolt. With the cut-off pushed in, the rifle became a single-shot weapon, and the rounds in the magazine remained there untouched while the soldier loaded one round at a time from his pouches. This was his normal course of action, and the full magazine was thus held in reserve against the time when the enemy would make his assault. When this came, the cut-off was opened and the soldier was then able to deliver rapid fire, secure in knowing that he started with a full magazine.

Another 1889 introduction was the Swiss Army's Schmidt-Rubin rifle, the only design other than that of Mannlicher to make a success of a straight-pull bolt. In this design the bolt handle was part of an actuating rod which lay alongside the action and terminated in a lug which engaged in a helical groove cut in a 'bolt sleeve'. The bolt sleeve surrounded the actual bolt body and also carried the locking lugs. Pulling the handle to the rear caused the lug, by its action in the helical groove, to rotate the sleeve and thus unlock the bolt assembly. Further movement of the handle withdrew the sleeve and bolt to open the action. As can be imagined, this meant an abnormally long stroke of the handle and the Schmidt-Rubin rifle is unique for the length of action behind the magazine. It was to remain in Swiss service for many years, but it is open to question whether it would have lasted so long had it ever been tried in earnest in a major war.

Finally in 1889 came the Danish Krag-Jorgensen rifle, a design which – for reasons best known to the inventor, Ole Krag, a Norwegian – departed from the universal idea of placing the magazine vertically below the bolt. In the Krag design the magazine was laid horizontally under the boltway, being loaded by way of a 'trapdoor' on the right-hand side of the action. This door hinged forwards and carried the magazine spring attached to it. The door was opened and the rifle tilted to the left; five cartridges were dropped into the magazine and the door closed, the spring then putting pressure on the cartridges. The inner end of the magazine curved up and round to deliver the cartridges to a slot in the left-hand side of the bolt way, so that when the bolt (a straightforward turn-bolt) was opened, the action of the spring thrust a cartridge through the slot, to be collected and loaded on the return stroke of the bolt. Unusual as this layout was, it did have the advantage that the magazine could be loaded or topped-up at any time without having to open the bolt. It also had a cut-off device so that the magazine contents could be held in reserve and the rifle used as a single-loader. After being adopted by Denmark, the Krag-Jorgensen was taken into use by Norway and then in 1892, by the United States Army, the only important army at that time not to be equipped with magazine rifles. The American and Norwegian designs differed slightly from the Danish in that the magazine door opened downwards.

The only other magazine system to be successfully applied to rifles was the rotary magazine. We have noted that Colt (among several others) had attempted to build rifles on the simple revolver principle. These weapons were, in essence, the same as a revolver pistol but with longer barrels and suitable shoulder stocks. Revolver rifles were never very successful, since the powerful cartridges considered to be essential to the rifle lost too much of their propelling gas through the gap between cylinder and barrel. Moreover, the construction, for long rifle cartridges, was cumbersome, and the support given to the barrel was not sufficient to ensure strength and rigidity.

In 1879 Antonin Spitalsky, chief foreman of the Austrian arms factory at Steyr, developed a rotary magazine which fitted into the stock of a bolt-action rifle. It resembled a revolver cylinder, held seven cartridges, and fed them to the bolt in succession. It was tested by various countries but not adopted, and in the following years a number of inventors tried to improve on Spitalsky's idea. It was not until 1900 that Mannlicher achieved a practical design, using a rotary magazine developed by Otto

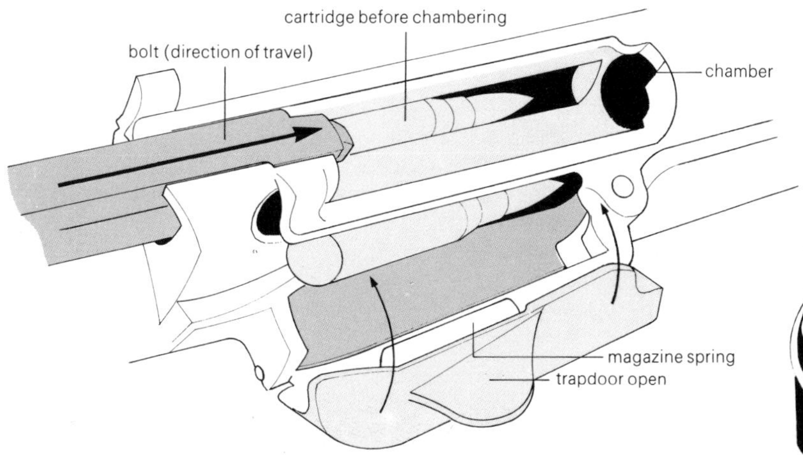

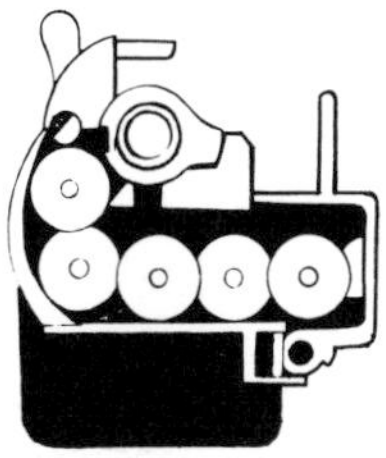

Left *The Krag-Jorgensen magazine is loaded from the side through a trap door which carries the magazine spring. The five cartridges then pass underneath the bolt up the left side of the rifle to the boltway. The magazine can be filled at any time without opening the bolt, but there is a risk of the contents falling out when the trapdoor is opened.*

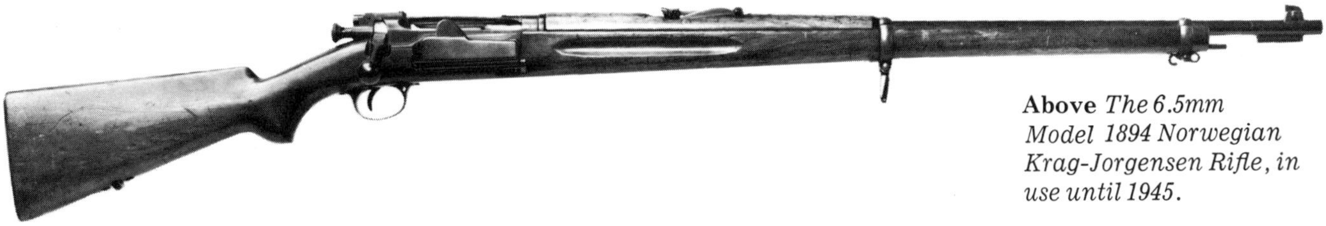

Above *The 6.5mm Model 1894 Norwegian Krag-Jorgensen Rifle, in use until 1945.*

Schoenauer and Josef Werndl. This magazine used a centrally-mounted, fluted spindle, driven by a spring. The cartridges were loaded through the open action (that is, with the bolt withdrawn) by stripping them from a charger. As they passed into the magazine so they each in turn engaged in a groove on the spindle and forced it round, placing the driving spring under tension. When the bolt was operated the spring forced the spindle round and delivered a cartridge into the boltway ready for loading. This design was adopted by the Greek Army in 1903 and has been widely used in sporting rifles. It is currently in use by the Austrian Army in their sniping rifle.

One last major step in magazine rifle design before the advent of the 'automatic' rifle came at the turn of the century. For hundreds of years it had been customary to produce two types of shoulder arm for soldiers – a long rifle for infantry, and a shorter carbine for use by cavalry, the latter because it was more convenient to carry on a horse. The changing tactics of war in the late nineteenth century had, in many instances, turned cavalry into 'mounted infantry', soldiers who rode to battle on their horses but then dismounted and fought as infantry. In such cases their short rifles were at a disadvantage since they had neither the range nor the accuracy of the long rifles of their opponents.

The US Army appears to have been the first to see the answer to this problem. In the 1890s, dissatisfied with the Krag-Jorgensen, it began studying the Mauser system and eventually designed a new rifle, based on the Mauser bolt action. This was the Springfield, named after the armoury in Massachusetts where it was developed, and the first experimental models of 1901 had a 760mm (30in) barrel; they were the traditional long rifles of the infantry. But before they were ready for issue it was decided to reduce the barrel length to 610mm (24in) to provide a short rifle – a weapon longer than the traditional carbine, shorter than the 'long' rifle, but with all the accuracy that any soldier needed. This was designated the Model 1903 and was first issued for field tests in 1905. At the same time the British Army had come to much the same conclusions and in 1904 it issued the first of the Short Magazine Lee-Enfield (S.M.L.E.) models. This had a barrel 640mm (25.19in) long instead of the 766mm (30.19in) of the preceding Lee-Enfield rifles, which was still longer than the usual 527mm (20.75in) of the cavalry's Lee-Enfield carbines. The Germans followed suit in the following year by adopting the Mauser Karabiner Model 1898 or 'Kar 98', which was the standard Mauser army rifle with the barrel shortened from 740mm (29.13in) to 600mm (23.6in).

By the turn of the century, then, regular infantry soldiers were universally equipped with magazine repeating rifles firing small-calibre, jacketed bullets by means of smokeless powder. In 1800, the universal weapon had been a muzzle-loading smooth-bore of about 12.7mm (0.5in) calibre, firing a lead bullet. A highly-trained man could load and fire some five shots a minute, and an enemy more than 180m (200yd) away was relatively safe. In 1900, by contrast, the trained man could get off 20 shots a minute and could hit a man-sized target at ranges of over 900m (1,000yd). An infantry platoon or squad could lay down a barrage of fire which could paralyze an attacking force. During World War I, the rate of fire achieved by well-trained British troops with their SMLE rifles was so high that the enemy thought they were facing the most effective of all infantry weapons – the automatic machine gun.

Lee-Enfield Rifles

The Lee-Enfield rifle was introduced in 1895, following from the adoption of cordite as the smokeless propellant for the British Army. Its predecessor, the Lee-Metford rifle, used the Lee bolt and box magazine allied to a barrel rifled according to a design by William Metford. The Enfield rifling, deeper and angularly cut, resisted erosion better and so the rifle got a new barrel and a new name.

The first Lee-Enfield was a long rifle for infantry use, having a 76.6cm (30.2in) barrel; it was supplemented in 1896 by a cavalry carbine with a 52.7cm (20.75in) barrel. But during the Boer War of 1899-1902 this traditional division was questioned. Two distinct weapons led to production and supply problems, and the long rifle, a hangover from the days of muskets and standing volleys, was not well-suited to modern warfare and firing from scanty cover. So in 1903 the distinction was swept away by the adoption of the 'Rifle, Short, Magazine, Lee-Enfield' or 'SMLE', with a 63.97cm (25.18in) barrel. This rifle would henceforth be common to all troops, long enough to give the accuracy the infantry demanded but short enough to be conveniently carried by mounted units.

The SMLE ran into a

Rifle, Magazine, Lee-Enfield Mark 1
(introduced 11 November 1895)

Carbine, Cavalry, Magazine Lee-Enfield Mark 1
(introduced 17 August 1896)

Rifle, Short, Magazine, Lee-Enfield (SMLE)
Converted Mark 2 (introduced 6 November 1903)

Rifle Number 4 Mark 1* (introduced 15 June 1941)

Rifle Number 5 Mark 1 (introduced 23 May 1945)

storm of criticism from various self-styled experts, whose principal objection was that it was not a long-range target weapon. Shaken by this, the War Office began a new rifle design, based on the Mauser bolt action and firing a high-velocity .276in cartridge. This was issued in some numbers for extended trials in 1913 but proved to be a failure. It gave excessive blast and recoil, over-heated badly, and the troops disliked its poor balance and cumbersome handling. The outbreak of war in 1914 killed the 'Pattern 13' rifle (though it was revived in .303in calibre as a wartime production measure) and also proved that the SMLE was, if not the best competition rifle, was certainly the finest combat long-arm ever seen.

After the war, the only criticism was that the SMLE was slow and difficult to produce in the vast quantities needed during wartime, and so it was slowly redesigned for easier manufacture. The result was 'Rifle No. 4' (the system of nomenclature having changed in the 1920s), formally introduced in 1941. The most obvious change was that the SMLE's characteristic blunt nosecap had been replaced by a naked length of barrel, and the sword bayonet replaced by a tiny spiky article which did not look like a real bayonet at all.

For jungle warfare the 'Rifle No. 5' was produced, a shortened and lightened version with a sporting style of stock and a bell-mouthed flash-hider on the muzzle. Though of dashing appearance, it was an unpopular weapon due to its excessive blast and recoil.

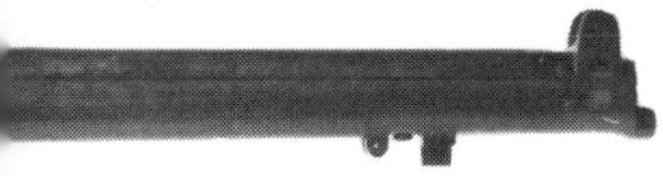

Far left *A British Boer War sergeant with the Lee-Enfield Mark 1 (seen top left; below it is the contemporary cavalry carbine). The NCO would have carried 120 rounds in his ammo pouches.*

Above *A Royal Marine Commando of 1944 with a Lee-Enfield No.4 Mark 1* (seen with 9in (228.6mm) bayonet, left). It was heavier (4.1kg) than the SMLE (3.91kg) and had the rearsight moved back.*

SMLE Mk III

Calibre .303in
Length 113cm (44.5in)
Weight 3.91kg (8.621b)
Barrel 63.9cm (25.19in)
Rifling 5 grooves, 1/hand
Foresight Blade
Rearsight U-notch, to 2,000yd (1,829m)
Action Bolt
Rate of fire 15rpm
Feed system 10-round removeable box magazine
Muzzle velocity 670m/sec (2,200ft/sec)
Bullet weight 13.9g (215gr)

AUTOMATIC MACHINE GUNS

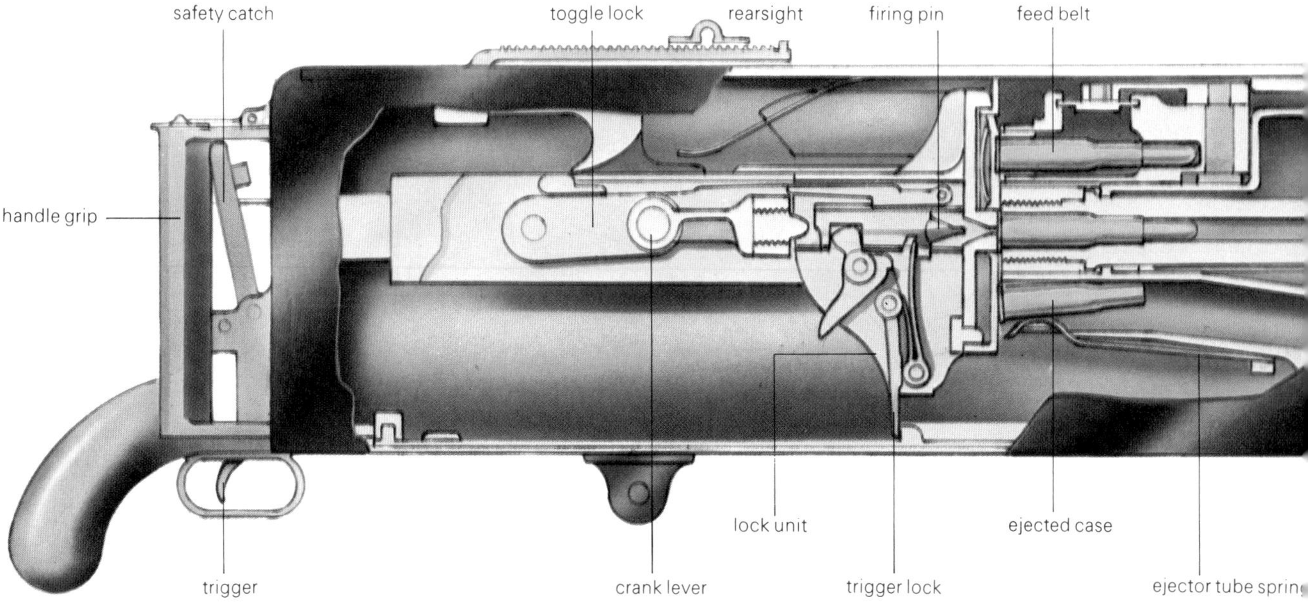

Previous page *The Vickers Mk 1 MG on a Mk 4B tripod. The condenser tube takes steam from the water-filled barrel jacket into the one-gallon (4.5l) can.*

Above *The Maxim Gun mechanism is recoil-operated. The barrel and lock recoil, locked together for a short distance. The toggle lock is then broken allowing (bottom right) the lock to continue to recoil while the barrel stopped. The face of the lock is a T-slot, into which the next cartridge is fed from the belt. It is then forced down into alignment with the chamber, knocking the spent case out of the way as it descends. The toggle, propelled by a spring, then thrusts the lock back to chamber the new cartridge.*

Although mechanical machine guns had been adopted in many countries and were in general use by about 1875, they were not entirely satisfactory. The principal reasons were that they were complicated, cumbersome, and, because they were manually operated (by the gunner tugging on the handle or crank), they were inaccurate, spraying rounds in a wide swath. But since there appeared to be no other convenient source of power to drive them, they remained in service until the first decade of the twentieth century. They would have survived much longer but for one or two enquiring minds.

Foremost among these was that of Hiram Maxim. Born in 1840 in America of French extraction, Maxim had been apprenticed to a coach-builder and then worked in a machine shop and a shipyard. With a highly inventive talent, he interested himself in the new science of electricity, and in 1881 he attended an Electrical Exhibition in Paris. There, so the story goes, he was approached by a friend who told him, 'Hang your electricity! If you want to make your fortune, invent something that will allow these fool Europeans to kill each other quicker!' Acting on this advice, Maxim went to London and set himself up in a small workshop, and between 1882 and 1885 he analyzed current firearms.

Maxim quickly appreciated the fact that the firing of a gun released a large quantity of energy, only a small proportion of which was devoted to driving the bullet – the rest was dissipated as heat, gas or recoil force, and went to waste. He eventually decided that the recoil force could be harnessed to operate a machine gun and in 1884 he produced his first model – the first automatic machine gun. It was chambered for the British service .45 Martini-Henry cartridge and was vastly different from any machine gun which had been seen before.

The barrel was carried in bearings which allowed it to slide back on recoil. When the gun was fired, the breech-block and barrel were securely locked together by a top-mounted hook. As the barrel and breech-block recoiled, the hook was lifted and the barrel brought to a stop, the block being allowed to continue the rearward movement which had been imparted to it by the recoiling barrel. Attached to the rear of the block was a connecting rod which led to a crank and flywheel at the rear of the gun body. At the moment of firing the crank stood at about 30° above the axis of the gun, so that the rearward movement of the breech was able to drive it backwards and begin a rotary movement of the flywheel. During the rearward movement the firing pin was cocked and the feed mechanism operated, the empty case ejected from the gun, and the feed belt pulled up to bring another cartridge into position. (By using a canvas belt of cartridges, fed in from right to left, Maxim got around the limitations of the hopper or box system which relied on gravity to feed a weapon with cartridges.) As the crank passed the dead-centre position, so the movement of the connecting rod was reversed and it began to drive the breech-block forwards again, chambering a

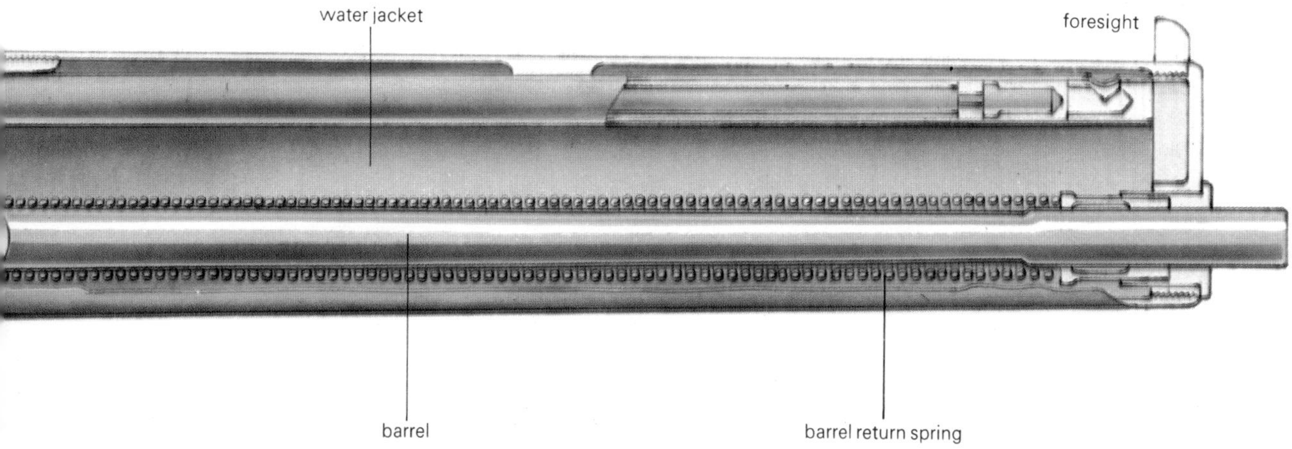

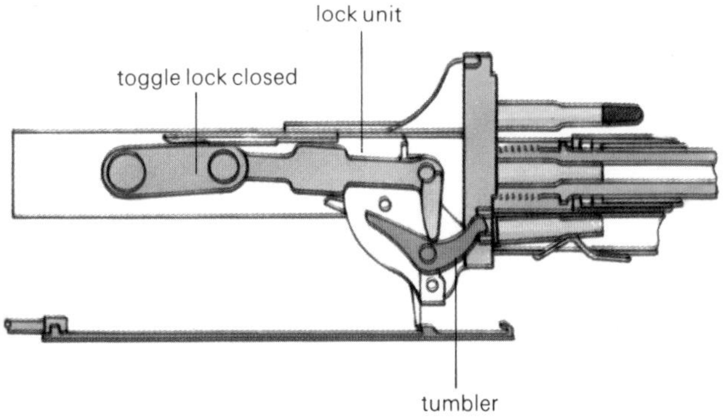

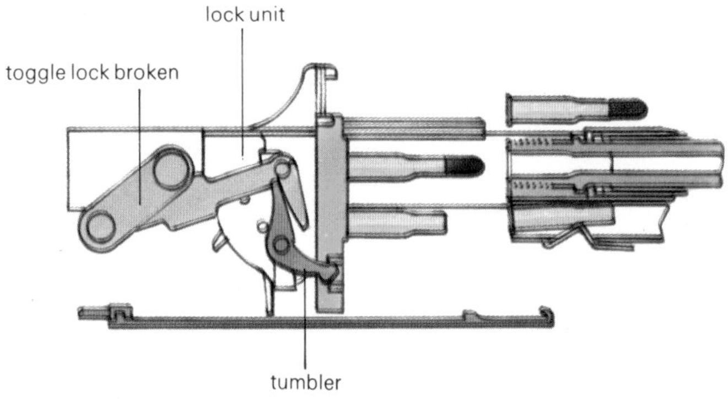

fresh cartridge. The hook dropped over the breech-block, locking it to the barrel, and the barrel and block were pushed forwards once more into the firing position. At this point the crank was now 30° below the axis of the gun and the firing pin was released to fire the chambered round. The action was then repeated, with the difference that the crank now rotated in the opposite direction, taking the connecting rod from bottom to top, as it were. Maxim elected to choose this to-and-fro oscillation of the crank rather than simply allow it to revolve (which could have worked the gun just as well) since he was afraid that the repeated impulses on a rotating unit would have built up speed until the gun 'ran away'.

Maxim demonstrated the 'Maxim Automatic Gun' to the press and military and stimulated a great deal of interest. Typical of the reaction is this contemporary newspaper report: '*No one can fail to be struck by the wonderful ingenuity and great capabilities of the weapon; it inaugurates a new departure in machine guns and opens up a new field of automatic action for other guns, which is being energetically worked by the inventor . . .*'

In fact, Maxim, not entirely satisfied, was 'energetically working' at a redesign. One of the senior military officers who had inspected his gun had taken the trouble to point out to Maxim that it would stand a far better chance of being accepted if it were made so that the essential parts could be stripped and replaced without tools and without special training. A soldier in the field could then keep the gun firing in spite of minor mishaps.

In 1885 Maxim introduced his new design, a design which was so well thought-out that it never needed modification and which was to serve unchanged in some armies until World War II. He kept the recoil-operated system, but completely abandoned the crank and connecting rod of the original model and introduced the 'toggle joint' instead. The barrel was extended into the body of the gun by a 'barrel extension' – two sideplates inside which the breech-block could slide. At the end of the barrel extension was a cross-shaft attached to the toggle unit.

The action of the toggle joint is best compared to that of the human leg. Both leg and toggle unit consist of two solid struts – the shin and the thigh – connected by a one-way hinging joint – the knee. Imagine the leg as the toggle in the Maxim gun; the hip is the connection to the cross-shaft at the rear of the barrel extension, while the sole of the foot is the breech-block. If the toggle – or leg – is extended in a straight line, any pressure on the foot – such as the firing of the cartridge – will pass straight up the leg and be resisted by the anchorage of the hip bone to the barrel extension. But if someone were to tap the underside of the knee joint, the resistance would be broken, the knee would fold up, and the foot – or breech-block – would move away from the barrel.

In the Maxim gun the toggle joint broke downwards. As the whole unit – barrel, barrel extension, breech-block and toggle joint – recoiled to the rear,

Maxim

'Whatever happens, we have got
The Maxim Gun, and they have not'

said a jingoistic Victorian poet, at a time when 'Maxim' meant machine gun and machine gun meant Maxim. Maxim's recoil-operated gun swept the world as no other gun has done before or since, to become the standard MG of almost every major army. Its first recorded use in combat was in 1888; one could not say that its last use has yet taken place.

The Maxim certainly remained in service with the Soviet Army until 1945 and with the Chinese Communist Army until 1952, and there are doubtless several thousand of them still in working order waiting to be called on. Short of a direct hit from a high explosive shell, Maxim guns are virtually indestructable.

The Maxim generated two variant models, one of which attained equal fame. This was the Vickers Gun developed by Albert Vickers in England after Maxim's original patents had expired. In this gun the Maxim toggle lock was inverted so as to break

upwards, which simplified the mechanism's assembly. The whole gun was redesigned to a slightly less safe standard and made of different materials to reduce weight from 27.2kg (60lb) to 18.1kg (40lb). The Vickers was the British Army's standard medium MG from 1912 to 1967.

The other derivative was the German Parabellum MG also developed in 1912. Its toggle was also reversed, the feed system improved, and a perforated jacket fitted for air cooling instead of the familiar water jacket of the Maxim and Vickers. Air cooling was feasible since the Parabellum was designed as an airborne gun; Zeppelins first, aircraft later. It eventually became the standard fighter armament in World War I. A number were adapted as ground MGs and showed that air cooling would work with army guns provided short bursts were fired. Reversing this process, the Vickers had its water jacket emptied and perforated by ventilating louvres for air force use.

The standard German Maxim was the Model '08'. and this was converted in 1915. Removed from its tripod, a wooden butt and pistol grip and a simple bipod were fitted to create a 'light' MG, the 08/15. This, too, opened military eyes to the value of an MG capable of being carried by one man among the advancing infantry, leading eventually to the whole light machine gun concept. Maxim wrought better than he knew.

Sir Hiram Maxim (1840-1916) is shown demonstrating his gun.

VICKERS-MAXIM
Calibre .303in
Length 107.9cm (42.5in)
Weight 27.2kg (60lb)
Barrel 67.3cm (26.5in)

MG08
Calibre 7.92mm (.312in)
Length 117.5cm (46.25in)
Weight 18.37kg (40.5lb)
Barrel 71.8cm (28.25in)

VICKERS Mk I
Calibre .303in
Length 109.2cm (43in)
Weight 14.97kg (33lb)
Barrel 72.2cm (28.72in)

-common to all three:
Rifling 4 grooves, r/hand
Foresight Blade
Rearsight (Vickers-Maxim) U-notch to 2,900yd (2,652m), (MG08) to 3,000m (3,280yd) (Vickers Mk 1) to 3,800yd (3,475m)
Action Recoil
Rate of fire (Vickers-Maxim) 550rpm (MG08) 450rpm (Vickers Mk 1) 500rpm
Feed system 250-round fabric belt
Muzzle velocity (Vickers-Maxim and Vickers Mk 1) 744m/sec (2,440ft/sec), (MG08) 892m/sec (2,925ft/sec)
Bullet weight (Vickers-Maxim) 11.25g (174gr), (MG08) 11.52g (178gr), (Vickers Mk 1) 11.27g (174gr)

the breech and barrel were securely locked together. After about 13mm (0.5in) of movement a crank handle on the end of the cross-shaft struck a fixed roller and this gave the toggle a downward impulse which broke the joint and allowed the breech-block to move back while the barrel stopped. At the same time the rotation of the cross-shaft wound up a spiral spring. When the toggle came to a halt, this spring reversed the movement and drove the breech-block forwards again to chamber a fresh round and lift the toggle until once more it became a solid strut. The whole assembly then ran forwards into the firing position again. During all this, of course, a bell-crank actuated by the movement of the barrel extension drove a set of pawls which lifted the ammunition belt and brought a fresh cartridge into place.

The heat generated by firing the Maxim gun at its normal rate of 600 shots a minute was considerable. Maxim placed the barrel inside a water jacket so that the barrel heat passed to the water; but even so, after one minute of steady firing the water would begin to boil. However, since continuous firing was not a general pastime – the demands of ammunition replenishment saw to that – this was no drawback, and the cooling effect of the water kept down the rate of wear of the barrel.

Maxim entered into partnership with an Englishman, one Albert Vickers, who had a factory at Crayford, in Kent, and they formed the Maxim Gun Company in 1884. Precisely which army was the first to purchase Maxim guns for service is not clear. The British Army bought three in 1887 for extended trials, but the official date of introduction is February 4, 1889. However, the first record of them being used in actual combat is on November 21, 1888 during a punitive expedition in The Gambia on the west coast of Africa, when a small British force under General Sir Francis de Winton took a Maxim gun and used it against a native fort.

Maxim, as good a salesman as he was an engineer, now toured Europe demonstrating his gun to every military authority he could find. Reactions were mixed; some countries appreciated what was happening and signed orders, while others were incredulous. The Russian officers refused to believe that anyone could manipulate the small crank on the side of the Maxim gun 600 times a minute and were astonished when Maxim demonstrated what an automatic machine gun could do. The King of Denmark is reputed to have asked him how much each round of ammunition cost. On being told, he replied that a single Maxim gun would bankrupt his Kingdom in six hours. But by the turn of the century the Maxim was firmly established as the premier machine gun. Indeed, 'Maxim Gun' was synonymous with 'machine gun' to most people.

Nevertheless, there were still plenty of inventors willing to bet that they could produce something either just as good or better, and a number of countries refused the Maxim gun, preferring to adopt a gun of their own design and manufacture. One of the first local designs appeared in Austria. In spite of being impressed with the Maxim gun, the Austrians bought only a few, and in 1888 the Archduke Karl Salvator and Lieutenant Ritter von Dormus patented a design which relied on a new principle, that of 'delayed blowback'.

If the breech-block of a gun is not locked to the barrel in any way, then when the cartridge is fired,

Left *A British .303in Vickers-Maxim MG team in a stone laager during the Boer War (1899-1902). The British Army adopted the Maxim in 1889. The introduction in 1891 of smokeless cordite cartridges improved the Maxim's recoil power and chances of concealment. Nevertheless it performed badly against elusive Boer marksmen in South Africa. Note the painted brass water jacket and tall sights.*

Right *A French Hotchkiss MG mounted in the nose of a Henri Farman biplane, 1914. This weapon is a Model 1909 with belt magazine for aerial use. The Henri Farman was also the first aircraft to take the Lewis Gun aloft.*

the explosion of the charge, as well as driving the bullet up the barrel, will also force the cartridge back out of the chamber and push the breech-block to the rear. The rate at which the block moves is, of course, in proportion to the relative masses of the bullet and the block. The bullet moves up the barrel very rapidly, since it is light in weight, while the block moves slowly since it is much heavier. As we shall see, this principle received wide application in pistols and small weapons in later years, but in 1888 it was an entirely new idea. It was, however, a little too simple for use in a machine gun firing a sizeable rifle cartridge, and it was necessary to 'delay' the opening of the breech-block by placing a heavy pivoting block behind it to add to the mass. This, due to its inertia, held the block closed just long enough for the bullet to leave the barrel and the gas pressure inside the bore to drop to a safe level before the breech began to open and the cartridge case was ejected.

Being a simple design, the Salvator-Dormus gun was quite reliable, but the lack of a really positive breech lock meant that only relatively weak cartridges could be used. Nevertheless, the Austrians adopted it as their Model 1893 for fortress defences and then a later model for use with field armies. It was manufactured by the Skoda company of Pilsen (then part of the Austro-Hungarian Empire) and was always known as the Skoda machine gun. Salvator and von Dormus never received much credit for it.

Another country waiting for the appearance of local talent was France, where the Hotchkiss company was now under the direction of another American, Lawrence V. Bénét. Hotchkiss were looking for a machine gun with which to compete against Maxim but were in difficulties because Maxim had secured patents on every possible method of recoil operation. In 1893 an Austrian, Captain Adolf von Odkolek, offered a design of machine gun to Bénét. Bénét saw that there were some good features in the idea, and he could also see that it was going to need some work in order to make it practical. So he bought the patent and design from von Odkolek.

In von Odkolek's design, below the barrel of the gun there was a cylinder in which ran a piston. A small port, or vent, connected the gun barrel with the end of the cylinder, so that when the bullet passed up the barrel, some of the expanding gas behind it was diverted through the port and into the cylinder to drive the piston to the rear. An operating rod attached to the piston unlocked the bolt by withdrawing a lug from the gun body and then thrust the bolt to the rear, extracting the empty case and compressing a spring. At the end of the stroke the spring expanded and pushed the bolt back, picking up a fresh round and chambering it, and as the piston went forwards so it forced the locking lug back into engagement with the gun body to securely lock the breech.

Ammunition was fed from a light metal strip into which 20 cartridges were clipped. The clip was fed into the gun from the left side and the rounds were stripped from it; at each stroke of the piston the strip was indexed across to present another round, and after the last round had been loaded the empty strip was ejected from the right side. By hooking a fresh strip into the end of one already feeding, it was possible to keep up a continuous fire.

The first prototypes of the Hotchkiss overheated badly, but Bénét designed a barrel with heavy fins which acted as a radiator to dissipate the heat. The gun was adopted by the French Army in 1897 and proved to be moderately reliable, though still suffering from overheating. The French Army then decided to redesign the gun itself, without reference to the Hotchkiss company, and set out on a disastrous journey. The first attempt was the 'Puteaux' of 1905, which was little more than the Hotchkiss with a lot more fins on the barrel and a complicated device to vary the rate of fire. Not a particularly efficient machine gun, it was relegated to use in fortresses.

The next attempt was the 'St. Etienne' of 1907, which is best described as a Hotchkiss with everything changed for the sake of changing it. It used the same gas piston but blew it forwards instead of backwards, so that a rack and pinion mechanism had to be interposed in order to convert the forward movement of the piston into a rearward movement of the operating rod. The Hotchkiss bolt was discarded and an odd device resembling a Maxim toggle was put in. The return spring was removed from the gun body and placed under the barrel where it rapidly heated up and lost its resilience. And the gas cylinder was fitted with an adjustable valve so that the amount of gas could be regulated to alter the rate of fire. All in all, it was a mechanical disaster. Its worst features were emphasized in the early weeks of World War I. The French Army eventually off-loaded them on to the Foreign Legion and went back to the Hotchkiss which, for all its little pecadilloes, was a far better weapon than the St. Etienne.

In spite of the troubles the French Army may have had with the Hotchkiss, it was sold widely throughout the world. One customer was the Japanese Army, as a result of which the Hotchkiss faced the Maxim in the first major machine-gun war. In the Russo-Japanese War of 1904-5, the Russians had Gorloff-Gatlings in their fixed defences and Maxim guns with their field armies, while the Japanese deployed their Hotchkiss guns. This, the first conflict between two first-class armies equipped with machine-guns, was monitored with interest by every other army in the world, all eager to find out just how effective the new weapons were.

The Russians got in the first blow when eight of their guns at the Battle of the Yalu River beat off several Japanese attacks, dealing out terrible casualties among the attackers. The Japanese, in their turn, demonstrated great skill in using the Hotchkiss guns, taking them well forward in the attack to give supporting fire to the assault and also firing them over the heads of their own infantry during an attack to keep the defenders' heads down.

The Russian cavalry were using another machine gun, the Danish Madsen – the first gun which could be called, by modern standards, a light machine gun. The definition of a light machine gun does not depend solely on weight; it revolves round the tactical use of the weapon as well. The early machine guns, such as the Vickers and Maxim, were intended for use either on tripods or on wheeled carriages, and were brought into position before the battle opened so that they could give covering fire to the infantry. Once the battle became fluid, the machine guns frequently fell silent since the movements of their own forces impeded their fire, and it took time

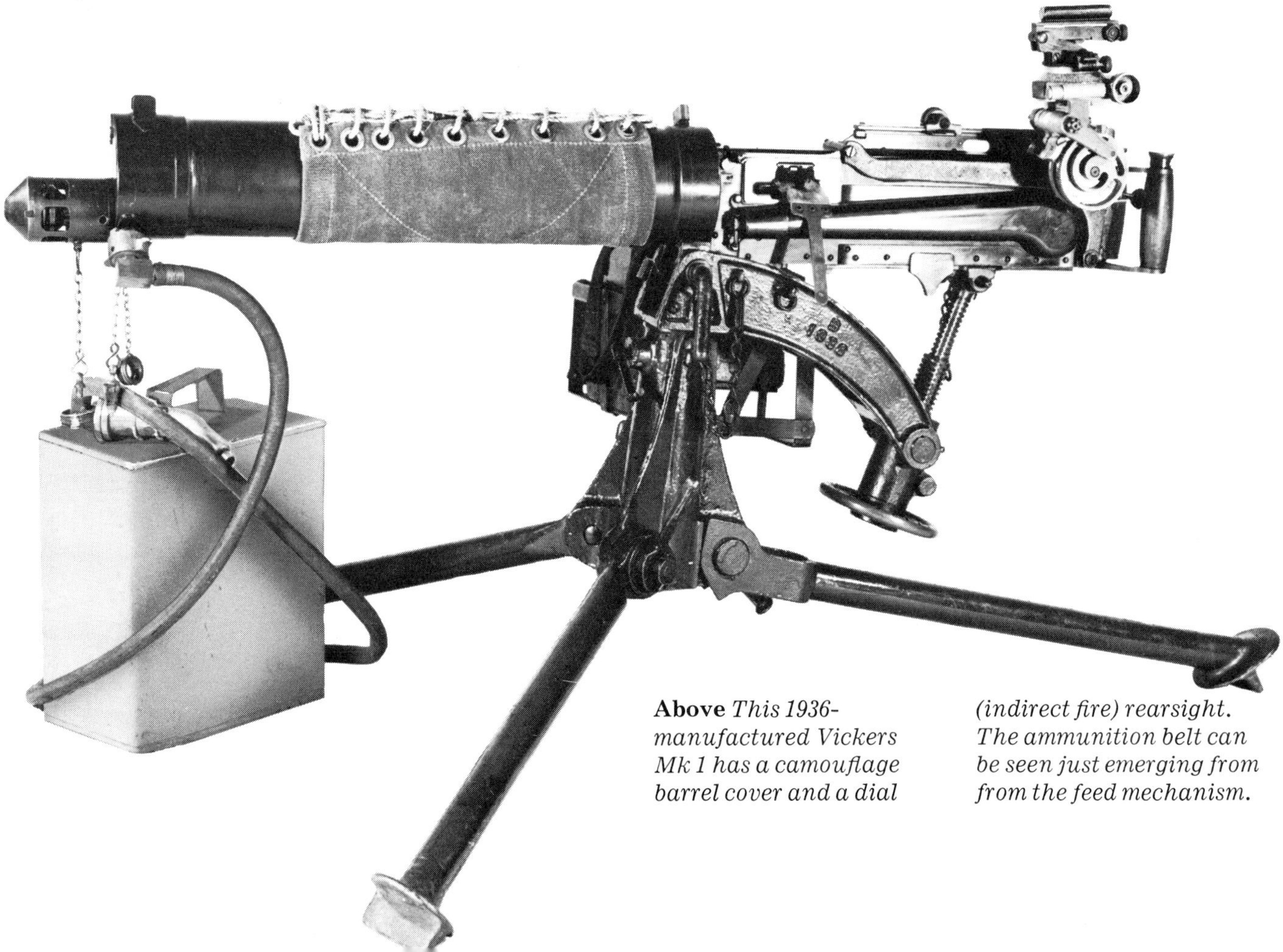

Above *This 1936-manufactured Vickers Mk 1 has a camouflage barrel cover and a dial (indirect fire) rearsight. The ammunition belt can be seen just emerging from from the feed mechanism.*

to select new positions and move the guns. The light machine gun, on the other hand, was readily portable by one or, at most, two men. It accompanied the infantry whenever they moved and provided fire support for the infantry squad or platoon at the most basic tactical level. It was this sort of handling which the Japanese pioneered with their Hotchkiss guns and the Russians with their Madsens.

The Madsen gun was designed by a Dane named Schouboe and adopted by the Danish cavalry in about 1902. It took its name from the Danish Minister of War who was responsible for introducing what has proved to be one of the most remarkable machine guns ever made. The Madsen was in production, practically unchanged, for over 50 years; though rarely adopted by any major power, it was used by 34 countries at one time or another; and yet it was one of the most complicated mechanisms ever to achieve success.

The mechanism was recoil-operated and is best thought of as a Martini or Peabody rising breech-block adapted to automatic action. The barrel and breech-block recoiled together on firing, and the action of the breech block was controlled by a 'switch plate' let into the side of the gun body. This plate was cut in a complex pattern of grooves, with a pin, attached to the front of the breech-block, riding in the grooves. On recoil, the pin, riding in the switch plate grooves, was moved so as to lift the face of the breech-block and expose the base of the spent cartridge in the chamber. A separate extractor, driven by a cam on the barrel, then extracted and ejected the case. As the barrel and block completed their recoil stroke, a hammer was cocked and a recoil spring compressed. When the recoil movement stopped, the spring forced block and barrel forwards and the stud in the switch plate rapidly dropped the face of the breech-block below the chamber. A separate rammer then moved forwards and rammed a cartridge from the overhead magazine into the chamber. The rammer retracted and finally the pin in the switch plate moved the breech-block up to take up its position behind the base of the cartridge, ready to fire. The hammer descended, struck the firing pin in the breech-block, and the cycle began once more.

Theorists never tire of pointing out that the Madsen gun should not work, just as it was once said that the bumble-bee should not fly. For one thing, the path of the cartridge as it enters the chamber is curved while the cartridge itself is, of course, straight. In spite of this, though, the Madsen works well, gives little trouble, and, as already mentioned, was to stay in production for over 50 years without modification. It also deserves credit for being the first machine gun to incorporate a wooden butt-stock and bipod so that it could be fired from the prone position by one man; the first to use a perforated jacket to allow heat to escape; and the first to use a top-mounted removable box magazine, all features which were to be widely copied in later years.

One last turn-of-the-century machine gun design which deserves mention was the Schwarzlose. The Austrian Army were not very happy with their delayed blowback Skoda, but the simplicity of the design had its advantages. So when another blowback design appeared, they took it more seriously

Above *A 7.92mm M1949 Madsen LMG with the anchor cypher of the Siamese (Thai) Navy. The magazine takes 30 rounds and the gun weighs 10kg (22lb). Its rate of fire is 400 rounds per minute.*

than might another country and eventually adopted it as their standard gun. The Schwarzlose was a heavy weapon which relied simply on a massive breech-block, a strong spring behind it, and a toggle joint to slow down the speed at which the breech-block opened. This toggle was unlike the Maxim version. When the breech was closed the toggle was not straight, but broken and almost folded back on itself. As the block moved back so it straightened out the toggle, but due to the interplay of leverage this 'straightening out' action slightly delayed the opening of the block. The Schwarzlose toggle never reached the fully opened and locked position, since the recoil stroke stopped before it got that far, allowing the toggle to be re-folded on the closing stroke.

Schwarzlose was a brilliant weapons designer, and his machine gun was a sound and simple weapon. But he discovered, as have many inventors since, that the apparent simplicity of the blowback system carries an inherent disadvantage. When the cartridge is fired, the rise of pressure inside the cartridge case acts equally in all directions – forwards to push the bullet out, backwards to push the breech-block back, and also sideways to stick the case firmly into the chamber. The grip of the case in the chamber is greatest at the front end, since here the case metal is thinner and the chamber, due to the constant firing, is usually roughened. As a result, the front end of the case resists the extracting movement; the rear end, being less tightly pressed outwards, tries to go back under the combined action of the internal gas pressure and the grip of the extractor on the breech-block. The net result is frequently that the brass gives up the struggle and splits, half the case being extracted and the neck end being left inside the chamber. The gun then jams when the mechanism tries to feed in the next round. Schwarzlose's solution was to fit a small oil reservoir inside the gun body which fed a pump operated by the gun mechanism. As each round was presented to the breech, the pump sprayed a small quantity of oil on to the case, lubricating it so that it would not stick to the chamber and extraction would be clean.

The same problem confronted an Italian inventor, Giovanni Agnelli, who developed a simple blowback gun in about 1912. But instead of adding the complication of an oil pump, Angelli cut very fine flutes in the length of the chamber. When the cartridge was fired, a proportion of gas leaked past the cart-

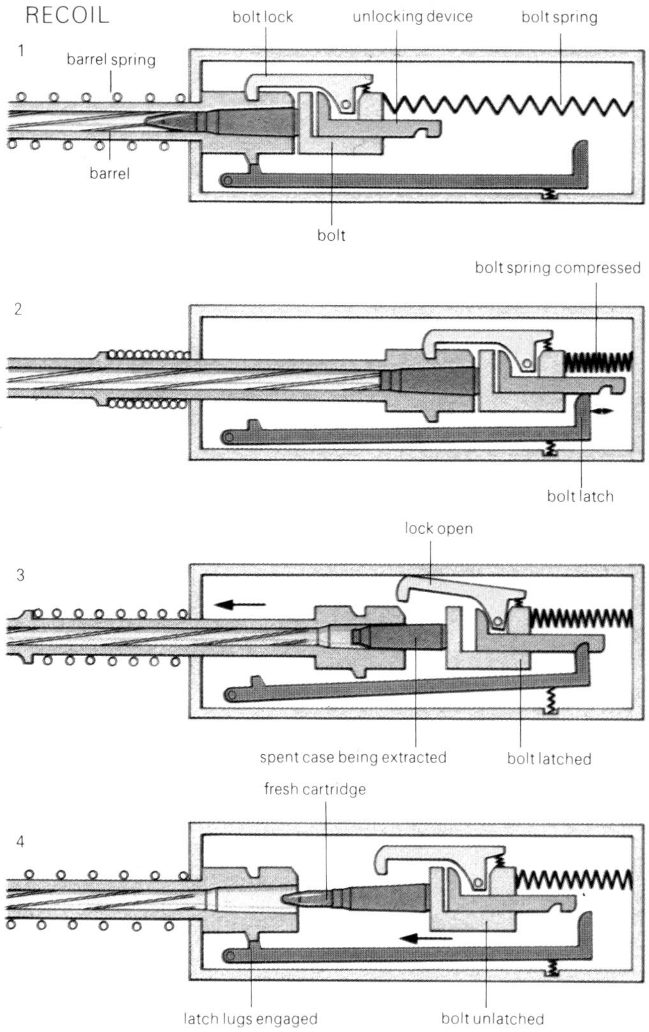

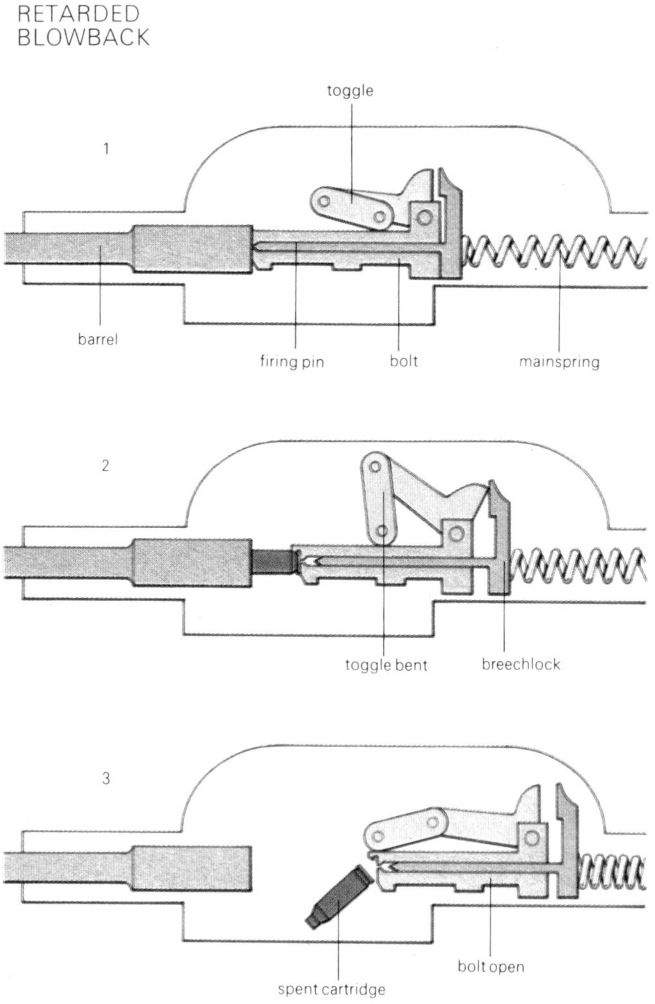

ridge case neck via these tiny grooves and, in effect, 'floated' the case on a layer of high-pressure gas, so preventing the case from sticking and allowing easy extraction to take place without the need to lubricate. His machine gun was never very successful, but the fluted chamber was a brilliant solution which has been widely used in recent years.

It will have been seen that there are, for all practical purposes, only three ways of making an automatic machine gun work – recoil, gas pressure, or the blowback of the spent case. And before World War I, all three systems had been tried, perfected and adopted. Each system had its advocates, and still has, and the reasons for adhering to any one system are as much a matter of personal preference by the designer as anything else.

By and large, the recoil-operated system stands up to sustained firing the best. Its resilience was dramatically tested during the famous action of the British 100th Machine Gun Company on the Somme in 1916. There, 10 Vickers guns were given the task of denying a piece of ground to the Germans for 12 hours, the range being about 1,800m (2,000yd). In the course of the subsequent 12 hours, just 250 rounds less than one million were fired by the 10 guns. It was reported that *'four 2-gallon (9-litre) tins of water, the company's water-bottles and all the urine tubs from the neighbourhood were emptied into the guns for cooling purposes'*, and about 100 barrels were used up. At the end of the action, the guns were firing as well as they had been at the start.

Gas operation is satisfactory for short bursts of fire, which is why gas-operated weapons usually appear as light machine guns. Their problem is the build-up of fouling from the powder which gradually chokes the gas port and slows down the action. Delayed blowback guns are not really satisfactory at all, though the people who use them usually manage to convince themselves that they have a good weapon. The delayed blowback system's chief problem lies in the vexed question of voilent extraction. To obtain satisfactory performance usually means producing ammunition with cartridge cases specially hardened to resist the still-high internal gas pressure as the extraction movement begins. For example, the current French machine gun, the AAT-52, is perfectly satisfactory with French cartridges, but cartridges manufactured in other countries, to a slightly different specification, show evidences of bulging at the base after extraction.

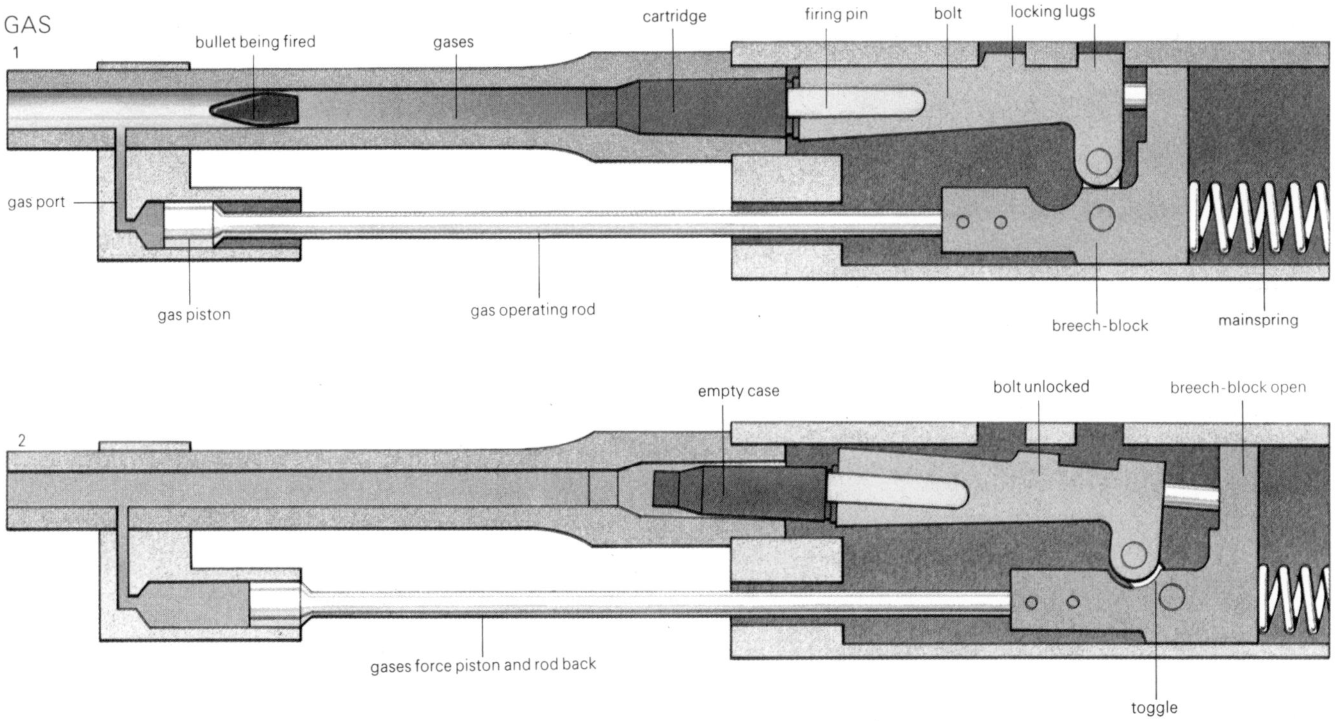

The three types of automatic MG mechanisms.

Far left *The recoil mechanism. (1) The instant of firing. (2) At full recoil, both barrel and breech block remained locked together. (3) The block is held back while the barrel is allowed to return. (4) As the barrel reaches the forward position, it releases the block which then runs forwards, chambering a fresh cartridge.*

Left *The 1902 Schwarzlose MG retarded blowback toggle action. (1) At the moment of firing. (2) As recoil begins the toggle is bent by the rearward moving breech-block. (3) The spent cartridge is ejected before the toggle is fully straight.*

Above *A gas-operated tilting block mechanism. (1) The breech-block is locked to the breech by lugs engaging in recesses in the gun body. (2) As the piston is pushed back by gas from the barrel, a toggle pulls the block down to unlock it before withdrawing it from the breech so as to extract the empty case and begin the feeding cycle once again.*

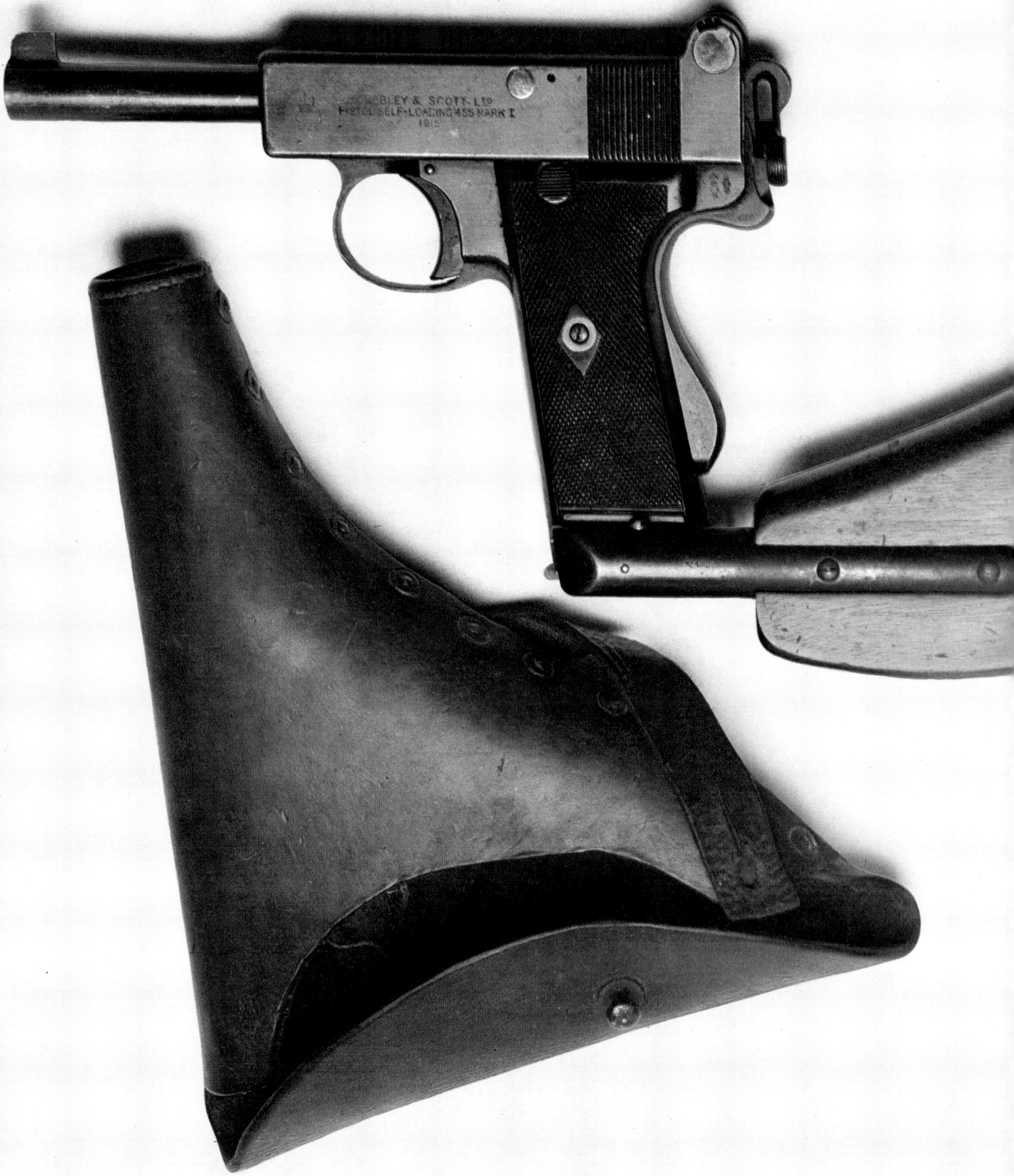
SCOTT LTD
SELF-LOADING .455 MARK I
1915

AUTOMATIC PISTOLS

Maxim's successful application of automatic principles to the machine gun aroused many inventors. Some of them concentrated on machine guns, but a few began to wonder whether or not similar self-actuating principles could be applied to handguns. Several people had tried to do this in the past, but they usually foundered on the poor quality of available ammunition – paper cartridges, black powder and soft lead bullets.

Noteworthy among early attempts at an 'automatic' pistol was that of Richard Paulson, an Englishman, who in 1886 took out a patent for a gas-operated revolver of extreme simplicity. A gas cylinder below the barrel carried a simple piston which extended back to butt against the lower face of the hammer. The revolver was a solid-frame weapon with a single-action lock, and after firing the first shot by thumb-cocking the hammer and pulling the trigger, subsequent shots were prepared by the piston being pushed back by gas pressure and thus cocking the hammer. Since the hammer carried the pawl, this also rotated the cylinder to the next chamber, so that all the firer had to do was pull the trigger again.

Unfortunately, no specimen of Paulson's gas-operated revolver exists, though he must have made at least one in order to prove that his idea worked. Again, the fouling generated by black powder would probably have brought the pistol to a halt after very few rounds had been fired, but it was a sound and simple idea.

Paulson had appreciated one significant point – that the mechanism has to include an 'interruptor' which disconnects the trigger after each shot. Otherwise the hammer would fall immediately and the gun would continue to fire until it was empty. The disconnector places the trigger out of action so long as it is being held pressed. The firer must consciously release the trigger for the disconnector to reconnect it with the firing mechanism before any further shots can be fired.

It is the disconnector which turns an automatic weapon into a 'self-loading' one. An automatic is defined strictly as a weapon which continues to fire so long as it is fed with ammunition and the trigger is held down. Pistols built in this way have existed, but they are impractical weapons. So-called automatic pistols have an interruptor which, technically, transforms them into semi-automatics or self-loaders. Nevertheless, definition or no, the word 'automatic' has stuck to pistols which are self-loaders, and we have continued to use it in this sense in these pages simply because it is common usage.

The automatic pistol had to wait until smokeless powder and the jacketed bullet appeared on the scene, promising freedom from fouling and a cartridge robust enough to stand the shaking and violent handling which occurs during automatic feeding in a pistol. The period which saw the introduction of the new ammunition was also the period which saw the appearance of the mechanical repeating pistols, and it was one of these designs, slightly modified, which was the first automatic pistol to be placed on sale.

The Schonberger automatic pistol began life as the Laumann mechanical repeater, worked by the usual finger-ring lever driving a reciprocating bolt back and forth. Laumann had a few pistols made by the Austrian Arms Factory at Steyr, and Anton Schonberger, the factory superintendent, began to modify the design, eventually producing an automatic weapon. It was a remarkable design, since Schonberger used a principle which has been frequently suggested but rarely used. He relied on the gas pressure in the cartridge to push the precussion primer out of the case by a very slight amount. This rearward movement – called 'primer set-back' – was detected and amplified by an arrangement of levers and used to unlock the bolt, after which the blowback action of the cartridge case performed the opening movement and a return spring then closed the action. A clip-loaded magazine, similar to that on the Mannlicher rifle, was positioned in front of the trigger and held five rounds of a special 8mm cartridge. Unfortunately, no specimen of this cartridge has been seen for some 70 years or more and no record exists of its dimensions or construction. It seems certain, however, that it incorporated an especially deep primer pocket and cap designed to make the unusual action function.

Cleverness, unfortunately, does not sell pistols. The Schonberger did not do well commercially, and this may well have been due to ammunition problems. The Schonberger was more dependent on ammunition than most designs, and in the early 1890s the quality of small-calibre ammunition tended to vary from batch to batch.

The Schonberger appeared on the market in 1892. In 1893 there came a weapon which was the forerunner of a legend. This was the Borchardt, generally admitted to be the first automatic pistol to be a success. Many stories are told of the Borchardt, the commonest being that Hugo Borchardt was an American who hawked his design around American manufacturers without success, finally coming to Europe to sell it to the Berlin company of Ludwig Löwe. There is, though, no truth in this tale. Borchardt was a German who, like many of his contemporaries, emigrated to America in the 1860s, and he became a naturalized American citizen in 1875. He worked for a short time for the Winchester company, designing revolvers, an area in which Winchester took a brief interest. None of his designs were accepted for production and, disillusioned, Borchardt returned to Europe in about 1882 to take up employment in the Royal Hungarian Arms Factory at Budapest. There he saw the Maxim machine gun at a demonstration, and he began to consider the application of Maxim's toggle lock to a pistol. Finding no enthusiasm in Austria he went back to Germany and offered his design to Ludwig Löwe. Löwe saw there was promise in the idea, employed him and gave him the facilities he needed to perfect his pistol.

Borchardt used the toggle to lock the breech in a

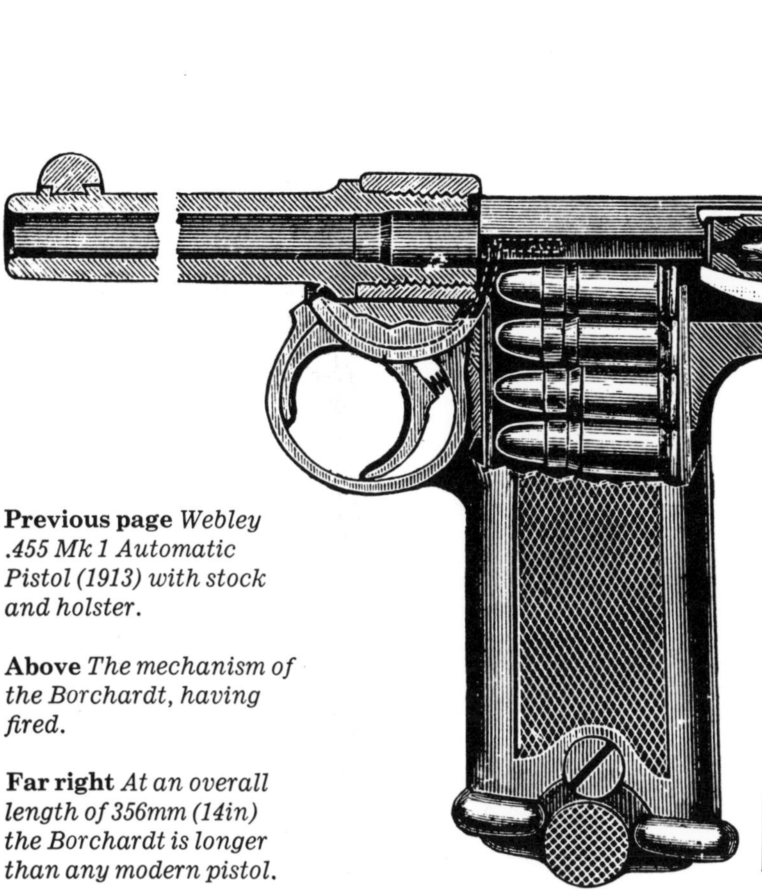

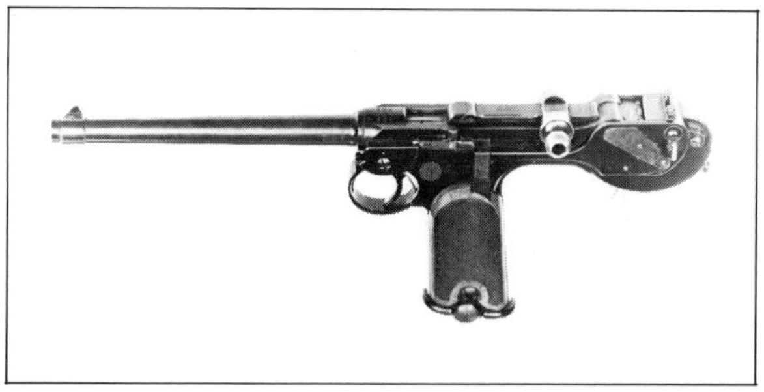

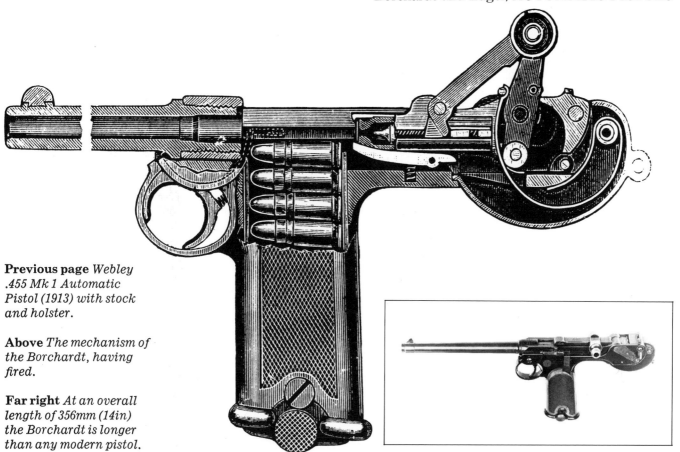

Previous page *Webley .455 Mk 1 Automatic Pistol (1913) with stock and holster.*

Above *The mechanism of the Borchardt, having fired.*

Far right *At an overall length of 356mm (14in) the Borchardt is longer than any modern pistol.*

similar manner to Maxim, but had it break upwards instead of down. He also pioneered the use of a detachable box magazine in the pistol butt, based on the Lee magazine and copied widely thereafter. Probably the most important feature, however, was the ammunition, a rimless 7.65mm round which Borchardt himself stated to be vital to the success of the weapon, claiming that he could make no progress until he had perfected the cartridge.

The Borchardt also introduced another feature which was to become commonplace on automatic pistols for some years. He supplied the weapon complete with a wooden butt-stock which could be clamped securely to the rear end of the pistol and thus converted it into a species of small carbine.

It is believed that about 3,000 Borchardt pistols were made between 1893 and 1896. Although the Borchardt worked, it was nevertheless a large and cumbersome weapon, and one critic called it *'awkward, clumsy and with a frail and easily dislocated mechanism, well-made as far as the limitations of its design allow . . .'*. But Borchardt appeared to be satisfied with it, and, apart from patenting some very small improvements to the design (which were never incorporated in the production models), he passed on to other things.

It was left to another employee of the Löwe company – one Georg Luger – to design an improved pistol, something rather less cumbersome and more reliable. It seems likely that Borchardt co-operated to some extent, but the facts are far from clear. Certainly, it was Luger who eventually took out patents for the new pistol in 1900. Putting it simply, Luger had retained the toggle lock of the original Borchardt, but had cleaned up the design by using an improved return spring and had reduced the dimensions of the pistol to produce a far more handy weapon. He developed a new cartridge in 7.65mm calibre, shorter and rather less powerful than the Borchardt, and also changed the angle of the grip so that the pistol lay more comfortably in the hand and assumed a more natural and instinctive 'point' when it was held.

The Luger pistol – known more properly as the Parabellum-Pistole – was adopted by the Swiss Army in May 1900. Patents were taken out in other countries. The application in the United States ran into opposition in the form of a lawsuit by John M. Browning and the Colt company on the grounds that Luger was infringing a Colt patent of 1897 (for a locked-breech recoil-operated pistol). In strict fact, the objection seemed to be no more than an assertion that the manufacture of any automatic pistol by anyone other than Colt and Browning was an affront, and the claim was thrown out. Luger obtained his American patent in 1904.

After acceptance by Switzerland Luger attempted to interest the German Army in the pistol. The Army, however, was not impressed with the 7.65mm bullet, since it did not have the 'stopping' or 'knock-down' power of the Army's contemporary 10.6mm revolver. Luger therefore took the 7.65mm cartridge, opened out the mouth to accept a 9mm bullet, and rebarrelled the pistol in 9mm calibre. Strangely

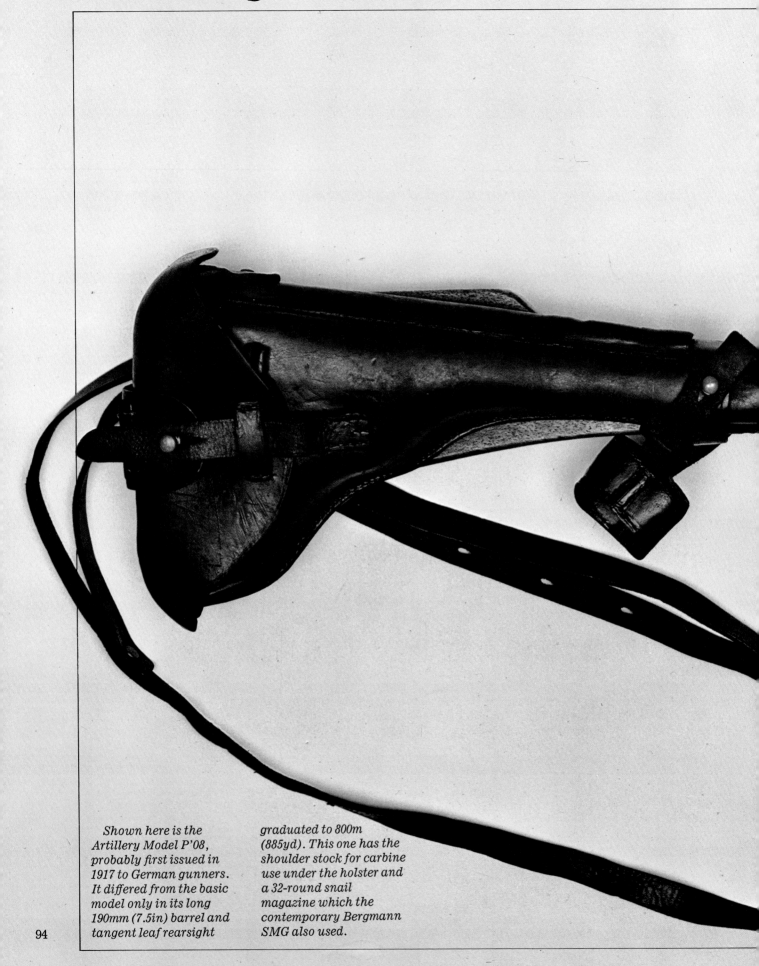

Shown here is the Artillery Model P'08, probably first issued in 1917 to German gunners. It differed from the basic model only in its long 190mm (7.5in) barrel and tangent leaf rearsight graduated to 800m (885yd). This one has the shoulder stock for carbine use under the holster and a 32-round snail magazine which the contemporary Bergmann SMG also used.

Luger Parabellum P08

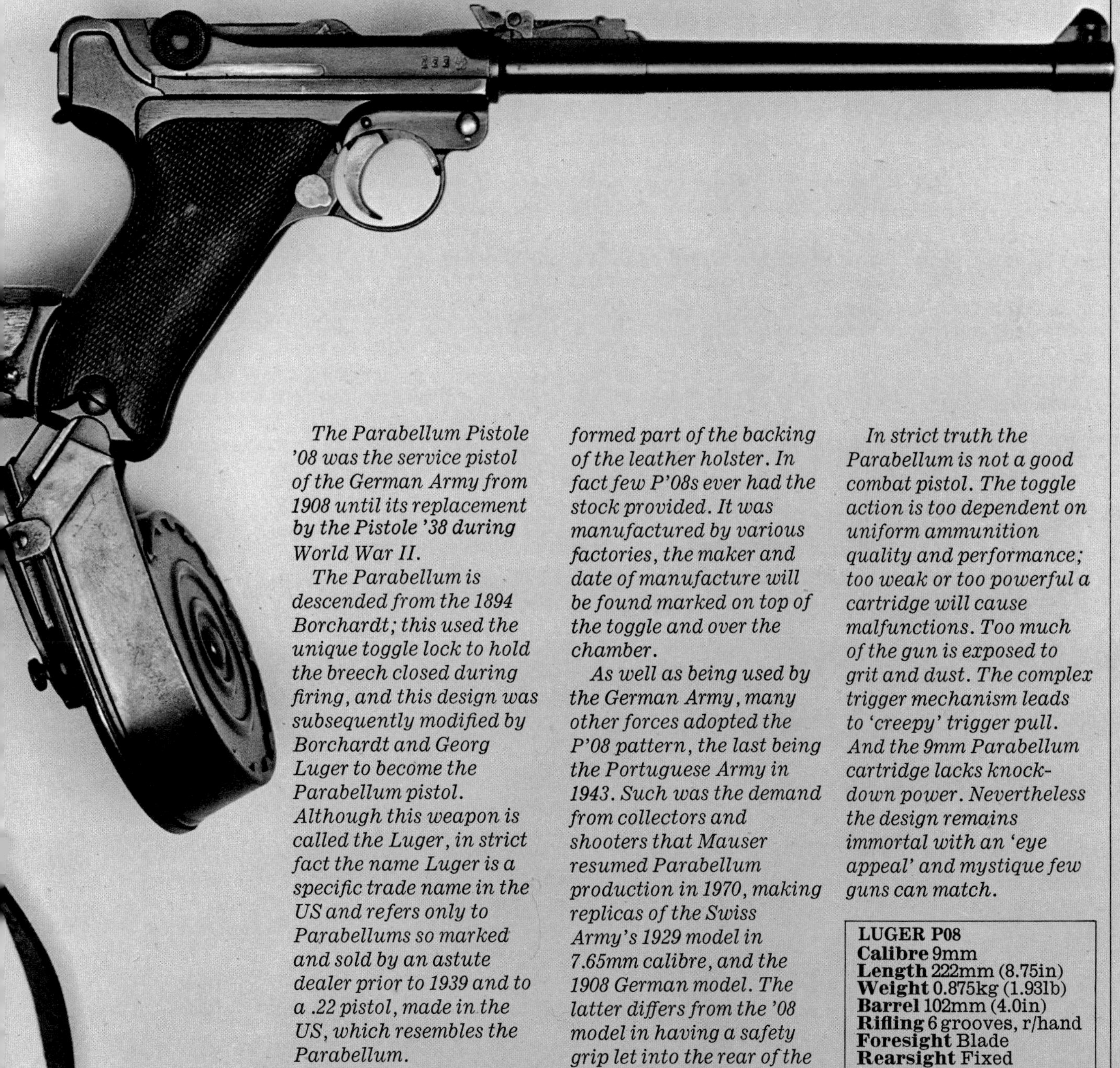

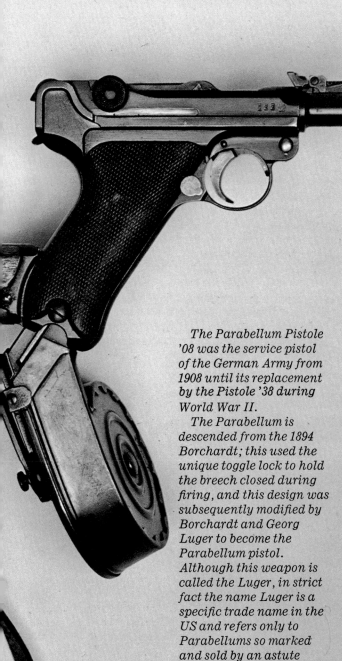

The Parabellum Pistole '08 was the service pistol of the German Army from 1908 until its replacement by the Pistole '38 during World War II.

The Parabellum is descended from the 1894 Borchardt; this used the unique toggle lock to hold the breech closed during firing, and this design was subsequently modified by Borchardt and Georg Luger to become the Parabellum pistol. Although this weapon is called the Luger, in strict fact the name Luger is a specific trade name in the US and refers only to Parabellums so marked and sold by an astute dealer prior to 1939 and to a .22 pistol, made in the US, which resembles the Parabellum.

The P'08 was in 9mm calibre with a 102mm (4in) barrel and an eight-round magazine, and had a lug at the rear of the butt for attaching a wooden stock which formed part of the backing of the leather holster. In fact few P'08s ever had the stock provided. It was manufactured by various factories, the maker and date of manufacture will be found marked on top of the toggle and over the chamber.

As well as being used by the German Army, many other forces adopted the P'08 pattern, the last being the Portuguese Army in 1943. Such was the demand from collectors and shooters that Mauser resumed Parabellum production in 1970, making replicas of the Swiss Army's 1929 model in 7.65mm calibre, and the 1908 German model. The latter differs from the '08 model in having a safety grip let into the rear of the butt and not having a butt-stock attachment (since this is disliked by the various licensing authorities). Some 50,000 of these Parabellums have been made so far.

In strict truth the Parabellum is not a good combat pistol. The toggle action is too dependent on uniform ammunition quality and performance; too weak or too powerful a cartridge will cause malfunctions. Too much of the gun is exposed to grit and dust. The complex trigger mechanism leads to 'creepy' trigger pull. And the 9mm Parabellum cartridge lacks knock-down power. Nevertheless the design remains immortal with an 'eye appeal' and mystique few guns can match.

LUGER P08
Calibre 9mm
Length 222mm (8.75in)
Weight 0.875kg (1.93lb)
Barrel 102mm (4.0in)
Rifling 6 grooves, r/hand
Foresight Blade
Rearsight Fixed V-notch
Action Recoil
Rate of fire 30 rpm
Feed system 8-round box magazine
Muzzle velocity 350m/sec (1,150ft/sec)
Bullet weight 7.44g (115gr)

enough, he seems to have offered this first, in 1902, to the British Army, who turned it down. The German Army, though, was more impressed and gave the pistol a comprehensive test. In fact, the German Navy was the first to adopt the Luger pistol, in 1905, followed by the Army in 1908, both models being in 9mm calibre.

Luger and the Löwe company – which was now known as the Deutsche Waffen and Munitionsfabrik – had achieved the target of all pistol makers. They had landed a fat military contract and, to make it better, were also providing the ammunition. But, before they reached that point, there were a number of other designers who had their eyes on the same goal.

Among them was Paul Mauser. Until now he had not paid much attention to the pistol market, having enough to do to supply half the world with his splendid rifles. He had made a handful of repeating pistols, and had produced his rather unusual revolver – the 'Zig-Zag' – in limited numbers, but in the early 1890s he saw the possibility of military adoption of a sound automatic pistol and set out to produce one. As it happened, two of his employees had been working on a design in desultory fashion, and he now encouraged them to perfect it, for the company's further glory. In 1895 the result was introduced, and it won almost immediate success, being reliable, accurate and beautifully made. It was the appearance of the Mauser Model 1896 which,

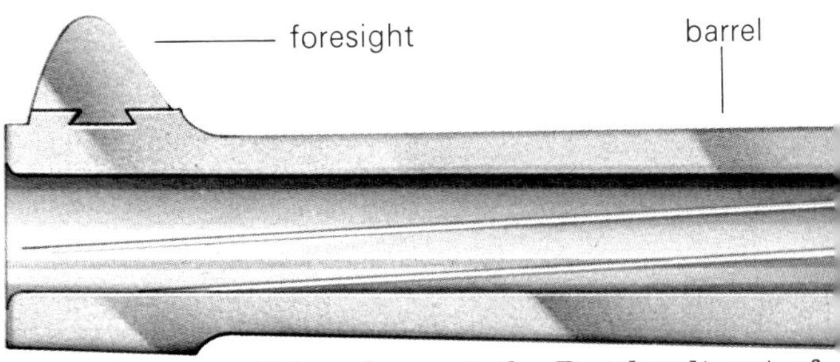

as much as anything else, put the Borchardt out of the market and spurred Luger to improve his design.

The Mauser pistol was of original design. It used a reciprocating bolt of square section moving inside a hollow barrel extension. A plate beneath the bolt was cammed up and down to lock bolt and barrel together for firing and to unlock it to allow recoil to actuate the bolt. The bolt carried a floating firing pin, struck by an external hammer which was automatically cocked as the bolt recoiled. The magazine was a fixed box ahead of the trigger into which 10 rounds could be loaded through the top of the action from a charger.

Like the Borchardt, the Mauser was provided with a wooden butt-stock, in the form of a hollow wooden holster which, after the gun had been withdrawn, could be clipped to the pistol butt. The connection was less rigid than that of the Borchardt, but it was sound enough to allow long-range firing,

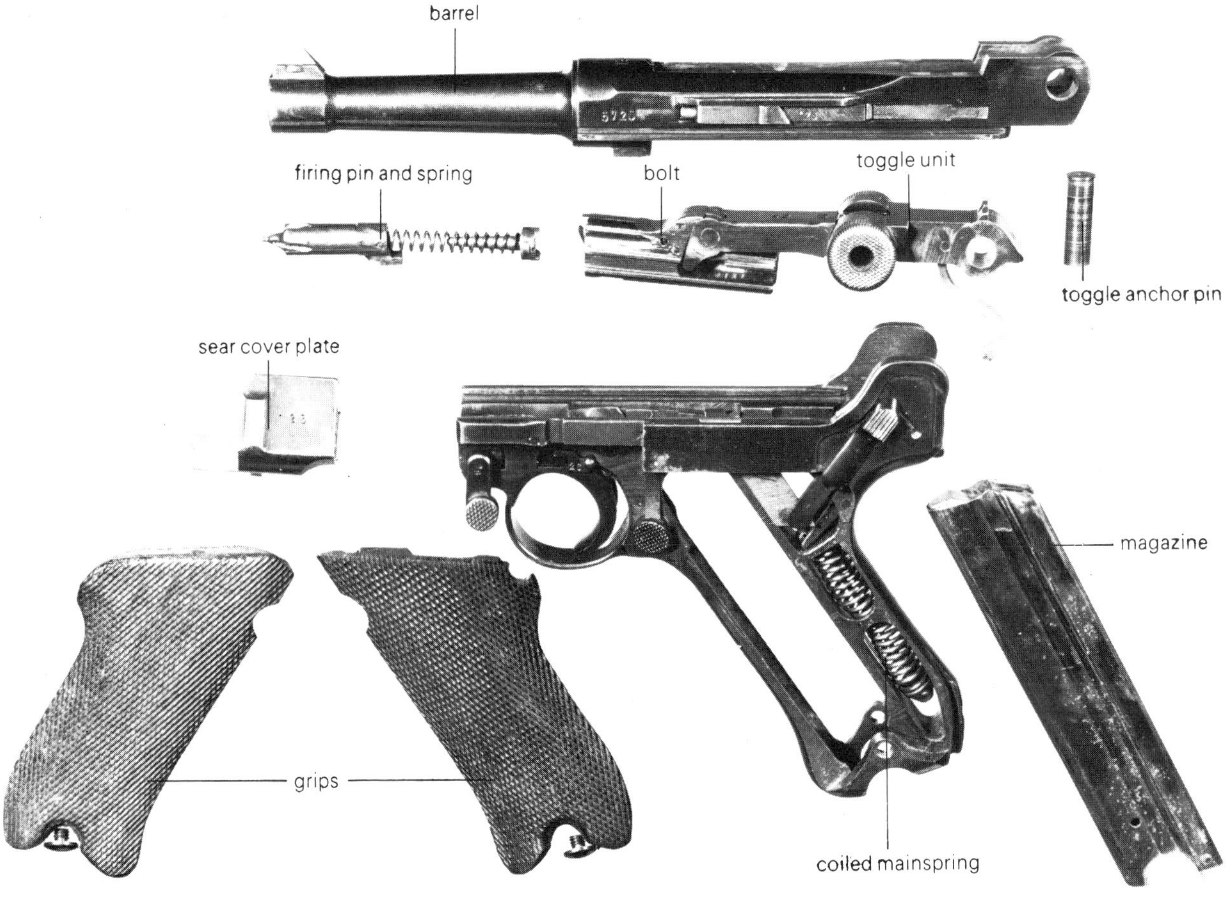

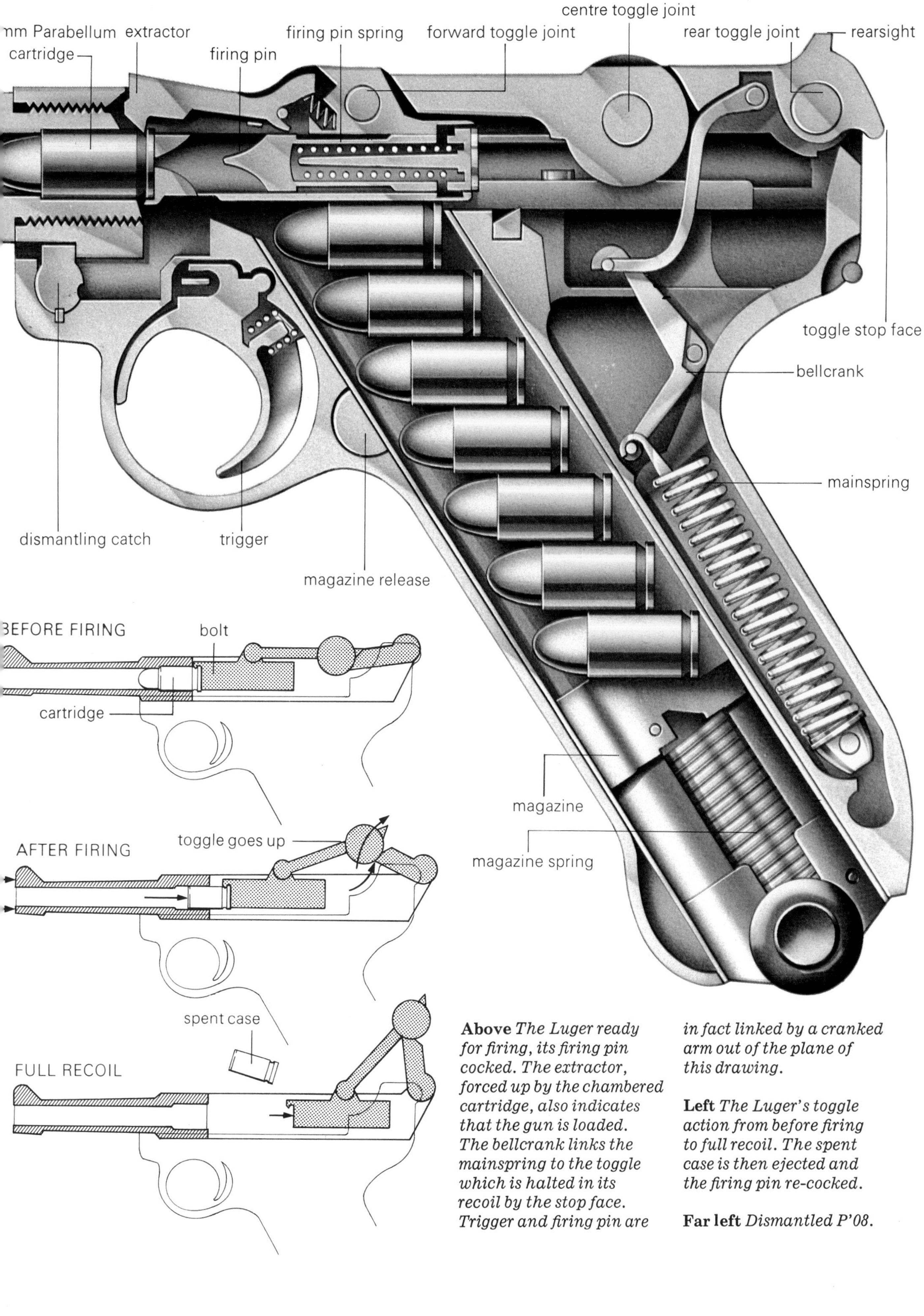

Above *The Luger ready for firing, its firing pin cocked. The extractor, forced up by the chambered cartridge, also indicates that the gun is loaded. The bellcrank links the mainspring to the toggle which is halted in its recoil by the stop face. Trigger and firing pin are in fact linked by a cranked arm out of the plane of this drawing.*

Left *The Luger's toggle action from before firing to full recoil. The spent case is then ejected and the firing pin re-cocked.*

Far left *Dismantled P'08.*

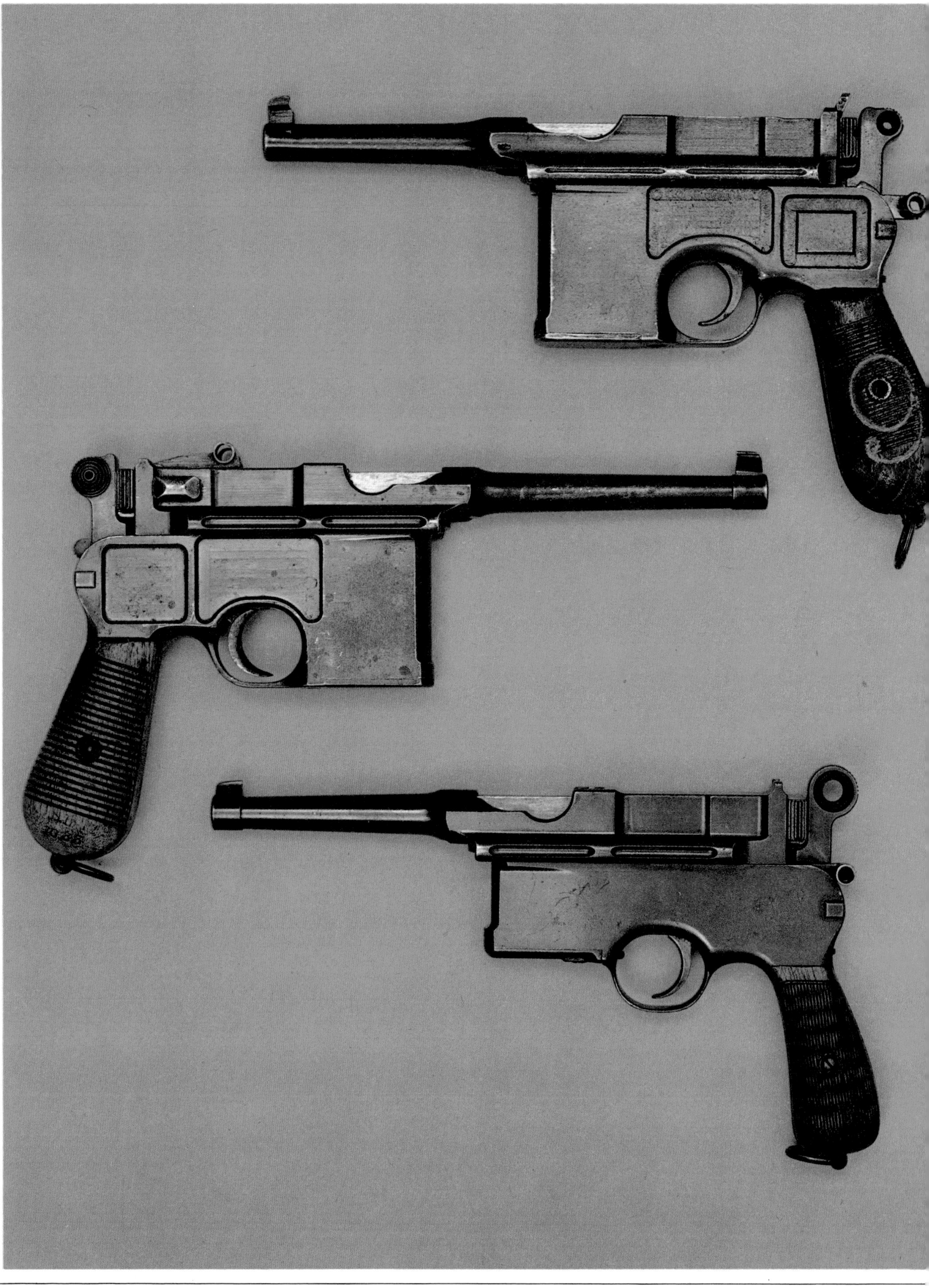

The Mauser Military Pistol was developed from a design by the Federle brothers, employees of the Mauser company in 1893. The following year Mauser decided to enter the automatic pistol field and used the Federle as a starting-point, the first prototype being completed in March 1895. Several experimental models were made before the design was completed, and full production began in 1897.

The Mauser C/96 (to give its correct title) is a recoil-operated pistol with its barrel fixed to a barrel extension, the two forming a single unit free to slide on the top of the pistol frame. Inside the barrel extension is the squarc-section bolt with return spring and firing pin, and underneath the bolt is a locking block with two lugs which engage in similar recesses in the under-surface of the bolt. Since the locking block is attached to the barrel extension, bolt and barrel are secured together when the block is lifted and the lugs engaged. As the barrel and extension recoil, the locking block is allowed to ride down a steel cam surface so that the lugs come away from the recesses in the bolt. This then allows the bolt to part company with the barrel and move back on its own, extracting and ejecting the spent cartridge case. On the return stroke of the bolt a cartridge is collected from the 10-round magazine and loaded into the chamber, whereupon barrel, extension and bolt all move forwards and the block, riding back up the cam, goes back into engagement with the bolt and locks everything up for the next round to be fired.

The basic design did not alter on the various models; variations were in barrel length, safety-catches, hammers and sights. The calibre was 7.63mm, except for a 1916 government order that required Mausers to be chambered for the 9mm Parabellum cartridge.

One variant model was the '712' or 'Reihenfeuer pistole' developed in 1932. This had a selective mechanism which allowed automatic fire, so that when fitted with the standard wooden holster-stock, it could function as a form of submachine gun or machine pistol. It was not very successful. A more elegant and rarer variation was the 'Mauser Carbine', a permanently-stocked, long-barreled pistol intended for shooting small game. A limited number were made before 1914. The final version of the C/96 ceased production in 1937.

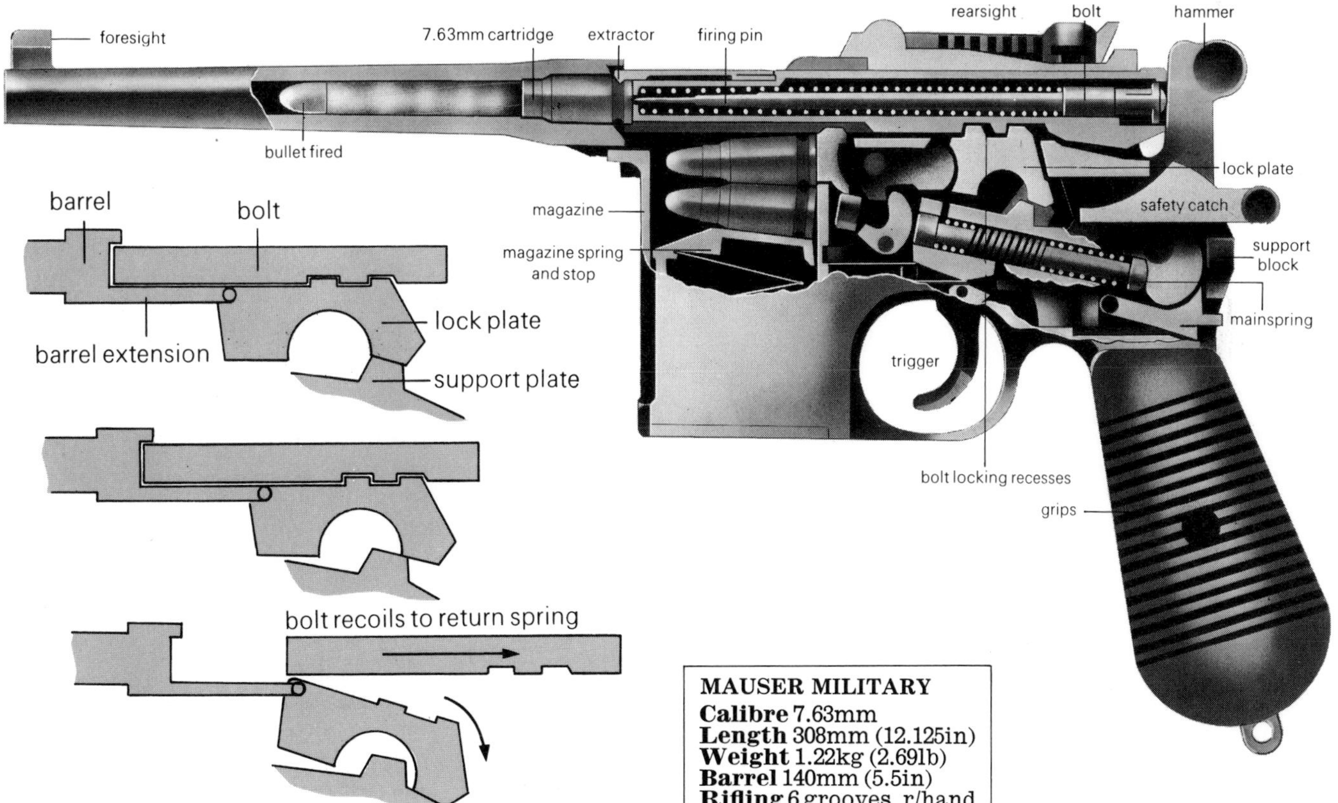

MAUSER MILITARY
Calibre 7.63mm
Length 308mm (12.125in)
Weight 1.22kg (2.69lb)
Barrel 140mm (5.5in)
Rifling 6 grooves, r/hand
Foresight Blade
Rearsight Fixed U-notch or adjustable V-notch, to 700m (765.5yd)
Action Recoil
Rate of fire 30 rpm
Feed system 10-round integral magazine
Muzzle velocity 435m/sec (1,425ft/sec)
Bullet weight 5.5g (85gr)

Left *(Top to bottom) Mauser M1915 marked with a red-stained '9' shows it uses 9mm Parabellum cartridges. Mauser C/96 basic model. The Mauser M1895 with 6-round 7.65mm Borchardt cartridge magazine.*

Above *The Mauser's recoil. (1) The breech is locked. (2) Recoiling the breech remains locked. (3) The lock plate, now over the support, frees the bolt for full recoil. The bolt is halted and thrust back by the return spring.*

Above *The compact layout of the Mauser's locking mechanism and mainspring unit. Except in the wooden grips, no screws or pins were used. All parts were fitted by coupling, bayonet-joint assembling or interlocking.*

and it appears to have been developed in the hope of selling it as a cavalry carbine. In the event no army ever took to it and most of the carbine applications of the Mauser were by hunters who wanted a lightweight, medium-range shoulder arm which was conveniently portable. The Mauser was chambered for a 7.63mm cartridge which was dimensionally the same as the Borchardt but loaded to a greater velocity. Indeed, Borchardt is said to have been somewhat upset by the success of the Mauser which he considered to have been built on his cartridge.

The fourth German pioneer of the automatic pistol was Theodor Bergmann, who was more of an entrepreneur with the sense to employ a brilliant designer, Louis Schmeisser. After some brief attempts at locked-breech pistols, in 1895 Bergmann marketed a simple blowback model, the first time the blowback principle had been applied to any firearm other than the Skoda machine gun. The layout was rather like that of the Mauser or Schonberger, with a clip-loaded magazine in front of the trigger and a bolt moving back and forth in the gun body. But there was no breech-lock, and the pistol fired only a low-powered 5mm cartridge. It was, therefore, of little interest to military buyers.

One feature of interest is that there was no extractor fitted to the bolt and the cartridge case had no rim nor any extraction groove. Ejection of the spent case from the chamber was done simply by the gas pressure forcing it back. This, of course, was how the blowback action of the bolt was achieved, but it is unusual to find a designer relying on the gas pressure to clear the chamber. In practice it worked well enough, but, lacking a proper ejector to throw the case clear of the pistol, it was common for the ejected case to land in the feedway and interfere with the return of the bolt. Eventually Bergmann saw that this irritating fault was probably costing him sales and he redesigned the pistol to incorporate a proper extractor and had the ammunition made with an extracting groove.

Nevertheless, when the Mauser pistol appeared, also in 1895, Bergmann realized that there was a chance of a military contract, but only if he could produce a locked-breech weapon. Locked-breech pistols, such as the Mauser or Parabellum, are pistols in which, due to the power of the cartridge, it is necessary to have the barrel and breech securely locked together at the time of discharge and for a short instant afterwards until the chamber pressure drops to a level at which it is safe to unlock and begin extracting the cartridge. Bergmann eventually produced a pistol of similar layout to the Mauser but with a vertically-moving yoke which locked the bolt before firing. It had a removable magazine and was chambered for a powerful 9mm cartridge, more powerful than that used with the Parabellum pistol.

With this design he achieved success – it was adopted in 1905 by the Spanish Army as their service pistol. But at Bergmann's moment of triumph, the rug was pulled from under his feet. Having no production facilities to make the huge number demanded by Spain, he had contracted the job to another firm. This was now taken over by a third party who cancelled the contract, leaving Bergmann an order, with penalties, but with no means of fulfilling it. In desperation, he licensed the manufacture to a Belgian company, A. E. Pieper of Liège, who completed the Spanish order and then since they had the

The civil version of the Bergmann-Bayard 9mm (with round) Automatic Pistol. It weighed 1.02kg (2.25lb), measured 254mm (10in) with 101mm (4in) barrel (6 grooves l/hand twist), and shot at 395m/sec (1,300ft/sec) with a 6- or 10-round magazine.

The mounted knight (Chevalier Bayard) trademark of the Belgian makers is on the magazine holder. As well as the Spanish Army, the Danes adopted it in 1911, Haerens Tojhus of Copenhagen making the weapon from 1922.

license, went on to make the pistol for sale to other countries for many years. This calamity killed Bergmann's own involvement in the pistol business.

An interesting point is that every pistol which Bergmann made was designed around a cartridge which he also designed, so that once you bought a Bergmann pistol you had to buy Bergmann cartridges. In the case of the 9mm pistol, the cartridge became known as the Bergmann-Bayard (Bayard from the Belgian licensees). In Spain it has always been known as the 9mm Largo and is still their service cartridge. This system of developing pistols to fit special ammunition, and vice versa, was common in the early years of the century, but once public and military preference had been evinced for one or two particular calibres, the idea weakened. Most designers became content to take an existing and popular cartridge and design around it.

In Britain the Army was quite happy with its heavy .455in Webley revolver. This, in one model or another, had been in service since 1887, and had a firm reputation.

The Army had examined several automatic pistols but found them all deficient in stopping-power. The effect of a bullet on its target is, broadly speaking, the product of the bullet weight and its velocity. One can fire a heavy bullet slowly or a light bullet at high velocity and obtain the same striking energy, although stopping-power is not dependent entirely on these factors. Nevertheless, the combination of small bullet and high velocity attracted one British inventor, Hugh Gabbet-Fairfax, who produced an automatic pistol in 1900 which he submitted for trial to the Royal Navy. The pistol was known as the Mars and was described by a contemporary reporter as a 'young cannon'. Gabbet-Fairfax made the pistol in three calibres – 8.5mm, 9mm and .45in – and all used extremely powerful cartridges of his own design. His 9mm, for example, fired a 156 grain bullet at 500m per second (1,650 ft/sec). This gave a muzzle energy of 1,282 joules (943 ft-lb-force). By comparison, the .45 Colt automatic of today fires a 230 grain bullet at 286m/sec (940 ft/sec) to give a muzzle energy of 613 joules (451 ft-lb-force), so the Mars had a theoretical stopping-power over twice as great as the Colt. (One should also bear in mind that 68 joules (50 ft-lb-force) is considered to be the amount needed to knock down a standing man.)

The mechanism was extremely complex, being of the class known as 'long recoil' in which the barrel and breech, locked together, recoiled for a distance greater than the length of a complete cartridge. At the end of the recoil stroke, the breech (which was a rotating bolt) was unlocked and held, while the barrel was allowed to run forwards almost to the firing position. During this recoil movement a 'lifter' had withdrawn a cartridge from the magazine and now lifted it up behind the breech. The bolt was then released to fly forwards and chamber the cartridge, and then rotate and lock into place. Pressure on the trigger then dropped an externally-mounted hammer which struck a firing pin in the bolt and thus fired the cartridge.

All this mechanical activity, plus the power of the cartridge, added up to a most unpleasant weapon to fire. It kicked like a mule and invariably finished pointing straight up. In the words of the Royal Navy's official report on the trials of the Mars pistol, '*Nobody who fired this pistol wanted to fire it again* . . .'. It was turned down for military adoption,

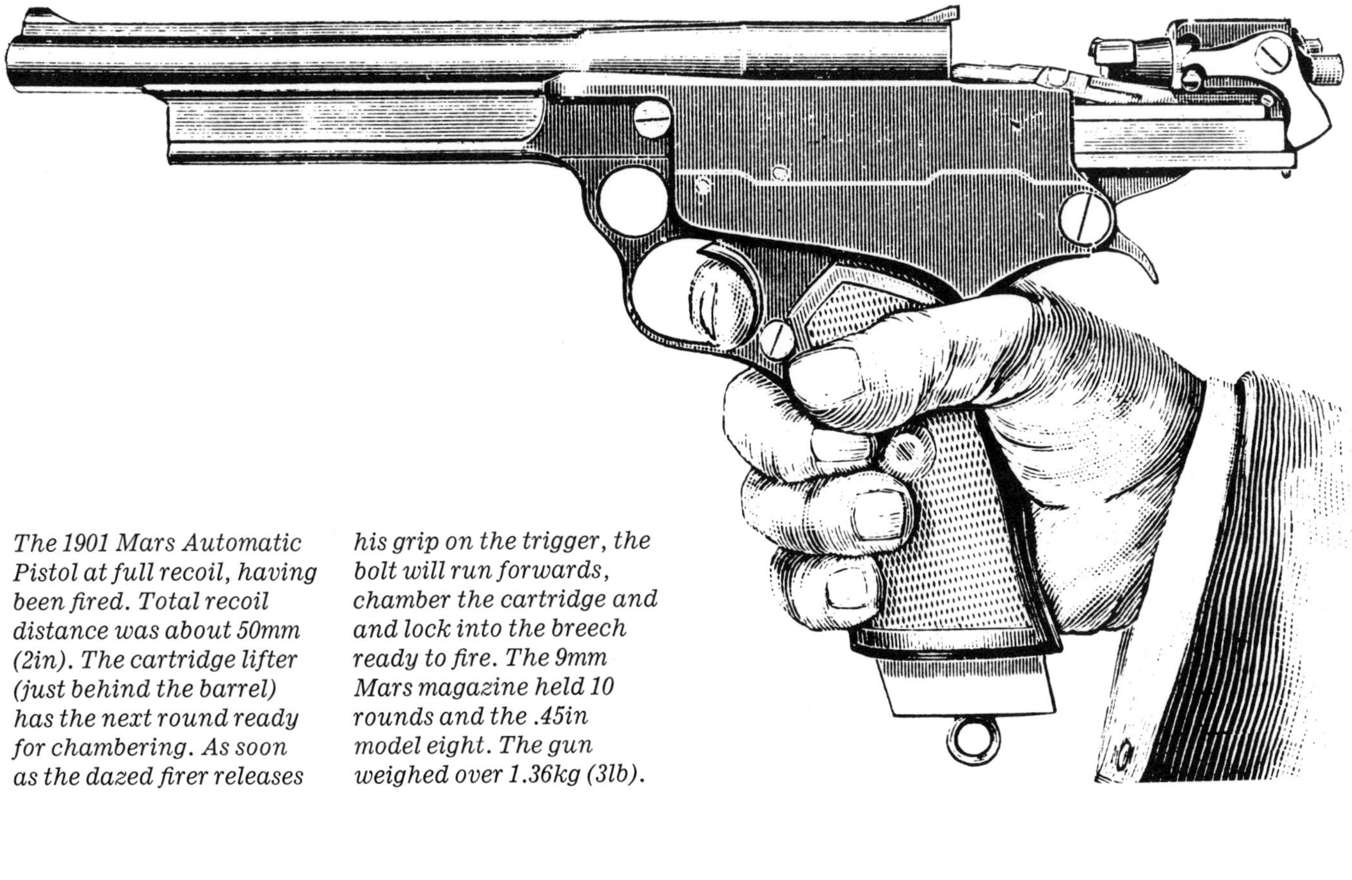

The 1901 Mars Automatic Pistol at full recoil, having been fired. Total recoil distance was about 50mm (2in). The cartridge lifter (just behind the barrel) has the next round ready for chambering. As soon as the dazed firer releases his grip on the trigger, the bolt will run forwards, chamber the cartridge and and lock into the breech ready to fire. The 9mm Mars magazine held 10 rounds and the .45in model eight. The gun weighed over 1.36kg (3lb).

The Birmingham firm of Webley was founded in 1838 by Philip and Joseph Webley, one of the earliest foundations of a modern gun-making company. The Webley brothers' first serious attempt at a heavy military revolver was the 'RIC' model of 1867, so designated because it was adopted as the standard sidearm of the newly-formed Royal Irish Constabulary in 1868. The 'RIC' appeared in several variants but was always a solid-frame revolver of some weight and durability. It was widely sold among police forces throughout the British Empire and was also available commercially.

In 1877 Webley began production of a hinged-frame revolver incorporating features patented by Charles Pryse. These 'Webley-Pryse' revolvers appeared in various calibres from .32 to .577in, being particularly popular among Army officers.

However, though Webley made and continued to to make a variety of revolvers, it was the long series developed and adopted by the British Army that brought the name into prominence. These pistols began with the Mk 1 in 1887, a .442in six-shot hinged-frame model with a 102mm (4in) barrel. Marks 2 and 3, which made progressive improvements in small details, followed in 1894 and 1897. In 1899 the Mk 4 appeared, the first to be made in the just-standardized Army .455in calibre. This was made in several barrel lengths, 102mm (4in) being the standard, 152mm (6in) being available to officers who wanted a pistol suited to target shooting (and were prepared to pay for it).

The Mk 5 of 1913 was a very minor change of design, the cylinder being of larger diameter and the barrel length standardized at 102mm (4in). Finally there came the Mk 6 of 1915, which, due to the demands of World War I, was produced in vast numbers.

The only drawback with the .455 revolver was that it demanded a high state of training in order to shoot well with it. The British Army decided to change to .38in as the standard revolver calibre and to produce its own pistol at Enfield. Webley produced a .38 revolver that was virtually a scaled-down .455 Mk 6, called it the .38 Mk 4, and sold it widely, particularly to police forces throughout the Empire.

In 1940, when revolvers were in short supply, the .38 Mk 4 was taken into military use. The last of the service Webleys, it remained until replaced by the Browning Automatic Pistol in 1957.

Picture shows, from bottom left to top right: .455 Automatic Pistol No.2 Mk 1 with special sights for Royal Flying Corps observers (1914-18). Webley-Fosbery Automatic of 1901 with Pryse barrel. .442 Webley Mk 1 of 1887. Webley-Wilkinson .45 Target Revolver of 1880. .455 Webley Mk 6 of 1915.

WEBLEY Mk VI
Calibre .455in
Length 286mm (11.25in)
Weight 1.075kg (2.371b)
Barrel 152mm (6.0in)
Rifling 7 grooves, r/hand
Foresight Blade
Rearsight Fixed V-notch
Action Revolver
Rate of fire 12 rpm
Feed system 6-shot cylinder
Muzzle velocity 198m/sec (650ft/sec)
Bullet weight 17.14g (265gr)

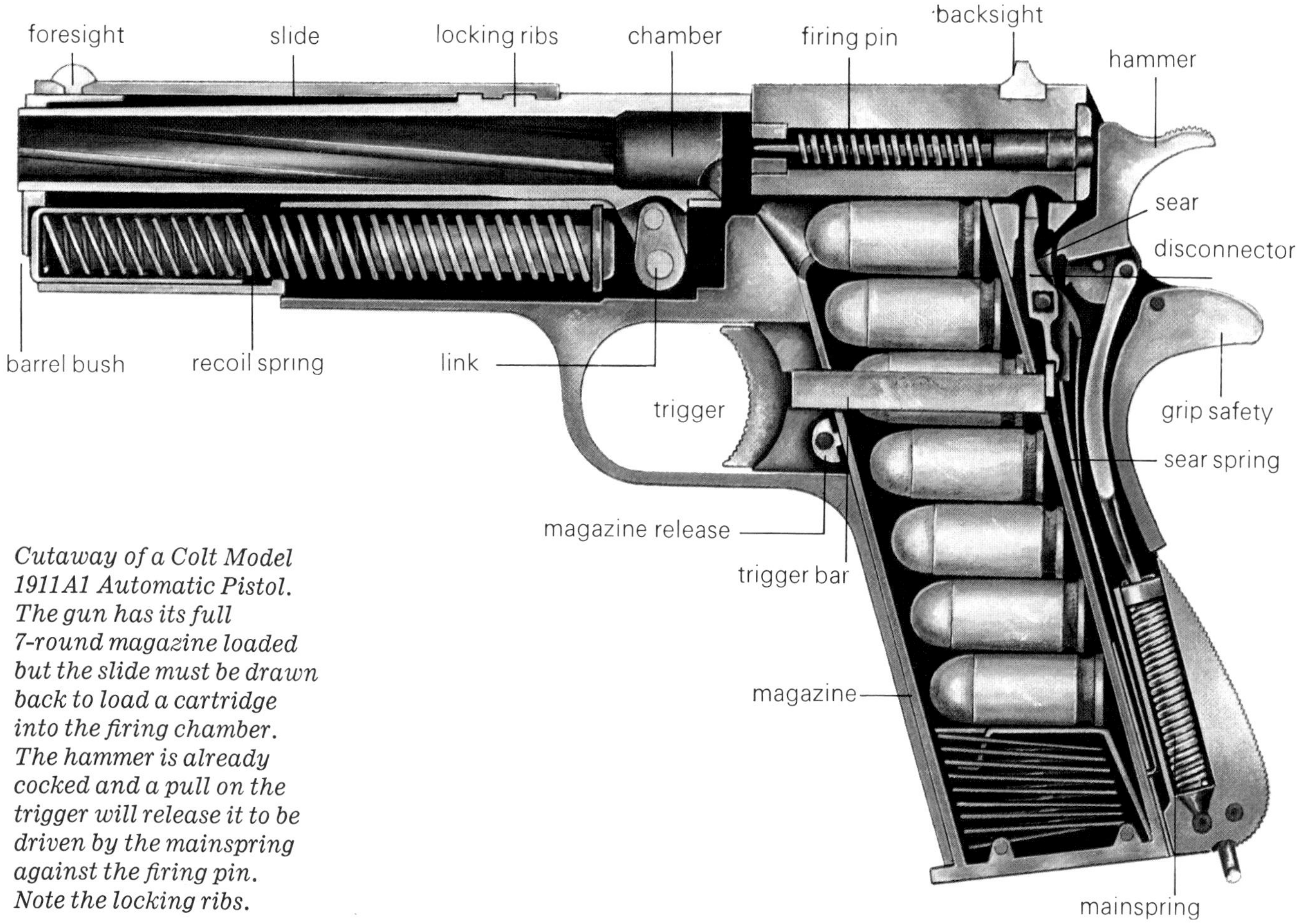

Cutaway of a Colt Model 1911A1 Automatic Pistol. The gun has its full 7-round magazine loaded but the slide must be drawn back to load a cartridge into the firing chamber. The hammer is already cocked and a pull on the trigger will release it to be driven by the mainspring against the firing pin. Note the locking ribs.

and Gabbet-Fairfax went bankrupt after 80 pistols had been made. They are probably the most rare and valuable of any automatic pistols in existence today.

On the other side of Europe, the Austro-Hungarian Army also began to examine automatic pistols. It had tested Luger's Parabellum, but there was a vast number of good firearms designers in the Austro-Hungarian Empire and the Army decided to wait and see what they could produce. Eventually it adopted the 8mm Roth-Steyr, which introduces us to yet another method of breech-locking – the revolving barrel.

In this pistol the barrel was free to revolve and was carried inside an all-enveloping sleeve. At the rear of the barrel was the breech bolt, also carried in the sleeve which actually formed the body of the gun. At the front of the barrel were two helical lugs engaged in grooves in the sleeve, and when the pistol was fired the barrel recoiled, pulling the helical lugs through the grooves and thus rotating the barrel through 90°. This rotation unlocked the breech, after which the barrel was halted and the bolt allowed to recoil and then run back to reload. As the fresh round was chambered, so the bolt pushed the barrel back, ran the lugs through the grooves in the reverse direction and rotated the barrel to lock the breech.

Another peculiarity of this design was the introduction of an integral magazine contained in the butt. The magazine had to be loaded by manually pulling back the bolt and then dropping a metal charger into two guides in the upper part of the sleeve. The cartridges in the charger were then pushed down into the magazine and the charger removed, allowing the bolt to go forwards and chamber the first round. In order to unload, since it was not possible to remove the magazine from the butt, the bolt was pulled back and a catch at the side of the butt pressed in. This retracted the feeding lip on one side of the magazine and permitted the magazine spring to eject all the rounds through the top of the gun.

The Roth-Steyr was adopted in 1907 for the Austro-Hungarian cavalry. In 1912 another Steyr design, probably attributable to George Roth but not acknowledged, was introduced for the infantry. This was the 9mm Steyr Model 1912, which looked more conventional than the Roth-Steyr (because it was slab-sided) but used much the same sort of rotating barrel breech-lock and the same integral magazine. It was chambered for yet another variation of the 9mm calibre, longer than the 9mm Parabellum but shorter than the Bergmann-Bayard round. It was, in fact, an extremely good design of pistol, reliable and accurate. Had it been chambered for a more common cartridge it might well have had greater commercial success.

In the United States the automatic pistol was

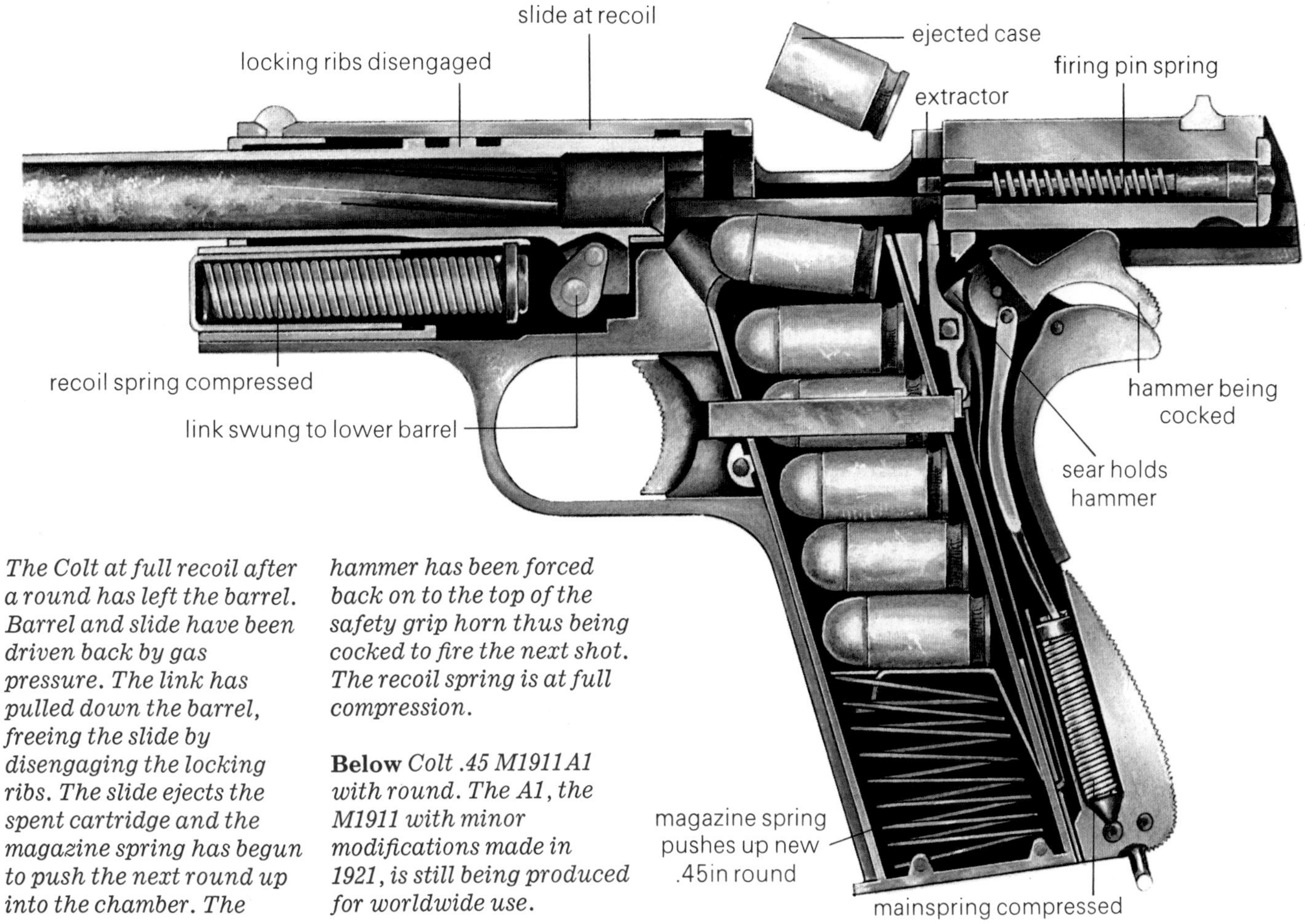

The Colt at full recoil after a round has left the barrel. Barrel and slide have been driven back by gas pressure. The link has pulled down the barrel, freeing the slide by disengaging the locking ribs. The slide ejects the spent cartridge and the magazine spring has begun to push the next round up into the chamber. The hammer has been forced back on to the top of the safety grip horn thus being cocked to fire the next shot. The recoil spring is at full compression.

Below *Colt .45 M1911A1 with round. The A1, the M1911 with minor modifications made in 1921, is still being produced for worldwide use.*

slow to get under way, probably because of the immense popularity and massive production of revolvers there. But in 1898, John Moses Browning, one of the foremost American firearms designers and one of the greatest and most successful inventors of automatic arms, took out patents for a blowback pistol. He was unable to interest an American manufacturer and took the design to Europe, where he arranged with the Fabrique National d'Armes de Guerre (F.N.) of Belgium to manufacture to his designs. Using the name 'Browning' they subsequently produced millions of blowback pistols.

The first Browning to be produced was the 1900 model, which was developed around a 7.65mm cartridge also designed by John Browning. This was succeeded by another of the same calibre but of simplified construction, known as the Model 1903.

The pistol frame of the Model 1903 carried a magazine in the butt and a hammer and trigger. On top of the frame rode a 'slide', an all-enveloping steel block which formed the breech-block at its rear end, carried a firing pin, concealed the hammer, and was hollowed out at the front to allow the barrel to be inserted. The barrel was a loose unit which was held in place in the gun by lugs around its breech end engaging in grooves in the gun body. This prevented lengthwise movement, while the close confines of the slide prevented it lifting away from the body. On firing, the slide unit was blown to the rear by simple blowback action, the empty case being extracted and thrown clear through a slot cut in the upper side of the slide. As the slide returned, driven by a return spring below the barrel, so the breech-block portion stripped a cartridge from the magazine and thrust it into the breech. During the recoil stroke, the interior shape of the slide had forced the hammer back and cocked it, where it was held ready for the next pressure on the trigger. A disconnector ensured that the trigger and hammer were not capable of functioning together until the slide had gone forwards and securely chambered the fresh cartridge.

This was one of the most successful pistol designs ever made, and it introduced the world to the pocketable automatic pistol. But it was of little interest to military authorities at that time, since they were still adamant that locked-breech pistols in heavy calibres were the only acceptable solution. (They were to change their minds in later years, and several armies adopted the 7.65mm Browning blowback as an official pistol.) John Browning con sequently applied himself to the design of a locked-breech weapon and – with the success of his blowback design for all to see – there was less resistance in the United States to his ideas this time. This model was taken up in 1900 by the Colt company with the aim, once it was perfected, of interesting the US Army.

The Colt Automatic, as it came to be known, relied on the same sort of slide with integral breech-block that was used on the blowback design. But in this case the barrel was anchored to the pistol frame by two hinged links, one under the muzzle and one under the breech, so that it could rise and fall relative to the frame but always parallel to it. The top of the barrel had two broad, locking ribs machined into the metal, and the interior surface of the slide had two corresponding grooves. With the pistol loaded and ready to fire, the slide was forced forwards by the action of a return spring, and the pressure of the breech-block on the bottom of the cartridge was transmitted to the barrel, forcing it to move forwards and upwards, due to its hinged link supports, so that the ribs on top engaged in the grooves in the underside of the top of the slide.

On firing, the slide recoiled due to the pressure on the base of the cartridge pushing back on the breech-block. But due to the meshing of the ribs and grooves, the slide carried the barrel back with it, the two being thus securely locked together for a short time until the action of the links drew the barrel downwards and disengaged the lugs. This period was quite long enough to allow the bullet to leave the barrel and the gas pressure in the breech to drop to a safe level. As soon as the lugs disengaged from the grooves in the slide, the slide was free to recoil while the barrel remained where it was. The recoil movement ejected the empty cartridge case and cocked the externally-mounted hammer. The return of the slide, under spring pressure, collected a fresh cartridge from the magazine in the butt and loaded it into the chamber, then put pressure on the barrel to force it forwards and upwards once more until it was locked in place by the engagement of the lugs and grooves.

Strangely enough, the one thing that Browning did not provide on his first model was a disconnector – with the result that the pistol smartly emptied itself after the first pressure on the trigger. This was soon rectified, since Browning saw that instead of an asset, such a rate of fire was a liability. A new cartridge in .38 calibre was developed for the Colt automatic and it enjoyed some sales in the early 1900s. But the US Army, though interested, were adamant that any pistol they adopted would have to

be of .45 calibre. In December 1906, the Chief of Staff of the US Army ordered the assembly of a Test Board to ascertain the design of an automatic pistol or revolver best suited to the Army's requirements and in 1907 the tests took place. Among the contesting pistols were the Parabellum, various revolvers, various designs of automatic, and the Colt model. Two pistols came out of the test with good marks – the Colt and an automatic using a revolving barrel designed by the Savage Arms Company of New York. Two hundred of each were obtained for extended troop trials, after which it was decided that the Colt held most promise and Colt were asked to make some improvements in the design.

The principal change was the abandonment of the two links. Only one was now used, under the breech, and the muzzle rode in a removable bushing in the front end of the slide. This simplified manufacture and assembly without interfering with the essential action of the locking system. More trials were carried out and the Colt was finally accepted into US service as the Model of 1911. Except for some very minor modifications made in the 1920s as a result of experience during World War I, it remains the standard US service pistol to this day and is, without any doubt at all, the best combat pistol ever made. Extremely reliable, robust, simple, easy to shoot, and with a powerful cartridge capable of stopping the most resolute or frenzied opponent, as a fighting man's pistol the Colt is above all competition.

One, at least, of the other contestants in the 1907 test deserves more mention, and that is the Webley-Fosbery Automatic Revolver from Britain. It might be expected that with the arrival of the automatic pistol on the scene somebody would try to apply automatic principles to a revolver. In fact several people tried, but only one person made any sort of a success of it and he was Colonel G. V. Fosbery, V.C. In effect, the Webley-Fosbery was a six-shot Webley revolver but with the pistol frame as one distinct unit and the barrel and cylinder as another. The frame had guides in its top surface, along which the barrel/cylinder unit could move backwards and forwards. The cylinder's outer surface was cut with a series of zig-zag grooves which engaged with a fixed pin on the top of the frame. A recoil spring kept the barrel unit to the front of the frame.

The barrel could be hinged down to expose the

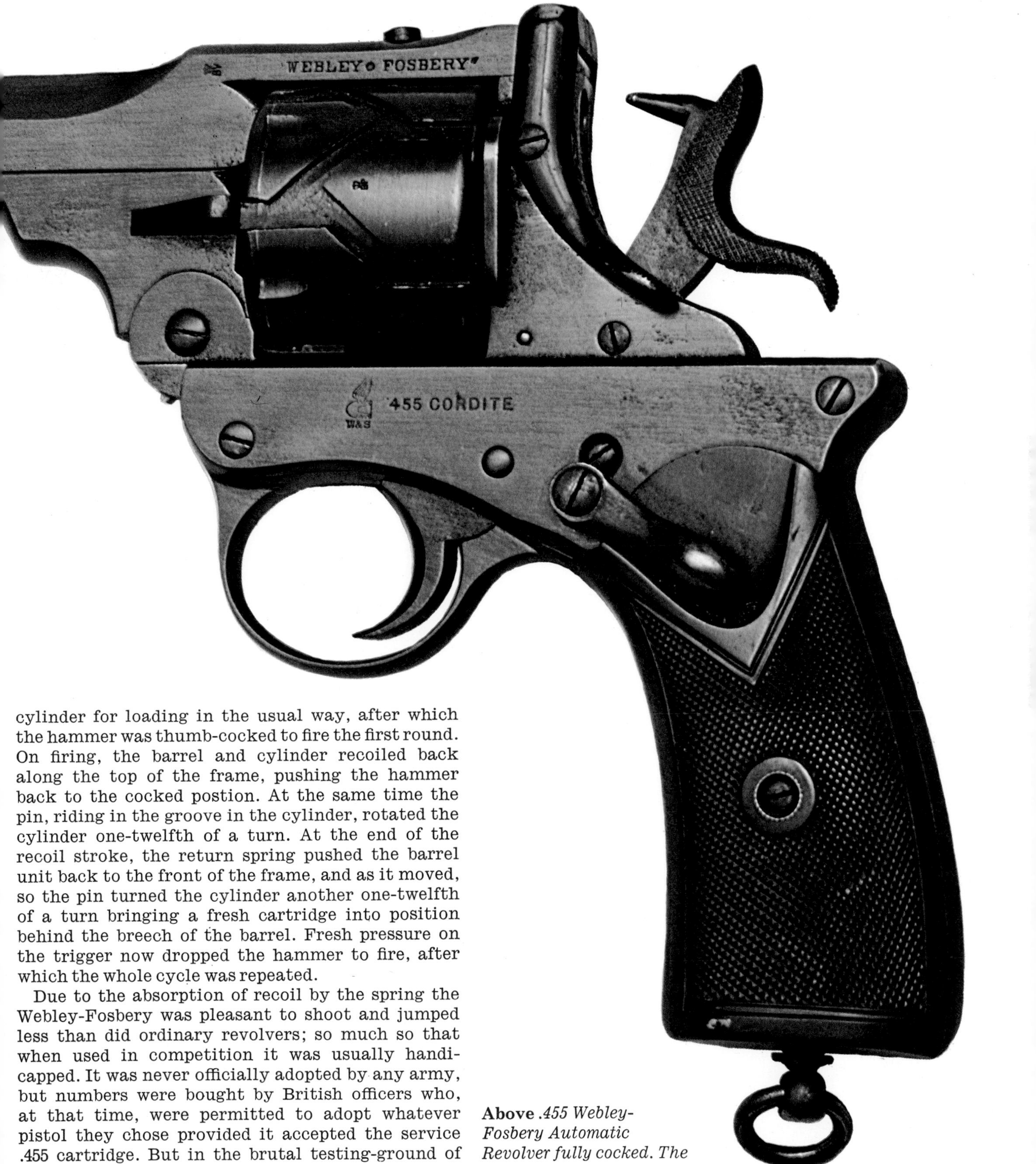

cylinder for loading in the usual way, after which the hammer was thumb-cocked to fire the first round. On firing, the barrel and cylinder recoiled back along the top of the frame, pushing the hammer back to the cocked postion. At the same time the pin, riding in the groove in the cylinder, rotated the cylinder one-twelfth of a turn. At the end of the recoil stroke, the return spring pushed the barrel unit back to the front of the frame, and as it moved, so the pin turned the cylinder another one-twelfth of a turn bringing a fresh cartridge into position behind the breech of the barrel. Fresh pressure on the trigger now dropped the hammer to fire, after which the whole cycle was repeated.

Due to the absorption of recoil by the spring the Webley-Fosbery was pleasant to shoot and jumped less than did ordinary revolvers; so much so that when used in competition it was usually handicapped. It was never officially adopted by any army, but numbers were bought by British officers who, at that time, were permitted to adopt whatever pistol they chose provided it accepted the service .455 cartridge. But in the brutal testing-ground of Flanders in 1914-18, the Webley-Fosbery was tried and found wanting. The mechanism was too exposed to mud and grit to be reliable in combat conditions.

Above *.455 Webley-Fosbery Automatic Revolver fully cocked. The firer had to keep his arm rigid to ensure that the recoil cocked the hammer.*

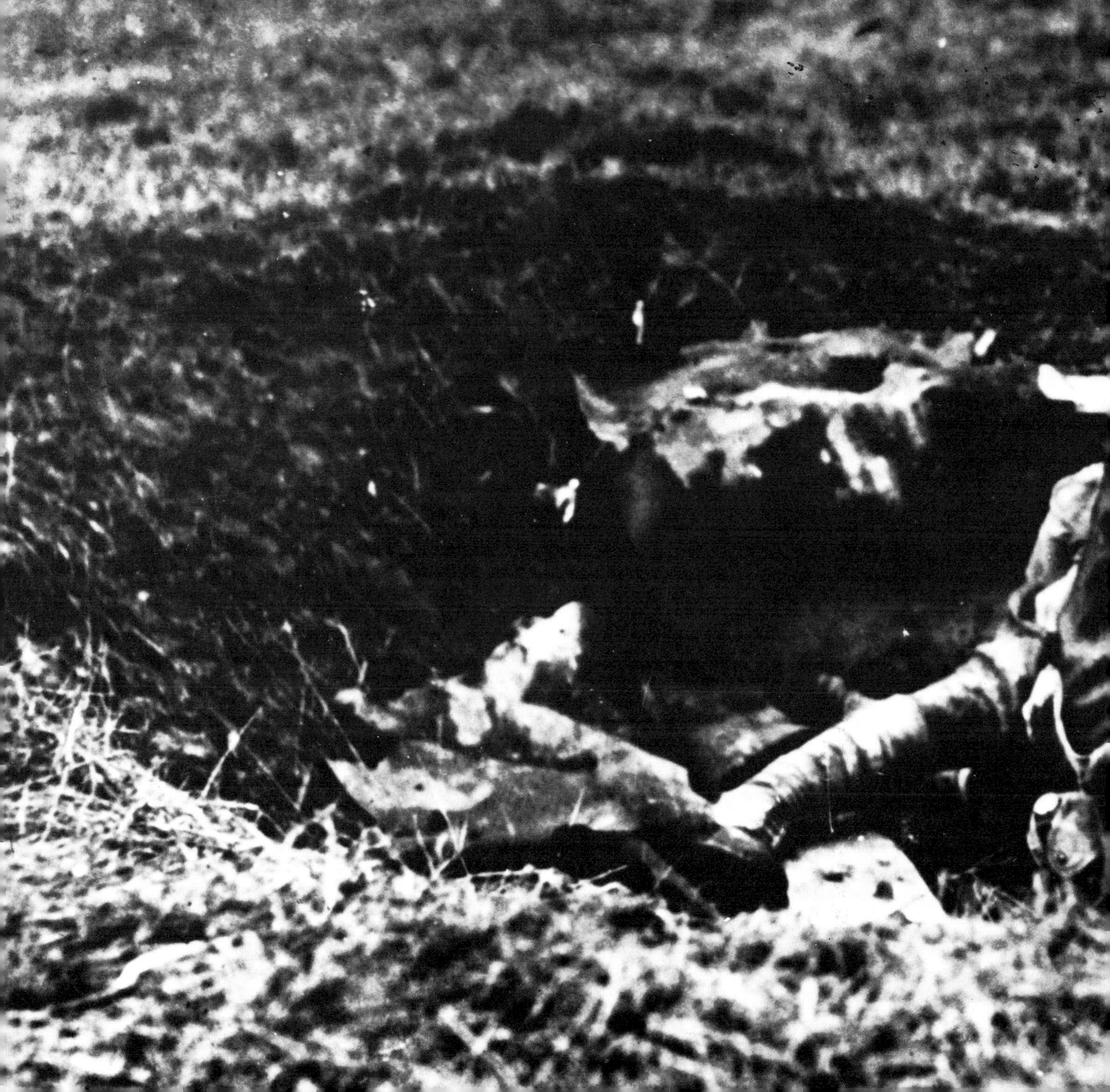

TEST OF BATTLE
GUNS OF WORLD WAR I

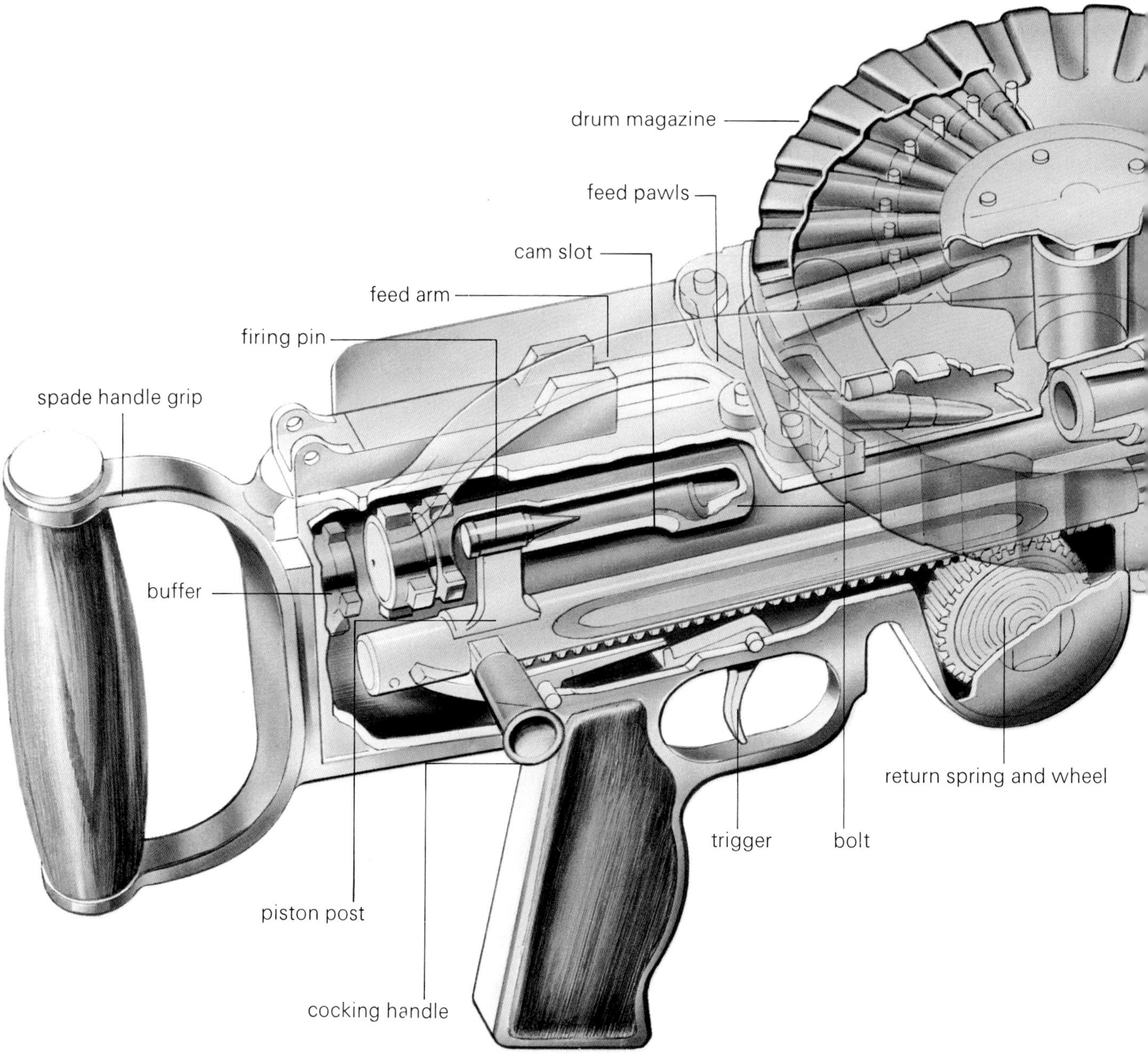

WORLD WAR I on the Western Front has frequently been likened to a great siege, in which the Allied powers – mainly Britain, France and, later, the United States – were trying to break into the fortress which was Germany; and the principal reason for the war taking that form was the use of the machine gun. Once the 'Race to the Sea' by the German Army had been checked and the trench lines drawn, the power of the machine gun to dominate 'No Man's Land' was the major factor in shaping the tactics, and it needed the invention of the tank to break the deadlock. When the war began, the general allocation of machine guns on both sides was some 24 guns per infantry division of 12 battalions. At the end of the war the division had been pared to 9 battalions, which in practice were seldom more than about 50 per cent of the strength of the 1914 formation, and it had 160 machine guns – which is an increase in gun strength of 1,778 per cent.

Increases of this sort demanded production to match, and while the war was begun with the Maxim, Vickers and Hotchkiss guns of prewar days, it was soon obvious that more weapons – weapons easier and quicker to make – were going to be needed. Another point which made itself known was the need for machine guns to be considerably more portable than the usual run of tripod-mounted, water-cooled heavyweights, so that infantry could carry them easily in an attack and bring them rapidly into action.

The choices were fairly limited, and on the Allied side they came down to the Madsen, the Hotchkiss, and a new design, the Lewis. The Danish Madsen was not considered acceptable, because of the complexity of its mechanism and the fact that what defects the gun had were magnified when it was asked to fire the British .303in rimmed cartridge.

The Hotchkiss was an improved model, known generally as the 'Light' Hotchkiss. It used the same gas piston system of operation as the earlier (1895)

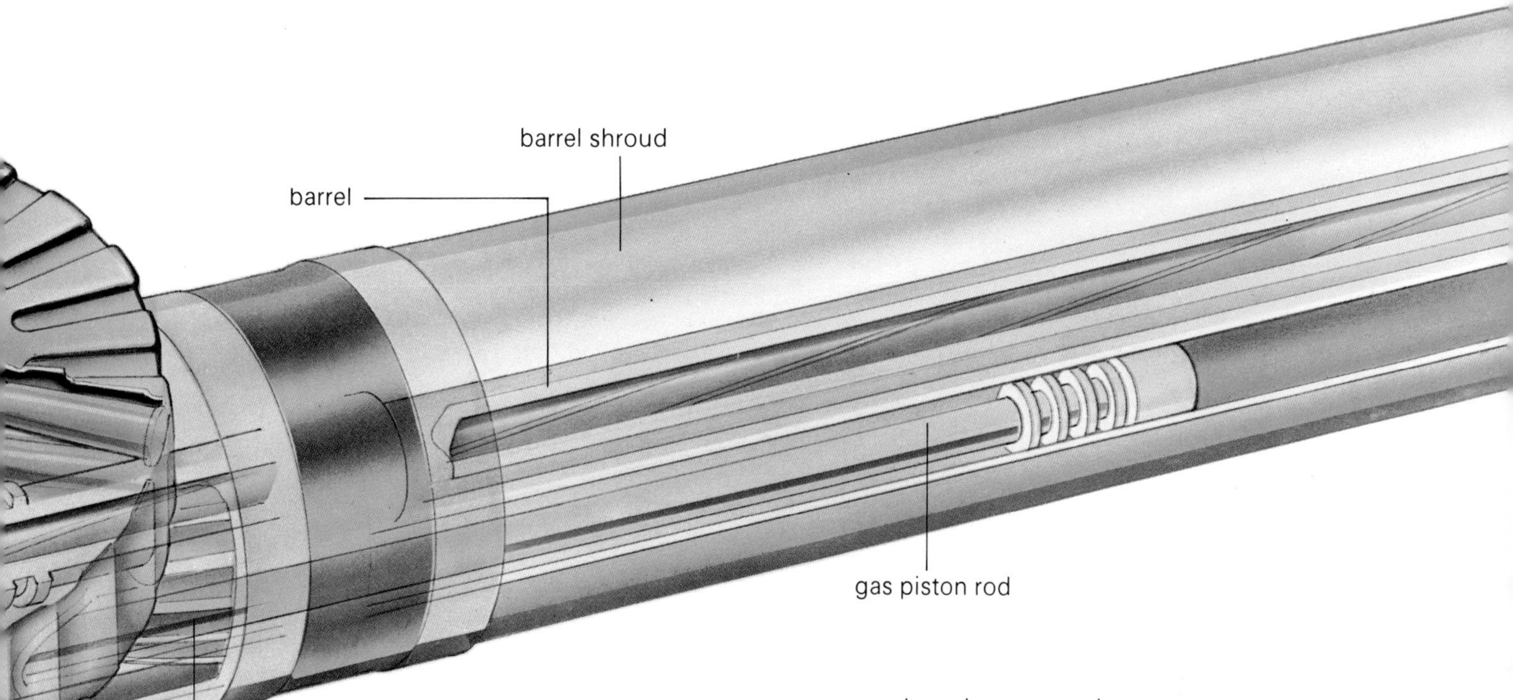

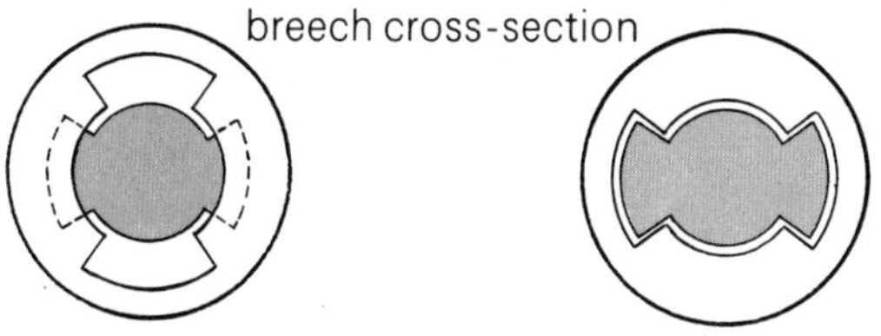

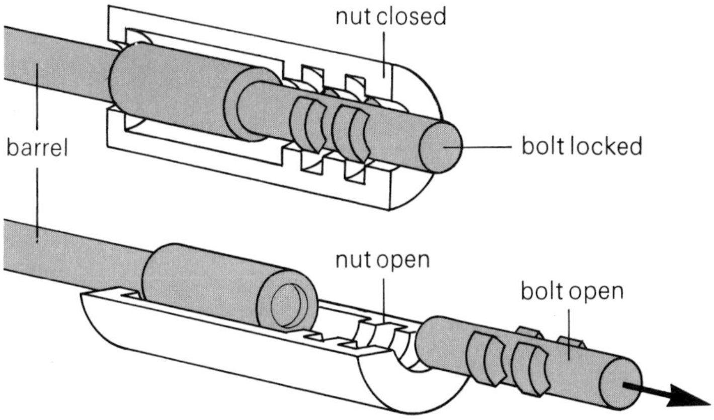

Previous page *US Marines man a .50in Browning M1917 MG on the Western Front in 1918.*

Above *The gas-operated Lewis Gun. The gas piston rod has a piston post and firing pin at its rear end. This rides in a cam slot in the bolt so as to rotate and move it to and fro. The movement of the bolt drives the feed arm which forces a round out of the magazine and actuates the feed pawls to rotate the drum and lock it. As the gas piston goes forwards, driven by the return spring, the firing pin pushes through the bolt to fire the cartridge. Muzzle blast draws air into the barrel shroud across the cooling fins and exhausts it at the muzzle.*

Right *Hotchkiss fermeture nut locking system.*

model, but locked the bolt by a new method, the 'fermeture nut' (instead of the pivoting locking lug). This was a hollow interrupted-thread nut around the breech which was rotated backwards and forwards by the action of the piston. As the bolt closed into the breech, so the fermeture nut was rotated, and the interrupted threads closed behind lugs on the bolt to lock it securely. On firing, the movement of the piston under gas pressure first unlocked the breech by rotating the nut and then forced the bolt back to start the operating cycle again. Feed was from a thin metal strip containing 30 rounds which was inserted upside down (making feeding complicated) into the right-hand side of the gun. This model of Hotchkiss, first introduced in 1909, had been taken into French service in calibre 8mm Lebel in small numbers, and was also adopted by the American Army as the 'Bénét-Mercié Machine Rifle', from the inventors' names and the fact that that it was light and came with a shoulder stock. It now went into production in vast quantities, both in Britain and France, and became the primary armament of cavalry units.

The British infantry received the Lewis Gun – one of the immortals. This gun had been designed by an American named Samuel McLean in about 1908, but it was perfected by Captain Lewis, who also found a manufacturer and got it into production.

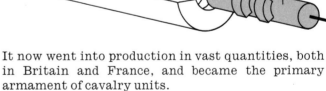

The Lewis was gas operated, using a rotating bolt similar to the Swiss Schmidt-Rubin rifle action, but had some very unusual features. The return spring, for example, was not the usual spiral spring lying along the axis of the bolt, but a clock-spring contained inside a toothed pinion, which engaged with the piston by means of a rack mechanism. This had the advantage that it could easily be regulated for strength by a key, and could in this way counteract a loss of power caused by dirt in the mechanism or could be used to regulate the rate of fire within small limits. Another innovation was the distinct-

Lewis Gun

This weapon was originally designed by Samuel N. Maclean and Lieutenant Colonel O.M. Lissak of the US Army as the 'Lissak-Maclean Rifle', but they were unable to raise any interest in the idea and eventually sold their patents to the Automatic Firearms Company of Buffalo, New York. This firm asked Colonel Isaac N. Lewis, US Army Retd, in 1910 to look at the design and see if he could turn it into a workable gun.

By 1911 Lewis had produced five pilot models which were demonstrated at Fort Myers to the Secretary for War, the Chief of Staff and other Army luminaries, after which four guns were handed over to the Board of Ordnance for testing. The Board proved reluctant to decide on the design, so Lewis took back his four guns and went to Belgium.

A new company, the Armes Automatiques Lewis, was set up and manufacture began, largely of specimens for assessment by European armies. The Birmingham Small Arms Company were interested and took out a licence to manufacture in Britain. Shortly after this, World War I broke out and the Lewis Gun entered service with the British and Belgium armies; production would be measured in hundreds of thousands.

Lewis never received much encouragement from the US Army. This was probably due to a clash between him and General William Crozier, Chief of Ordnance, an autocratic arbiter of what was right and what was wrong in military equipment. It was not until the Lewis Gun was shown to be the only possible choice as an aircraft gun that it was accepted. It was never accepted as a US ground weapon.

Since the Lewis achieved such fame as an air weapon it is noteworthy that it was first fired from an aircraft as early as 7th June 1912. It was taken up in a Wright Type B Pusher, flown by Lieutenant Milling and the gun fired by Captain Chandler. The target, a 2m (6ft) square of cloth, was fired at from an altitude of 76m (250ft) during three passes and was successfully hit.

On 22nd August 1914, two British pilots, Lieutenants Strange and Penn-Gaskell, took up a

LEWIS GUN
Calibre .303in
Length 128.2cm (50.5in)
Weight 12.24kg (27.0lb)
Barrel 66.1cm (26.04in)
Rifling 4 grooves, 1/hand
Foresight Blade
Rearsight Aperture, to 2,000yd (1,829m)
Action Gas
Rate of fire 550rpm
Feed system Drum magazines, 47 or 97 rounds
Muzzle velocity 745m/sec (2,450ft/sec)
Bullet weight 13.9g (215gr)

Lewis gun in a Henri Farman and engaged a German Albatross at some 1,520m (5,000ft) altitude without hitting it. On reporting this, they were immediately told never to do it again in case the Germans got the same idea and began firing back.

Although obsolete by 1939, there were 50,000 British Lewis guns in reserve stocks which were brought back into service when World War II broke out. In addition, Britain bought 1,157 guns in .30in calibre from the US. Many guns were issued to merchant ships, trawlers and minesweepers. They were also widely issued to the Home Guard for use as a section light machine gun.

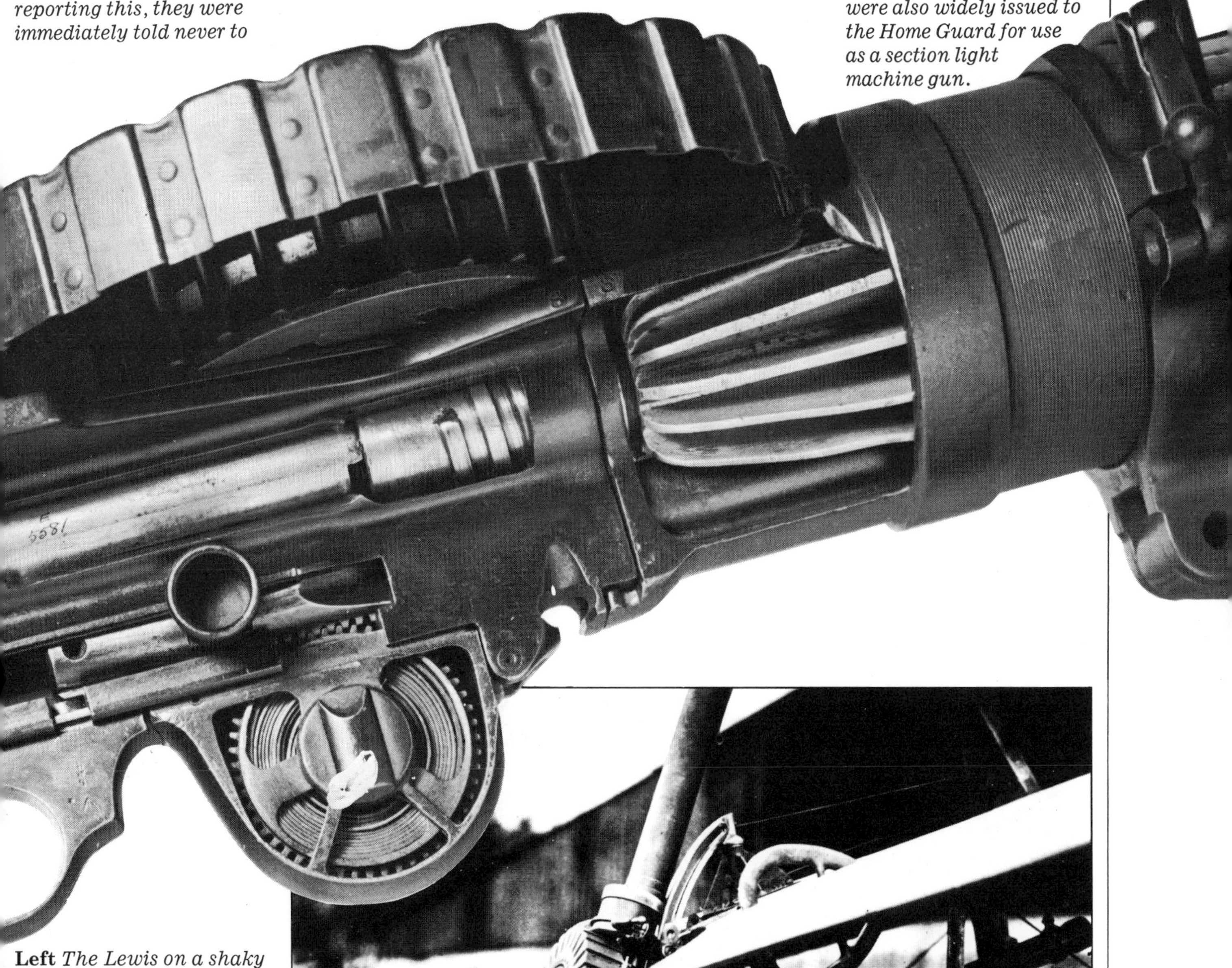

Left *The Lewis on a shaky anti-aircraft mount in 1916, with range-finder to the right.*

Above *The Lewis' breech and feed mechanism cut away. The radial fins for air-cooling the barrel are clearly seen to the right of the locked turning bolt. Beside the trigger guard is the coiled helical spring.*

Right *World War I air ace 'Billy' Bishop shows the elevation of his Nieuport's Mk 2 Lewis.*

ive method of feed – from a 47-shot drum mounted flat on top of the gun action.

Most peculiar of all was Lewis's method of cooling the gun. The barrel was surrounded by aluminium fins, parallel with the bore, and shrouded in a steel jacket, which was open at the rear but which projected a distance in front of the muzzle. According to Lewis's theory, the blast of gas at the muzzle as the gun fired set up a current of air which was induced past the gun breech, through the jacket between the fins, and out of the muzzle end, thus drawing cool air across the barrel as long as the gun was firing. This idea was accepted. But during World War II a number of Lewis Guns without this cooling system were used as infantry weapons and never over-heated; which led some people to suspect that Lewis may not have been entirely correct, and that the poor infantryman had been carrying a lot of extra weight around to little purpose. Nevertheless, the Lewis was successfully manufactured in large numbers during World War I, one reason being that six could be made in the same time as one Vickers.

When the United States entered the war in 1917 the US Army could muster 282 Maxim guns, 158 Colt-Browning M1896 machine guns, and 670 Bénét-Mercié 'rifles' – not an impressive collection for a nation about to enter the Great War. The Army's first reaction was to order 4,600 Vickers guns to be made by the Colt company, and they also bought some Lewis guns. But the Lewis was under some sort of cloud in American service, due largely to a personality clash between Lewis and his old commander, General William Crozier, who was the Chief of Ordnance and therefore had the last word on what weapons the US Army obtained. The US Marines managed to equip with Lewis guns, but the Army were never permitted to have them in any number.

Instead, when they got to France they were encumbered with the *worst* machine gun ever built – the Chauchat. This had been put together by a commission set up to provide the French Army with a light machine gun to supplement the Hotchkiss. It used the 'long-recoil' system of operation – in which all the recoiling parts, including the barrel, travel back the entire length of the cartridge – and fed from a peculiar half-moon magazine fixed under the gun. The Chauchat's list of faults is impressive: the enormous movement of the long-recoil functioning caused excessive vibration; the barrel support bearings (which the gun required for the barrel to recoil a long distance) soon wore and caused a loss of accuracy; and the complex mechanism almost guaranteed that no one ever fired a full magazine without the gun jamming at least once in the process. In spite of all this, the Americans accepted 37,000 of them, chambered for the .30-06 Springfield rifle cartridge. This was more powerful than the original 8mm French cartridge and the Chauchats almost shook themselves to pieces. It has been reliably estimated that over 50 per cent of American Chauchats were thrown away by their disgusted crews.

Above *Lt. Val A. Browning fires his father's water-cooled .30in M1917 MG.*

Below *This US corporal carries the Chauchat LMG with 20-round magazine.*

Salvation, however, was just around the corner. John Browning had been working on a new design of machine gun for some years, basing the operation on short recoil of the barrel. In this system, the barrel recoils for only a portion of the total recoil stroke before it is unlocked from the bolt and is stopped. The bolt continues to move back under its own momentum (or it may be helped, as in Browning's gun, by the action of a mechanical device known as an 'accelerator') until stopped and returned by the bolt spring. Because less time is needed before the barrel has returned to a position in which it can receive a new round, the short-recoil system can achieve a much higher rate of fire than the long-recoil system.

Browning had been unable to raise any interest in prewar days, but in February 1917 he was invited to demonstrate the gun to the Army. This was successful, but another demonstration was called for in May 1917. At this, the gun fired 20,000 rounds non-stop, and then, after a pause, another 20,000. The inspecting board were reluctant to believe that this sort of reliability could be expected from run-of-the-mill production weapons, so Browning produced another gun, loaded it, and then kept feeding it ammunition until he ran out. After firing non-stop for 48 minutes 12 seconds, and after using up 28,920 rounds, the gun stopped. Browning then had himself blindfolded and he stripped and reassembled the gun, ready to fire but for ammunition. That did the trick. Within weeks, contracts for 10,000 guns were placed.

The machine gun became the standard article in aerial combat in World War I. Allied machines began carrying Lewis guns, operated either by an observer as a 'free' gun – that is, one which could be swung from side to side, up and down, to point in any direction – or as 'fixed' guns – mounted on the upper wing of a biplane to fire forwards, so that aiming the gun became a matter of aiming the aeroplane.

The French flyer Roland Garros is credited with the idea of mounting a machine gun on top of his engine cowling, where he could aim along it, and of then fixing pieces of steel plate to his propeller so that any bullets striking the propeller were deflected and did not cut off the spinning blades. This allowed greater precision of aim and Garros was soon carving a swath through the German aircraft. But when he crashed in German territory, his secret was out.

The standard German aviation machine gun was the Parabellum, a redesigned and much-lightened Maxim gun which was air cooled. Fokker, the aircraft designer, now took this gun and developed a synchronizing mechanism which, attached to the trigger linkage, prevented the gun from firing whenever a propeller blade was in front of the muzzle. With this, the German fighters did great execution until, in their turn, they lost an aircraft behind Allied lines and their secret became known. Finally the Allies adopted the Constantinesco hydraulic synchronizer and mounted two British Vickers guns on their fighter aircraft.

On the ground, the siege gradually turned again into mobile warfare, and part of this was due to a German general, von Hutier, who had developed a technique of advancing in small parties of 'Storm Troops' instead of in the rigid lines so beloved of the traditionalists. These small squads of well-trained men could, under cover of gas and smoke bombardments, filter through the front lines, bypassing difficult positions, to cut communications and isolate the front so that it could be neutralized by the following infantry. To do this, the Storm Troops had to be more than well-trained. They had to be well-armed with something light, fast-firing and accurate at short ranges. No existing weapon filled this specification, and so von Hutier went to the German gun designers and asked them to make something entirely new.

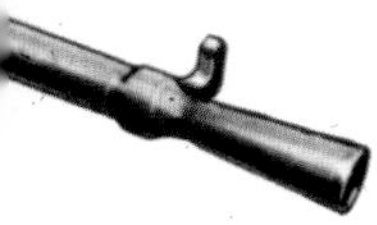

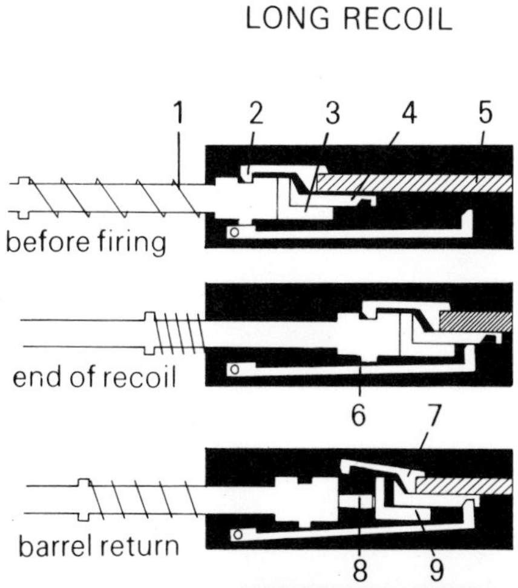

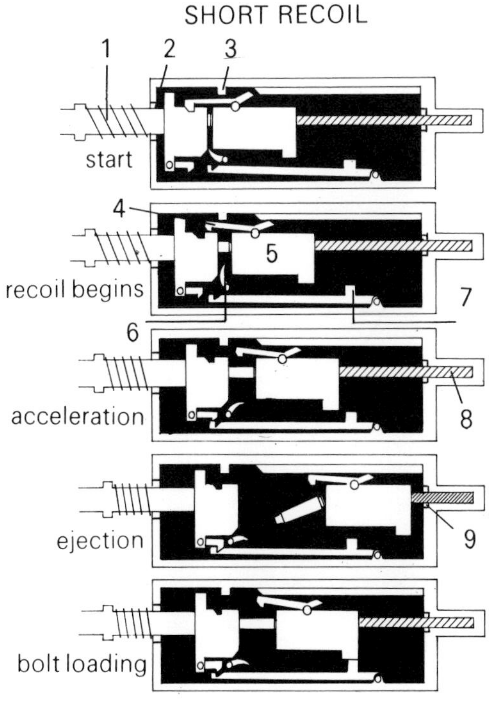

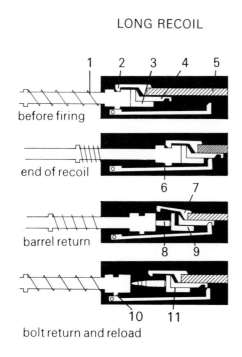

Right *Long recoil: (1) barrel spring, (2) bolt lock, (3) bolt, (4) unlocking device, (5) bolt spring, (6) bolt latch, (7) lock open, (8) spent case, (9) bolt latched, (10) latch lugs engaged, (11) bolt unlatched. Short recoil: (1) barrel spring, (2) moving barrel, (3) recoil buffers, (4) bolt lock, (5) bolt, (6) accelerator, (7) unlocking cam, (8) bolt spring, (9) backplate buffer.*

RAPID FIRE

Von Hutier's specifications for a gun – lightweight, hand-held, short-range but fast-firing (that is, automatic) – for use by his advance 'Storm Troops', fairly well sums up the definition of the submachine gun, although the name 'submachine gun' did not come into use until the 1920s. The gun has also been known variously as a machine pistol and machine carbine. The definition of a submachine gun traditionally includes the qualification that it fires pistol ammunition.

Von Hutier's needs were answered by Hugo Schmeisser, designer for the Theodor Bergmann company. The weapon Schmeisser produced in 1917 was the 'Bergmann Muskete', the world's first submachine gun. (It is ironic that the gun which Schmeisser designed was always called the Bergmann, while a gun which he did not design went into history as the 'Schmeisser', as we shall see.)

The design of the Bergmann was deceivingly simple. It consisted of only four basic parts – the barrel with its perforated casing; the body; the bolt; and the wooden stock. The barrel lay at the front of the body, and in the body ran the cylindrical bolt, controlled by a trigger below the stock. Into the side of the body, through an angled housing, went the magazine, and, in order to utilize existing production components, the magazine was the 'snail' helical magazine which had been developed for a long-barrelled version of the Parabellum Pistol 08 and which held 32 rounds of 9mm Parabellum ammunition.

On the face of it, the gun operated by simple blow back action. The bolt was pulled back by a cocking handle until it was held against the power of the recoil spring by the trigger mechanism. On pulling the trigger, the bolt flew forwards in the gun body, collected a cartridge from the magazine, chambered it, and then fired it by the firing pin which was inside the bolt. The pressure exerted on the base of the cartridge case by the exploding charge then blew the bolt back against its spring, allowing an ejector on the bolt to pull the empty cartridge case from the chamber. As the bolt reached the end of its travel, it was either held by the trigger mechanism ready for the next shot, or, if the firer kept the trigger pressed, then the recoil spring sent the bolt forwards to fire the next round.

That was the commonly accepted method of operation, but in fact there was rather more to it than that. The 9mm Parabellum was a powerful cartridge, and in order to use an unlocked breech in this blowback model, the bolt would have had to be much heavier and the recoil spring much stronger. To get round this, Schmeisser adopted an artillery design technique called 'differential recoil' and turned it into something generally called 'advanced primer ignition' or 'differential locking'. To understand this system it is necessary to know two things about the Bergmann bolt. Firstly, the firing pin, inside the bolt, is the bearing surface on which the recoil spring pushes, and the pin's shoulders, hard against the bolt, transfer the thrust. This means that the firing pin is always protruding from the front of the bolt. Secondly, the extractor claw, which snaps over the cartridge rim, is a strong and broad item, stiffly sprung. Now consider the operation again.

When the bolt picks up the new cartridge from the magazine and forces it into the mouth of the chamber, as the cartridge lines up with the barrel it is the *extractor* which is actually pushing it, thus keeping the base of the cartridge clear of the face of

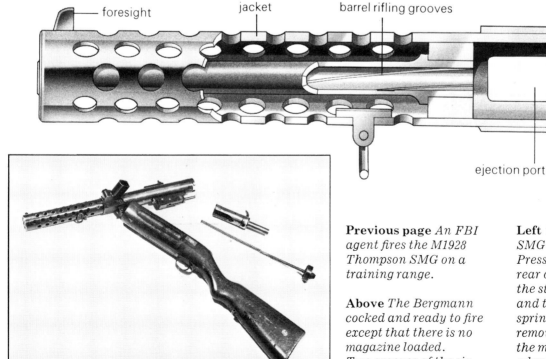

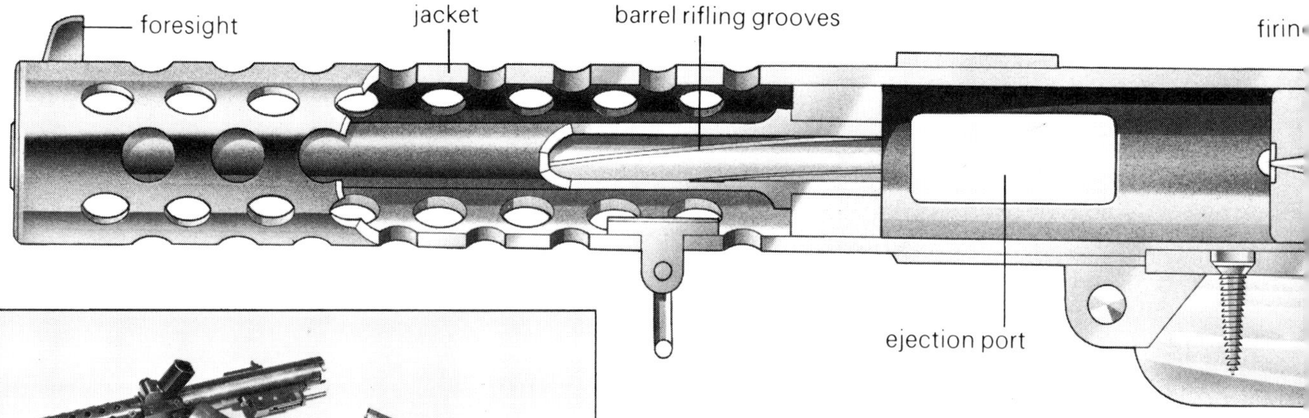

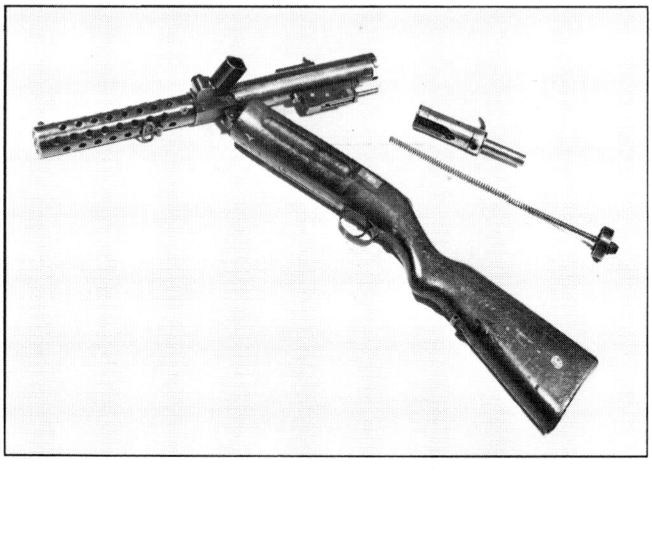

Previous page *An FBI agent fires the M1928 Thompson SMG on a training range.*

Above *The Bergmann cocked and ready to fire except that there is no magazine loaded. Two grooves of the six-groove rifling can be seen.*

Left *The Bergmann M1918 SMG disassembled. Pressing a catch at the rear of the body allowed the stock to be folded and the main operating spring with bolt to be removed. Not shown are the magazine and its adapter-sleeve (to prevent it fouling the bolt).*

the bolt – and of the firing pin. As the cartridge enters the chamber its progress is checked by friction, and at a certain point this is enough to overcome the spring pressure of the extractor claw, which then rides up and snaps over the rim of the cartridge and into the extractor groove. As this happens, so the bolt snaps forwards, the firing pin hits the cap on the cartridge, and the cartridge is fired. At that instant the bolt, which weighs over 680g (1.5lb), *is still moving forwards* and the recoil blow on the cartridge case has first to stop that forward movement, then reverse it to drive the bolt back. It is this absorption of the forward movement which makes the operation possible without excessive weight or length, because this uses up a high proportion of the recoil force which would otherwise be blowing the bolt back at high speed.

The Bergmann Muskete was issued in the summer of 1918, being officially known as the Maschinenpistole 18 or 'MP18'. Plans were afoot to provide all officers, NCOs and 10 per cent of the soldiers in infantry battalions with the weapon, but it came too late and only about 36,000 were ever made. They were issued to von Hutier's Storm Troops, who used them very successfully in one or two actions, but by that time the odds were against the Germans and the submachine gun failed to make much impression.

At much the same late stage of World War I, the Italian Army had discovered the submachine gun by accident. Most of their activity during the war took place on the mountainous border with Austria, and the mountain troops had requested a machine gun a good deal lighter and more handy than the usual Maxim pattern. A suitable weapon was designed in 1915 by Bethel Revelli, who had also designed a full-sized machine gun for the Army, and it was built by the Officine Vilar Perosa, from which it took the name of 'VP' or Vilar Perosa. This fired a 9mm bullet, using either the Italian service 9mm Glisenti cartridge or the 9mm Parabellum; both are the same in dimensions though differing in power.

The mechanism was on a different principle to that of the Bergmann, for the VP used delayed blowback. The bolt, travelling back and forth in the gun body, has a lug on it which engages in a groove in the body. This groove is curved at the forward end, so that as the bolt reaches the breech, so it is turned by the action of the groove on the lug. But note that the bolt is not actually locked to the breech. The firing pin, floating in the bolt and propelled by the recoil spring in the same way as that of the Bergmann, also has a lug which rides in the same groove. But due to being positioned further back than the bolt lug, it moves only in the straight section of the groove and simply ensures that the firing pin cannot rotate when the bolt does. The face of the striker had a shaped cam which mated with a cutaway portion inside the bolt, so that only if the bolt was rotated through about 45° at the end of the closing stroke could the firing pin be pushed forwards by the spring to hit the cartridge cap. On firing, the recoil force on the bolt had to overcome the friction of the lug in the groove and thus turn the bolt back through 45° before it could move straight back. At the same time, the mating faces of the cam and bolt ensured that the firing pin was withdrawn inside the bolt before recoil began. The net result was, firstly, that the blowback action was slightly delayed, allowing breech pressure to drop before the breech was opened, and, secondly, that the gun could not possibly be fired unless the breech was properly closed.

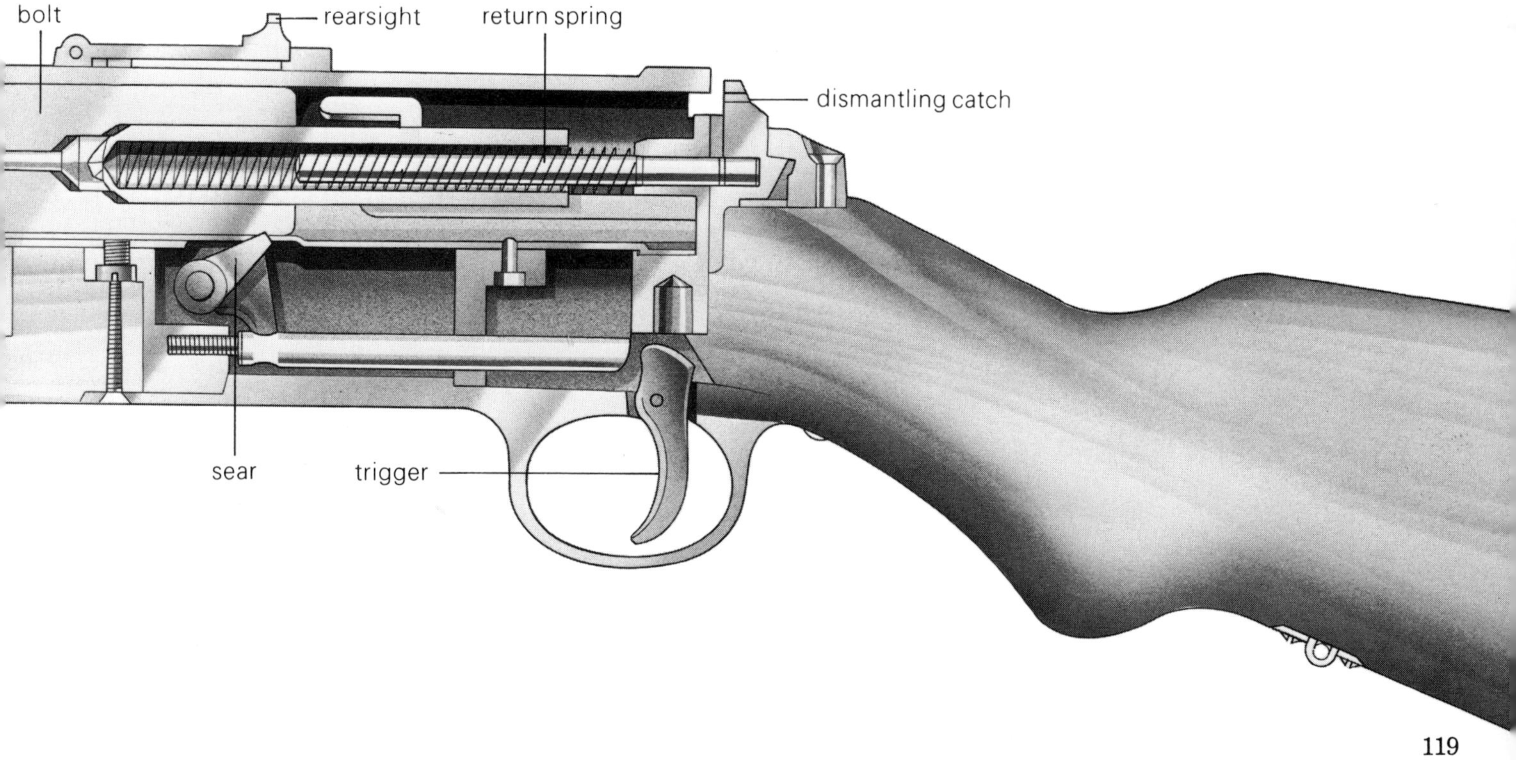

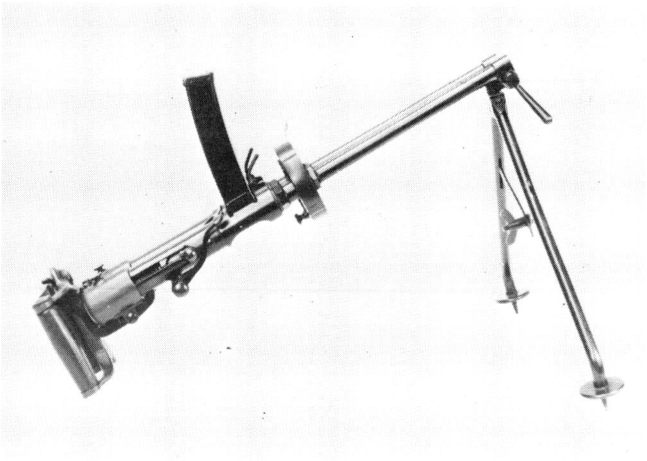

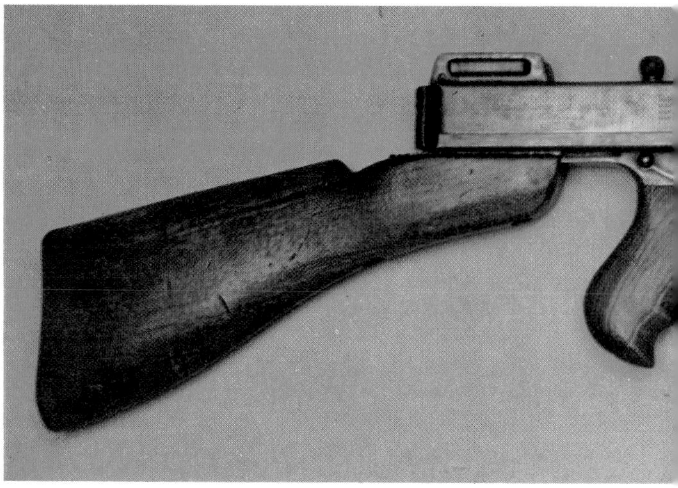

This was a sound mechanism but Revelli then put it into a somewhat peculiar weapon. The gun itself was a simple straight-line affair of body and barrel, feeding from a top-mounted magazine, but Revelli anchored two guns together side by side, controlling them by a common spade grip at the rear end which carried two thumb-triggers. It was then mounted into a steel shield for use in defensive positions or it could be fitted to a tray-like board suspended around a soldier's neck, who then marched into action with the gun in front of him like a match-seller's tray.

Needless to say, because it used pistol ammunition, the VP was not very effective in the light machine gun role since its range was nothing worth speaking of and its rate of fire was astronomical. Due to light bolts and strong recoil springs, 3,000 rounds a minute from the twin gun was commonplace. After trying it for some months, the Italian Army asked the Beretta company to have a look at it and see if they could turn it into something more useful. The task was given to a young engineer named Tullio Marengoni, who was later to become Beretta's principal designer. Marengoni split the VP in half and put the single guns so obtained on to wooden stocks resembling rifles. He added a trigger mechanism and a folding bayonet and arrived at the Beretta Model 1918 submachine gun, a far more practical weapon than the VP had ever been. The Italian Army was so impressed that it withdrew almost all the VPs and sent them to Beretta to be converted.

When World War I ended, the submachine gun was almost ignored. The Allied Disarmament Commission did not consider them to be military weapons at all and forbade the German Army to own them, though it permitted the German police forces to possess a few. The great problem was that of fitting such a weapon into the military vocabulary. It was not a rifle, and infantry always carried rifles, so it was no use to them. It was not a machine gun, because it did not have the range, so it could not be used in that role. The best thing to do, it seemed, would be to ignore it and hope it would go away.

But it was not going to go away, and this was to be due largely to one man, Brigadier-General John T. Thompson. Thompson had been an officer in the US Ordnance Department responsible for small arms design and development until he retired in 1914. He then set about designing an automatic rifle. He considered that recoil operation would mean too heavy a weapon and gas operation too complex, and he was convinced that he ought to be able to design a blowback weapon. Unfortunately he was aiming at a military rifle, and the cartridges were far too powerful for blowback functioning.

In 1915 a Commander Blish, a retired US Navy officer, patented a delayed blowback system which Thompson thought would solve his problem. The Blish system used a floating 'H-Piece' which slid up and down an oblique groove in the bolt and locked into a similar oblique groove in the body of the gun when the bolt was closed. The sudden pressure on the bolt following the firing of the cartridge caused this H-Piece to jam solidly in the two grooves due to friction and pressure, but as the pressure dropped after the bullet had left the barrel, the friction was eased and the bolt was free to move back, its oblique groove lifting the H-Piece from its locking groove in the gun body. The whole process, therefore, depended upon a very fine balance of friction and pressure.

Thompson, with Blish and a financial backer, formed the 'Auto-Ordnance Corporation' in 1916 with a view to developing a rifle. One Mr Eickhoff was engaged as engineer and in 1917, when Thompson was recalled to military service, Eickhoff continued to work on the rifle, assisted by a colleague, Oscar W. Payne. Between them, they soon found that the

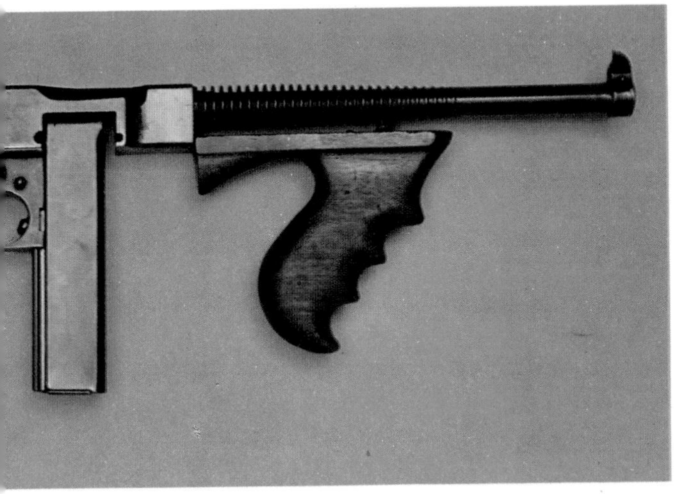

Far left *The twin-barrel Vilar Perosa (top) was the first SMG in the world. It weighed a hefty 6.52kg (14.375lb) unloaded. This model is on the normal bipod mount with two 25-round curved box magazines. The VP's successor was the M1918 Beretta (bottom) which had the same barrel, retarded blowback action and magazine, but weighed only 3.26kg (7.2lb) unloaded.*

Left *The M1921A1 Thompson with a 20-round box magazine and without the Cutts Compensator on the muzzle (see artwork overleaf). Two seconds automatic fire would exhaust a magazine.*

Below *The Cutts Compensator's four vertical slots diverted muzzle blast gases upwards after the bullet's passage. This helped counteract the muzzle's tendency to lift.*

Blish lock would not function with a high-powered rifle cartridge, but that it could be made to work quite well with the US Army's .45in pistol round. Thompson therefore changed the concept of the weapon from an automatic rifle to a hand-held machine gun which he called the 'Trench Broom' because it would sweep the trenches clear of enemies. Work continued but the end of the war came before the weapon was perfected.

After the war Thompson, retired again, began promoting the sale of his new 'Submachine Gun' – a descriptive phrase which he invented and which has since passed into common use. Sales were poor, because it was a complex and expensive gun to make, but Thompson had the Colt Company build sufficient components to make up 15,000 guns. What undoubtedly saved the 'Tommy gun' from an early demise was the publicity which it attracted from its use by the gangs and gang-busters during the Prohibition era in America in the 1920s and the subsequent portrayal on the films. Yet, equally certainly, it was this gangster image which bedevilled the chances of military acceptance for a long time.

The first military adoption of the Thompson was by the US Marines, who used it in Nicaragua in 1927, and as a result of their favourable reports, a 1928 or 'Navy' model was produced. This featured a 'Cutts Compensator' on the muzzle, a device which directed a proportion of the muzzle blast upwards, thus tending to force down the muzzle during automatic fire and counteract the tendency for the muzzle to rise. This 1928 model also had a straight wooden fore-end instead of the familiar pistol grip of the original 1921 version.

The early Thompson guns showed up in some odd places, and one of those was the Baltic States, who were having various civil commotions in the 1920s. Whether this drew attention to the submachine gun idea is not certain, but the next design to come forward was from Finland. The noted Finnish designer Aimo Lahti began experimenting with submachine gun designs in the early 1920s and eventually produced one for sale in 1926. This was in 7.65mm Parabellum calibre – an odd one for a submachine gun – and it featured some interesting design ideas. The barrel could be quickly removed by

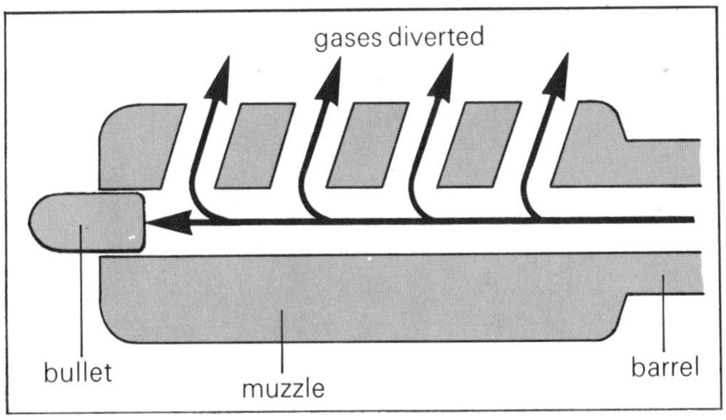

operating a locking clamp; the bolt was cocked by a retracting rod with an operating knob at the rear of the gun body; the 36-round box magazine was a peculiar semi-circular device which protruded forwards below the barrel; and the bolt was a two-piece construction with separate firing pin, though this was later removed and a fixed firing pin in the front end of the bolt was substituted.

It was a remarkably good weapon for its day, but it could stand improvement and Lahti worked on it for a few years. He eventually produced his Model 1931 which was adopted in large numbers by the Finnish Army and then made available commercially as the 'Suomi 1931'. It was used by the Swedish, Norwegian and Swiss Armies and sufficient numbers were sold to other countries for the Suomi to take part in almost every major conflict for many years.

The 1931 improved on the earlier model in several ways. The peculiar semi-circular box magazine was dropped in favour of a 71-round drum below the barrel; the weapon was chambered for the 9mm Parabellum cartridge; the firing pin was fixed and the operation became the same as that of the Bergmann; and the somewhat fiddly retracting knob was replaced by a handle resembling a rifle bolt. The barrel was surrounded by a perforated jacket to allow it to be gripped without burning the hand, and a muzzle compensator, doubtless based on the Cutts device, was frequently fitted. But like all successful gunmakers, Lahti was quite ready to bend his design to suit the wishes of individual customers, and so Suomis with bipods, with remov-

The 'Thompson' submachine gun commemorates Brigadier General John Taliaferro Thompson (1860-1940) though the actual design is due to Theodor Eickhoff and Oscar W. Payne, while the breech-locking system was devised by Commander John B. Blish, US Navy.

The original model, called the 'Persuader', was belt fed. But the rate of fire was too great for the feed system and it was re-designed as the Annihilator', using a box magazine. The final version, which appeared in 1919, was called the 'Submachine Gun' and featured the 50-round drum magazine that came to be associated with the Thompson. It was first demonstrated during the National Match shooting contest at Camp Perry, Ohio, in 1920.

Thompson's Auto-Ordnance Corporation had no manufacturing facilities, so he had the components for 15,000 guns made by Colt's Patent Firearms Company. The first batch were delivered in March 1921 and Thompson's son, Marcellus, sold 495 to American agents of the Irish Republican Army, a fact discovered when the Department of Justice raided a ship in New York Harbor and found the guns. The subsequent publicity was unpleasant, but certainly brought the Thompson to public notice.

On 4th October 1925 the Sallis-MacErlane gang of Chicago attempted to kill Spike O'Donnell, a business rival, by spraying his HQ with a Thompson fired from a speeding car. The 'Tommy Gun' was born. In 1926 Al Capone bought a Thompson, killed three men with it, filed off the serial number and threw the gun away. Unfortunately for him, there was a second, secret serial number on the gun, by means of which the purchase was traced back to him, leading to his eventual imprisonment.

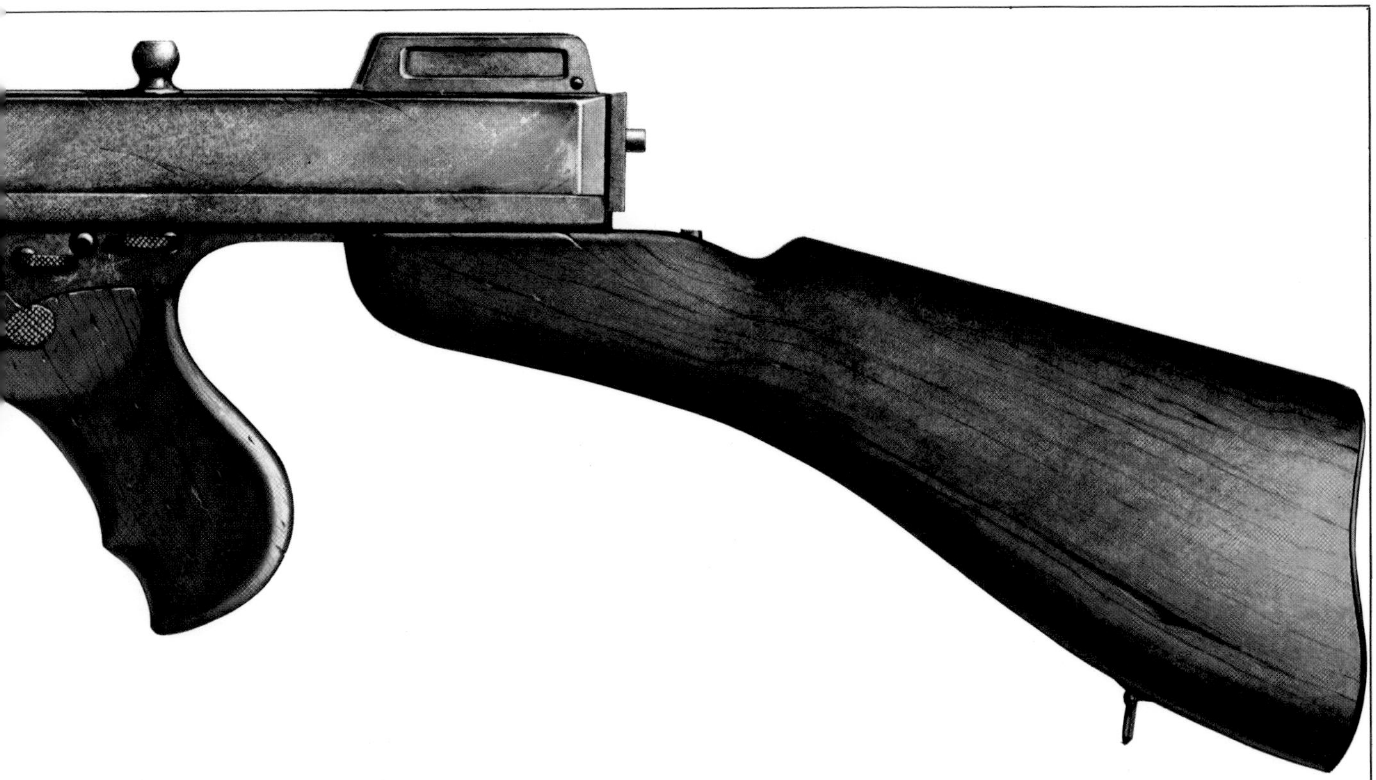

In 1927 the US Marines took Thompsons to Nicaragua and Shanghai for the weapon's first military use. But in 1930 the Thompson family was bought out by Thomas Ryan, its financial backer. In 1938 he sold what was left of the company to Russel Maguire. Maguire's hunch that a European war would lead to a demand for Thompson guns came true in 1939. In November the French Army ordered 6,000, then the British Army ordered 107,500 and the US Army 20,450. Colt refused to make them, having been less than pleased with the 'gangster' publicity, so the Savage Arms Company obtained the contract. Eventually 1.75 million, plus enough spare parts to make another 250,000, were made during the war including a simplified version which did away with the controversial Blish lock.

After the war the company changed hands twice more, but the Thompson is still available today. John T. Thompson died of a heart attack in June 1940 just as his dream was being fulfilled.

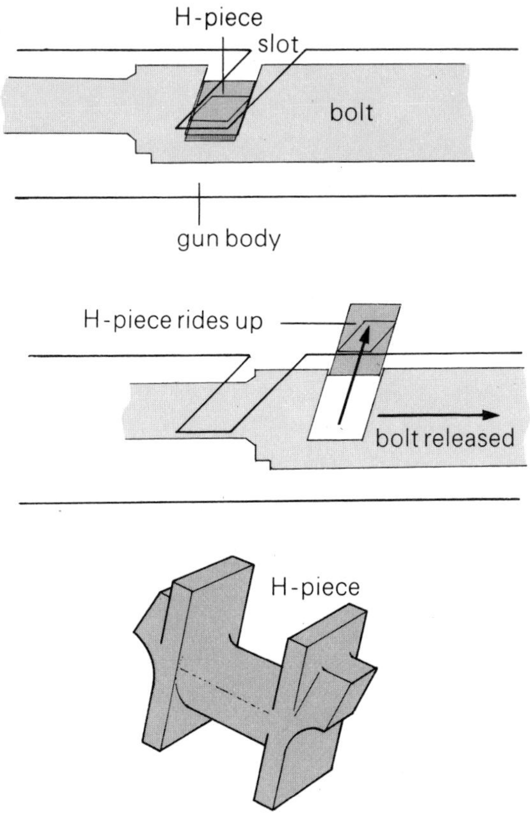

Far left *Winston Churchill poses with the M1928A1 Thompson in 1940. This one has the vertical pistol fore-grip and Cutts Compensator.*

Above *A side-view of the famous M1928A1 Thompson with horizontal fore-grip (optional sling swivel attached), Cutts Compensator and 50-round drum magazine. The single-shot and safety catches can be seen just to the right and above the trigger guard.*

Left *How the Blish delay device worked in the Thompson. The phosphor bronze H-shaped piece locked the gunbody to the bolt until falling gas pressure released the bolt to full recoil.*

THOMPSON M1928A1
Calibre .45in
Length 85.7cm (33.75in)
Weight 4.88kg (10.75lb)
Barrel 266mm (10.5in)
Rifling 6 grooves, r/hand
Foresight Blade
Rearsight Aperture, to 600yd (548m)
Action Blowback
Rate of fire 700rpm
Feed system 20 or 30-round box magazine, or 50 or 100-round drum magazine
Muzzle velocity 282m/sec (920ft/sec)
Bullet weight 14.88g (230gr)

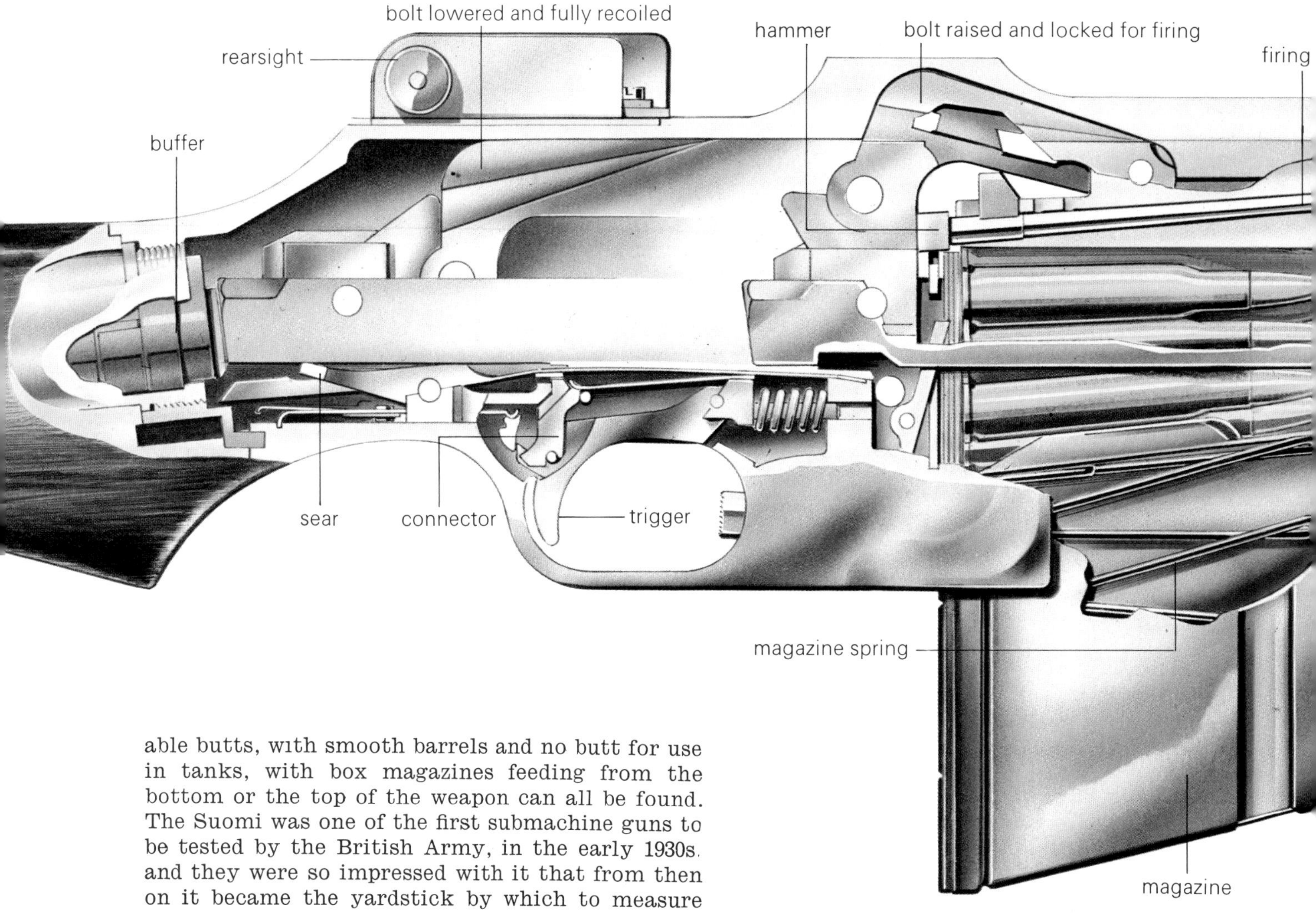

able butts, with smooth barrels and no butt for use in tanks, with box magazines feeding from the bottom or the top of the weapon can all be found. The Suomi was one of the first submachine guns to be tested by the British Army, in the early 1930s, and they were so impressed with it that from then on it became the yardstick by which to measure others – and very few ever managed to combine the Suomi's mechanical reliability, accuracy, and economy in one package.

Shortly before the Suomi appeared, a submachine gun was placed on the market in Switzerland – the Steyr-Solothurn S1-100. This weapon had a peculiar history which demonstrates the shifts to which German armament manufacturers were prepared to go in those days. The weapon was originally designed in 1920 by a German named Louis Stange, for the Rheinische Metallwaaren und Maschinenfabrik of Düsseldorf, who are better known by the name they later adopted, Rheinmetall. Due to the restrictions imposed by the Versailles Treaty, Rheinmetall could not produce the gun in Germany. They therefore acquired a large holding in the Austrian Weapons Company at Steyr and also bought a moribund Swiss engineering company, Solothurn AG. In effect Rheinmetall in Germany now became the design office, Solothurn AG became the development engineers, and Waffenfabrik Steyr the production factory, with a fourth subsidiary, Steyr-Solothurn Waffen AG of Zurich being the market outlet. In this way tracks were effectively covered. So effectively, in fact, that it was not until after World War II that the connection was unravelled, explaining why several German army weapons appeared to be of Swiss origin.

The Steyr-Solothurn submachine gun was very much in the same style as the original Bergmann – a wooden-stocked weapon with perforated barrel jacket – except that the recoil spring was contained in a tube running down inside the butt. It was exceptionally well-made and finished and has, in the past, been called the 'Rolls Royce' of submachine guns. One minor but interesting detail was the provision of a magazine loader in the magazine housing; several of these guns were chambered for 7.63mm Mauser cartridge, which was always supplied in 10-round clips for use in the pistol. To get the rounds out of the clip and into the submachine gun's box magazine could have been an awkward job, but for the magazine loader. The empty magazine was clipped under the side-entry magazine housing; above it, through the magazine housing, was a slot into which the clip was placed, after which a sweep of the thumb pushed the cartridges out of the clip and into the magazine. Three quick moves like that and the magazine was full.

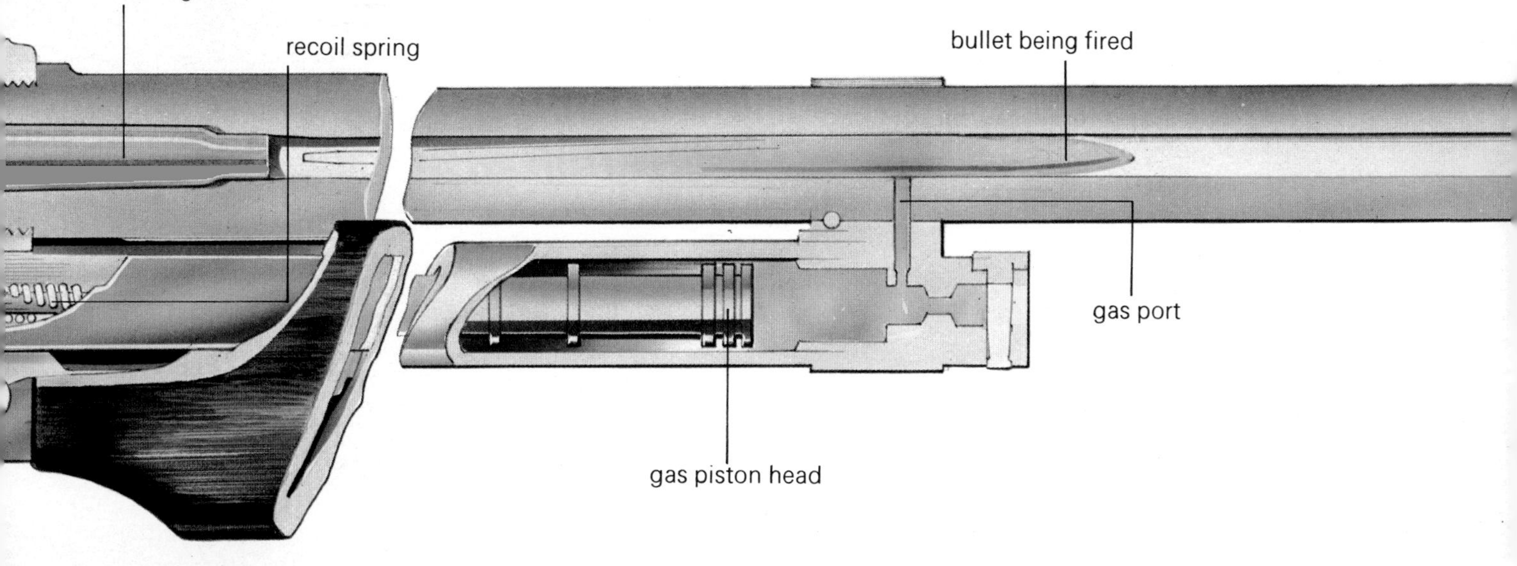

Top *'Phantom' drawing of the Browning Automatic Rifle's mechanism in two positions: breech closed and locked; and breech open and fully recoiled. In the forward position the breech-block has been lifted to fit a recess in the top of the gun body. On recoil, the gas piston rod lowers the bolt to unlock it and drives it back to extract the empty case. The buffer in the butt halts the bolt and a spring concealed in the buffer throws the bolt back to load a fresh round.*

Above *A World War I period US soldier aims the Browning Automatic Rifle M1918. It could fire single shots or bursts. As it weighed 7.28kg (16lb), a bipod was added to the next model, the 1918A1. Sights were graduated to 1,500yd (1,372m).*

The Steyr-Solothurn was widely used by the German Army during World War II. The Austrian Army adopted the gun as their 'MP34', having it chambered for the 9mm Mauser 'Export' cartridge – probably the most powerful round ever used in a submachine gun. South America and China bought it in 7.63mm Mauser and 9mm Parabellum chambering, while the Portuguese Army bought it in 7.65mm Parabellum; they were later to buy the last batch ever made, in 1942, these being 9mm calibre.

It will be recalled that General Thompson had been trying to perfect an automatic rifle but changed his direction and developed the submachine gun instead. Once he had the submachine gun under way, he turned once again to the automatic rifle, since he and many others were convinced by what they had seen during World War I that an automatic rifle was a necessity as a military arm.

At the same time as Browning had demonstrated his machine gun in 1917, he also displayed another weapon, which he called his 'Automatic Rifle'. This was operated by a gas piston which ran under the barrel and actuated the bolt. The bolt was locked on firing by means of tipping up its rear edge to jam firmly against a face inside the top of the gun body. Feed was from a removeable box magazine which fitted under the gun, and a small bipod was provided to allow it to be fired from the prone position. It was, in fact, a light machine gun, but it had been produced in answer to a tactical theory which called for 'walking fire' – troops carrying light automatics and firing from the hip as they advanced across 'No Man's Land' – and thus it came to be called the

Browning Automatic Rifle, or 'BAR' for short. But designing weapons and having them accepted was one side of the story; producing them was another. Few machine guns or automatic rifles were actually in the hands of the US Army by the time the war ended, though production was to continue after the war and Browning had in fact designed what was to become the standard automatic weapon of the American forces for many years.

Ever since the introduction of repeating rifles, inventors had tried to perfect an 'automatic' or 'semi-automatic' rifle, the difference being that an *automatic* rifle fired like a machine gun, so long as the trigger was pressed, while a *semi-automatic* or *self-loader* fired a single shot for each pressure of the trigger. The advantage claimed was that with either of these weapons the soldier would have nothing to do, once he had loaded it, but lay the sights on the target and press the trigger. However, limited experience with the earliest models soon showed that to fire a full-automatic rifle with the heavy service cartridges of the day was out of the question, since the arm leapt and bucked all over the place. So the semi-automatic came into vogue, though still called an 'automatic' to distinguish it from the conventional hand-operated weapon. After the advent of the BAR, though, the distinction was necessary between full and semi-automatic weapons.

Semi-automatic rifles had been marketed for several years as civilian arms. The Winchester company, for example, marketed a thoroughly serviceable weapon in 1905 in two calibres – .32in and .35in – while the Remington company produced a .35in model in the following year, a gun designed by John Browning. Similarly, German, Belgian and French gunmakers made sporting semi-automatic rifles, but every one was a simple blowback using a fairly low-power cartridge. Indeed, many of them had special rounds designed for them in order to obtain the best possible ballistics within the limitations of the blowback system. But when military authorities expressed any interest in automatic rifles, they invariably did so by issuing a list of 'desirable features', and heading the list was always the demand that the breech had to be securely locked at the moment of discharge and not unlocked until the chamber pressure dropped to a safe level.

The first automatic rifle to gain service acceptance was a Danish design, adopted in limited quantities by the Danish Navy in the 1880s. It was not a success, however. The mechanism, suitably reworked, went on to become the Madsen machine gun. Then came the Italian Cei-Rigotti, using a gas piston to operate a normal type of bolt-action. But the first automatic rifle to gain wider acceptance came, strangely, from Mexico, not usually thought of as being a source of firearms designs. There General Manuel Mondragon invented a gas-operated rifle which was adopted in 7mm calibre with an 8-round box magazine by the Mexican Army in 1908. The lack of manufacturing facilities in Mexico meant that it had to be made elsewhere – in Switzerland – and a number were bought from the Swiss by the German Army in

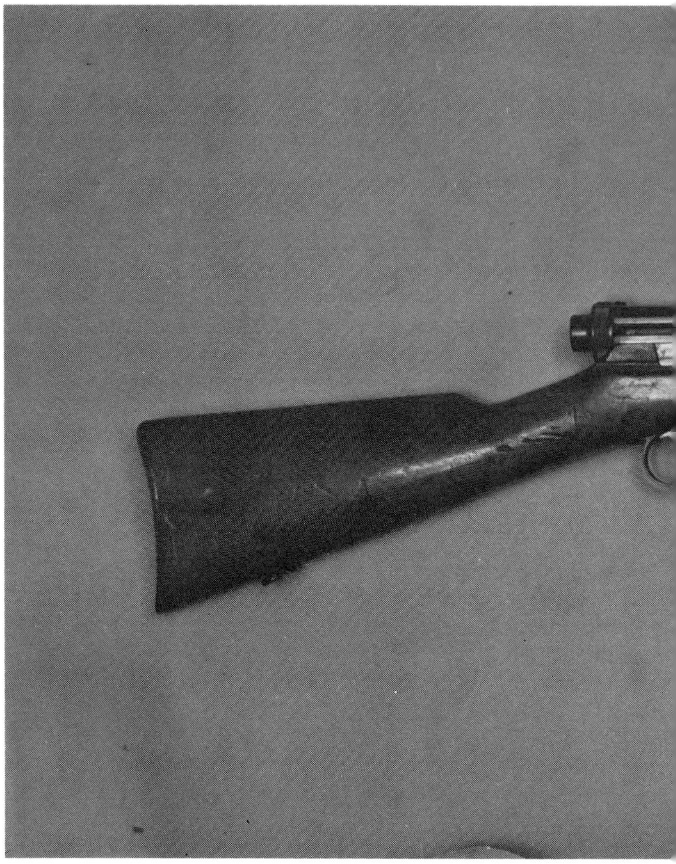

Top *The Mondragon Automatic Rifle of 1903 with German magazine. The gas operation could be shut off and the bolt worked manually.*

Above *Breech detail.*

1915. The Germans soon found that the mechanism was too delicate to stand up to the testing conditions of the mud-logged Western Front and most of the rifles, fitted with a special 30-shot drum magazine, were issued to aviators. The German experience with automatic rifles on the ground seems to have confirmed everyone's worst suspicions about the things, and little more was heard of the idea during the war years. The only other design to come forward, also in 1915, was a Mauser, but this too was relegated to use by the German air forces after some

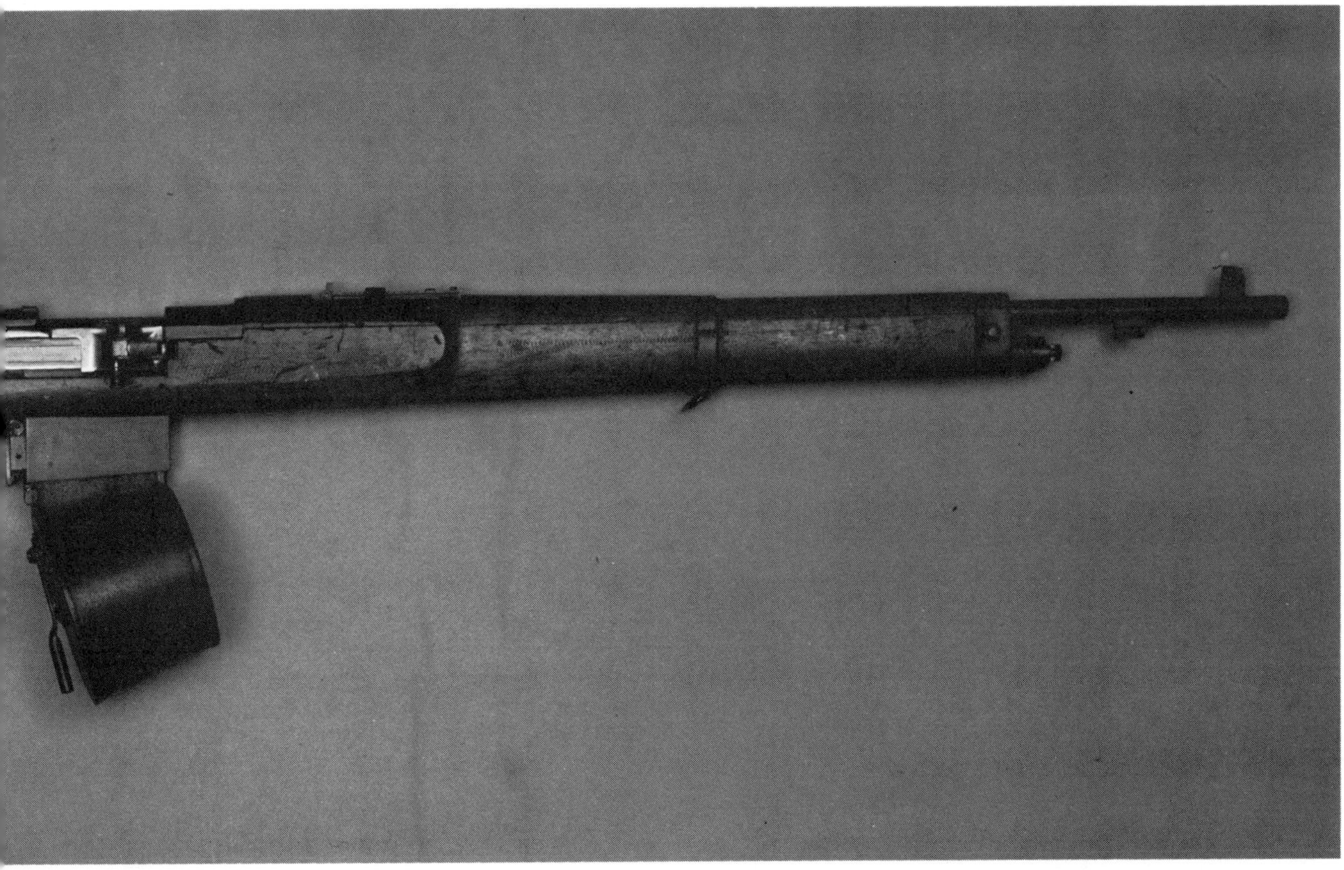

trials in the trenches.

World War I had seen more attempts at building an acceptable semi-automatic rifle after the Mondragon and Mauser failures. In Russia a designer named Vasiliy Federov had begun working on a design as early as 1908; by 1916 it was good enough to be ordered into production and was used at the front. Only the wretched supply and manufacturing situation in Russia at that time prevented the Federov 'Automat' from going into major production and service. One of the most unusual things about the Federov was that it was not designed for the standard Russian cartridge. This was a fat, rimmed-case, 7.62mm round which was an awkward shape for automatic feeding, and often of inconsistent manufacture. After the Russo-Japanese War, on the other hand, the Russian Army, which had captured stocks of Japanese 6.5mm rifles and ammunition, did some design exercises based on the Japanese Meiji cartridge, probably for no more than interest's sake. Federov designed his rifle around this smaller round, accepting the lower power in exchange for the lesser stress and lighter weapon which resulted. It is quite remarkable that an Army generally considered to be ultra-conservative – not to say hide-bound – was willing to accept a weapon which demanded its own special ammunition, and it says a great deal for Federov's design that it was good enough to overcome this objection.

The French also fielded a semi-automatic rifle, known as the St. Étienne (from its place of manufacture) or 'RSC' (from the initials of the designers, Ribeyrolle, Sutter and Chauchat — yes, the same Chauchat who helped to design the ill-fated Chauchat machine gun). It was a poor design, long, heavy and badly-balanced and its 8mm Lebel cartridges had to be loaded into a special 5-round clip to suit the feed system of this gas-operated rifle. The designers persisted with it, producing a shorter, lighter model in 1918, but no amount of tinkering could improve what was basically a bad weapon and eventually, in the 1930s, they were converted to manual, straight-pull bolt operation and given to French colonial troops.

There was, therefore, a fair amount of knowledge in the 1920s about semi-automatic rifles and how they could be expected to stand up to combat, though it is doubtful if anyone in the West knew of the Federov. As a result, the late 1920s saw a number of semi-automatic rifle designs put forward, notably in the United States and Britain. One of the first was the Farquhar-Hill, which had first appeared in Britain before 1914 as a recoil-operated rifle and was then changed to gas operation. It was tried several times by the British Army but was never accepted. At first the grounds were its admitted early stage of development and consequent unreliability, but later there was a hardening of military arteries against semi-automatic rifles in general and it is also believed that there was a personality clash between the inventors and the authorities. Whatever the reason, the Farquhar-Hill rifle, although continuously developed until 1930 to a very sound weapon, never got any further.

Another contestant, tried in both the US and Britain, was the aptly-named 'Bang' rifle, invented

by Soren H. Bang, a Dane. This rifle used an idea first patented by Maxim in the 1880s but then abandoned as impractical, the idea of trapping the escaping gas at the muzzle, behind the bullet, and using it to operate the mechanism. A cone surrounded the muzzle and this caught the blast and was thus pulled forwards. By suitable linkage, a rod connected to this cone unlocked and retracted the breech-block, the usual spring being used to complete the return action. One minor advantage of the Bang rifle was that since the bullet had left the barrel before the gas could impinge on the muzzle trap, the breech opening was always delayed until breech pressure had dropped. But apart from that there was little to commend the Bang rifles. They were expensive to make, easily deranged, and prone to overheating, and no one ever adopted them.

One design which very nearly made it was the American Pedersen. John Pedersen was a designer who had worked with the Remington company until the war, when he had gone to the government's Springfield Arsenal. There he perfected a self-loading rifle which used a toggle-joint lock, similar to that on the Parabellum pistol, but which was designed to act as a delayed blowback mechanism. It required careful design of the various cam surfaces in the toggle to obtain a slow initial movement so that the chamber pressure could drop before the breech began to open, followed by a rapid actuation to extract the case and reload. Unfortunately, this meant that the extraction movement actually began while the cartridge case was still tightly expanded against the chamber walls, and this friction led to cartridge cases being torn in half. The only solution to this sort of problem was to lubricate the cases, and Pedersen developed a dry-wax coating applied during manufacture which made the rifle work very well. But lubricated cases are not popular with military authorities. They tend to gather dust and carry it into the rifle chamber which actually makes things worse. So the Pedersen rifle was turned down.

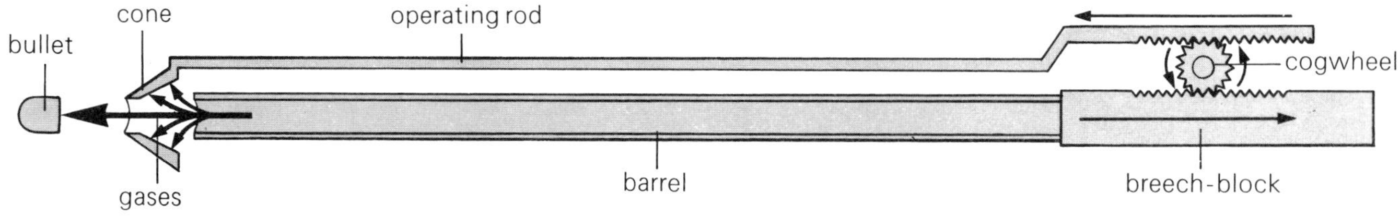

A schematic diagram of the muzzle cone actuation system used on the Bang Rifle and Walther M1941 German semi-automatic rifle. A cone surrounding the muzzle traps some of the emergent gases. This blows the cone forwards and this movement is transferred, by an operating rod, to the breech-block which is driven back to open the breech. Springs return the cone and breech-block.

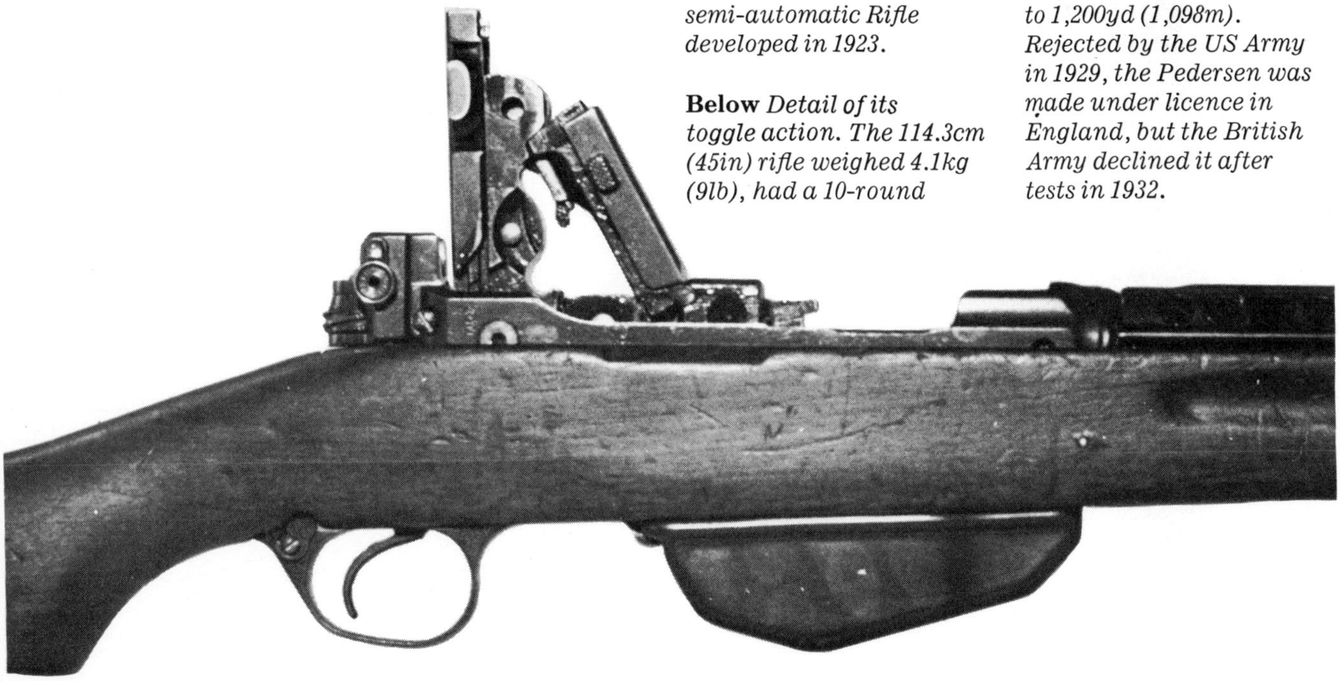

Above *The .276 Pedersen semi-automatic Rifle developed in 1923.*

Below *Detail of its toggle action. The 114.3cm (45in) rifle weighed 4.1kg (9lb), had a 10-round magazine, and was sighted to 1,200yd (1,098m). Rejected by the US Army in 1929, the Pedersen was made under licence in England, but the British Army declined it after tests in 1932.*

At the same time, and in the same arsenal, another American designer had produced a gas-operated semi-automatic rifle which fired the same .276in cartridge as the Pedersen, though without requiring it to be lubricated. John Garand had first developed, in about 1920, a primer-actuated rifle in which the set-back of the primer unlocked the bolt, after which blow-back action completed the loading cycle. He offered the design to the US Navy who examined it, considered it to be impractical and turned it down, but offered Garand a post on the design staff at Springfield which he accepted. There he continued working on his rifle, changing the operation to a gas piston, and eventually, in competitive tests held in 1929, the Garand was selected to be the future US Army service rifle.

The Chief of Staff at that time was General Douglas MacArthur and he, while approving of the rifle, was not in favour of the .276in cartridge. MacArthur based his decision not on any ballistic grounds, but on the purely logistic viewpoint that the Army had stocks of several million rounds of the existing cartridge plus the machinery for making several millions more, and that, with finance so short, it would be folly to change cartridges. He therefore ruled that the Garand had to accept the standard .30in calibre cartridge, and the rifle had to be re-designed. It was finally ready in 1932 and was standardized as the 'Rifle .30 M1', but due to the prevailing financial climate, production did not begin until 1936. Even with this delay, the American Army became the first army in the world to adopt a semi-automatic rifle as the standard arm of her infantryman.

Springfield Model 1903 Rifle

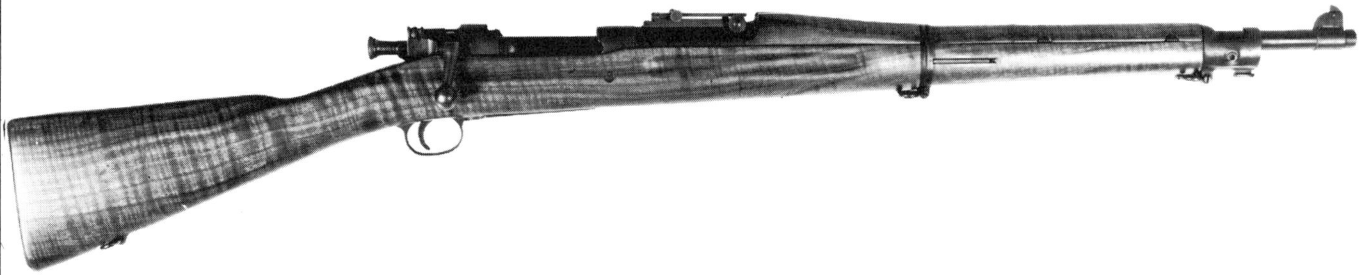

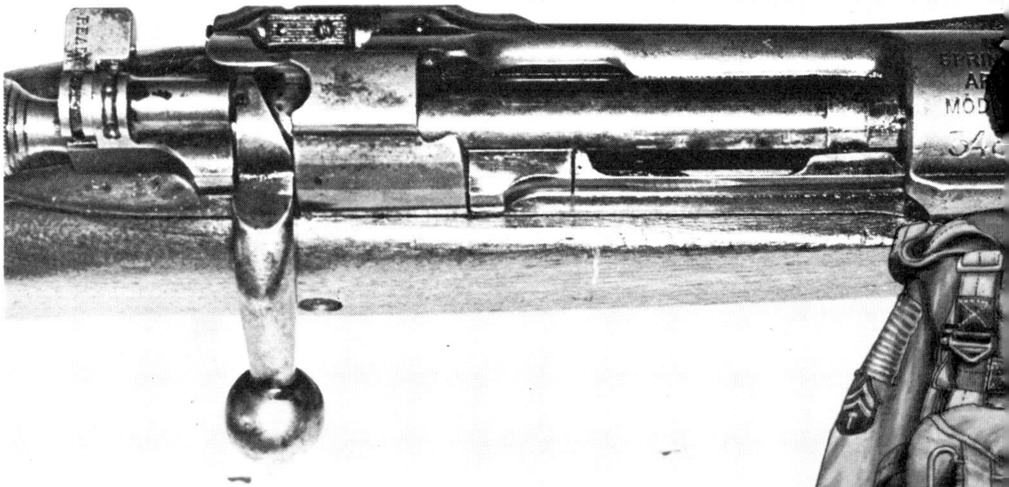

Above *The Springfield's breech closed. The rear sight is graduated to 2,700yd (2,469m).*

In 1892, after examining no fewer than 53 patterns of breech-loading rifle, the US Ordnance Department standardized the Krag-Jorgensen as the US Army's new rifle. It was a poor and inexplicable choice, and in 1898 the Spanish-American War ruthlessly exposed the Krag's deficencies when it came up against the latest Mauser rifles in the hands of Spanish forces defending Cuba. In a nutshell the Krag was too weak to fire a reasonably powerful cartridge and it could not be clip-loaded.

During 1900-1 the Ordnance Department deliberated again, testing Spanish and German Mausers. Eventually they decided that the Mauser system was the one to adopt and they designed a new rifle around the Mauser bolt and magazine. According to one story, a license was obtained from Mauser. In another version this formality was overlooked until Mauser claimed indemnification for the use of their design. Whichever way it was, Mauser was paid $200,000 for the patented features. Development work was done at the Springfield Arsenal, Massachusetts, whence came the rifle's popular name; officially it was 'Rifle, US, M1903'. As with the British Lee-Enfield of the same year, it was a short rifle for use by infantry and mounted troops.

Like all Mauser's later designs, the Springfield used a bolt with two locking lugs on the front end which locked into recesses in the mouth of the chamber, plus an auxiliary lug on the bolt body. This made for an extremely strong bolt and an accurate weapon though like all Mauser bolts it could not be manipulated as quickly as the Lee bolt action.

Although officially replaced by the M1 Garand in 1936, the Springfield remained in service until the end of World War II, since there were never enough Garands to arm every GI. After 1945 the Springfield was relegated to training and home defence. Even so, the US Marine Corps used it in the Korean War (1950-53). About 2,250,000 Springfields were made and the pattern remained basically unchanged. The main variants were the easier manufactured M1903A3 adopted in 1942 and the M1903A4 sniper rifle with telescopic sights. Production was 945,846 and 26,650 respectively.

SPRINGFIELD M1903

Calibre .30in
Length 109.7cm (43.2in)
Weight 3.94kg (8.69lb)
Barrel 61.0cm (24.0in)
Rifling 4 grooves, 1/hand
Foresight Blade
Rearsight Aperture, to 800yd (731m)
Action Bolt
Rate of fire 12 rpm
Feed system 5-round integral magazine
Muzzle velocity 853m/sec (2,800ft/sec)
Bullet weight 11.25g (174gr)

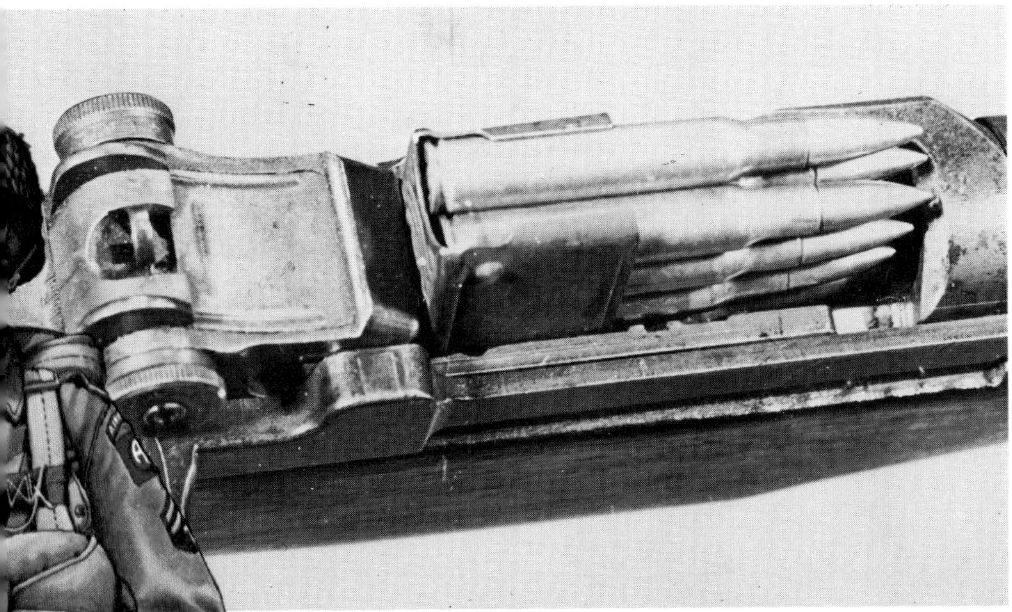

Above *Loading an 8-round clip of .30in M1906 cartridges into the Garand's breech. The cartridges are in two staggered rows of four.*

Left *US paratrooper of 82nd Airborne Division (1944-45 period) shown with his Garand rifle.*

The Garand, or Rifle, US M1, was the first semi-automatic rifle to be adopted by any army, and there is no doubt that it helped establish the automatic rifle worldwide. By September 1941 only 60,000 had been issued to the US Army but another four million were supplied in World War II.

It had been designed by John C. Garand at Springfield Arsenal during 1922-32. Originally developed in .276in calibre, it was changed to .30in due to ammunition availability.

Operation of the Garand was by a gas piston below the barrel which drove an operating rod. This, by means of a cam, rotated the bolt to unlock it, and thrust it back to open the breech and eject the spent case. A return spring around the piston rod then pulled the rod and bolt back, stripping a round from the magazine and chambering it before rotating the bolt to lock it. A hammer, cocked by the returning bolt, was then released by the trigger to strike a firing pin inside the bolt. The loading system used an 8-round clip dropped complete into the magazine. A spring-loaded follower then forced the cartridges out of the clip. After the last shot had been fired the bolt remained open and the empty clip was automatically ejected from the magazine.

In postwar years various modifications were designed, finishing up with the M14 Rifle that replaced the original M1. The M14 is, in fact, little more than a Garand with the less desirable features removed. The eight-round clip loading system was discarded because it was impossible to top it up with loose rounds between shots and the ejected clip could give away the firer if it dropped on hard ground. The replacement was a removeable 20-round box magazine. The port for tapping gas to the piston was moved nearer the breech. A cut-off gas system was installed to give a more gentle action without sacrificing power. Finally, the calibre was altered to 7.62mm NATO. Garand M1 rifles were adopted by many nations after the war and they were also made under licence by Beretta of Italy. That firm's BM59 rifle series evolved from the Garand and M14.

GARAND M1
Calibre .30in
Length 110.7cm (43.6in)
Weight 4.31kg (9.5lb)
Barrel 61.0cm (24.0in)
Rifling 4 grooves, r/hand
Foresight Blade
Rearsight Aperture, to 1,200yd (1,100m)
Action Gas
Rate of fire 20rpm
Feed system 8-round clip-fed magazine
Muzzle velocity 853m/sec (2,800ft/sec)
Bullet weight 11.25g (174gr)

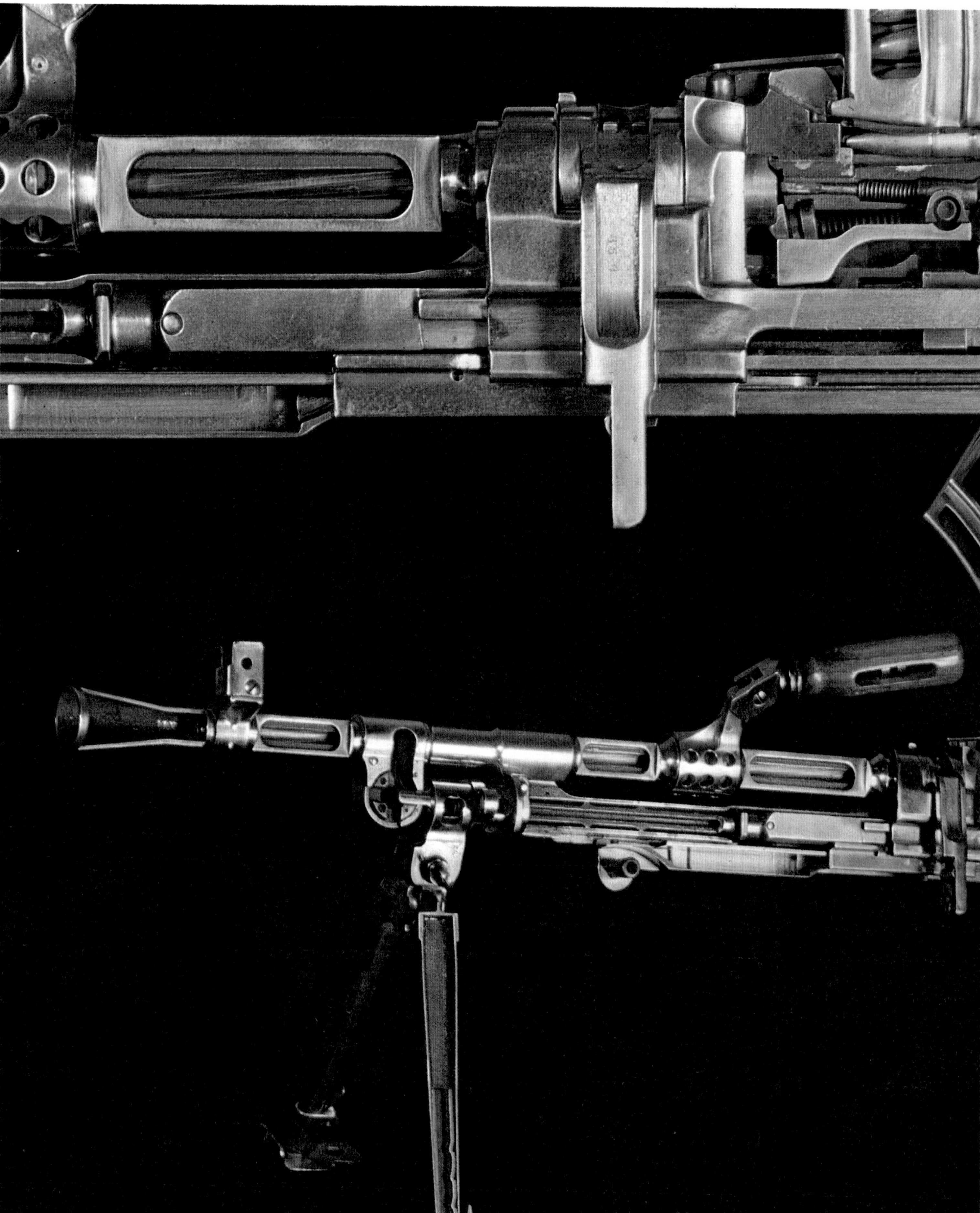

ROAD TO WAR
GUNS OF WORLD WAR II

It was not only the inventors of submachine guns and semi-automatic rifles who were at work in the 1920s and 1930s. The clouds of war were gathering over Europe, and every class of firearms came under scrutiny, their performance during World War I being weighed and examined. The most obvious area of interest was the light machine gun field, since although light guns had been used during the war, they were not, as a rule, satisfactory.

The French, having been the owners of the worst gun – the Chauchat – were early in the race and set about designing a replacement weapon in the early 1920s. They were astute enough to see that the biggest obstacle to a successful gun was their 8mm Lebel cartridge – a fat, conical, rimmed case, totally unsuitable for automatic feed. Their task, therefore, was to develop a new service round. After some work with the 7.92mm Mauser cartridge, they decided to take the 7.5mm Swiss service round as their model, and in 1924 produced a cartridge and a machine gun to suit. But instead of issuing it to the French Army, it was offered for sale to the Jugoslav and Rumanian governments. At demonstrations arranged for them, the gun performed erratically, finally disgracing itself by blowing up and seriously injuring the man who was firing it. The purchasing commissions went elsewhere for their machine guns while the French went back to the workshops to try and improve matters. The fault was eventually traced to the ammunition. The cartridge was redesigned with a shorter case and the weapon appeared once more in 1929 as the Chatellerault machine gun, named after the manufacturing arsenal.

The Chatellerault used a gas-piston arrangement and a method of breech-locking which owes a great deal to the Browning Automatic Rifle. A gas piston below the barrel drove the bolt back and, on the return stroke, chambered a fresh cartridge from the magazine. As the breech closed, the rear end of the bolt was thrust up so that it became wedged firmly against shoulders formed inside the gun body, so that the breech was securely locked. It was fed from a box magazine mounted above the body, and had a short bipod. One unusual feature was the provision of two triggers, the rear trigger giving automatic fire and the front trigger used for firing single shots. In its final form the Chatellerault was a reliable and successful weapon.

Britain was also looking for a machine gun. The Hotchkiss and Lewis both had their defects, and in 1932 a series of tests of possible replacements took place. The most favoured gun was the Vickers-Berthier, designed by a French Army officer, André Berthier, in the early 1920s and manufactured in Britain by Vickers. A gas-operated gun which used a similar bolt-locking system to the Browning Automatic Rifle, it fed from a top-mounted magazine, had very few moving parts, and could be rapidly dismantled without the use of any tools. The Indian Army adopted it in 1933, but while the British Army were still considering the matter they were advised of a new design by the military attaché at the British Embassy in Prague. He had seen specimens of a

Czech machine gun made by the Zbrojovka Brno company and he thought it so good that the powers-that-were back in Whitehall ought to hear about it. Surprisingly, the authorities took some notice, bought a gun and some ammunition, and tried it out.

The ZB Model 26, as the Czech gun was known, was a gas-operated light gun which, like so many of its contemporaries including the Chatellerault, locked the bolt by tipping it up to wedge in front of shoulders in the gun body. A box magazine fed into the top of the action, and the barrel was finned in order to assist cooling. The gas was tapped off close to the muzzle, giving a slow rate of fire and a very smooth action, and the piston and gas cylinder were of stainless steel in order to resist corrosion. One unique feature was a quick-release device at the front of the gun body which allowed the barrel to be removed in a couple of seconds and replaced by a fresh, cool, barrel. This allowed sustained fire to be kept up and also, by changing barrels before they got too hot, reduced the erosive wear caused by the high temperature of the internal gases.

Tests in Britain showed that the Model 26 was definitely the best gun available, but the British Army felt that one or two minor improvements

Previous page *The working parts of the Bren LMG cut away. The piston and bolt, magazine and spring, and attachment of the interchangeable barrel can all be seen. Cutaway weapons of this type were made in the Royal Small Arms Factory (Enfield, Middlesex), often by apprentices, for use as demonstration and instructional models.*

Above *Bren Mk 1 mounted unusually on a tripod for the sustained fire role, especially fixed-line firing at night. The tripod could also be re-assembled as an AA mount.*

Left *Two Australian Bren gunners advance in New Guinea, 1943. One man has lowered the gun's bipod to rest its 10.15kg (22.3lb) weight on the tree stump. The other carries his Bren on a sling with the bipod folded forward.*

would make it nearly perfect. In the first place, it had to be chambered for the British .303in rimmed cartridge, and not the 7.92mm rimless Mauser in which calibre the test gun had been supplied. The barrel was then to be shortened, to make the gun rather more handy to carry; the gas port brought nearer the breech; the sight graduated in Imperial yards; and the magazine changed from a straight box to a curved one, to cater for the rimmed British cartridge. These were done in a surprisingly short time. The resulting gun was officially called the ZB Model 33. Only about a dozen were made in Czechoslovakia, solely as sales specimens for demonstration in Britain. There the gun was approved, and production facilities were set up at the Royal Small Arms Factory, Enfield. Drawings were received in January 1935 and the first guns came off the production line in September 1937.

By the time World War II broke out in September 1939, guns were coming off at a rate of 400 a week. All that was left was to give it a name, since the British Army, at that time, did not follow the rest of the world in giving numbers and dates to their weapons. Taking the BR from BRno, the place where the gun had been designed, and adding EN from ENfield, where it was being made, gave BREN – and so the Bren gun was born.

The Bren gun was undoubtedly among the best machine gun designs of all time. It offered absolute reliability; very good accuracy; and steadiness in firing and a fairly low rate of fire which allowed better aim and did not waste ammunition. It was easy to teach; easy to use, with very few drills to learn (the Lewis, for example, had 23 different kinds of possible stoppage and the gunner had to know them all by heart – the Bren had just three); and it was easy to strip and maintain. Not only did it serve the British Army (and Commonwealth armies) throughout World War II, but it was also made in Canada for the Chinese Nationalist Army and, in its original Model 26 form, was used by the German Army as well. Re-chambered for the 7.62mm NATO cartridge it still serves today in Britain and many other countries.

Although the German Army used the ZB26, this was simply because they needed every machine gun they could lay their hands on by the middle of the war. Their stated doctrine, though, did not embrace the light machine gun as such. The German Army was the first to perceive the need for a 'universal' machine gun – one which could function as the squad light machine gun today, and tomorrow function as a sustained-fire medium machine gun for long-range harassing fire – tasks which, in every other army, were split between two distinctly different types of gun.

On the face of it, trying to reconcile these two tasks was attempting the impossible. The light gun

Germany's two general purpose MGs in World War II designed for tripod, bipod or AA mountings. This all-purpose concept originated after World War I when Germany was forbidden to make heavy MGs.

Right
The 12.1kg (26.7lb) MG34 is being carried by a Volksgrenadier *corporal with a pannier full of spares and cleaners.*

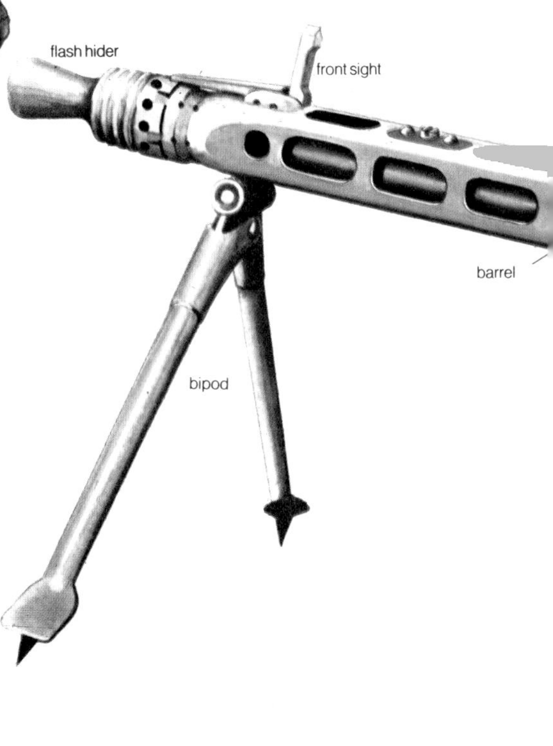

Far right *The MG42 was .44kg (1.2lb) lighter with a 95mm (3.75in) shorter barrel. It had a roller-tipped bolt as opposed to the MG34's rotating bolt. Once the bolt is locked into the breech another forward movement by the bolt (red arrow) fires the round. The MG42 could not fire single shots but had a top cyclic rate of 1,300rpm as against the MG34's 900rpm.*

needed to be light, so that it could be easily carried by one man with the infantry section; it did not have to fire more than short bursts, so cooling was no particular problem; and its function in life was to provide covering fire for the riflemen who were the basis around which the infantry section was built. The medium machine gun, on the other hand, needed the ability to keep up sustained fire; a long range; a tripod or other heavy mounting; and usually some form of optical sight so that the guns could be sited in concealed positions and still fire on indicated targets.

The Germans argued with much of this, particularly with the role of the light machine gun. In their view, the gun was the base of fire for the infantry section, the rifles being there solely to keep the enemy off the machine-gunner's back. Therefore the gun had to be the best available. It had to be just light enough to be carried, but it also had to be tough enough to do duty as a medium gun.

When the restrictions imposed on Germany by the Versailles Treaty began to lose their teeth, one of the first guns to be offered to the German Reichswehr was from the Solothurn Company of Switzerland which, as we have already seen, was a 'front' for Rheinmetall of Düsseldorf. The Solothurn MG30 (Maschinengewehr 1930) designed by Louis Stange, was an extremely advanced design which used barrel recoil to drive back the bolt, which was then rotated to unlock by two rollers riding in cam tracks in the tubular gun body. It was a very slender weapon, the body being a prolongation of the barrel and the butt a prolongation of the body, giving a 'straight line' configuration. This delivered the recoil in a straight line to the firer's shoulder, instead of via a bent butt-stock, and this helped to prevent the gun muzzle from rising when fired. The barrel was surrounded by a perforated jacket which allowed cooling air to circulate, and the barrel could be rapidly changed simply by twisting the butt through 90° and pulling it off, drawing out the bolt, and then pulling the barrel out through the back of the gun body.

About 5,000 of these were made, being sold to Austria and Hungary. The German Army took only a few because they were not entirely convinced that it was the best weapon available. They passed some samples of the gun to the Mauser company and asked for the design to be improved.

When Mauser had finished with it, the MG30 bore very little resemblance to the gun the Army had given them. The MG30 originally used a box magazine feeding from the left side. That had gone, and the new design fed either from a 250-round belt or, by changing the top cover of the body, from a 75-round 'saddle drum' magazine. The rotating bolt went, replaced by a bolt in which only the head rotated, locking into the breech by interrupted threads. A gas trap was fitted to the muzzle to make the gun recoil faster and thus boost the rate of fire to 850 rounds a minute. The barrel changing system was modified by making the gun body hinge to the back end of the barrel jacket, so that by swinging the gun body to the side, the barrel could be pulled straight out of the jacket. And finally the trigger mechanism was changed and a double trigger fitted. Pressure on the top portion of the trigger gave single shots, while pressure on the bottom gave automatic fire. A bipod was fitted to the barrel jacket for squad work, while a tripod was available for sustained fire. The German Army was delighted. It called it their MG34 (Maschinengewehr 1934) and it became Germany's standard machine gun.

The MG34 only had one fault – it was too good. The quality of workmanship demanded meant extremely precise and long manufacturing processes, and the

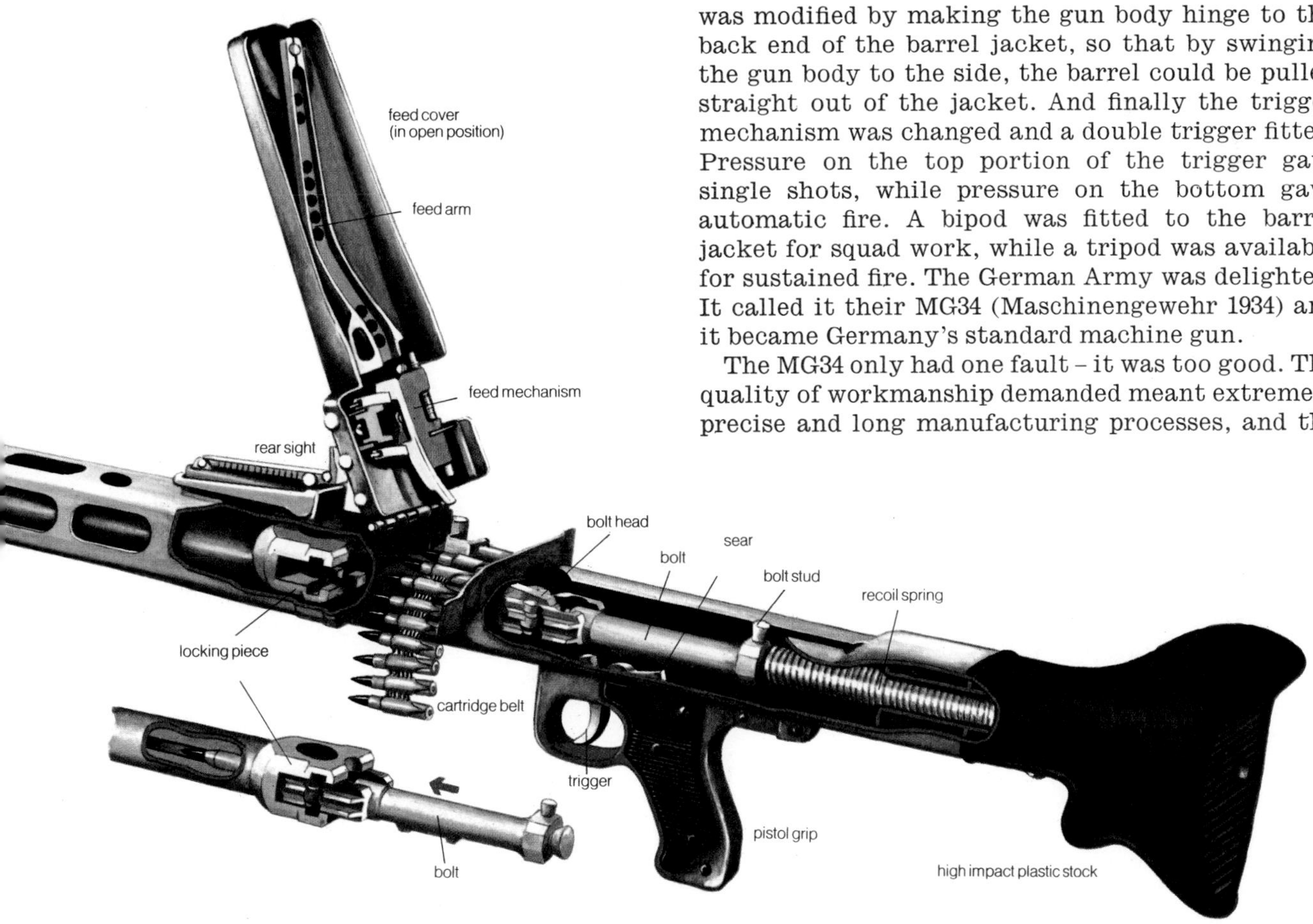

Browning GP35

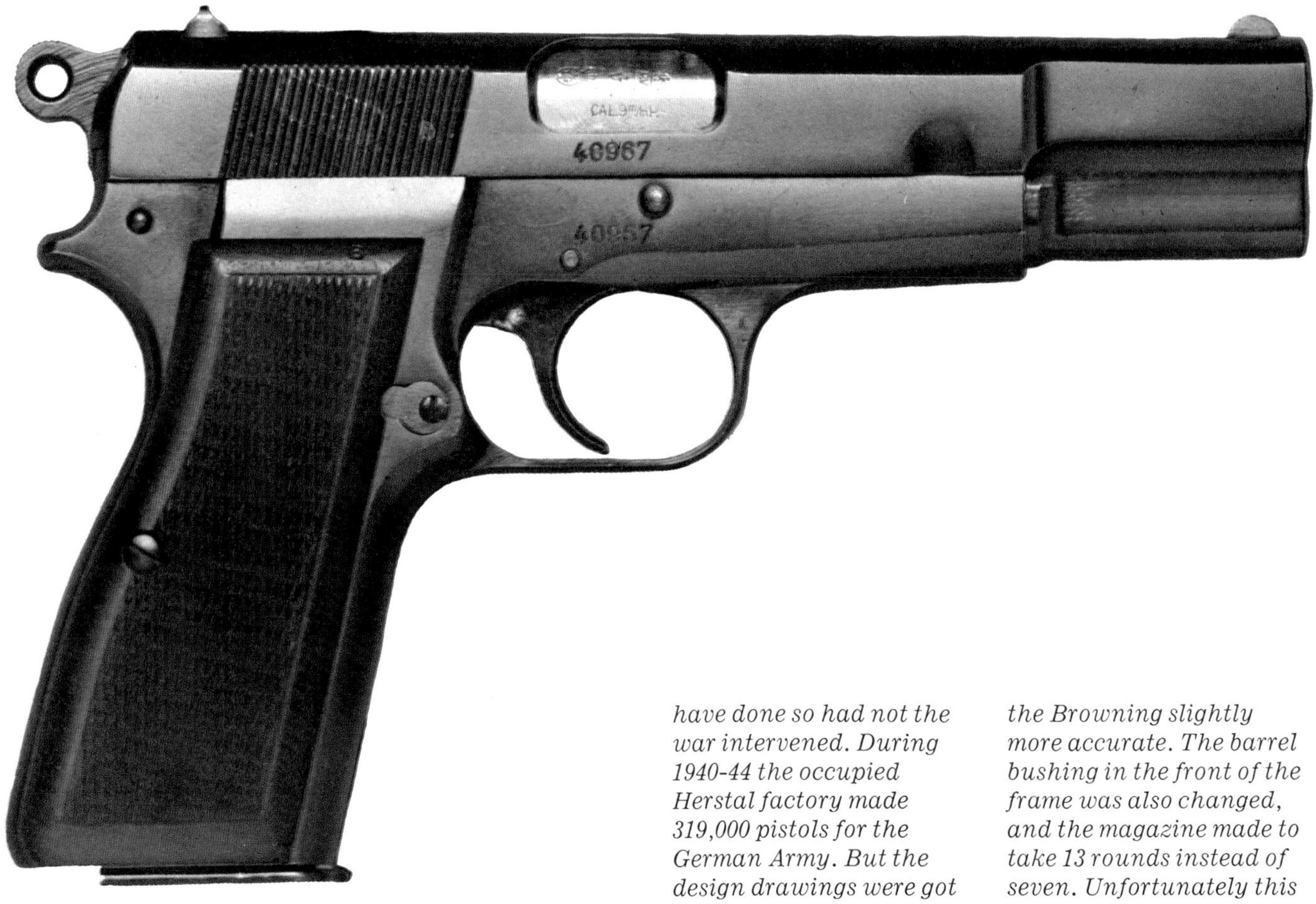

John Browning was never a man to sit on his hands if he thought something needed improving. No sooner had the Colt M1911 pistol gone into service with the US Army than Browning was designing a better one. Due to World War I the idea was shelved until the 1920s. In conjunction with Belgian Fabrique National D'Armes de Guerre of Herstal (near Liège), Browning had completed the first prototype by the end of 1923. This was a striker-fired pistol chambered for the 9mm Parabellum cartridge. In 1924 the striker was abandoned in favour of an external hammer and more prototypes followed. Browning died in December 1926, the design was finished in February 1927, FN continued their work and in 1928 the pistol had reached its final form – a hammer-fired weapon with a double-row magazine holding the unprecedented number of 13 cartridges.

Unfortunately the Wall Street Crash of 1929 put an end to any hope of putting the pistol on the market. Firearms sales slumped and FN's management decided to withhold capital investment until things improved. Production finally got underway in late 1934, and in 1935 the 'Grande Puissance, Modèle 1935' was adopted as the Belgian Army's service pistol. The Baltic States, China, Peru and Rumania soon bought GP-35s and others would have done so had not the war intervened. During 1940-44 the occupied Herstal factory made 319,000 pistols for the German Army. But the design drawings were got out to England and thence to Canada where the John Inglis Company of Toronto produced 151,800 Brownings for the Chinese Nationalist Army followed by the Canadian Army and British airborne troops.

After the war production reverted to FN. Since then the GP-35 has become the standard NATO military pistol and been adopted by many other countries.

Browning's design changes from the Colt M1911 pattern were small but effective. The swinging link was changed into a fixed ramp under the breech end of the barrel. This worked against a cross-pin on the pistol frame. The effect is the same, to pull down the barrel's breech end and free the locking lugs from the slide. But the shaping of the ramp avoids tipping the barrel as soon as recoil starts and thus makes the the Browning slightly more accurate. The barrel bushing in the front of the frame was also changed, and the magazine made to take 13 rounds instead of seven. Unfortunately this led to a change in the trigger mechanism layout that has caused complaints from target shooters, but since this pistol was designed for battle, this objection can hardly be sustained. The GP-35 is undoubtedly one of the world's great guns and a fitting tribute to the genius of Browning.

Above *Browning 1935 High Power Automatic Pistol (US nomenclature).*

GP35
Calibre 9mm Parabellum
Length 197mm (7.75in)
Weight 0.99kg (2.18lb)
Barrel 118mm (4.65in)
Rifling 4 grooves, r/hand twist
Foresight Blade
Rearsight Fixed V-notch
Action Recoil
Rate of fire 25rpm
Feed system 13-round box magazine
Muzzle velocity 335m/sec (1,110ft/sec)
Bullet weight 7.45g (115gr)

Beretta Modello 1934

The Beretta Company, with a long and distinguished record of making sporting arms, went into the pistol field during World War I to produce a sidearm for the Italian Army. The Model 1915 was a 7.65mm blowback pistol designed by Tullio Marengoni, later famous for the Beretta SMG designs, and it laid down the basic outline that has characterized Beretta pistols ever since. The barrel was pinned to the frame, with a slide unit forming a breech behind the barrel and with arms reaching alongside the barrel to contain a recoil spring below. The pistol was fired by an internal hammer.

This weapon found immediate favour with its users; the contemporary service pistol was the 9mm Glisenti which had a number of defects. The small size and complete reliability of the Beretta more than compensated for the reduction in calibre. The design was gradually refined until in 1934 the Model 1934 became the standard-issue pistol. This used the same sort of open-fronted slide, but had an external hammer, and the barrel could be removed by pulling back the slide and rotating the safety catch to lock it back. As the catch rotated, so its shaft, inside the frame, came clear of the lug holding the barrel and only a smart tap on the barrel was needed to take it out for cleaning.

The Model 34 was chambered for the 9mm Short cartridge, a round low-powered enough to work safely in a blowback pistol but with enough bullet mass to make a practical combat weapon if not a devastatingly lethal one. Its only serious drawback was a lack of accuracy, since the sights were not on the barrel and wear soon caused the slide to move and misalign the sights. But this was less important over the short ranges the Beretta was normally fired.

The Model 1935 was the 1934 pistol chambered for 7.65mm cartridges and adopted by the Italian Air Force. The basic design has been retained since for commercial pistols in various calibres. The Model 84, introduced late in 1977, looks much like the M1934 except for streamlining and a double-action lockwork.

After World War II the 9mm Short cartridge was no longer acceptable as a combat round. After joining NATO, which standardized on the 9mm Parabellum for pistols and SMGs, the Italian Army adopted a new Beretta, the Model 51, in 1957. This still uses the open-fronted slide layout with external hammer but locks the breech with a wedge similar to that used on the Walther P-38. The result was a very good military pistol used also by the armies and secret services of Egypt and Israel.

It has also sold widely in the commercial market, and, at the time of writing, has just been revamped into the Model 92 with a 15-shot magazine and a double-action lockwork. There seems to be little doubt that this will become a popular military pistol in the tradition begun by the Model 1915.

Below *Beretta 9mm Modello 1934, standard service pistol of the Italian Army and Navy. The date of manufacture indicates the calendar year and also the 21st year of the Fascist regime.*

BERETTA Modello 1934
Calibre 9mm Short
Length 152mm (6in)
Weight 0.66kg (1.46lb)
Barrel 94mm (3.75in)
Rifling 4 grooves, r/hand
Foresight Blade
Rearsight Fixed U-notch
Action Blowback
Rate of fire 20rpm
Feed system 7-round box magazine
Muzzle velocity 250m/sec (825ft/sec)
Bullet weight 6.16g (95gr)

fit and finish of the parts was so fine that relatively minor quantities of dust or dirt could upset it. After the war broke out, there were five major factories in Germany doing nothing but making MG34s as hard as they could, backed up by a number of smaller firms making components. By 1941 it was obvious that a new design, easier and quicker to make, was needed, but even so the MG34 continued in production until the end of the war. It has been reliably estimated that there were probably more MG34s in use during the war than any other single model.

Its replacement, easier and quicker to manufacture, was the MG42. The mechanism was changed to use a non-rotating bolt which locked into the breech by means of two rollers which were cammed outwards. Movement of the bolt drove a pivoted arm in the gun's top cover and this, in turn, drove feed pawls which lifted the ammunition belt into the gun. Barrels could be changed in a matter of seconds by unlatching the breech end and swinging the barrel out through a slot in the cooling jacket. Some 750,000 MG42s were made before the war ended. In postwar years many nations took them into use, and when the German Army was reformed in the 1950s they looked no further than the MG42 when a new machine gun was required. Now in 7.62mm NATO chambering, the MG1 (as it is now known) continues to serve with distinction.

The other field of inter-war activity lay with pistols. World War I marked, for many nations, the borderline between military revolvers and military automatic pistols, and the vast numbers of pistols used up during the war meant that many second-rate weapons had to be bought. In the aftermath of the war, many countries decided to make a clean sweep, get rid of the various handguns they held, and start with a fresh model.

Some degree of argument still arose over the relative advantages of the revolver and the automatic pistol, even though the war had shown that automatics were quite viable combat weapons. Briefly, the arguments in favour of either can be summed up as follows:

The *revolver* is more robust and reliable; it is readily seen to be loaded or empty; and is not stopped by poor ammunition, since simply pulling the trigger places a fresh cartridge under the hammer – with an automatic pistol, the failure of one cartridge jams the gun.

The *automatic*, on the other hand, carries more rounds in the magazine than the revolver; it is faster to reload if spare magazines are available; it is ballistically more efficient, since there is no leak of gas at the cylinder/barrel junction; and it is generally more compact than a revolver of equal calibre.

Such apparently clear-cut statements obviously invite a number of qualifications, and even today there is still room for argument and discussion. Nevertheless, the 1920s saw a great deal of development in automatic pistols for the simple reason that most of the service revolvers were of pre-1900 vintage and were feeling their age, and something fresh had to be provided in order to build up stocks.

John Browning had never been completely satisfied with the Colt M1911 .45in pistol which the US Army had adopted, and he kept playing with the design throughout the war years. Colt, however, were happy with the M1911, so Browning took the road to Belgium once more and interested the Fabrique Nationale of Liège, and with their engineers he produced a prototype pistol in 1923. Modifications and more prototypes followed until Browning died in 1926. In the following year the FN engineers took out the patents for the new pistol. It had been intended to put it into production in 1929, but the Depression put paid to any such plan and the FN company decided to conserve their capital until things got better. This happened in 1934 and the new design went into production in the following year as the 'Pistolet à Grande Puissance, Modèle 35'. Since 'Grande Puissance' translates as 'High Power', it has since become known as the Browning High Power or the GP35.

Browning's principal innovation was to alter the 'swinging link' system of locking, changing it to a fixed cam under the breech. He also improved the magazine (in the butt) so that it would now hold thirteen 9mm Parabellum cartridges in a double column and yet still keep grip dimensions which the average hand could hold. The GP35 was an instant success, being purchased by several European armies, though, since the Belgian Army had first priority, deliveries were relatively small. After World War II it was widely adopted elsewhere.

The Polish Army had considerable weapons problems in the 1930s because it was armed with a haphazard collection of equipment left behind by the previous occupying forces, dumped as the course of World War I had flowed to and fro, and acquired as reparations and free gifts after the war. To bring some order into the pistol inventory, a competition was advertised to which all comers were invited in order to select a standard service pistol.

Against some very powerful competition, the winners were two Polish designers, Wilniewczyc and Skrzpinski, who produced a pistol built on very similar lines to the GP35. It used a similar sort of cam beneath the barrel to withdraw the locking lugs from the slide, which argues some sort of licence from Fabrique Nationale of Belgium, though no public disclosure of such an arrangement has ever been made. One rather unusual feature of the Polish Model 35 was that, with the pistol loaded and a cartridge in the chamber, pressing a catch at the rear end of the slide would lower the hammer and disconnect it from the trigger so that the pistol could be carried safely. To make it ready for use, all that was necessary was to thumb the hammer back to full cock.

The French Army's standard handgun was the Mle 1892 8mm revolver, a venerable weapon of great robustness but one which was outclassed by this time. During the War, vast numbers of cheap Spanish blowback automatic pistols of dubious quality had been purchased in order to provide the numbers of pistols needed, and in the late 1920s it was decided to sweep all these away in favour of a new French design. Eventually a design from the Société Alsacienne de Constructions Méchanique (SACM) was adopted as the Modèle 1935. It seems that 1935 was a good year for pistols.

This Mle 35 was designed by Charles Petter, an enigmatic Swiss who had worked for SACM as a designer for some time and, once again, there is little doubt that Petter was influenced by the Browning-FN patent of 1927 since he also used the fixed cam in place of the swinging link. Generally speaking, the pistol was a sound and reliable weapon, but it was handicapped by being designed around an odd cartridge – the 7.65mm French service 'Longue' round – which had insufficient calibre or energy to be a worthwhile military cartridge. It is said that experimental pistols in 9mm Parabellum were made for the Rumanian government shortly before the outbreak of World War II, but no production of these ever took place. This was a pity, since in 9mm Parabellum it could have been a very good pistol.

The German Army, of course, had the Parabellum pistol, which had served them well since 1908. But the Parabellum had been designed in those spacious days when skilled workmen came cheap, and making a pistol was a matter of taking a slab of steel and machining about 90 per cent of it away until you had what you needed. This sort of design was, by the 1930s, becoming outdated. What was needed was a design specifically aimed at mass production, speed of manufacture, and, where possible, cheapness; all, of course, without sacrificing reliability, robustness or accuracy. It was a tall order, but the Walther company felt they could meet it.

Walther had been making pocket pistols since about 1908, but except for a brief excursion under pressure in 1916-18, they had not attempted a military pistol, nor had they made a locked-breech model. They had won considerable fame in 1929 when they placed their Model PP (for Polizei Pistole) on the market. This was in 7.65mm calibre, and was a shapely blowback pistol which introduced something quite unusual in automatics – a double-action lock. With the average automatic pistol, the options for carrying it about were two. Having inserted a full magazine, you could then either leave it at that, keep the chamber empty, and, when the need arose, grasp the slide and pull it back so as to cock the hammer and load the chamber; or you could work the slide as soon as you had put the magazine in, set the safety catch, and walk around with the hammer cocked over a loaded chamber, relying on the safety catch to prevent any untoward accident.

Neither of these options were entirely satisfactory for police or military applications. If the gun were carried loaded and cocked, there was danger of an accident. If it was carried with the chamber empty and the hammer uncocked, then two hands were needed to bring it into action.

Revolvers, of course, did not have this problem. The six chambers were loaded, and the hammer rested clear of the cartridge, in perfect safety. When danger threatened, the revolver could be drawn, and a quick pull through on the trigger would cock and release the hammer to fire the pistol immediately.

What Walther did was to take the revolver's 'double action' and apply it to the automatic pistol. It must be said that Walther was not the first to do this, but he *was* the first to do it efficiently and to make a commercial success of it. With the Walther Model PP, you inserted a full magazine, then pulled back on the slide and released it so as to chamber a cartridge and cock the hammer. You then pushed down the safety catch, which was, unusually, on the slide instead of the pistol frame. Pressure on this catch first rotated a steel block into place between the firing pin and the hammer, and then released the hammer to fall on to the block. The pistol could now be carried in perfect safety. When required, the safety catch was pushed clear, turning the block out of the way, and the trigger pulled, causing the hammer to rise to full cock and then fall on to the firing pin to fire the round in the chamber. Once the pistol fired, the normal recoil action of the slide re-cocked the hammer at each shot, so that the second and subsequent shots were fired in the usual 'single-action' mode.

Walther's pistol was an instant success and was widely adopted by police forces all over the Continent. It was followed by his PPK (Polizei Pistole, Kriminal) intended for concealed carriage by plain-clothes police. This pistol was simply a slightly smaller version of the PP, also chambered for the 7.65mm cartridge, and having the same double-action lock.

When the Army began looking for a new service pistol to supplant the Parabellum, Walther's first reaction was to enlarge the Model PP to take 9mm Parabellum, call it the Model MP (Militarisches Pistole) and offer that. The Army were not particularly impressed. A blowback pistol in 9mm Parabellum demanded a powerful recoil spring to hold the breech closed until chamber pressure had dropped to a safe level, and once the spring began to age and lost its original power, troubles followed.

Walther then went away and came back with something totally different – a locked-breech pistol firing 9mm Parabellum which used a wedge below the barrel to hold barrel and slide together until the bullet was out of the muzzle. It also had the double-action lock, but had the hammer concealed inside the slide. This was sound engineering, but it does not appeal to armies, since one cannot tell whether or not the pistol is cocked by simply looking at it. Walther therefore went away again and redesigned the pistol to have an external hammer. This time the Army approved, and the 'Pistole 38' or 'P-38' was authorized as the standard German Army pistol. Issues began in 1939, but production of the Parabellum P-08 was to continue until 1942, so great was the demand for pistols.

Germany's other requirement was a submachine gun. The Spanish Civil War (1936-39), which elements of the German forces had attended, brought the submachine gun into prominence, and demonstrated

Walther P38

The Pistole '08 had a sound reputation in the German Army but by the early 1930s it had to be admitted that it was not a design which lent itself to mass production. The Army therefore asked for a new design, and the outcome was the Walther P-38.

The principal novelty of the P-38 was the double-action lock, used for the first time on a military pistol. Also new was the rather complex safety mechanism. Several commentators had misgivings about these features, but Walther had been using them on smaller weapons since 1929. With the gun loaded and the hammer locked, pressing on the safety catch lifted the firing pin and moved it inside the slide. The firing pin then pressed on a sear catch which released the hammer to drop until its face struck the rear end of the slide. The pistol could then be holstered and carried in absolute safety. When required, all that was needed was to release the safety catch and pull the trigger. Releasing the catch dropped the firing pin back into line and pulling the trigger lifted and dropped the hammer to fire the pistol. Thereafter, shots could be fired in the usual semi-automatic fashion.

In fact the Army P-38 made a slight change to this mechanism in the interests of quicker manufacture, by omitting the mechanism which withdrew the firing pin into the slide. In the military version, the firing pin was merely locked solidly so that when the hammer fell, the pin could not go forwards and fire a round. This demanded high-quality material, and it is known that some of the pistols made by a sub-contractor late in the war used poor quality steel in the firing pins. These, after some use, crystallized and fractured when the hammer fell, firing the cartridge in the chamber, to the surprise of the pistol owner and probably to the discomfiture of some unsuspecting by-stander.

That flaw apart, the P-38 was a fine pistol. The breech was securely locked when firing by a wedge unit under the barrel. The wedge moved back with the barrel and this in turn forced the slide back, until the rear edge of the wedge locked into a recess in the pistol frame. This held the barrel but allowed the slide to go back and complete the unloading-loading-cocking cycle. On the return slide stroke, the barrel was forced forwards, the wedge lifting to lock barrel and slide together again.

As well as being adopted by the German Army, the Walther was sold to the Swiss Army to become the P-39. A small number were made available to the civil market but during the war this production was taken over by the Luftwaffe. The Army's heavy demand led to contracts going to Mauser and Spreewerke GmbH of Berlin.

In postwar years the P-38 returned as the P-I of the West German Armed Forces. It is also available in 7.65mm and 9mm Parabellum, and .22in rimfire chambering.

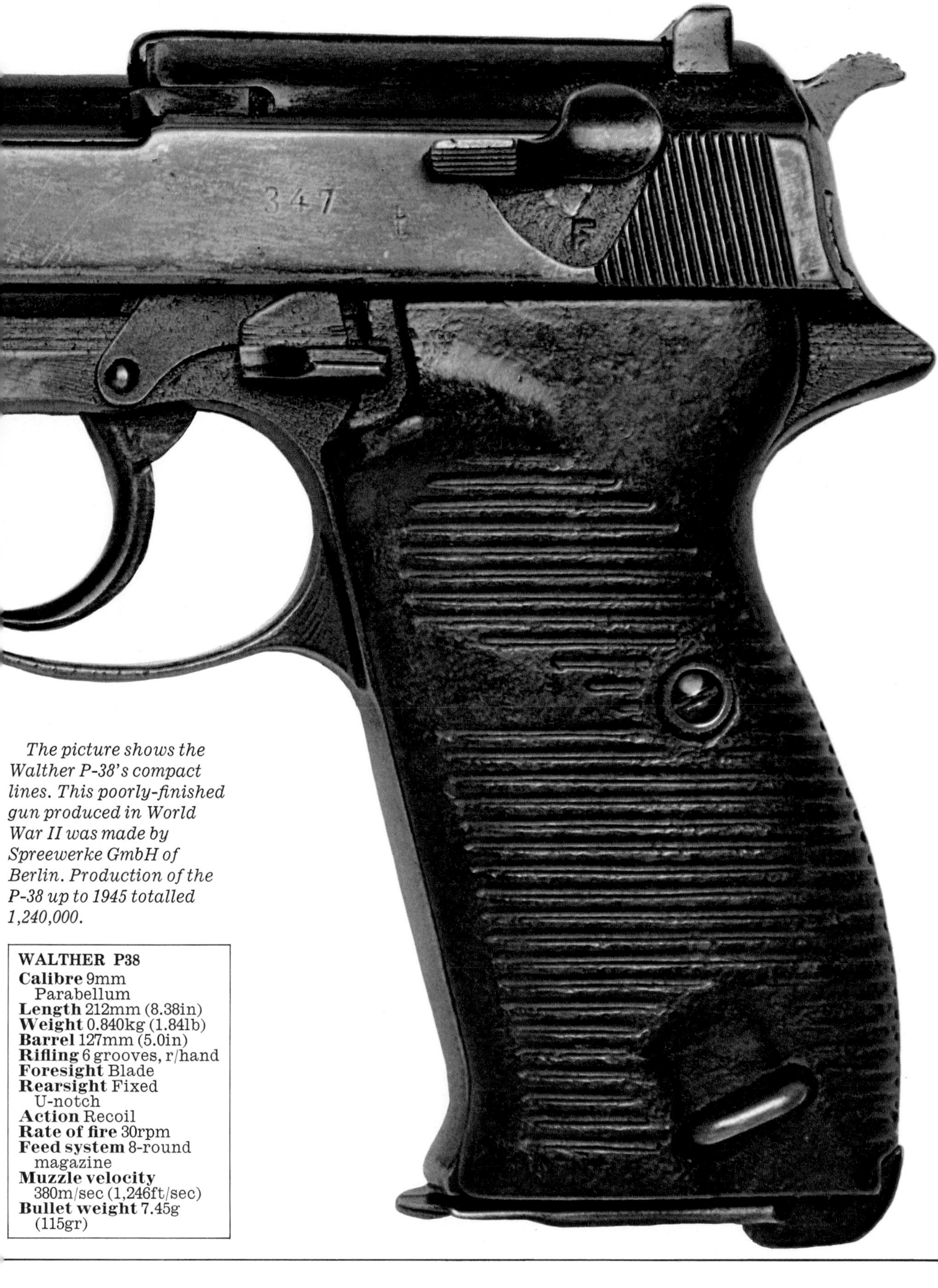

The picture shows the Walther P-38's compact lines. This poorly-finished gun produced in World War II was made by Spreewerke GmbH of Berlin. Production of the P-38 up to 1945 totalled 1,240,000.

WALTHER P38
Calibre 9mm Parabellum
Length 212mm (8.38in)
Weight 0.840kg (1.84lb)
Barrel 127mm (5.0in)
Rifling 6 grooves, r/hand
Foresight Blade
Rearsight Fixed U-notch
Action Recoil
Rate of fire 30rpm
Feed system 8-round magazine
Muzzle velocity 380m/sec (1,246ft/sec)
Bullet weight 7.45g (115gr)

some of its overlooked virtues. It was simple to teach, easy to use, and cheap to make. The battle-grounds of Spain showed that it was an ideal weapon to put into the hands of hurriedly-enlisted troops with little training, and, by extension from this, it was obviously an ideal weapon for large conscript armies suddenly mobilized for war.

As with every other army, the Germans had looked at submachine guns, even bought a few, but, also like every other traditional army, they were not quite sure where the submachine gun fitted. Spain showed the answer – it fitted well with the *blitzkrieg* ('lightning war') idea, because the submachine gun was essentially a weapon for the attack. With a submachine gun you did not sit in a trench and snipe away at, say, 300m range; you got out of the trench and got in close, otherwise the gun was useless. And this sort of tactic went well with the Panzer theories. So the Wehrmacht began looking for a submachine gun.

As it happened the Ermawerke factory of Erfurt was ready with a design. Erma had a designer called Heinrich Vollmer who had been working on submachine guns since the 1920s and had developed a unique telescoping recoil-spring unit which formed the heart of a number of Erma designs. The bolt was much the same as the original Bergmann, a hollowed-out unit which carried inside it the firing pin. But in the Vollmer design the firing pin formed part of the foremost of three light metal tubes which telescoped into each other and contained the recoil spring. This meant that the spring unit could be easily removed for cleaning and maintenance.

In 1938 the German Army asked the manager of Ermawerke to produce them a compact, reliable and cheap submachine gun. He was back within weeks bearing a prototype, since the design had already been under way. The Army found it acceptable and it was immediately adopted as the MP (Maschinen-pistole) 38. It was to become the archetypal German submachine gun. No present-day television play or film portraying the German Army would dare be without an MP38 across somebody's chest. It broke new ground in several respects. It was the first weapon to use nothing but metal and plastic – no wooden stock or pistol grip; the first to utilize stamped steel components; and the first to adopt a folding steel butt-stock. It has, ironically, gone down in popular history as the 'Schmeisser' submachine gun, though Hugo Schmeisser – designer of the 'Bergmann' MP18 – had nothing whatever to do with its design.

Another army which had some practical experience in Spain and which saw the advantages of submachine guns was the Soviet Army. It too had dabbled with submachine gun designs and in fact

Above *Cutaway of the Maschinenpistole 38. Like the Bergmann MP18 it fired from the open-bolt position. During firing the bolt was blown back against the firing pin unit, so compressing the telescoping recoil-spring unit (the MP38's novel feature) against the rear of the frame. The magazine held 32 rounds of 9mm Parabellum ammunition that could be fired at up to 500 rpm. Foresight was an open U-notch with an L rear flip sight graduated for 100 and 200m (110/219yd). Over 1,047,400 of this weapon and its development, the MP40, were produced, 1938-1945.*

Right *The ubiquitous PPSh41 7.62mm SMG in the hands of a Black Sea Fleet sailor. This version has the 35-round box magazine instead of the more common 71-round drum housing. (The ammunition belts are not for the SMG.)*

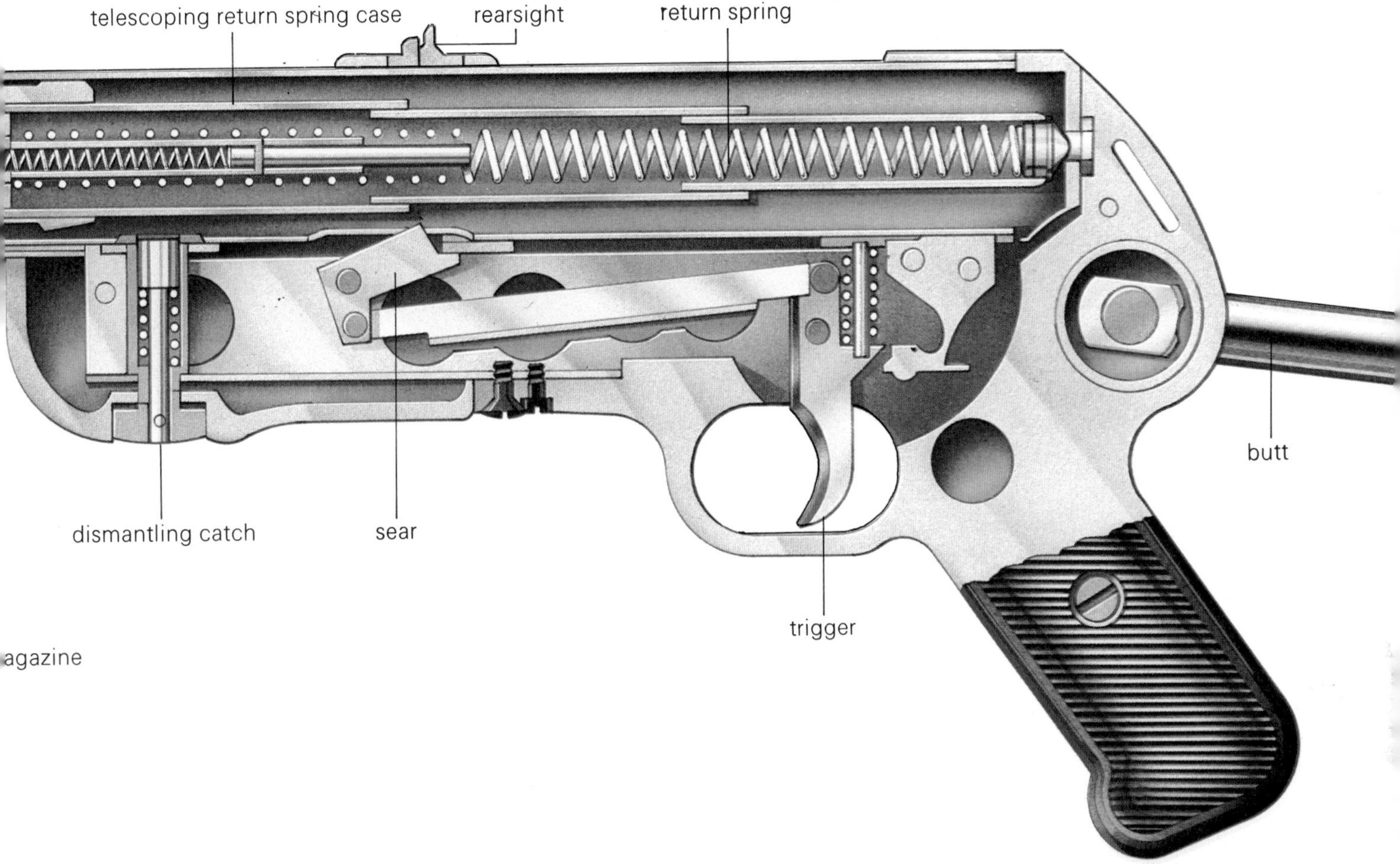

had one in limited production. This was the PPD-34 (Pistolet Pulemyot Degtyaryova or 'Machine Pistol designed by Degtyaryov'), and in 1938 it was slightly modified and the production stepped up. It was a fairly conventional design, which appears to have leaned heavily on the Bergmann MP18 and the Suomi for its inspiration, to the extent of copying the Suomi drum magazine. However, a box magazine was also provided, and in order to simplify the magazine housing, the drum was given an odd upward extension, resembling the top 5cm (2in) of the box magazine, so that it could be pushed into the box-magazine housing. This was not a particularly good idea, and Degtyaryov set about redesigning the weapon, at the same time making it easier to produce. The result became the PPD-40, since it was first made in 1940, and while it retained much the same mechanism and layout as the earlier model, it used the Suomi magazine without alteration, the gun's housing being suitably altered and the alternative box magazine dropped.

1940, of course, found Britain faced with the possibility of invasion, and having lost far too many weapons on the far side of the Channel. Submachine guns appeared as a quick and cheap way to provide ample firepower for the Home Guard, volunteers, airfield guards, Commandos and just plain soldiers. The only question was, which design to adopt? In late 1939 a number of Thompsons had been bought from the US and used by fighting patrols on the

Franco-German border. These troops had reported favourably on the Tommy gun's reliability, but were less enthusiastic about the characteristic drum magazine. Apparently the cartridges inside were prone to slap back and forth as the weapon was carried, advertising the patrol's presence for kilometres around. The drum magazine vanished at once, never to be seen again on a military Thompson.

Unfortunately, while the Thompson was considered to be the best submachine gun available, it was extremely expensive, slow to manufacture and, of course, had to be brought across the Atlantic. Something cheaper and capable of manufacture in Britain was wanted, and after looking at various designs, it was decided to take the original Bergmann of 1918, as later modified to take a straight box magazine, and build it in England. Some slight redesign was done in order to suit British dimensioning and methods, and the 'Lanchester' submachine gun was born. The Lanchester was tested, and plans were drawn up for putting it into production.

But at the proverbial eleventh hour, two designers, Major R. V. Shepherd and Mr H. J. Turpin, of the Design Department of the Royal Small Arms Factory at Enfield, appeared with a submachine gun they had developed. It was demonstrated in January 1941, passed all the acceptance tests, and became the immortal Sten gun – the name being derived in a similar fashion to that of the Bren, from the initials of the designers and the place of birth of the design.

The Sten was the British Army's introduction to the 'functional firearm', and it horrified many of the old school. It was simply a metal tube, one end of which held a barrel and the other end of which had a bolt and return spring working in it, held in by a simple bayonet-cap. The magazine entered from the left side of the weapon, so that it could lie across the firer's forearm for additional stability and it did not interfere when the gun was being fired from the prone position. The butt was a simple frame of welded tube, the trigger mechanism was concealed by folded sheet metal and a short wooden handguard, and there was a plain folding fore-grip. It was also provided with a spoon-like flash hider and muzzle compensator. But even this simple design was capable of being pruned, and subsequent models did away with the flash hider, the wooden fore-end and the fore-grip until the design was as basic as it could possibly be.

Due to its simplicity, the production figures were staggering. BSA Ltd made over 400,000, plus 350,000 spare barrels. The Royal Ordnance Factory at Fazacklery, near Liverpool, turned out 20,000 guns a week for much of the war. There were other factories in Britain turning them out at the same rate. There was the Canadian factory at Long Branch turning them out by the tens of thousands. And there were even underground resistance workshops in France and Denmark making them. Finally the Germans copied it with the intention of arming their own home guard, the 'Volkssturm'. It is doubtful if anyone knows how many Stens were made, but the figure must run into millions.

A curious by-product of the Sten Gun was the adoption of silenced weapons. Commando and other raiding parties using Sten guns asked if a silent version could be developed for use in night raids. The silent firearm had long been the target of a number of inventors, and it had been popularized by novels and films, but the hard facts of the matter were very different to the popular impression.

The noise arising when a firearm is discharged comes from two sources – the explosion of the cartridge in the chamber, which becomes audible when the high-velocity gases emerge from the gun muzzle; and secondly from the bullet itself as it goes through the air faster than the speed of sound. Today, people are familiar with sonic booms, but in the early 1940s few but scientists had ever heard of them. To silence a weapon effectively, therefore, not only had the cartridge to be muffled, but the bullet had to be sub-sonic, otherwise it announced its arrival with a distinct crack.

Since the Sten gun fired the 9mm Parabellum cartridge with a muzzle velocity of about 365m per second (1,200ft/sec), and since the speed of sound is about 335m/sec (1,100ft/sec), both sounds had to be dealt with. The solution was to fit a special short barrel, drilled with holes so as to release gas from behind the bullet and thus lower the velocity to a sub-sonic level. This barrel was then surrounded by a long tubular casing containing cupped baffles and sealed at the muzzle by a rubber disc. The casing was perforated, and around it went an outer casing, separated from the inner by a series of felt rings. Thus, when a shot was fired, the bullet had its velocity reduced by the perforated barrel, and the gases which left the barrel were trapped by the baffles and swirled around inside the inner casing before escaping into the outer casing. All this movement gradually reduced the gases' velocity until, by the time they escaped to the atmosphere, they were moving too slowly to generate any sound waves. Just 15m (50ft) away from the silenced Sten, the only noise discernable was the mechanical noise of the bolt moving forwards.

Silencers found other applications during the war years. They were often provided for automatic pistols used by various resistance and partisan groups, though, as with the Sten gun, the noise made by the slide moving back and forth tended to nullify some of the advantages of the silencer. (A silencer is not effective on a revolver, since the slight leak of gas at the cylinder/barrel joint generates most of the noise.)

Probably the most effective silenced weapon of World War II was the De Lisle Carbine – a .45in calibre weapon firing the US automatic pistol cartridge (since this was sub-sonic) and using a modified Lee-Enfield action. The barrel went into a very large silencer carried on a Lee-Enfield type of rifle stock, and since there were no moving parts other than the firing pin when the gun fired, it really was silent. Moreover, since the barrel was rather longer than usual for the calibre, it was highly accurate and had a good range.

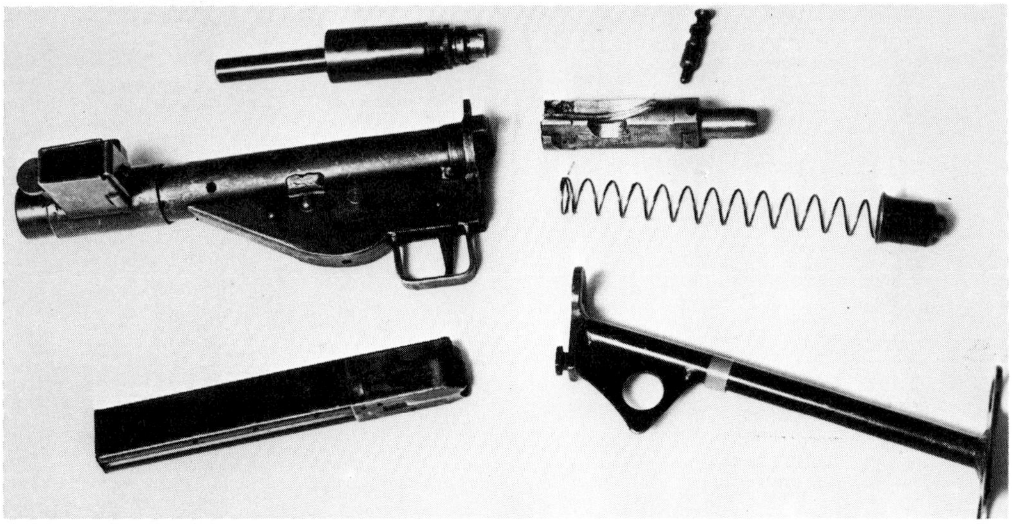

Above *The Sten Mk II(S) (silencer) with a very early infra-red sight. The canvas heat-resistant cover on the silencer is in the firer's left hand.*

Left *Disassembled Sten Mk II. Clockwise from bottom left, the magazine, receiver (gun body), barrel, firing pin, bolt, main spring and metal stock.*

Below *Sten Mk V, a quality 1944 model with wooden stock, pistol grip and rifle foresight.*

NEW DIRECTIONS

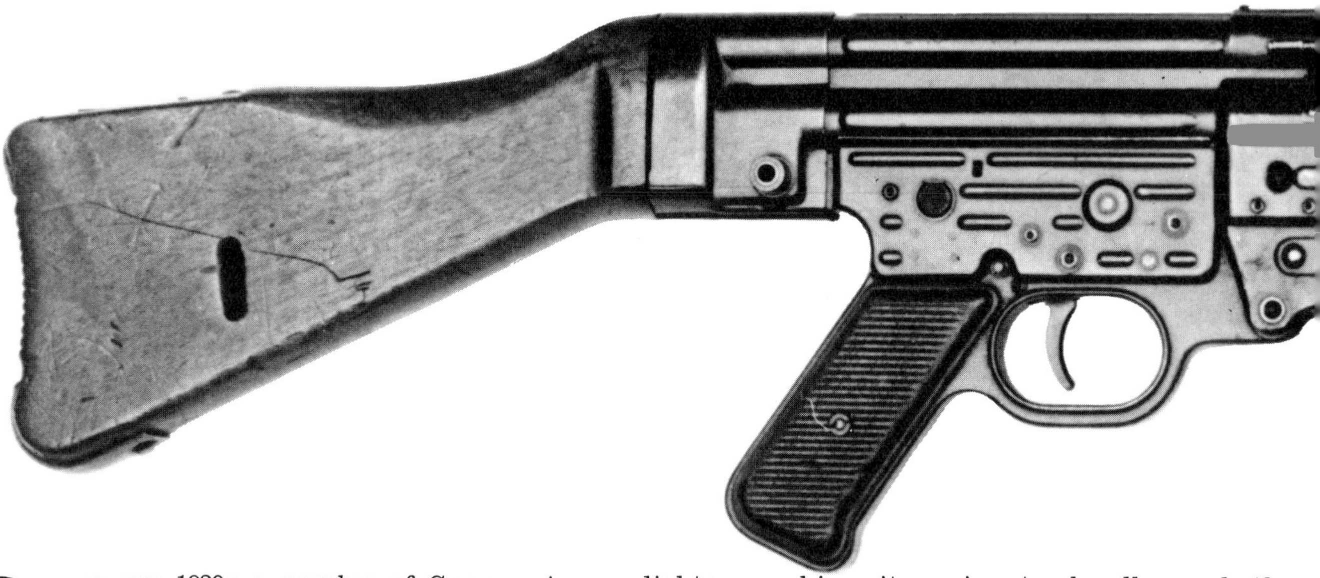

During the 1930s a number of German Army officers sat down to contemplate the possibility of a new service rifle, and instead of simply asking for the mixture as before, they began to question some of the absolute fundamentals of rifle design. Broadly speaking, the military rifle of the period was a fairly heavy, long, powerful weapon, firing a cartridge which was accurate to 1.6km (1 mile) distant and sometimes better than that on the hands of an expert. It was the cartridge which governed the rifle. With powerful cartridges, light rifles were impossible, since the recoil is proportionate to the ratio between bullet weight and velocity and rifle weight, so that firing a heavy bullet at high velocity demanded a heavy rifle in order to keep the recoil energy within the limits that the average man could accept.

But, asked the Germans, how often did the average soldier shoot at targets 1.6km away? Come to that, how many average soldiers could *see* a target that far away? They were not speaking of practice targets – 3m (10ft) squares of white board – but of active service targets – men in drab uniforms covered in mud, creeping under hedges and close to the ground – and it takes exceptional eyesight to see such a target even at 400m (440yd). Examination of records of World War I showed that few soldiers ever had the chance to fire a rifle at much more than 400m range, so that the heavy and powerful bullet was a waste of energy. It still had a useful role in the support machine gun, but in a rifle? There were grave doubts.

From these and similar arguments, the conclusion was reached that what was needed was a new cartridge, less powerful than the traditional military round. If it were less powerful it could be made shorter. If it were shorter, then the rifle could be shorter, since the length of a rifle's mechanism was largely governed by the length of the cartridge it had to feed. If it was less powerful, the rifle could be lighter, making it easier to handle, and the cartridges would be lighter, so that the soldier could carry more of them. And, in spite of the reduced power, it would still be effective to ranges of 500m or 600m (550-650yd), all that appeared to be needed.

As a result of this reasoning, a new 7mm cartridge was developed, having a shorter bullet and cartridge case than the conventional rifle cartridge, and work began on developing a suitable automatic rifle. By the time the cartridge design had been resolved, the war had begun, and the designers were astute enough to realize that, while suggesting a new cartridge would be bad enough, suggesting a change of calibre would be worse, so the cartridge was redesigned in the standard 7.92mm calibre, thus allowing much of the manufacture to be done in existing machinery.

The Haenel and Walther companies were asked to develop rifles to suit the new 'short' cartridge, their instructions being that the weapon had to be designed with mass-production and cheapness well to the fore, and in 1942 they both produced prototypes. These were known as the MKb42(H) and MKb42(W), for Maschinen-Karabiner (Machine Carbine), the letters showing the manufacturer. Several thousand of each were made and sent to the Russian Front for evaluation in combat, and as a result the Haenel design was selected for further development. It is of interest to see that it had been designed by Hugo Schmeisser, who had also designed what amounts to the World War I equivalent.

At this point in the story, politics entered into it. The Army was convinced that it had an ideal service rifle. It was gas-operated, using a rotating bolt, and offered 'selective fire' – that is, it could be fired in the single shot mode as a rifle, or at 500 rounds a minute as a light machine gun. It was reliable, and was well-liked by those who had used it. But when approval was sought for putting it into production, the idea was vetoed by Adolf Hitler on the grounds

Previous page *(top) Armalite AR-15; (middle) Gyrojet, VP70, and Sig pistols; (bottom) EM2.*

Above *The futuristic lines of the Sturmgewehr (Assault Rifle) 44. Weighing 5.1kg (11.25lb), it soon exhausted its 30-round magazines at 500 rpm.*

that it did not have sufficient range. He, having been a soldier on the Western Front in 1917-18, knew all about rifles and knew, of course, that long range was vital. No argument would move him, and the short rifle appeared to be doomed before it began. But the soldiers had their own ways of dealing with this. Like all good soldiers, they saluted, fell out – and then went away and put the rifle into production anyway. But in order to conceal it in the monthly production returns which Hitler always studied, they gave it a new name. It became the Machine Pistol 43 and thus appeared in the submachine gun totals; and since Hitler was a believer in submachine guns, he was quite pleased to see the monthly production increasing.

Inevitably, of course, the cat got out of the bag in the end. At a conference of commanders from the Russian Front. Hitler is reputed to have asked them what equipment they wanted, and was somewhat astounded when they all asked for more supplies of the new rifle. He was more astounded when he found that a shrewd High Command had actually armed his personal bodyguard with the new weapon. Eventually the uproar died down and Hitler gave the new rifle his blessing, bestowing on it a new title – the Sturmgewehr 44 or 'Assault Rifle'.

After the war the Allies interrogated the German designers, discovering the reasoning which had led to the new weapon, and began to take an interest in the idea themselves. The Russians, who had developed a healthy respect for the StuG 44 from being the principal opponents of it, had already begun work on their own design of short cartridge and now set to work to produce a rifle to match. This was the work of Mikhail Kalashnikov and was to enter service in 1947 as the Automat Kalashnikova or AK47. The AK47 has since earned its place as one of the best automatic rifles ever developed and certainly one of the most widely distributed, having been supplied to the various satellite nations. Over 35 million are said to have been made in the last 30 years.

In Britain, the post-World War II years seemed to be a good time to institute a change of rifle, since the .303in bolt-action Lee-Enfields were now obsolete, and a new short cartridge in .280in calibre was developed. It was followed in 1949 by a new rifle, simply known as the 'EM2' for Enfield Model 2, which was quite revolutionary in its design. All things being equal, the longer the barrel of a rifle, the greater the bullet velocity it will develop and the better the ballistics. But short cartridges suggested short rifles and short rifles meant short barrels.

This dilemma was resolved by Noel Kent-Lemon, the designer of the EM2, by using a layout known (for no very good reason) as the 'bull-pup' layout. This had been invented many years before by competition shooters who were also trying to get the longest possible barrel into a manageable rifle, and it meant placing the barrel on the rifle stock so that the breech mechanism was just in front of the butt-plate. In other words, when the firer lay down and took aim in the usual way, the chamber of the rifle was alongside his ear. Since the barrel now started at the butt end of the stock, it could be longer than normal without exceeding the usual overall length of a rifle. Such an arrangement in a bolt-action

rifle was obviously unsatisfactory for military use (where the bolt had to be manipulated rapidly without taking the rifle from the shoulder), but it was quite satisfactory for some kinds of competitive shooting. But now that the mechanism could be actuated automatically, there was no constraint to having it on a military weapon – except the horrified faces of some traditionalists.

The EM2 was produced in small numbers for evaluation. Gas-operated, and with a revolutionary optical sight, it was well-balanced and reliable, accurate and robust. All seemed well, but it ran into political trouble. The other countries in the North Atlantic Treaty Organization, particularly the Americans, were less convinced of the virtues of the short cartridge, and after much bitter argument, NATO settled on a new round – the 7.62mm cartridge – which was little more than a slightly-shortened US .30in round. Attempts to redesign the EM2 to take this round were not successful, and the design was abandoned.

During the immediate postwar years almost every army in the world decided to get rid of its bolt-action rifles and equip with an automatic, and as luck would have it the Belgian Fabrique Nationale company was ready with a suitable design. Work on this had begun well before the war but had been put into cold storage during the German occupation. As soon as work could be resumed, the design was completed and the rifle offered for sale.

Known as the 'Modèle 49' or SAFN (Semi-Automatic, FN) it was a gas-operated rifle, the piston being above the barrel and being driven back to strike a 'bolt carrier'. This was a hollow unit sliding back and forth in the gun body and with cams on its inner surface. As it moved back, after being struck by the gas piston, the cams lifted the bolt and unlocked it from engagement in faces cut in the gun body. Then bolt and bolt carrier recoiled and were returned by a spring, collecting a fresh round from the bottom-mounted magazine on the way and chambering it. As the bolt closed on the cartridge, the carrier continued to run forwards so that the internal cams now pressed down the rear end of the bolt and locked it. The Modèle 49 was a successful weapon, numbers being sold throughout the world, and it was used in the Korean War by the Belgian contingent. But Fabrique Nationale were not satisfied and continued to work on the design, eventually producing the FAL or Fusil Automatique Léger.

This weapon was fortunate enough to appear just as NATO had decided on their 7.62mm cartridge and when many of the NATO members were looking for a suitable rifle to adopt. FN astutely produced the FAL in 7.62mm and put it on sale. It used the same basic mechanism of gas piston and bolt carrier as did the Modèle 49 but in a more reliable and more easily manufactured package. After trials had shown its ability, orders followed, and from about 1953 onwards it was bought by some 36 different countries. It was adopted by the British Army as their 'Rifle L1A1' to replace the Lee-Enfield instead of the unfortunate EM2.

With the widespread adoption of the 7.62mm NATO cartridge (for it was taken into use by many other nations outside NATO) it might be thought that the 'short' cartridge and assault rifle idea had died except in Russia, and for several years this seemed to be the case. But in the 1950s the US Air Force required a 'Survival Rifle' – a lightweight collapsible rifle which could be carried by aircrews and used by them for either self-defence or hunting if their

Left *Cutaway of British L1A1 Self-Loading Rifle (SLR), a modified Belgian FN. The carrying handle, a special Trilux night sight, and 20-round magazine are prominent.*

Below *South Vietnamese soldier of 1970-75 with US 5.56mm M16A1 (Armalite) AR15 Rifle. Its low weight of 2.88kg (6.35lb) suited Asian troops, pleased also with its performance.*

aircraft was forced to land in a hostile or isolated environment. The order for this went to the Armalite Company, who had been formed to make civil weapons and who had amalgamated with the Fairchild Engine and Airplane Corporation. Since they made more profit out of the Air Force order than they had from selling civilian weapons, Armalite began to concentrate on military designs and employed a designer named Eugene Stoner, a former US Marine and soon to become one of the world's leading firearms designers.

Stoner knew all about the 'short' cartridge idea, and he began by developing a new cartridge based on a Remington deer-hunting round. The calibre was 5.56mm and Stoner re-worked the round until he had a 55-grain bullet travelling at 990m/sec (3,250ft/sec) and lethal up to 450m (500yd) range. He then developed the 'AR-15' rifle around the cartridge. The AR-15 broke new ground in many directions. It used a direct gas system of operation in which there was no piston of the conventional type, merely a tube which led gas back to the face of the bolt carrier and simply blew it back. Extensive use was made of light alloy and precision casting to simplify manufacture and reduce weight. All the furniture was of plastic, and the design was laid out in a straight line, instead of the butt dropping as in traditional rifle designs. The sights were high set, the rear sight forming part of the permanently attached carrying handle. The whole thing looked very 'space-age', but it also looked 'cheap and nasty', which gave it a considerable handicap to overcome.

Although the US Army was unenthusiastic, in 1962 the US Air Force bought numbers of AR-15s for use by guards at Air Force bases. Again, that might have been the end of the matter, except that in 1963

Above *An AKM with pressed steel gun body. The easiest way to distinguish an AKM from an AK47 is to look for the semi-circular gas relief cut out above the barrel. The AK47 has four circular holes. It is estimated that over 35 million Kalashnikovs have been made, more than any other gun in history.*

Below *Communist People's Militia of Ho Chi Minh City (Saigon), Vietnam, on parade with Chinese Type 56/1 AK47 Assault Rifles in 1975. The folded knife bayonets are quite apparent.*

This rifle, probably the most successful automatic rifle so far introduced, was designed by Mikhail Kalashnikov (born 1920) who developed an unsuspected talent for firearms design while convalescing after being wounded in the Battle of Bryansk (1941), where he had been a tank commander. Kalashnikov first designed an SMG, then a carbine, both sound designs with no current military requirement. In 1943 the Soviets developed their 7.62mm M1943 'short'

AK47
Calibre 7.62mm
Length 87.0cm (34.25in)
Weight 4.80kg (10.58lb)
Barrel 415mm (16.34in)
Rifling 4 grooves, r/hand
Foresight Post
Rearsight U-notch, to 800m (875yd), 1,000m (1,093yd) for AKM
Action Gas
Rate of fire 600rpm
Feed system 30-round box magazine
Muzzle velocity 600m/sec (2,350ft/sec)
Bullet weight 7.89g (122gr)

cartridge around which Kalashnikov designed his automatic rifle. It was taken into service in 1947 as the Avtomat Kalashnikova (AK-47). The designer later improved the system of manufacture, leading to the introduction of the AKM Rifle in 1959. Subsequently the basic Kalashnikov mechanism was adapted to a series of MGs.

The AK rifle is gas operated; a piston above the barrel being driven back to impart rearward motion to a bolt carrier. This rotates and unlocks the bolt and then draws it to the rear, cocking the firing hammer simultaneously. The carrier and bolt are then returned by a spring, chambering a fresh round from the 30-round magazine. A selector lever allows either single shots or automatic fire at a practical rate of about 100 rpm.

The AK47 was made in the conventional manner, most of it being machined from solid steel while the butt and fore-end were of seasoned wood. The AKM uses pressed and formed sheet steel in its construction. Though early models had wood furniture, later models use a folding metal stock. The AKM is therefore 1.1kg (2.5lb) lighter than the AK-47.

As well as Soviet models, several variations have appeared in other countries: the East German model has a folding steel butt; the Rumanian has furniture of laminated wood; the Chinese Type 56 can be found with a wooden stock and a permanently attached folding bayonet or with a folding steel stock and no bayonet; the Hungarians use a version with a forward pistol grip as an SMG; the Bulgarians dispense with a cleaning rod and a bayonet lug; the Poles fit a grenade-launcher on the muzzle; and the Finns have bought a license to produce a modified version as their service rifle and also sell it commercially in single-shot form.

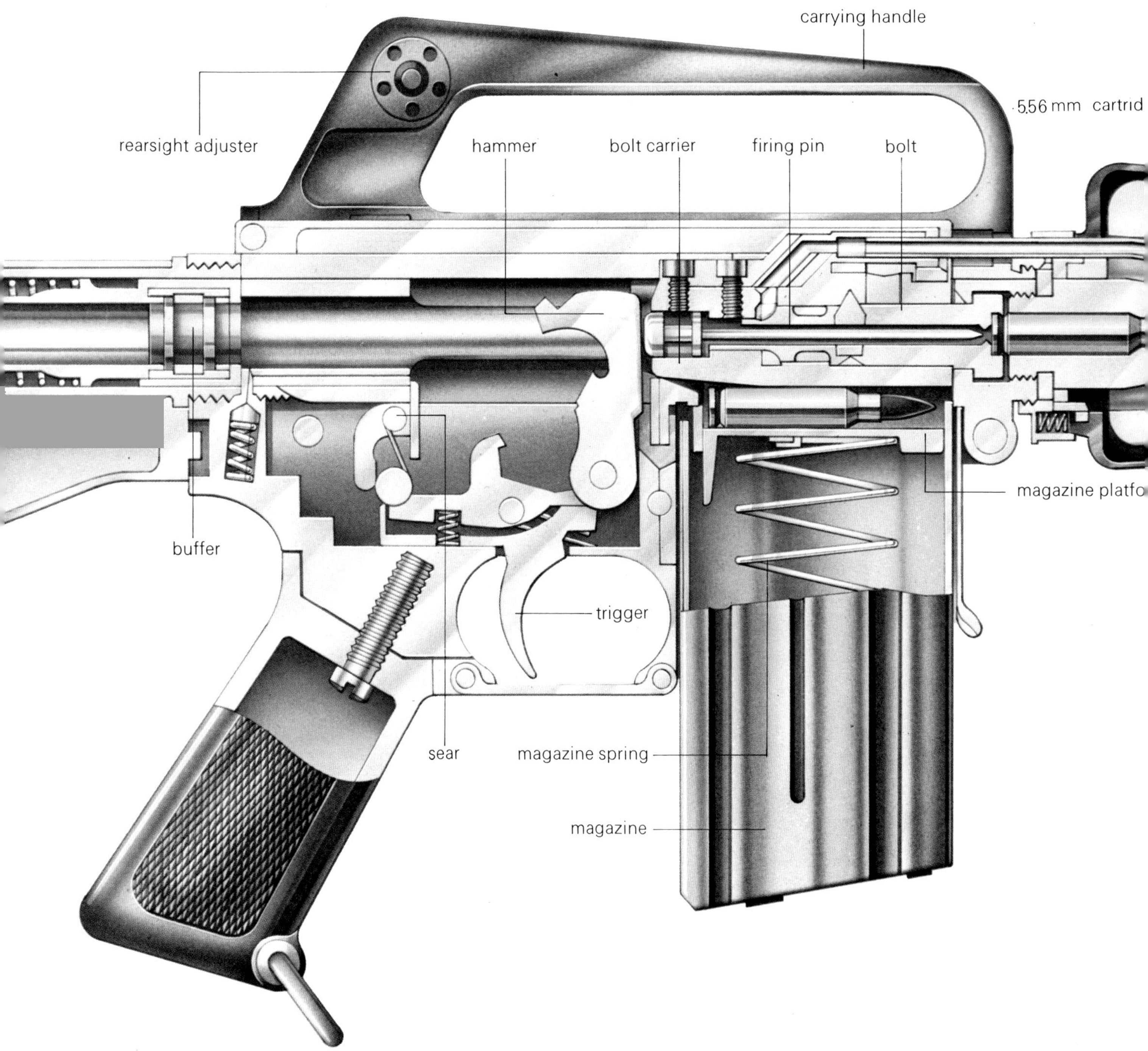

Above *The Armalite action (barrel has been shortened). Gas is passing down the tube above and parallel to the barrel. It will cause the locked bolt to unlock and move back. The spent case will be ejected through the open dust cover after being withdrawn from the chamber by an extractor on the bolt. A port in the bolt carrier's side exhausts the gas.*

Right *Colt Commando with 5.56mm x 45mm (.223in x 1.77in) round, developed as a handier version of the AR15 for SMG use. The 254mm (10in) barrel is half the length of the AR15's. The telescopic butt has been fully extended for shoulder firing. A 102mm (4in) flash-hider is fitted. It is used by US Special Forces (the Green Berets) and perhaps the British SAS.*

the USAF sent a detachment to Vietnam, armed with AR-15s. The South Vietnamese Army saw them and realized that these small, light rifles were just what was wanted, since the average Vietnamese soldier was only about 150cm (5ft) tall and weighed under 45kg (100lbs). The Vietnamese Army bought AR-15s and reported enthusiastically; US Special Forces serving in Vietnam tried them out and also reported favourably. Eventually, the AR-15 was taken into regular US Army service as the M16 rifle, and the US Army, who had scorned a 7mm cartridge as too small some years earlier, now embraced the 5.56mm round.

Since that time the 5.56mm cartridge has been taken into use all over the world, many manufac-

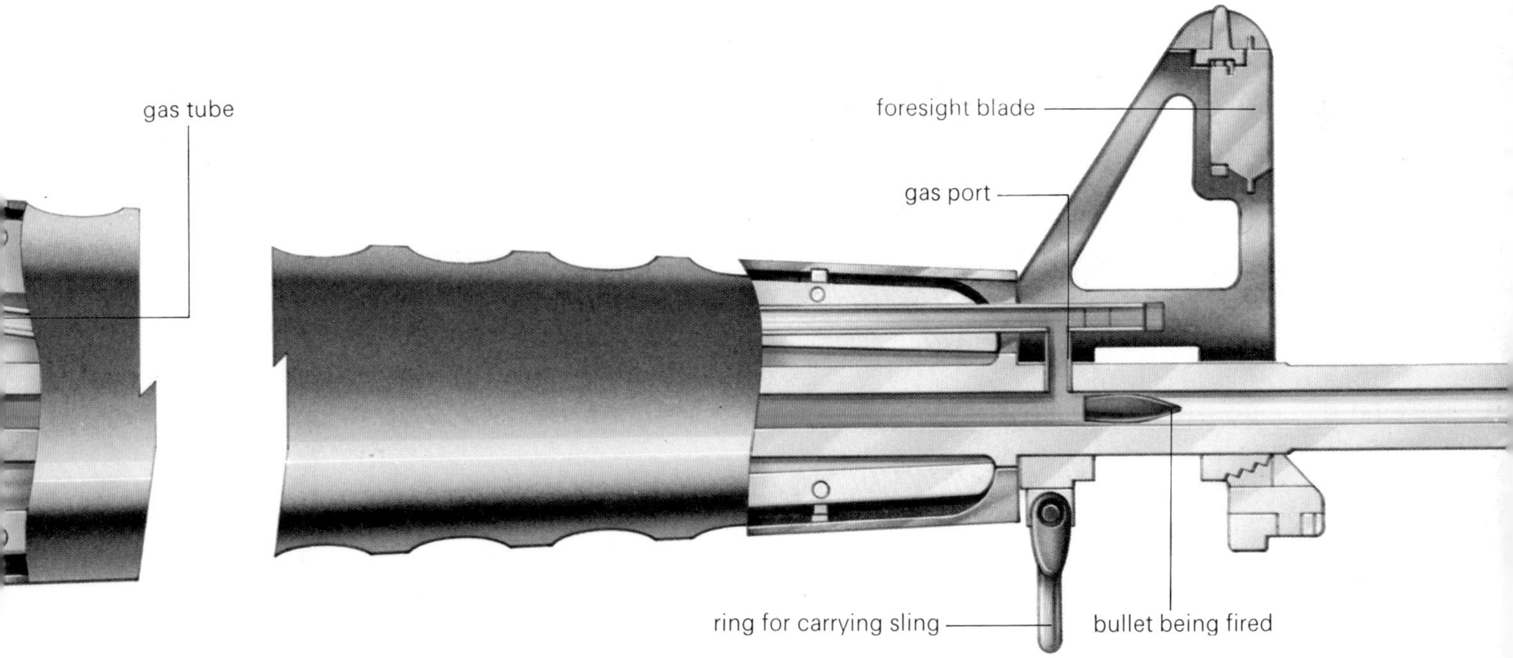

turers producing rifles to suit. And with the reduction in rifle size which the 5.56mm cartridge has allowed, there is now a considerable body of opinion which suggests that the day of the submachine gun is over, since a modern assault rifle in 5.56mm calibre is little larger or heavier than the average 9mm submachine gun, can fire as rapidly, can also be used as a rifle, has longer range, and eases the supply problem by having but one weapon and one cartridge instead of two.

However, this point of view does not appear to have daunted the submachine gun makers as yet, and in the years after the war the submachine gun was a growth industry. The only major innovation in submachine gun design first appeared in a production weapon in 1949 when the Czech VZ-23 was placed on the market. Until this design appeared, the overall length of a submachine gun had been determined by the length of the barrel plus the length of body necessary to allow the bolt to reciprocate sufficiently far to soak up the recoil and reload. Vaclav Holek, the Czech designer, changed all this by bringing the barrel back into the gun body for a considerable distance and then hollowing out the bolt so that when the breech was closed, most of the bolt lay in front of the breech face and surrounded the barrel. Behind the breech there was only sufficient thickness of bolt to withstand recoil and mount the firing pin and extractor. Slots in the bolt allowed for the ejection of the spent case and feed of the fresh cartridge.

As a result of this design, the barrel length was 280mm (11in), the bolt 'over-hung' it by 165mm (6.5in), and the entire length from muzzle to end of the body was only 445mm (17.5in). By comparison, the German MP 38, which had a 250mm (9.9in) barrel, had a body and barrel length of 630mm (24.8in). Another advantage of the design was that the pistol grip could be brought close under the centre of balance and also used as the magazine housing. This location of the magazine makes magazine-changing in the dark much easier, since one hand always tends to find the other.

The 'over-hung' bolt design soon spread, and probably the most famous post-war submachine gun, the Israeli-made 'Uzi', was one of the first to adopt it. The Uzi also popularized another fitting – the grip safety. A metal plate at the rear of the pistol grip had to be securely pressed in, by gripping the weapon properly, before the bolt could be moved or the gun fired. This answered one of the greatest defects of the submachine gun, its liability to go off accidentally if dropped or jarred. With a blowback submachine gun, jarring the butt on the ground could cause the bolt to move back, not far enough to engage with the firing mechanism and be held, but far enough to go past the magazine and load and fire a cartridge as it bounced back. Many soldiers were

The Uzi SMG was developed in the late 1940s by Major Uziel Gal of the Israeli Army and went into production in 1951. Major Gal had closely studied almost every SMG then available and his design was much influenced by the Czechoslovak VZ-23 model.

The main mechanical novelty of the Uzi was the principle of the 'overhung bolt'; the breech face is not at the front end of the bolt, but is recessed 88mm (3.5in) farther back. Thus, at the moment of firing, the bolt surrounds the rear end of the barrel and much of the bolt's mass is in front of the breech face. As a result of this, the barrel can be set into the gun body and it is possible to have a 26cm (10.2in) barrel in a gun whose overall length (without butt) is only 44.45cm (17.5in).

Another advantage is that due to the shorter bolt movement, the pistol grip can be brought forwards to the centre of balance and can act as a magazine housing. This gives extremely good mechanical support to the magazine, avoids a shift of balance as the

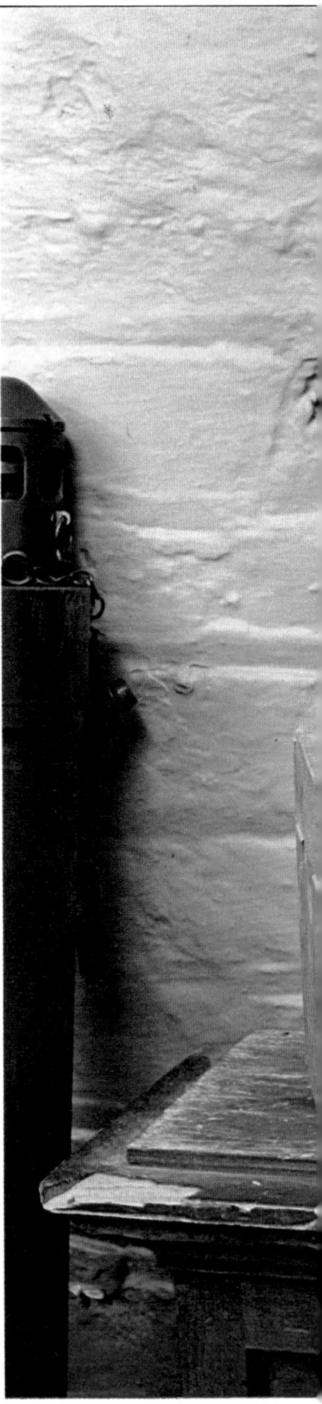

Left *An Israeli infantryman with the Uzi SMG in front of his M3 White half-track. Being so short, the Uzi is ideal for troops in armoured vehicles.*

Right *The same wooden-stocked Uzi with carrying sling. The detachable 203mm (8in) stock makes it 640mm (25.2in) long. It can be fired one-handed like a pistol.*

UZI
Calibre 9mm
Length 64.0cm (25.2in)
Weight 3.5kg (7.7lb)
Barrel 260mm (10.2in)
Rifling 4 grooves, r/hand
Foresight Blade
Rearsight Two-position aperture, 100 and 200m (110/219yd)
Action Blowback
Rate of fire 600rpm
Feed system 25, 32 or 40-round box magazine
Muzzle velocity 390m/sec (1,280ft/sec)
Bullet weight 7.44g (115gr)

magazine empties, and also makes magazine changing much quicker, especially in the dark.

The Uzi is largely made from sheet metal pressings welded together. The first models were fitted with wooden butts, fore-end and pistol grip, but these were soon changed to high-impact plastic material for the grip and fore-end and an ingenious folding metal stick.

Safety was carefully considered from the very start and two special features incorporated in the Uzi. First, a grip safety at the rear edge of the pistol grip prevents the gun being cocked or fired unless it is pressed in by a hand holding the pistol grip in the firing position. Second, a ratchet device under the top of the body cover is linked with the cocking handle. This prevents a shot being fired if the handle is accidentally released during the cocking stroke. Once the bolt has been drawn back about 2.6cm (not enough to pick up a cartridge) it cannot go back into the forward position without first being fully drawn back and cocked.

The Uzi was an immediate success and even though it is almost 30 years old, it remains one of the best SMGs in existence. After the Israeli Army, it was adopted by the West German and Dutch armies and then by many African and South American forces. It was also built under licence by FN of Belgium.

killed or wounded in this way in the early days of World War II, and various extempore safety measures – slots into which the cocking handle could be turned, or clamps which held the bolt securely – were added to designs. But the Uzi grip safety was probably the best solution, and one that has been widely copied.

The present tendency is for submachine guns to get smaller and smaller. They are losing their place in the foot soldier's armoury to the assault rifle, as we have already noted, but there is still a useful role for them as personal weapons for crews of armoured vehicles or combat aircraft. And in both these applications, the smaller the weapon is, the better it will be liked.

Probably the best example of this type of weapon is the Czech Army's 'Skorpion'. With the wire stock folded across its top, the Skorpion is no more than 270mm (10.65in) long, has a 115mm (4.5in) barrel, and can be carried in a holster and fired single-handed like a pistol. But when more firepower is needed, the stock is unfolded and the lever selector set to 'Auto' to give a rate of fire of 700 rounds a minute.

One problem with a weapon of such a small size is that the necessarily light bolt will move very fast and thus give a very high rate of fire. This was countered in the Skorpion by putting an inertia mechanism inside the pistol grip. As the bolt recoiled, it drove a weight down the grip against the resistance of a spring. At the same time, the bolt was held by a trip-catch in the rear position. The weight rebounded from the bottom of the grip and, when it reached the top, tripped the catch and released the bolt to fire the next round. The duration of this action is very brief, but sufficient to delay the bolt's return and thus reduce the rate of fire to manageable proportions.

The Skorpion actually seems to be a rationalization of a much older idea – the 'machine pistol' – a weapon which came about more or less by accident. In the middle 1920s, when the German gunmakers were finding life difficult, those of Spain saw their opportunity. One or two Spanish companies began making outright copies of the Mauser Military pistol for sale in South America and the Far East, markets which had traditionally been filled by Germany. One shrewd manufacturer, appreciating that some

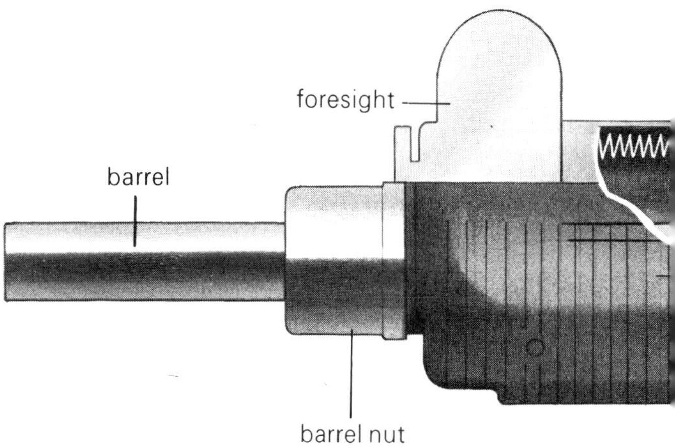

of his customers were more enthusiastic than knowledgeable, converted his Mauser copy – sold as the 'Royal' – to fire full automatic and provided it with a detachable magazine. With the holster-stock fitted, it became a 'machine pistol' or submachine gun of sorts, sold well, and was copied by other Spanish makers.

In fact, it was a pretty dismal sort of weapon by any account. Due to the lightness of the bolt and the power of the cartridge – it was chambered for the 7.63mm Mauser round – the rate of fire was astronomical – well over 1,000 rounds a minute – so that the entire magazine was loosed off in less than a second. This made the weapon uncontrollable, the violent recoil action and muzzle blast causing the muzzle to rise rapidly so that only the first shot was near the target, the remainder of the burst being shot into the sky. In self-defence, the Mauser company had to put similar designs on the market in the early 1930s but in spite of being better engineered, these could not overcome the inherent disadvantages of the design, and few were produced.

The idea then died for some years but was revived in the Soviet Union in the 1950s with the issue of the Stechkin pistol. This was a blowback pistol, loosely based on the Walther PP design but rather larger and without the double-action lock. In place of that, it was provided with a full-automatic ability, to be used when the pistol was clipped to its wooden holster-stock, a similar fitment to that of the Mauser. It was chambered for a peculiar 9mm cartridge invented by the Russians – the 9mm Soviet, or 9mm x 18 (the second figure being the length of the cartridge case in millimetres). This is more powerful and longer than the 9mm Browning Short cartridge, but shorter and less powerful than the 9mm Parabellum cartridge, and seems to have been designed in order to have the most powerful cartridge possible to be used with a blowback pistol. The Stechkin could fire this at 725 rounds a minute, but recent reports indicate that the Soviet Army has had second thoughts about the idea and has withdrawn the Stechkin from service.

In the early 1960s a new idea suddenly appeared in

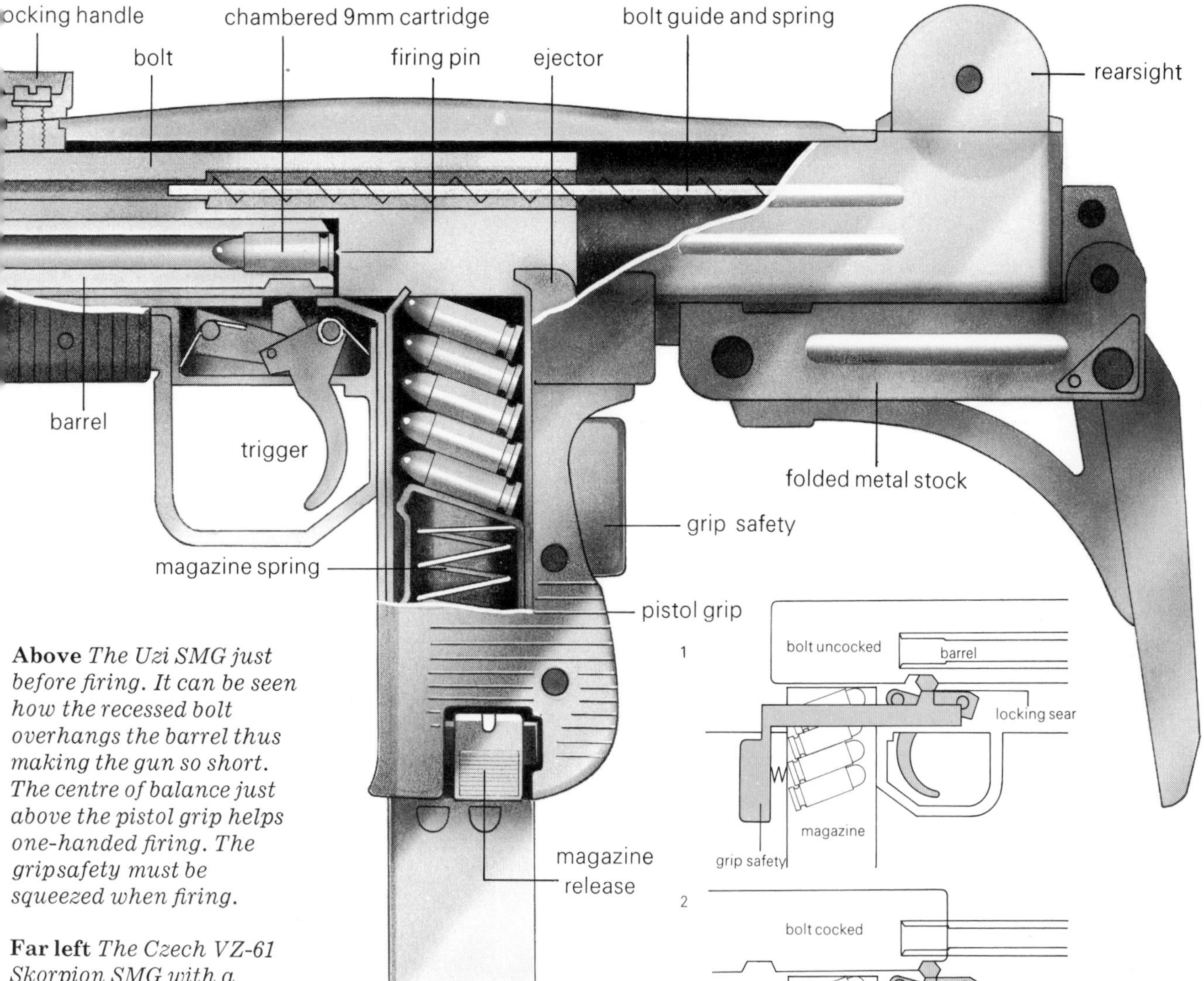

Above *The Uzi SMG just before firing. It can be seen how the recessed bolt overhangs the barrel thus making the gun so short. The centre of balance just above the pistol grip helps one-handed firing. The gripsafety must be squeezed when firing.*

Far left *The Czech VZ-61 Skorpion SMG with a 7.65mm round. The 251mm (9.9in) metal stock is retracted but the gun could still be fired. It weighs only 1.31kg (2.87lb) unloaded.*

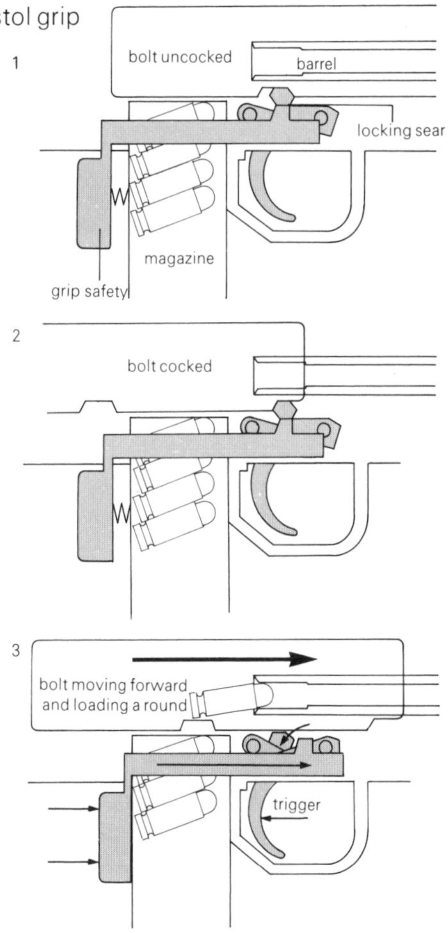

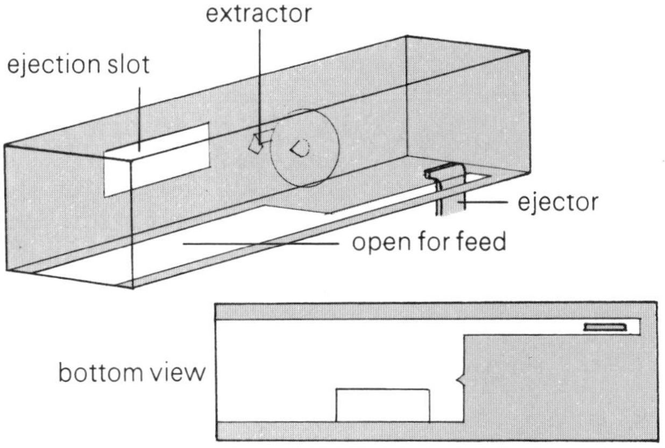

Left *Two views of the Uzi's bolt, hollowed out in front. The firing pin is an integrally formed pip on its face. The bolt has openings at the bottom for feeding cartridges and, top right, to eject them.*

Above *The grip safety works by means of a locking sear when the Uzi is (1) uncocked or (2) cocked. Pressing the safety (3) frees the locking sear and allows a trigger pull to free the bolt.*

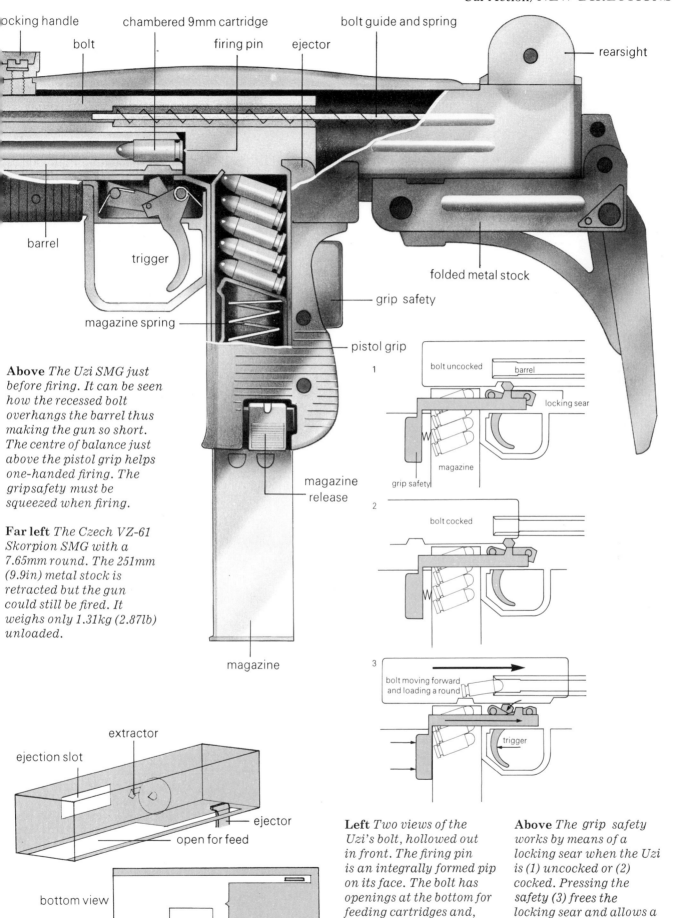

automatic rifle designs. It is hard to say who invented it, since it seemed to appear in several places at the same time. The idea was called the 'burst-fire facility' and took the form of an additional position of the rifle safety catch. When turned to this position, an internal mechanism was engaged which resulted in a fixed number of shots – usually three or five – being fired for one pressure on the trigger. The reasoning behind it ran something like this: if single shots are fired and the first one misses, the soldier instinctively takes pains over aiming his second and subsequent shots in which time the enemy may escape. If automatic fire is used and the first shot misses, the 'climb' of the gun may very well spray the shots in the wrong place. But if the first squeeze of the trigger brings three shots, then if the first misses, the second and third, being fired without pause, will be slightly dispersed and may well strike the target. There are, of course, several loopholes in this argument, as doubtless can be seen, but it seemed to have merit and for some years it was a considerable arguing point. It seems to have died away, however, and no current service weapon uses the burst-fire facility.

But, thinking back to the drawbacks of machine pistols, there is some merit in providing a burst-fire capability on a machine pistol. In such weapons, as we have already pointed out, the rate of fire is such that only the first two or three rounds have any chance of going near the target, since the climb of the gun disperses the remaining rounds harmlessly. So if the burst is confined to just those first three shots, there will be a saving of ammunition and a probable increase in accuracy. This seems to have been the theory which has prompted one West German firm, Heckler and Koch GmbH, to produce a modern design of machine pistol, their 'VP70'. This is a blowback pistol, chambered for the 9mm Parabellum round, which can be used as a normal handgun. By attaching the plastic holster-stock, a connection is made with the trigger mechanism which allows selection of either single shots or a three-round burst-fire facility. At present the pistol is still being evaluated.

The pistol field has been rich in unusual ideas in postwar years, and one of the most unusual was the 'Gyrojet' pistol. This was the product of two Americans, Mainhardt and Biehl, who had set up a company to develop engineering patents. As it happened, nothing very good came their way, and they began to look at firearms, feeling that since the existing technology was fairly ancient, there might be room for improvement. At this time (1960), rockets were the coming thing, and they set about developing what amounts to a handheld rocket launcher in the shape of a pistol. The heart of the design was the projectile, a tiny rocket little bigger than a conventional .45in pistol cartridge, which had a number of angled 'venturis' in the base, surrounding a percussion cap. The offset angle of the venturis not only propelled the rocket but also gave it spin in order to stabilise it in flight.

The launcher was pistol-shaped and carried a magazine in the butt in conventional fashion – but

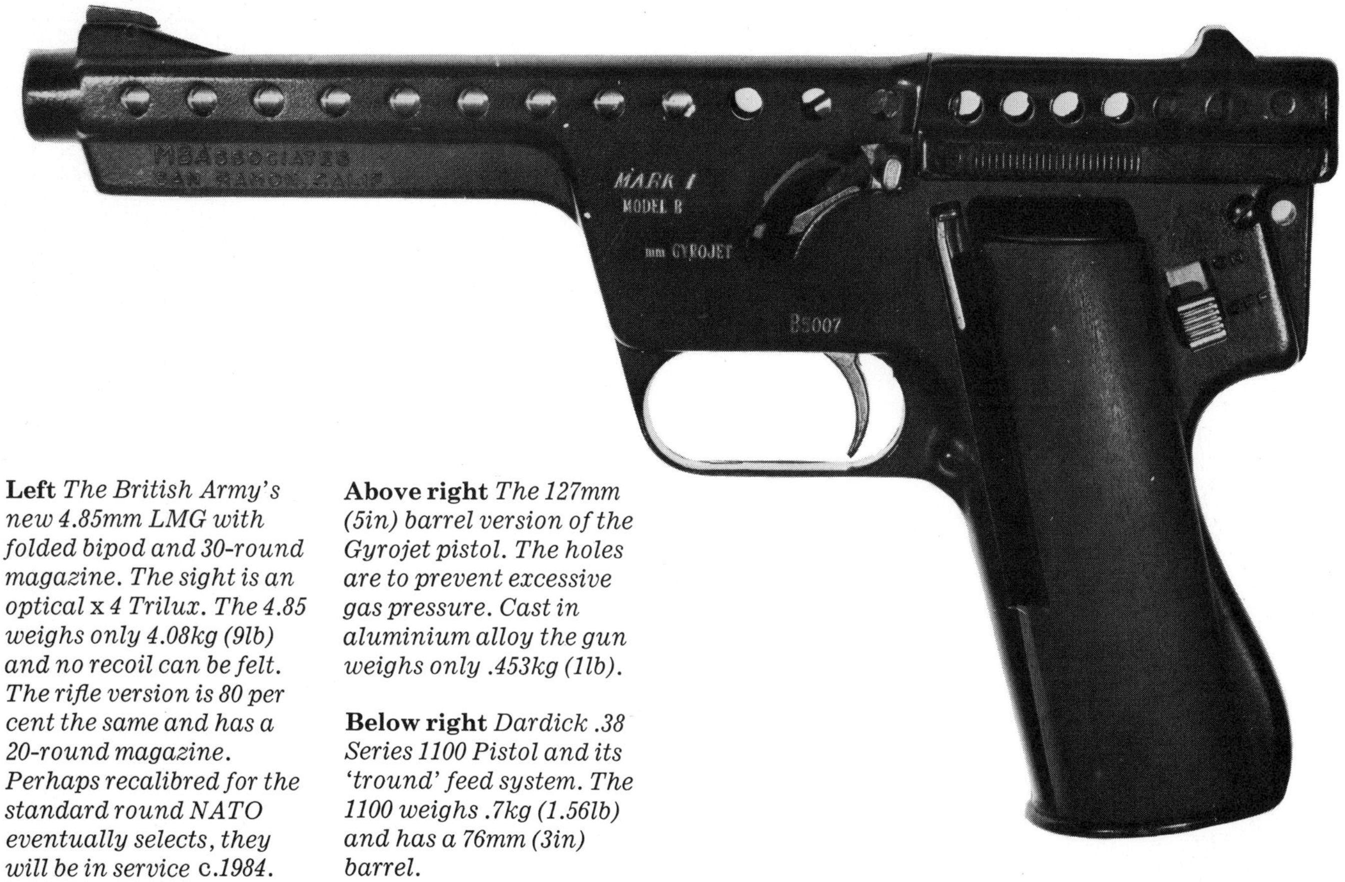

Left *The British Army's new 4.85mm LMG with folded bipod and 30-round magazine. The sight is an optical x 4 Trilux. The 4.85 weighs only 4.08kg (9lb) and no recoil can be felt. The rifle version is 80 per cent the same and has a 20-round magazine. Perhaps recalibred for the standard round NATO eventually selects, they will be in service* c.*1984.*

Above right *The 127mm (5in) barrel version of the Gyrojet pistol. The holes are to prevent excessive gas pressure. Cast in aluminium alloy the gun weighs only .453kg (1lb).*

Below right *Dardick .38 Series 1100 Pistol and its 'tround' feed system. The 1100 weighs .7kg (1.56lb) and has a 76mm (3in) barrel.*

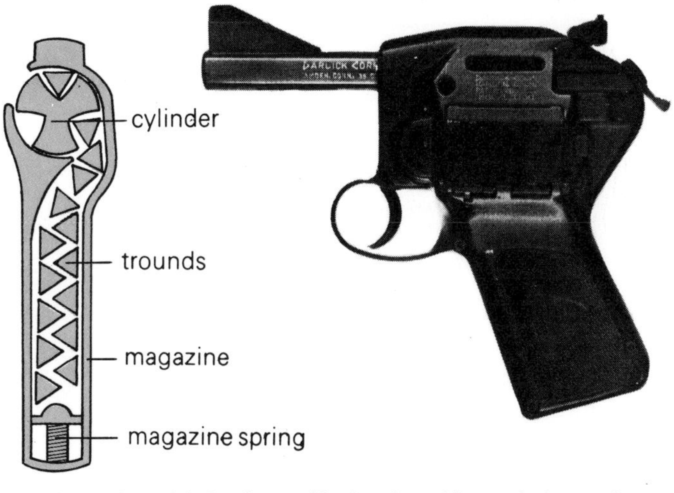

that was as far as resemblance with convention went. The firing mechanism was a hammer mounted in front of the trigger. It struck backwards to hit the nose of the rocket at the top of the magazine column and thus it sat at the end of the launcher – in the same position as a conventional cartridge would be in the breech of a conventional gun. Behind the rocket, forming part of the standing breech,was a fixed striker. Thus, when the trigger was pulled, the hammer sprang up, hit the rocket on the nose, and drove it back so that the percussion cap in its base struck against the fixed striker. As a result, the rocket propellant was ignited and the rocket was launched from the weapon. The rocket weighed about 11.3g (0.4oz), attained a maximum velocity of about 365m/sec (1,200ft/sec), and was of 13mm calibre. Pistol launchers and small carbine-pattern launchers were developed, and the Gyrojet 'pistol' went on sale in 1965 at the then high price of $250. But efforts to interest the military failed. The accuracy was far below that of a conventional pistol – one report spoke of 280mm (11in) groups at 9m (10yd) range – the velocity falls off rapidly once the rocket fuel is burned out, and the cost of ammunition was high. Apart from achieving some spectacular publicity in one of the James Bond films, the Gyrojet failed to make an impression and the company eventually turned to other things.

More conventional in some respects, was the Dardick pistol, conceived by an American, David Dardick, in 1949. His invention was what he called the 'open chamber gun'. It can be best likened to a revolver in which the cylinder has three triangular cut-outs which, to some extent, resemble conventional chambers. But this cylinder does not function as a magazine. It is a transport and firing device, the cartridges being carried in a conventional box magazine inside the pistol's butt. The cartridges were triangular – Dardick coined the word 'tround' to describe them – and were in fact standard commercial cartridges encased in a polycarbonate plastic sleeve. These were fed up the magazine in the usual way and entered one of the cut-out sections in the cylinder. This was then indexed round by the trigger mechanism. During its travel, the tround was prevented from falling out by a thin metal cover, and when the tround arrived in line behind the pistol barrel, it was kept in place by the

Walther PP

This pistol appeared in 1929, the culmination of a line of pocket sidearms begun in 1908. In 7.65mm calibre, the Model PP's greatest novelty was a double-action lock (later used on the military P-38). This permitted the Walther to be carried with the chamber loaded and the hammer down in perfect safety, yet allowed it to be fired by simply releasing the safety catch and pulling the trigger. Another innovation was the adoption of a 'signal pin' in the top of the slide, a spring-loaded pin whose front end rested on the rim of a cartridge in the chamber. This forced the pin back so that the rear end exposed itself above the hammer. Thus a loaded chamber could be seen or felt, a most useful safety feature.

The PP became the standard police pistol throughout Europe in the 1930s and was widely sold commercially. Although the standard calibre was 7.65mm, versions in .22in rimfire, 6.35mm and 9mm Short chambering were also made, in fewer numbers.

The PP's success as a holster pistol prompted development of a more compact model for pocket or concealed use. This was introduced in 1931 as the Model PPK. It was simply a smaller PP, though after the first few had been made there was a change of butt design to allow a one-piece plastic grip to be used. The PPK was also made in the same alternative calibres.

After the war patents for these pistols were still valid so Walther licensed the French company of Manurhin to make both models for some years. By the mid-1960s the Walther factory had been reorganized in Ulm and production then reverted to the parent firm once more. Numerous licensed and unlicensed copies and near-copies have also appeared in other countries.

In 1968 the US Government passed the Gun Control Act, which, among other restrictions, forbad the importation of any pistol measuring less than 101.6mm (4in) from the bottom of the butt to the top of the slide. At that time the PPK was selling widely among plain clothes policemen in America, but was banned because it measured 99mm (3.9in). Walther developed the PPK/S for the US market, simply the PP frame with the PPK's barrel and slide. Length remained the same but the vital depth measurement was increased to 104.14mm (4.1in), thus allowing its legal importation into the US.

Below *A compact 9mm Walther PPK (of post-1965 manufacture) with its magazine loaded.*

WALTHER PP

Calibre 7.65mm
Length 172mm (6.8in)
Weight 0.680kg (1.5lb)
Barrel 100mm (3.9in)
Rifling 6 grooves, r/hand
Foresight Blade
Rearsight Fixed V-notch
Action Blowback
Rate of fire 25 rpm
Feed system 8-round box magazine
Muzzle velocity 290m/sec (950ft/sec)
Bullet weight 4.65g (72gr)

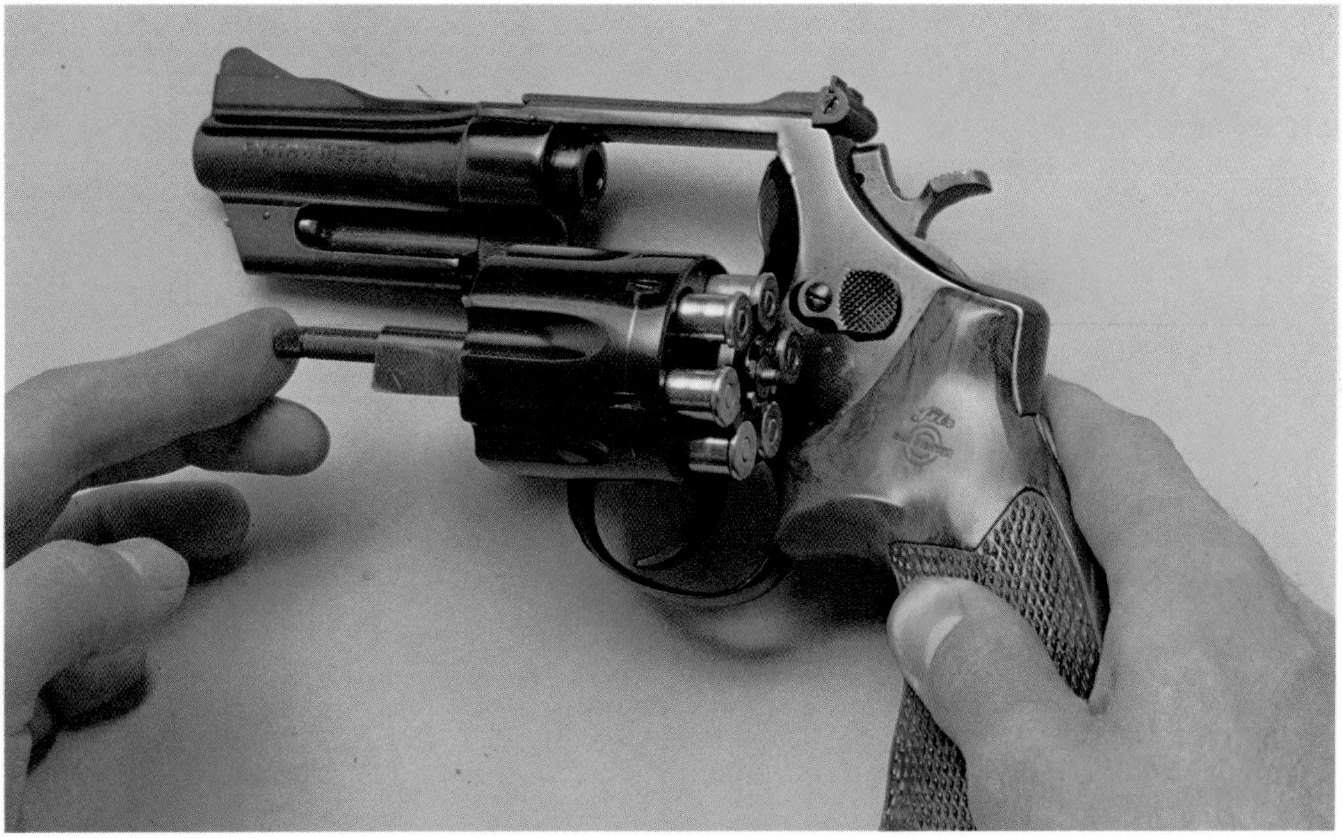

In the early 1930s, Elmer Keith, an American pistol user of considerable repute, developed his own design of .38 revolver cartridge. He used a 11.2g (173grain = 0.39oz) bullet with a powerful charge, firing it from a .38-44 'Outdoorsman' revolver. Major Douglas B. Wesson, of the Smith and Wesson Company, became interested and in 1934 began designing a revolver to shoot a 10.22g (158 grain = 0.36oz) Keith bullet at as high a velocity as possible. The resulting weapon was the .357 Magnum Revolver, introduced in 1935.

The revolver was built using the .44 Target model's frame as a basis, in order to obtain ample strength. The barrel was 222.25mm (8.75in) long, with a stiffening rib along the top, and the pistol weighed 1.36kg (3lb). The bullet developed 435.86m/sec (1430ft/sec) with a striking energy of 972 joules (717 ft-lb force). For several years the .357 Magnum was the most powerful handgun available. The calibre designation of .357 (which is the barrel diameter of all .38in revolvers) was chosen to distinguish the Magnum from the general run of .38s. The cartridge case was made about 2.5mm (0.1in) longer than the normal .38 case so that it would not fit chambers of lesser revolvers.

The .357 Magnum was at first available only to special order, but demand became so great that it went into general production. The 222.25mm (8.75in) barrel was supplemented by other lengths, from 88.9mm (3.5in) upwards, and about 5,500 were made before production stopped in 1941.

After the war it began again, the pistol now being called the Model 27. It is offered in the same barrel lengths, the shorter being more popular, and is fitted with a target rear sight. A less luxurious version is the Model 28 'Highway Patrolman', available with 101.6mm (4in) or 152.4mm (6in) barrels, and, as the title implies, popular with US police forces.

Finally there came the Model 19 'Combat Magnum', a light weight Model 27 on a slightly smaller frame. Normally with a 4in or 6in barrel, a special 'snub' version with 63.5mm (2.5in) barrel and rounded butt is also made.

The .357 Magnum was the gun which began the 'Magnum' fashion and its reduction in size is interesting. In 1935 the Smith and Wesson Company said that 'we do not recommend this gun for the ordinary user' but that it was 'intended for men of large build and more than ordinarily powerful physique'. If that was true of a 1.36kg (3lb) gun with 222.25mm (8.75in) barrel, one is inclined to speculate about the physique of whoever is firing the 878g (1.93lb), 63.5mm (2.5in) barrel Combat Magnum. Since ammunition is the same, the lighter gun generates much more recoil force.

Above *A .357 Smith and Wesson Magnum is shown with its cylinder open and cartridges being extracted.*

MAGNUM MODEL 27
6in Barrel

Calibre .357in
Length 285mm (11.25in)
Weight 1.25kg (2.75lb)
Barrel 152mm (6.0in)
Rifling 5 grooves, r/hand
Foresight Blade
Rearsight fixed V-notch
Action Revolver
Rate of fire 12 rpm
Feed system 6-shot cylinder
Muzzle velocity 442m/sec (1,450ft/sec)
Bullet weight 10.22g (158gr)

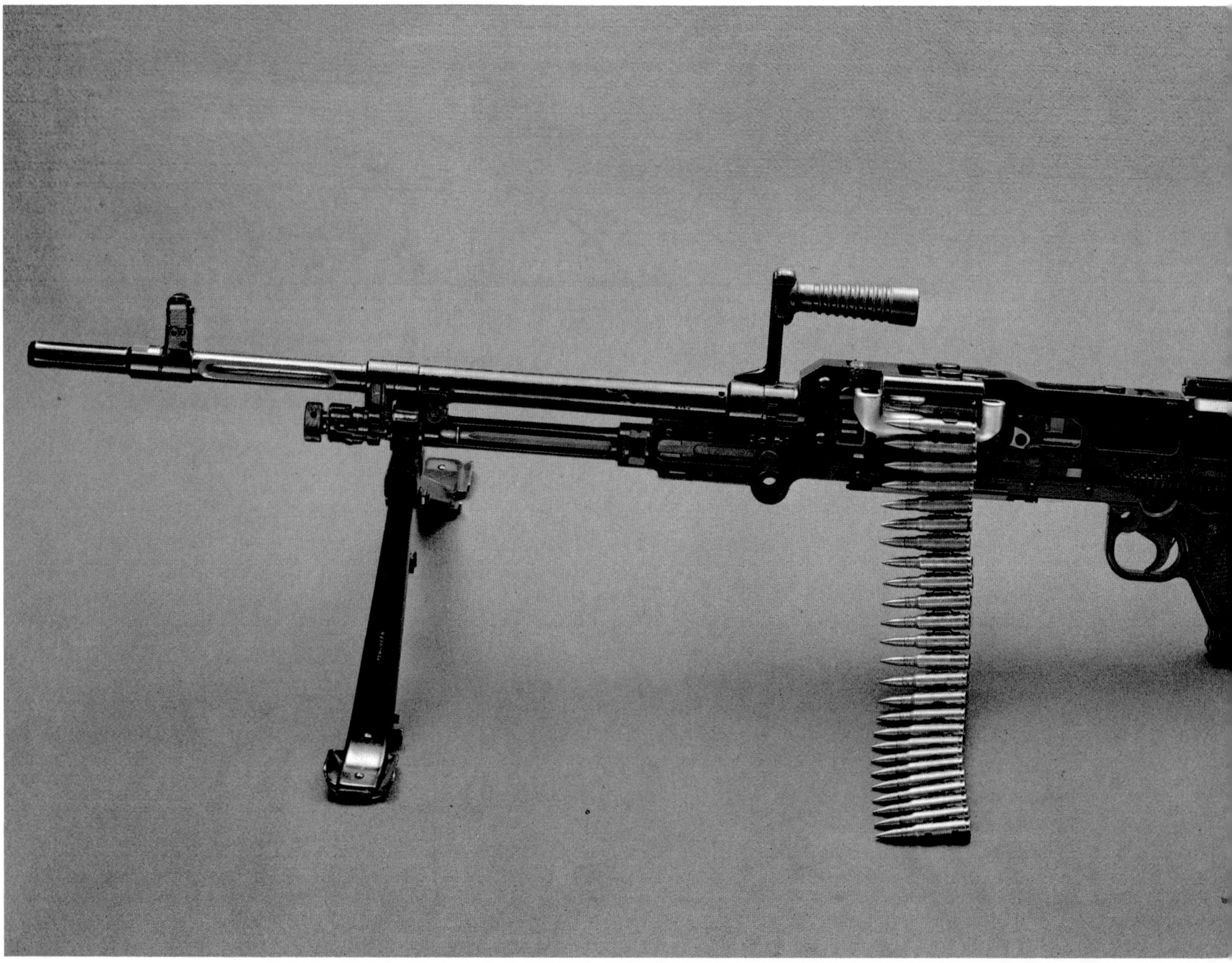

top strap of the pistol frame forming the third side of the triangular 'chamber' in which the tround lay. The hammer now fell and fired the 'tround', the bullet passing up the barrel in the usual way. The next movement of the trigger revolved the cylinder to eject the fired 'tround' and bring the next one in line with the barrel.

Dardick produced two models of pistol, both in .38in calibre, though by the use of interchangeable barrels and adapters they could be made to fire 9mm Parabellum or .22in rounds. Although they worked, they were sufficiently different to meet a certain amount of customer resistance. Moreover, the ammunition was not readily available, and, in comparison with conventional pistols, they were expensive. Due to a combination of these factors, the pistol was discontinued after a few years. The idea, however, has continued to be developed and is currently being evaluated as a possible means of operating an aircraft cannon.

One pistol development which appears to have prospered beyond the original intention is that of the 'Magnum' pistol. There have always been shooters for whom the available firearms are not enough, either because they feel that their own potential as marksmen is not being sufficiently stretched or because they feel that there is a need for a weapon of some particular characteristic, be it high velocity, heavy bullet, long barrel, or what-have-you. The United States, with its less repressive firearms laws, ready availability of weapons and components, and firearms-oriented population, has been the home of most of these innovators, and they have been responsible for innumerable developments in the firearms world.

In the 1930s the Smith and Wesson company began the magnum trend by developing the .357 Magnum revolver. This was, in effect, a high-velocity .38 built on the frame of a .44 revolver and thus endowing it with the weight and strength needed to withstand the heavy loading of the new Magnum cartridge. Calibre .357in is actually the bore dimension of all .38in revolvers. How they came to be called '.38' is a question which has never been thoroughly answered. Smith and Wesson chose to use the correct dimension in the title in order to differentiate between the new cartridge and the rest of the .38 world, and they also made the cartridge case rather longer so that it would not chamber in their ordinary .38 revolvers, which were not built to withstand the new cartridge.

The .357 Magnum became a popular cartridge with target shooters, hunters and police, and in postwar

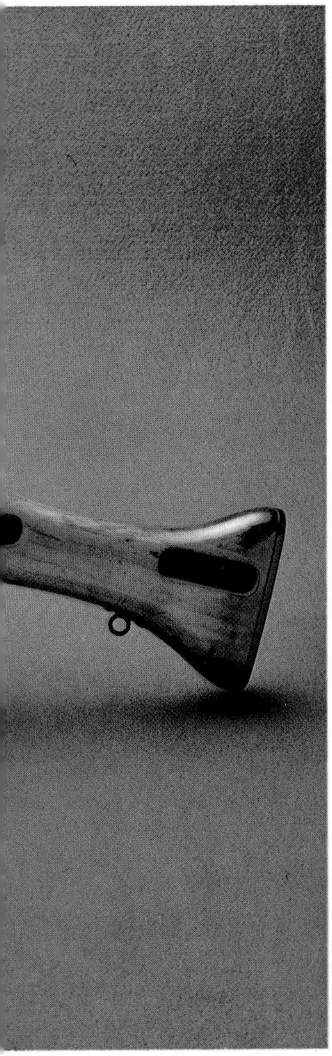

Left *Demonstration model of the British General Purpose MG L7A1 which is a slightly altered Belgian FN Mitrailleur à Gaz (MAG). A 250-round belt of 7.62mm NATO ammunition is shown loaded. This gas-generated tipping bolt gun weighs 10.89kg (24lb) with its bipod.*

Above *Night strafing by a 7.62mm Vulcan Mini-gun.*

years other magnum cartridges appeared, each being accompanied by a suitably strengthened pistol. Some have prospered, some have not – there seems to be no rule-of-thumb which can forecast how well a magnum cartridge will be received. The latest introduction has been the .44in Magnum automatic pistol called the 'Auto-Mag', the cartridge for which was put together from a .44in revolver bullet and a cut-down 7.62mm NATO rifle cartridge case. The pistol is a recoil-operated weapon using a rotating bolt controlled by cam tracks in the pistol frame. It weighs over 1.55kg (3.5lb), fires the .44in bullet at 544m/sec (1,785ft/sec), and develops a recoil energy of about 16.25 joules (12ft-lb) force). Considering that the US service rifle develops a recoil energy of 15 joules (11ft-lb force), it can be seen that the Auto-Mag is something of a handful to fire. It seems probable that with this monster, the end of the magnum trail has been reached.

The machine gun world has also seen some new developments in postwar years. largely due to the demands of modern fighting aircraft. With aircraft speeds into the four figures, the amount of time available to engage a target has dropped to fractions of a second, and it became necessary to develop machine guns which would deliver as great a weight of bullets as possible in the shortest possible time. This demand was stated as early as 1944 by the US Air Force, and some inspired engineers removed an old Gatling gun from a museum, geared it to an electric motor, and fired short bursts at rates up to 5,000 shots a minute. This was far in excess of the rate which could be achieved by any other type of machine gun, and it was therefore decided to take the Gatling design and bring it up to date. The project was given to the General Electric Company and became 'Project Vulcan'.

In 1949 an electrically-driven prototype gun in .60in calibre was fired at 6,000 rounds per minute (rpm). The mechanism was exactly that of the original Gatling, a few changes being made to suit modern production methods and the modern ammunition. Development continued, changing the calibre to 20mm in order to be able to use high explosive projectiles and thus do more damage to the target, and in 1956 the 20mm Vulcan aircraft gun went into service. The designers then turned to smaller calibres and developed a 7.62mm version, the Vulcan M134. This uses six barrels driven by a 28-volt electric motor. An electronic control system allows selection of any two rates of fire between 400 rpm minimum and 6,000 rpm maximum. As a ground weapon it is scarcely practical – due to the need for power supply, and the need for cumbersome ammunition-feed arrangements to cater for the gun's enormous appetite – but mounted in a vehicle as an anti-aircraft weapon, or in a helicopter for ground attack, it delivers a devastating stream of bullets which can literally chop their way through undergrowth or light buildings.

With the acceptance by the US Forces of the 5.56mm cartridge, the General Electric Company quickly produced a 5.56mm version of the Vulcan which they called the 'Six-Pak'. This is more feasible as a ground weapon, since the whole gun, with power supply and 1,000 rounds, weighs only 38kg (85lb), and it is currently being evaluated by the US Army.

SPORTING GUNS

THE HUNTING SCENE is currently dominated by the shotgun. Far more people use shotguns than use rifles, largely because of the availability of suitable game such as game birds – the grouse, pheasant, partridge and waterfowl – and because the limited range of a shotgun permits bird shooting to take place close to inhabited areas.

The double-barreled shotgun, with the barrels side-by-side has, for years, been the archetypal shotgun, but in recent years other types have gained favour. The 'over-and-under', with the barrels superimposed, has its adherents, who hold to the view that aiming is more certain since there is a well-defined line across the one upper barrel rather than a somewhat nebulous line of sight up the rib in between the two barrels of the traditional gun. Thus the over-and-under appears where more precise pointing is demanded, such as in trap shooting.

Multiple-loading guns are favoured by some people, though it has to be said that there are 'traditional' shooters who regard them as an abomination. The 'slide-action' or 'trombone' gun, with a tubular magazine and with the breech operated by sliding the wooden fore-end back and forth is perhaps looked on with more favour than the pure automatic weapon. These usually accept five shots and are either gas or recoil operated in much the same way as an automatic rifle. Their principal virtue is that they hold two-and-a-half times as much ammunition as a traditional double gun and can be 'topped up' without having to unload, so that one is always ready for a suddenly-presented shot as a bird swoops into range. On the other hand it seems true to say that they do tend to encourage the less responsible type of hunter in indiscriminate gunfire. Anyone doubting this should walk through the Portuguese countryside on August 1, when the hunting season opens. The fusillade of gunfire resembles the Battle of Mons.

The use of the rifle in hunting begins with shooting rabbits with a .22 and ends with shooting elephants with a .500 Express rifle. And, we might add, there are hunters who consider that rifle shooting is too easy and go armed with pistols to do the same thing. Once out of the 'vermin class' – rabbits, woodchucks and so forth – there are few, if any, rules about what rifle should be used for what game. Every hunter has his own ideas about what calibre and cartridge is best for a given target, though it is noticeable that there do tend to be fashions in this.

In the 1920s there was a sudden swing away from the massive calibres which had been popular for 'big game' shooting. For years the standards had been in the .45in, .476in, .500in calibre area, firing massive lead bullets at median velocities to achieve a powerful knock-down blow. Then came the sudden fashion for small calibres fired at extremely high velocities. Their protagonists argued that the product of bullet mass times velocity worked out the same way, so that the result would be the same. The ballisticians knew, the shooters knew, but nobody remembered to tell the elephants and lions – and there is a neat row of crosses in a Nairobi graveyard to prove it.

Today the fashion has moved back to large calibres,

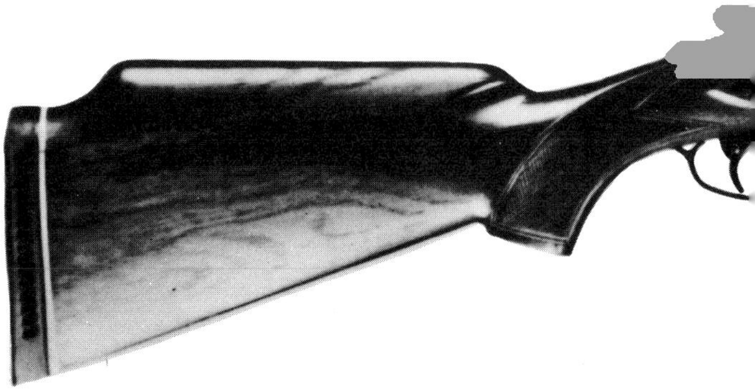

though coupled with high velocities. One American expert, asked his opinion on the best rifle for game shooting, is said to have answered, 'The heaviest damn gun you can carry all day', and there is a lot to be said for that. In years gone by the 'double rifle', a rifle with two side-by-side barrels and, at first glance, indistinguishable from a shotgun, was the preferred weapon of English hunters. Such a gun, chambered for the .500 Express cartridge, was a formidable weapon both for the target and for the man who fired it. Today the calibres have dropped – .300 Magnum, .375, .335, .476, .458 are standard loadings. The double rifle has almost disappeared in favour of the bolt action, usually based on the Mauser bolt, or, in less powerful calibres, the lever-action based on the Winchester design.

The airgun has made a surprising return in recent years. Fifty or more years ago, airgun clubs were common in Britain, but by the 1930s the airgun had become little more than a child's toy, particularly in the United States. But legislation and economics have, between them, brought the airgun back into prominence in both Britain and the US. Airgun clubs are once more flourishing, tournaments are being contested, and some highly sophisticated and expensive weapons are appearing.

The airgun is, in its basic form, a simple machine. A piston is pulled back against a spring and held there by a trip mechanism. A lead pellet is inserted

Previous page *Venere Extralusso 'Side-by side' double barrel, side-lock 12-bore shotgun, made by the Italian firm of Abbiatico Salvinelli. It has double Purdey-type under bolting, selective automatic ejectors and special bouquet engraving.*

Above *A 12-bore 'over and under' (one barrel above the other) double barrel shotgun for trap shooting. A ventilated rib above the barrel dissipates heat sideways to avoid air turbulence, giving a better sight along the two small beads.*

Below left *This side-by-side barrelled shotgun breaks forward and downward for loading or cartridge ejection.*

Below right *Duck shooting with decoys and a pump action 'over and under' 12-bore.*

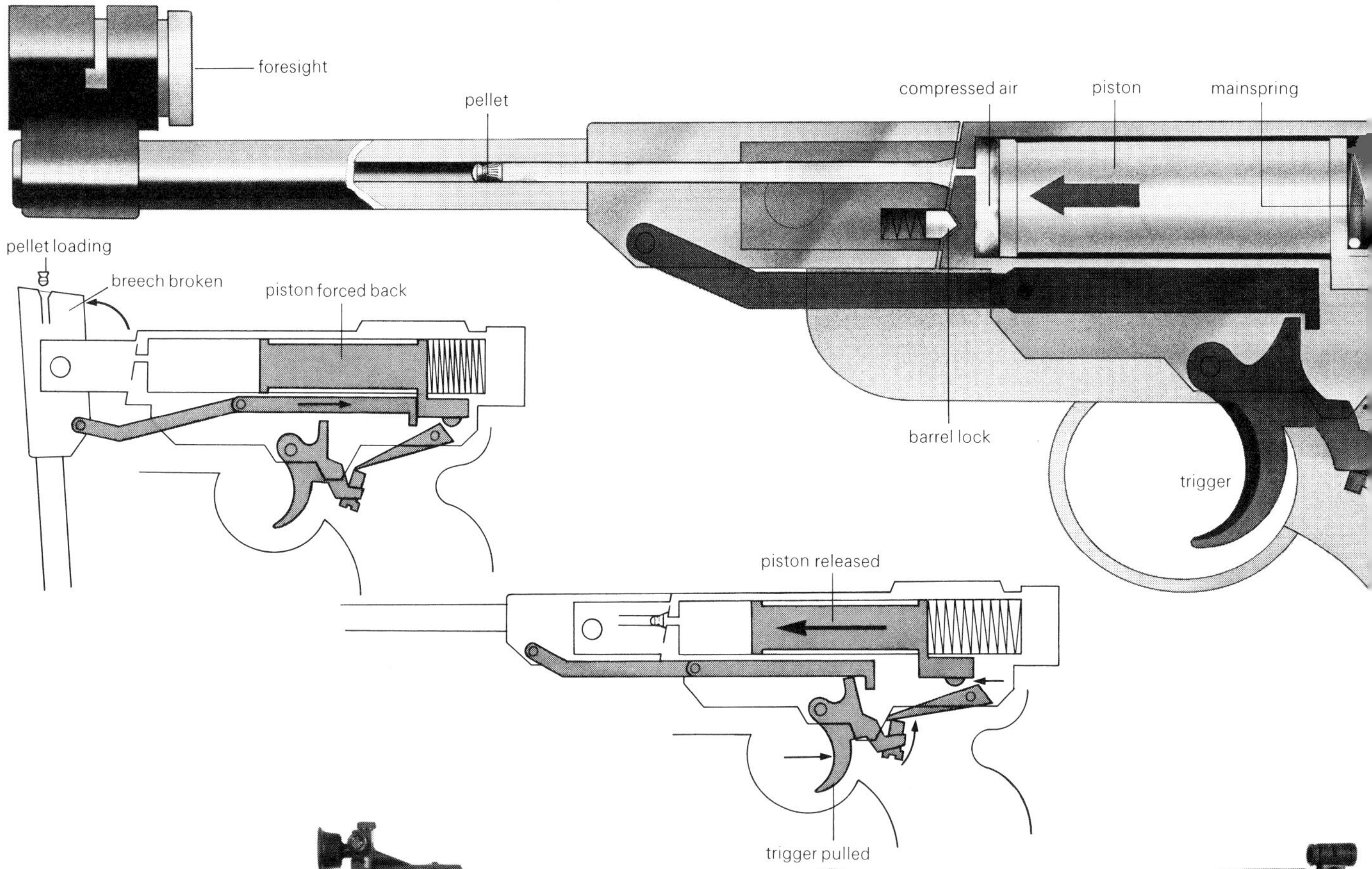

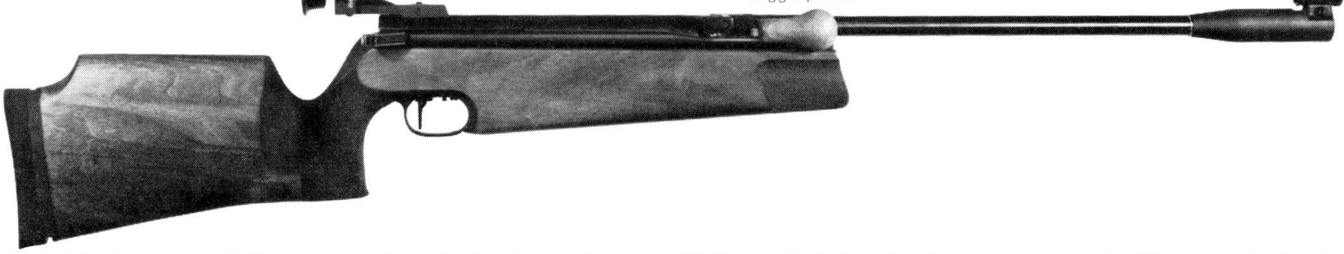

into the barrel and the trigger is pulled. This releases the piston which flies forwards in a cylinder, compressing air which is then channelled into the breech to blow the pellet from the barrel. Within this simple framework many refinements are possible. For example, it will be apparent that when the piston flies forwards there will be a sensible change in the balance of the weapon, and this is countered in some modern designs by arranging for a similar weight to be propelled in the opposite direction in order to cancel out the piston's effect. Rifling of the barrel needs to be carefully tailored to suit the airgun. The deep rifling needed with the high velocities of power-burning weapons is not required with the low-powered airgun, and with less pressure behind the pellet, there is less deformation into the rifling, so shallow grooves are needed.

The matter of expense is one which is continuing to shape sports shooting. The only way to become a proficient shot *is* to shoot. A noted American exhibition shooter was once asked what was needed to become a first-class shot. 'About ten years', he replied, 'and several car-loads of ammunition.' In 1979, .45 automatic pistol 'Match grade' ammunition cost about £23 per hundred rounds (about $23 in the US), and .308 Winchester – the civilian equivalent of 7.62mm NATO – about £26 per hundred (about $39 in the US).

At prices like this, the traditional sort of rifle and pistol shooting can soon become expensive. One way out of the dilemma is to manufacture one's own ammunition – 'handloading' as it is termed. One can start either by purchasing a quantity of commercial ammunition, firing it, and preserving the cartridge cases. Or one can buy fired cases (or even new ones). The cases then have the primers removed, are cleaned, checked, and brought to 'new' dimensions once again by a special tool known as a 'resizing die'. Powder is then bought in bulk, weighed into charges and filled into the cases; bullets bought and fitted; primers bought and pressed into the cases.

The result is a round of ammunition ready for firing at a cost considerably less than the cost of commercial ammunition – once the expenditure on reloading tools has been amortized. The other advantage of this system is that the shooter is not restricted to the charge and bullet prescribed by the ammunition manufacturer. He can experiment with lighter or stronger charges, different weights and shapes of bullet, until he arrives at a loading

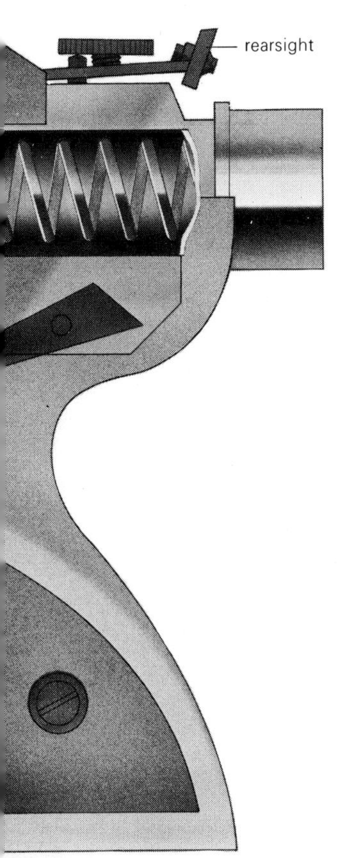

Left *The air gun mechanism. The weapon is shown being fired and loaded. Breaking the breech (far left) not only enables the pellet to be loaded but also forces back the piston, cocking it to fire.*

Below left *This Walther LGR .177 Match Air Rifle is recoilless (piston and counterweight system) and weighs 5.44kg (12lb). The large knob is the cocking lever and the rifle has finely adjustable micrometer aperture sights.*

Below *A Brown Bess flint lock musket being fired by a latter-day enthusiast. The ignition of the priming powder in the pan, a moment before the main charge is fired, has not made the firer flinch.*

which precisely suits his particular weapon and his particular method of using it.

Handloading also benefits a class of firearms enthusiast most common in the United States, the 'wild-catter'. The term has no bearing on the object of the shooter's expertise. It is of doubtful etymology but it indicates that the shooter was not satisfied with the calibres which the gunmakers have seen fit to provide, but, instead, has developed a calibre and loading of his own. Some wildcatters are undoubtedly frustrated firearms designers who would be happiest in a military arsenal somewhere, designing and building weapons. Others are simply hunters or target shooters who are quite convinced that their pet project is the answer to flatter trajectories, higher velocities, or better killing power.

Wildcat cartridges are usually characterized by commercial cases which are modified to accept a totally different bullet. For example, the .22in Varminter began as a .250in Savage case with the neck reduced to take a special jacketed .22in bullet. This was one of the more successful designs and later appeared in commercial form. Another, the '8mm-06' was developed when owners of 8mm Mauser rifles found that the supply of commercial ammunition had dried up. They therefore expanded the rifle chamber to take the standard US Army .30-06 cartridge case, and then modified the case neck to take the 8mm bullet. One expert has estimated that there have been upwards of 200 different wildcat rounds developed in the US alone, and there appear to be new ones coming along to replace the failures at a rate which will probably keep this figure fairly constant.

Another way of economizing which has gained ground in recent years has been to revert completely and go back to using gunpowder and percussion caps or even flintlocks. 'Black Powder Shooting' has become immensely popular in the last ten years, both in the US and in Europe, and there are several companies fully engaged in producing factory-built replicas of old weapons – from 'Kentucky Rifles' to imitations of Brown Bess, from flintlock dragoon pistols to copies of the early Remington and Colt cap-and-ball revolvers.

It must be said that economy is not the whole story. There is a good deal of sensuous satisfaction from firing a black-powder gun. The recoil and report differ from those of a smokeless-powder arm, and the cloud of powder smoke which wreathes the shooter has its own peculiar attraction. Originally this movement was devoted to target shooting, but there is now a growing band of devotees using black-powder rifles and shotguns for hunting. Not only do they have the pleasure of using their older weapons, but there is also the element of a 'handicap' favouring the hunted animals, giving them rather more of a sporting chance than they are likely to get with the very latest products of the gunsmiths' art.

In the last 600 years, the hand firearm has come a long way – from a roughly cast lump of bronze, to the intricate and finely-machined target pistol or rifle or the lovingly-crafted shotgun of the present day. It may seem premature to say that future advances will be relatively minor, but it certainly looks as if the powder-fired projectile-discharging firearm has reached the point where major further development is extremely unlikely.

There has been no significant advance in principles of operation since the development of the automatic rifle and the submachine gun, and even they were founded on basic principles which had been known for years. There have, it is true, been attempts to devise something entirely different – a solenoid gun, for example, in which a magnetic field is employed to discharge a missile – but these have been aberrant curiosities which have come and gone, while the traditional gun has stood the test of time. It may well be that in future years, historians will point to the latter part of the twentieth century and say, 'This was the zenith of firearms development'.

BY WAY OF ACCOMPANIMENT

IT MAY SEEM OBVIOUS, but it is frequently forgotten that the best of guns is nothing without ammunition. The *bullet* is the weapon – the gun merely a means of getting the weapon to the target.

It is not unknown for a good gun to be spoiled by poor ammunition, or an indifferent gun to be improved out of all recognition by well-designed ammunition. A case in point is the Smith and Wesson .44in 'American' revolver. As originally produced, its accuracy was no more than average due to the poor fit of the bullet in the barrel. When the Russians decided to adopt the weapon, they redesigned the cartridge, increasing the size of the bullet and making it a better fit into the rifling. This small alteration transformed the .44 into a first-class target pistol.

Modern ammunition began with the researches of the Swiss designer Major Rubin, who developed the compound bullet having a lead core and a hard-metal jacket. This gave the combined advantages of mass (from the core) and freedom from fouling in the barrel (from the jacket) and, allied with smokeless powder, enabled automatic arms and repeating rifles to become a practical possibility. It also changed the shape of rifle bullets from short, fat lead slugs to long, thin, jacketed bullets which retained their velocity better through the air.

The matter might have rested there but for the discovery of high-speed spark photography. This enabled pictures to be obtained of bullets in flight and also showed the air flow and shock waves which were built up around the bullet. The photographs made it possible to obtain positive information about the effect of changes in bullet shape, and one of the first benefits of this came in 1905 when the German Army adopted a pointed rifle bullet in place of the round-nose pattern previously used. This gave better flight characteristics and maintained velocity to a greater distance. This lead was followed by most other nations, the French adding a twist by introducing their 'Balle D', made entirely of bronze.

The pointed bullet with its base at right angles was selected as there are two factors which affect the flight of a bullet – the shock wave generated at the nose due to exceeding the speed of sound; and the turbulent drag caused by the airflow passing into the area behind the base as the bullet cleaves the air. The spark photographs and practical experiments showed that the shock wave was the biggest factor, and that tapering the nose reduced the effect. The base drag was negligible in comparison. But during World War I the long-range machine gun came into greater use, and field experience indicated that at long range there was a serious fall-off in accuracy. More experiments were carried out and these showed that once the bullet dropped below the speed of sound, as it did at long ranges, the base drag became the more important of the two factors, causing instability and inaccuracy of flight. This was cured by the development of the 'streamlined' bullet, one in which the base was slightly tapered so as to give the airflow a smoother run to the base of the bullet.

Unfortunately, streamlining or 'boat-tailing' the base upset one of the basic mechanical features of the bullet, its 'set-up' into the rifling. The average rifle bullet had a base which was not precisely flat but slightly concave, and the effect of the propelling gas on this was slightly to expand the base and thus make a perfect gas-tight seal in the rifling. But once the bullet was streamlined, this 'set-up' did not take place, and inaccuracy began before the bullet had even left the barrel, since there was a tendency for gas to leak around the bullet, and this led to erosion of the gun barrel. The answer to this lay in special dimensioning of the bullet and careful selection of the jacket metal so as to achieve even engraving into the rifling. Nevertheless, the streamlined bullet was difficult to manufacture and still caused barrel erosion, and most countries restricted its use to machine guns, in which the barrels could be changed periodically, and retained flat-based bullets for rifles in order to preserve their accuracy.

Previous page *Rifle cartridges. Left to right: US .30 M1941 Tracer M1; Austrian 8mm Mannlicher M1888; Soviet 7.62mm x 39 M1943; .600 Express Rifle; French 7.5mm x 54 M1929; NATO 7.62mm x 51 M1954; .450 Martini-Henry M1871 in Boxer wrapped brass case; French 8mm Lebel M1886; British .303in.*

Having got the bullet to fly through the air accurately, the next consideration is its effect at the target. Apart from specialist military bullets (such as tracer or armour-piercing), most bullets are designed to kill, either animals or people. In the earliest days of the gun there was little finesse about this. The bullet was a solid lump of soft lead which struck the target's body, deformed due to its impact, and tore its way through, causing serious injury. But – strange as it may seem – the criterion of efficiency of a bullet is not whether it kills, but whether it incapacitates. A dead soldier is a dead soldier, but a wounded soldier often means two or three enemy out of the line since, human nature being what it is, when a man goes down wounded, often a companion or two will go to his aid, at which point they are no longer combat-effective. Moreover, it is of little use to wound a man if the wound is such that he can continue to fight, or to wound an animal so that it can still run, seek cover, and escape the hunter. So, over the years, the criterion of bullet efficiency has come to be its 'knock-down' power – whether the impact puts the victim flat on the ground, irrespective of the seriousness of the wound.

The best examples of this come from the late nineteenth century, when wars against fanatic tribesmen and the like were still commonplace. The British service revolver bullet was a pointed .455in of hard lead/antimony compound, and experience soon showed that a charging fanatic, armed with a spear or sword, could be hit more than once with these bullets and could still keep coming, moving fast enough to overcome the impact of the bullet and still slice the pistol-holder with his blade. To counter this, a new bullet – known as the 'Man-stopper' – was developed. It was a simple lead cylinder, with the nose formed into a concave cup. When this struck, the head mushroomed out and delivered such a massive blow that even a charging fanatic would be knocked off his feet.

To give rifle users a similarly powerful bullet, the Dum-Dum Arsenal in India produced the 'Dum-Dum' bullet. In recent years any soft-nosed bullet has come to be called 'Dum-Dum', but the genuine article was the British .303in rifle bullet with the metal envelope slit back from the nose for about 6mm (0.25in). It was invented by Captain Bertie Clay, Superintendent of Dum-Dum, and was first used to horrible effect at the Battle of Omdurman (1898). The object of the design was that on impact, the soft lead core would, due to its momentum, pass through the slit envelope and 'mushroom' out to give a greater impact and stopping power.

The American Army learned the same lesson in the Phillipine Insurrection of 1900. They had, some time previously, adopted the .38 revolver as the service pistol instead of the .45in calibre, and they were distressed to find that the .38 had little effect on charging tribesmen. It was this experience which led to the Ordnance Department specifying a .45 bullet for their future arms.

The Hague Convention of 1899 however, outlawed such bullets as the 'Man-stopper' and since then military bullets, except those for some revolvers, have been fully-jacketed types which tend to pierce rather than knock down. Recently, however, there has been a great deal of ill-informed notoriety attaching to the 5.56mm bullets fired from the Armalite and other rifles. Frequently it has been alleged that they are explosive or that they 'tumble in flight, end-over-end, so as to tear into their target'. A moment's thought would make it clear that any bullet which tumbled end-over-end would scarcely be accurate, yet these stories persist. The truth is that the 5.56mm bullet can deliver a devastating knock-down blow and a serious wound, in spite of its small size, simply because the designers of the rifles take advantage of ballistic facts.

A bullet passing through the air carries, stored within it, so many joules (or foot-pounds) of energy, the product of its mass and velocity. It can lose this energy gradually, by friction and air drag, until gravity takes over and it falls to the ground at the end of its flight. Or it can lose it suddenly by striking a target and, stopping, transferring the energy to the target as a blow. In most cases, of course, the strike of the bullet falls somewhere between these two extremes, since the bullet passes through the target and only yields a portion of its energy.

This is where the spinning of the bullet comes to play. If the bullet is well stabilized, the spin persists during the passage through the target, and this tends to keep the bullet on course and encourage it to pass through. In the case of the 5.56mm bullet, however, the amount of spin given to the bullet is only just sufficient to keep it stable throughout its calculated effective range, say to 1,000m (3,300ft). Any interference with the bullet's flight – either by striking a target or even a leaf or blade of grass – is sufficient to upset the stability. The bullet then topples in flight and no longer follows its theoretical trajectory. If the upsetting factor is a target, then the toppling bullet delivers all its energy to the target in one massive blow – and it is this which accounts for the effect of the 5.56mm bullet.

For hunting, however, there are no restrictions on the shape or form that a bullet can take, probably

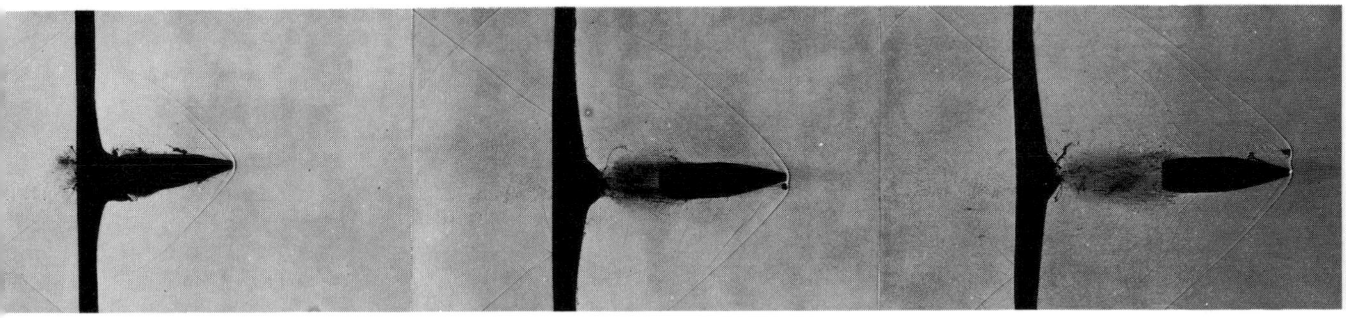

Above *Six shadowgraphs (high-speed silhouette photographs made with high-voltage spark illumination) of a 7.62mm L2A2 British Rifle bullet. In (1), velocity is about 840m/sec (2,755ft/sec) or 2½ x speed of sound. In (2) to (6) a bullet penetrates a polypropylene sheet at c.520m/sec (1,700 ft/sec).*

because there were no animals present at The Hague in 1899. And in order to obtain the greatest possibility of a clean kill, partially-jacketed bullets, which leave the core exposed at the tip, are the most popular. The exposed soft point spreads on impact and delivers more energy to the target, ensuring greater wounding power and more certain knock-down of the game. Obviously, the choice of bullet, both calibre and type, is governed by the type of game to be hunted – the bullet which would stop a charging rhinoceros would be unsuited to hunting rabbits, and vice versa.

Since the effect of a bullet is governed by considerations of its mass and its velocity, achieving high velocity in rifles has always been desirable. This is true not only for the effect of the bullet on the target, but also because a high velocity means a flat trajectory, that is, the bullet travelling closer to the ideal straight line between gun and target and thus simplifying the design of the sights. The easy way to achieve high velocity is simply to put a bigger cartridge behind the bullet, as in the various 'magnum' rounds; but this brings problems of recoil and weight in its train. Other ways have been tried. One method, originally patented in the early 1900s, is to make the rifle barrel with a gradually diminishing calibre as it reaches the muzzle, the breech calibre being, say, 7.5mm and the muzzle calibre, say, 6.5mm. Having done this, the next task is to design a bullet which is 7.5mm when loaded but which will conform to the reduction in calibre and emerge as a 6.5mm. The advantage in this is that since the velocity of the bullet is governed by the gas pressure on its base, reducing the base area will increase the unit pressure and boost the velocity.

Rifles on this plan were built in the 1920s and 1930s by a German gunsmith named Gerlich, who not only promoted the idea for use in hunting rifles but also tried to interest various military authorities in the idea for sniping rifles. The bullets were made with 'skirts' on the jacket which were squeezed in during travel down the rifle bore, or with the jacket swelled out in the wall so that it could be squeezed without deforming the core. The idea worked, and several hunters were enthusiastic about the 'Halger' rifles which used Gerlich's bullets, but they were expensive, and so was the ammunition, and they did not make the inventor a fortune. Gerlich later applied his talents to heavier weapons and was the guiding hand behind some of Germany's most potent anti-tank guns of World War II, which used the 'taper-bore' system.

In the 1960s the 'flechette' made its appearance as a new type of rifle projectile. This was a small dart, resembling, in general, a 2.5cm (1in) nail with three fins. This weighed but a fraction of the weight of a conventional bullet, and it could be launched at extremely high velocities. At the target, because of the high velocity, the impact was considerable and, like the 5.56mm bullet, the flechette gave up its energy instantly and was severely incapacitating. The only problem lay in actually launching it. The flechette could not plug the bore like a bullet, and had to be surrounded by a plastic sheath. This filled the bore and acted as a gas seal, and dragged the flechette up the barrel. Once they both arrived at the muzzle, the plastic sheath was discarded and the flechette left to travel to the target at velocities in the order of 1,370m/sec (4,500ft/sec). Unfortunately the early promise of flechette was not fulfilled – its accuracy at anything but extremely short ranges is poor, and it is expensive and difficult to manufacture to the degree of precision demanded. By the 1970s, little had been heard of it.

One of the more entertaining ammunition ideas to appear in recent years has been the multiple-bullet cartridge. In fact, like almost everything else in the ordnance world, the idea is not new. It was patented by (among others) none other than Georg Luger as early as 1910. But it was not until the 1950s that the idea began to prosper, as a result of various US Army investigations into marksmanship and the lack of it among soldiers. By fitting two bullets in the cartridge case, and cutting the base of the second bullet slightly obliquely, it was then possible to discharge both at one shot, the first bullet going where the rifle was pointed and the second, because of the cut base, taking a course slightly to one side of the first. Which side it took – or, indeed whether it went to the side or went above or below – was entirely random since it depended on the position of the bullet inside the breech. The theory was that if the first bullet was reasonably well-aimed but missed by a small margin, then the second bullet's slight dispersion might well result in a hit and save the day. A 'Duplex' round in 7.62mm NATO calibre was standardized in the US Army in about 1960, but

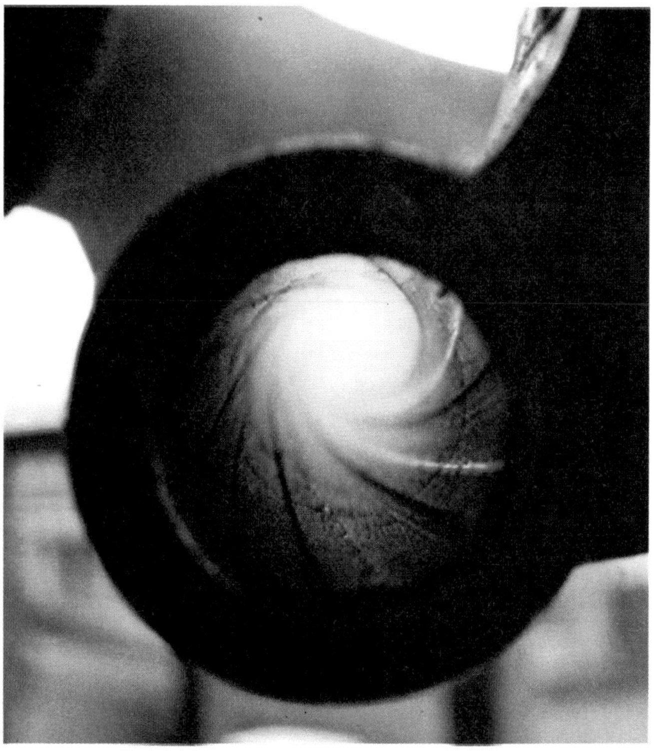

Top *Inside view of a rifled barrel, showing the 'lands' – the spiral ridges and grooves of the rifling.*

little has been heard of the idea since.

Military ammunition, of course, has to perform other functions besides simply producing casualties. Special types of ammunition (and the specific tactical requirements which provided the initial impetus for their development) include the incendiary bullet (developed after Zeppelin's dirigibles appeared during World War I); the tracer bullet (a product of aerial combat); the explosive 'observing' bullet (used in long-range machine-gun firing); and the armour-piercing bullet (designed to counter the tank). All these manage to produce their specialized effect while keeping within the confining envelope of the standard-sized bullet.

The tracer bullet serves as a good introduction to this group since its construction is very basic. It is, in effect, a normal bullet except that the rear half of the core is drilled out to form a receptacle into which a chemical composition is pressed, leaving the bottom of the filling exposed. When the cartridge is fired, the flash of the powder ignites this exposed portion, and the tracer compound then burns away layer by layer, emitting flame and smoke. Thus the passage of the bullet through the air is 'traced' by a visible marker and the firer can correct his aim as necessary.

Obviously, as the tracer material burns away, the weight and balance of the bullet changes, and it no longer performs precisely as a standard solid bullet – commonly called a 'ball' – of the same size. This is catered for in the design, the tracer being arranged to match the trajectory of the ball bullet up to some specified range. In this way, with, for example, a belt of machine gun bullets arranged with one tracer to every four balls, the tracer gives reliable register up to the average fighting range of the gun.

The incendiary bullet resembles the tracer except that the incendiary composition is designed to burn particularly fiercely to set on fire anything it touches. So that the composition is not entirely consumed in flight, the first part of the filling is a 'delay' mixture which burns relatively slowly, allowing the incendiary substance to blossom forth at the mean fighting range. Another way of achieving the same desired effect was to hollow out the nose of the bullet and fill it with phosphorus. When the bullet struck, the phosphorus splashed out and – being spontaneously inflammable – raised fire in the vicinity. But phosphorus is touchy stuff, and is rarely used for this purpose today.

The same sort of construction is used for observing bullets, the nose of the bullet being filled with an explosive substance which detonates on impact. This type of bullet is proscribed for use against personnel, but it can be found in, for example, tank machine guns which are used for determining the range to a target prior to opening fire with the heavy armament. The explosive bullet, fired against another tank, bursts with a flash and bang which makes it quite obvious that hits are being scored. In a similar manner, long-range machine guns have used these bullets for observing the fall of their shot at ranges which made it impossible to detect the fall of inert ball bullets.

The armour-piercing bullet consists of a core of hard steel or even of tungsten encased in the normal bullet envelope. This gives an additional piercing power which the usual sort of lead/antimony core of the ball bullet does not have. There is, of course, nothing except the technical manufacturing problem to stop the incorporation of more than one of these features in one bullet. One can have, for ex-

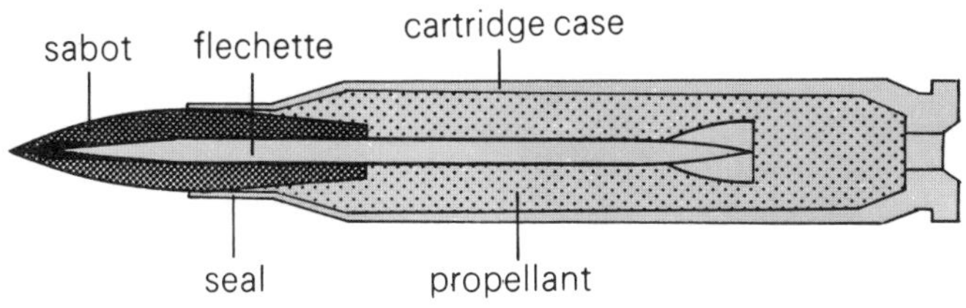

Left *Diagram of a flechette cartridge. The sheath or sabot is discarded at the gun muzzle and the 0.324-0.648g (5-10gr) flechette flies on at four times the speed of sound. Multi-flechette rounds have also been tried.*

Below *Four bullet types. AP rounds are for penetrating the steel plates of light armoured vehicles. The nose is longer and slimmer than the ball type to reduce all resistance and penetration is also helped by the flat nose.*

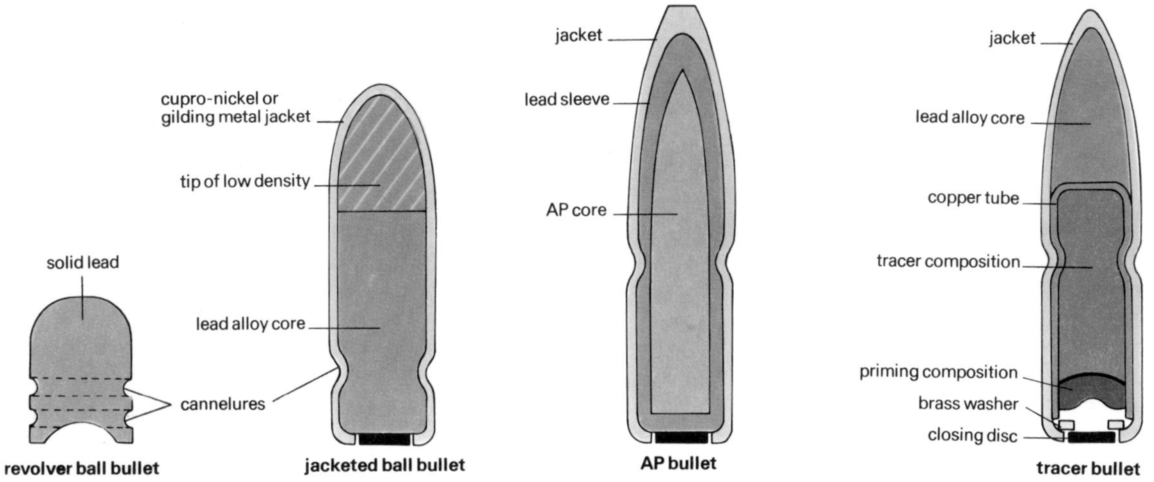

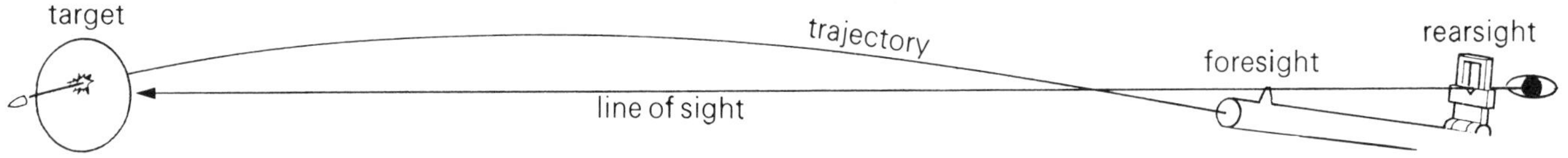

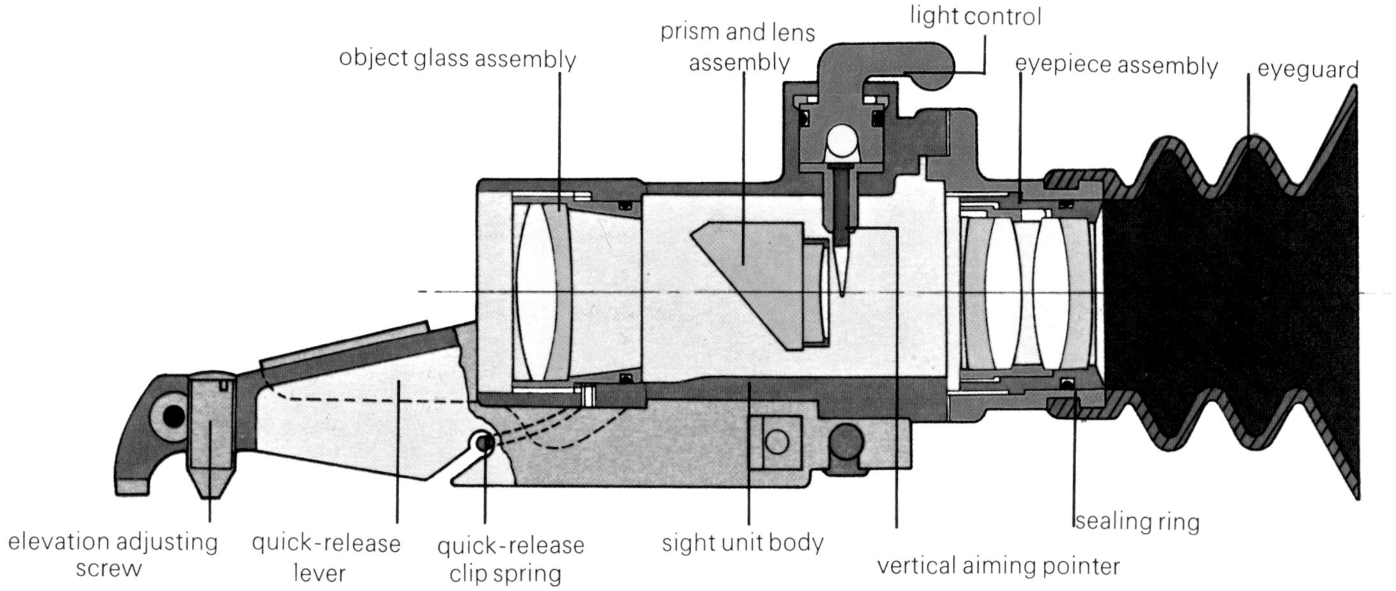

ample, armour-piercing/incendiary bullets.

Having acquired a gun and some ammunition, all that remains is to hit the target – and for this, sights are needed. The simplest form of sight is that found on shotguns and which was used on early muskets. A bead, or block, above the muzzle acts as a foresight, and there is no backsight, as the aim is taken by simply looking down the length of the barrel or barrels.

With the adoption of rifling and the consequent increase in range of weapons, something more precise was needed, in particular a method of applying the correct elevation to the weapon. The object of a sighting system is to correlate the optical line of sight with the axis of the gun barrel in such a way that the trajectory intersects the line of sight at the target. If the rifle is fired when perfectly horizontal, the effect of gravity is to pull down the bullet and thus bend the trajectory or line of flight. To counter this, it is necessary to lift the muzzle of the rifle so as to start the bullet off on an angle of elevation. If this amount of elevation is correctly chosen, then the curvature of the trajectory due to gravity will eventually bring the bullet on to the target.

To attain the correct amount of elevation, the backsight is made to extend some distance above the line of the bore. Thus, a line drawn through the back and fore sights to the target will cause the muzzle of the rifle to be elevated to the necessary amount. As to what the necessary amount may be, this is a question which is affected by the type of rifle, the propelling charge and the flight characteristics of the bullet, and it can only be determined by actual firing.

The sights on a rifle usually take the form of a blade or triangle in the front and a notch at the back. This arrangement gives the best compromise between accuracy and speed of use, since the eye can rapidly pick up the target across the top of the sights. For greatest accuracy, the two sights should be as far apart as the size of the weapon permits, but at this point anatomy intervenes. The human eye is not capable of focusing backsight, foresight and target all at once with complete accuracy – one of the three will be more or less blurred. It is for this reason that the ideal position for the sight was frequently abandoned on military rifles and the backsight placed about half-way down the weapon, in front of the chamber, since this gave a better likelihood of obtaining a sharp sight picture.

To overcome this defect, the aperture backsight was introduced at about the turn of the century. The principle on which this sight is based is that no attempt need be made to focus on the backsight. The sight is merely a piece of metal with a hole in it, through which the firer sees the foresight and the target. Because the hole is circular, the human eye automatically aligns itself with the centre since this is the position giving the greatest luminosity. Thus the foresight is the nearest object on which the eye has to focus, and if a small enough rearsight aperture is used, this tends to deepen the amount of focus of the eye so that both the foresight and the target can be comfortably accommodated. The backsight can also be brought well back, since the closer it is to the eye, the more effective it is, and this improves the sight base, the distance between fore and back sights.

Every improvement, of course, has to be paid for. With the aperture sight, the problems are, firstly,

Left *Setting the line of sight to raise the gun's muzzle will compensate for the bullet's curved trajectory in flight.*

Below left *An example of a modern rifle sight. The Trilux, in service since 1974, has a suspended vertical aiming point with a red triphium light source that illuminates the target not only at night but also in poor daylight.*

Right *The Trilux on the L2A1 British service rifle it was devised for. The soldier is from the Royal Corps of Transport, an indication of how seriously the British Army takes rifle marksmanship in which every rank up to lieutenant-colonel is tested.*

that the surround to the sight obscures the target when bringing the rifle to the aim, and, secondly, that for the best results the aperture should be small, but a small aperture is only usable in good light. Target shooters and hunters can get around this by having adjustable apertures or completely interchangeable apertures, but on military rifles this sort of solution is not practical and the aperture has to be a compromise.

The ultimate form of sight is, of course, the optical or telescopic sight. This, mounted above the rifle and carefully aligned, has definite advantages. In the first place, it removes the focusing problem since all the elements of the sight 'picture' – the target and the telescope's cross-wires – are in the same plane of focus. Moreover, since it magnifies the field of view, it enables a more precise aim to be taken and allows small or indistinct targets to be engaged which could not even have been seen with the naked eye. It also allows targets to be engaged in light too poor to allow the use of open sights and, theoretically, increases the accuracy by a factor which is the magnifying power of the telescope.

There are, though, some problems. Probably the greatest of these is the actual mounting of the telescope on to the rifle. The mounts on to which the telescope fits can rarely be more than about 15cm (6in) apart, and thus must be aligned with the utmost precision and the telescope held there with complete rigidity. If there is 0.25mm (0.01in) play in the mount, then the bullet will be 15cm (6in) off the target at about 100m (110yd) range. The problem is made worse by the rifle's recoil which tends to shake the telescope loose from the mount. This also effects the telescope itself, loosening the optical elements. The mount must also be made in such a fashion that the telescope can be removed and replaced and yet always go back in precisely the same alignment. And, finally, the mount and telescope must be positioned so that they do not interfere with the loading or ejection of the cartridge, or the action of the rifle, and must leave the normal open sights available for use in an emergency.

Several recent designs of military rifle have used a 'unity' optical sight in which there is no magnification of the image. This gives the advantages of focus and good light-gathering power, but retains the target at the same size as its background and does not exaggerate movement as does a magnifying telescope. This makes it a better sight for snap shooting and for shooting at moving targets. It is, moreover, a much simpler and more robust device than a magnifying telescope, and can be permanently mounted on the rifle.

For specialized military purposes, it is possible to go even further and use electronics to improve vision, particularly at night. These night-vision devices are extremely expensive and involved, and depend upon electronic amplification of the perceived light, the amplified picture being presented in the 'telescope' eyepiece in the normal way. Early versions used infra-red techniques, either relying on the infra-red emission from the target – for example, human body heat – or on an infra-red light source mounted on the weapon and 'floodlighting' the target area. While these systems worked, they were relatively imprecise and were only effective at short range. The modern techniques of light amplification can be effective to almost the maximum range of the weapon and, quite literally, turn night into day.

Calibre Conversion

The number of calibres, both metric and 'inch', which have been tried over the years is legion, but no practical purpose would be served by listing all of them. The following are what might be called the 'standard' calibres, for which ammunition was most commonly used. It must be kept in mind that much of the designation of calibres is traditional: weapons developed in the United States and Britain used 'inch' calibres; those developed on the Continent used metric calibres. And these calibres stay with the weapons thereafter, irrespective of who speaks of them or where. A Frenchman will still refer to the '.45 Colt Frontier', not the '11.43mm Colt Frontier', just as an Englishman speaks of the '9mm Parabellum' and not the '.354 Parabellum'.

Another difficult point is that the commonly accepted equivalents between inch and metric calibres are not always strictly correct. The same round of pistol ammunition would be called 7.65mm in Europe and .32 Auto in America, but .32in measures 8.13mm and not 7.65mm. There are no set rules to be learned in this game; you just have to learn each one individually. Ours not to reason why . . .

Inch	Metric (mm)	Metric (mm)	Inch
.22	5.58	4.25	.167
.223	5.66	5.5	.216
.243	6.17	5.6	.22
.25	6.35	6	.236
.257	6.52	6.35	.250
.276	7.0	7.5	.295
.280	7.11	7.62	.300
.303	7.7	7.65	.301
.308	7.82	7.92	.312
.32	8.13	8.0	.314
.357	9.06	8.5	.334
.375	9.53	9.0	.354
.38	9.65	9.3	.366
.41	10.4	10.6	.417
.44	11.12	11.5	.452
.45	11.43	12.0	.472
.455	11.55	15.0	.590
.50	12.7		
.577	14.6		

Weights and Measures

American and British ammunition charges and bullets are usually measured in grains or, less frequently, drams, again a matter of traditional usage. For those unfamiliar with these units, some equivalents are given:

1 grain = .0648 gramme (g)
1 dram = 1.772 g
27.3 grains = 1 dram
437.5 grains = 1 ounce (oz) = 28.349 grammes
16 drams = 1 ounce
7,000 grains = 16 oz = 1 pound (lb) = 453.6 g

Shotgun and Musket Bores

Shotguns, muskets and early pistols were calibrated according to the number of bore-sized lead balls which went to make up one pound (1lb =543.6g). Thus a 12-bore gun will accept a lead ball weighing one-twelfth of a pound. The exceptions which prove the rule are the .410in and 9mm shotguns which came late on the scene and were given 'proper' calibre notation.

4-bore	.930in calibre (23.622mm)
8-bore	.835in calibre (21.21mm)
10-bore	.775in calibre (19.7mm)
12-bore	.729in claibre (18.52mm)
14-bore	.693in calibre (17.60mm)
16-bore	.662in calibre (16.81mm)
20-bore	.615in calibre (15.62mm)
24-bore	.579in calibre (14.70mm)
28-bore	.550in calibre (13.97mm)
32-bore	.526in calibre (13.36mm)

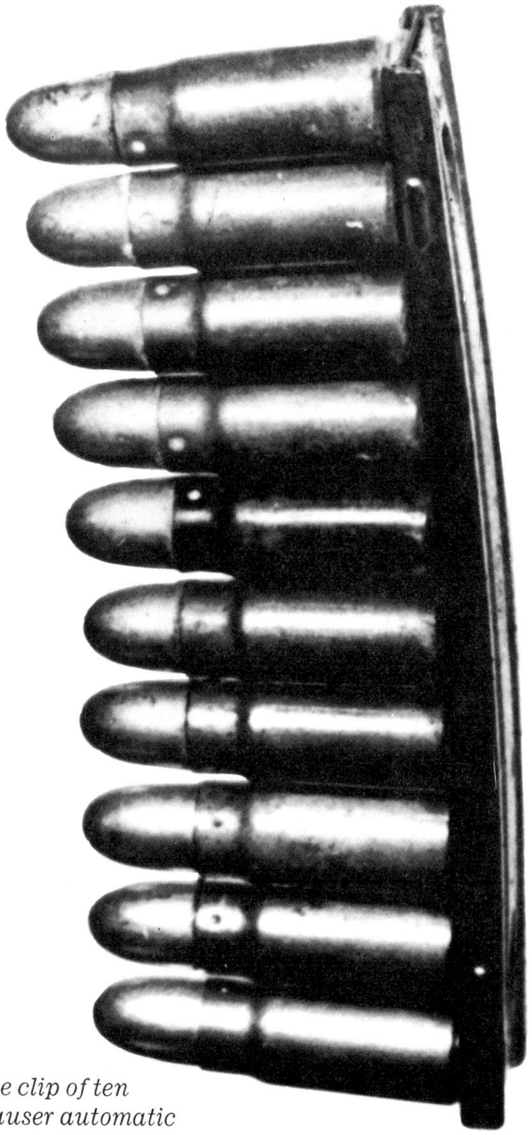

A magazine clip of ten 7.63mm Mauser automatic pistol rimless cartridges, first issued in 1896.

INDEX

Page numbers in roman type indicate text references. Page numbers in **bold** indicate diagrams. Page numbers in *italics* indicate photographs and other illustrations.